Renshaw and Davison climbing the crest of south ridge of
Kusum Kanguru. Rock pillar above.

(Stephen Venables)

THE
HIMALAYAN
JOURNAL

✳✳✳✳✳✳

Honorary Editor
HARISH KAPADIA

Honorary Assistant Editor
M. H. CONTRACTOR

VOLUME 49

1991-1992

Published for

THE HIMALAYAN CLUB

OXFORD UNIVERSITY PRESS
DELHI   LONDON   NEW YORK
1993

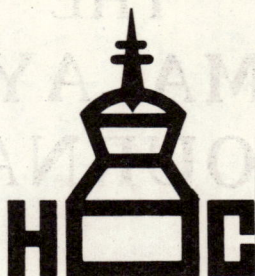

THE HIMALAYAN CLUB

(FOUNDED 17TH FEBRUARY 1928)

'To encourage and assist Himalayan travel and exploration, and to extend knowledge of the Himalaya and adjoining mountain ranges through science, art, literature and sport.'

Published by:
J.C. Nanavati, Hon. Secretary
The Himalayan Club
Post Box 1905
Bombay-400 001
INDIA

Printed by:
S. V. Limaye
India Printing Works
India Printing House
42 G. D. Ambekar Marg
Wadala, Bombay-400 031

CONTENTS

1991 (Giancarlo Contalbrigo) 10. Nilkanth — The Enigma (Graham Little) 11. Ascent of Chaukhamba I (Col. Amit C. Roy) 12. Mana Peak (Capt. S. P. Malik) 13. Yogeshwar, 1992 (Simon Yearsley) 14. Matri Expedition, 1991 (Swapan Kumar Ghosh) 15. Across Dhumdhar Kandi Pass (Sanjib Kumar Mitra) 16. Sahastra Tal (Sandeep Dutt) 17. Temptations of Kedar (Harish Kapadia) 18. From Sangla to Netwar Over the Rupin (William McKay Aitken) 19. Rubal Kang Expedition, 1991 (Apurba Chakrabarti) 20. Kugti Pass (Prashant M. Tale) 21. Karcha Parbat Expedition, 1991 (Satyajit Kar) 22. Matho Kangri, 1992 (Michael Ratty) 23. Sani Pakush (Hubert Bleicher) 24. Shimshal — Malangutti Glacier Expedition, 1991 (Paul Hudson).

───────────────PANORAMAS───────────────

Facing Page

Cover: Panch Chuli peaks (front) and the Milam valley (Eastern
Kumaon panorama). From an original water-colour by
Serbjeet Singh.

Correction: The front cover of H.J. Vol. 48 was of Broad Peak.

PHOTOS

EDITORIAL

MOUNTAINEERING was never a game of numbers. There were no runs to be scored or goals to be counted. Other than the heights of peaks, only human endeavour mattered. But now a new number game is emerging, recording the same endeavours and achievements. By 1992, there were 107 ascents of Cho Oyu, 112 ascents of Ama Dablam and the 150th ascent of Everest. 52 persons climbed Everest in the summer of 1992, with 32 persons standing on the summit on one day. By 1993 even these records were bettered and more than 500 persons have now climbed Everest. At this rate, soon we will have the 259th ascent of Rum Doodle!

Amidst this rush, mountaineers have also been enterprising, as is evident in the following pages of this volume. Exploring Gorichen, and Basingthang peaks in Bhutan, breaking new ground (and a leg) in Mongolia, reaching Danu Dhura and Rupin Ghati passes, and many other adventures were undertaken. The expedition to the Panch Chuli group is covered in detail; climbs, achievements, the rescue and above all its great fun. The correction of the mistaken so-called ascents of Panch Chuli III, IV and V after 28 years, goes to stress the maxim that truth ultimately prevails. In similar vein, in the Book Reviews, facts about the 1939 K2 tragedy and the 1984 Indian Everest expedition are stated and discussed. The variety of books on mountaineering, covered here, show that mountaineers can write as vigorously as they can climb.

In the year of the 40th anniversary of the first ascent of Everest, the highest peak also receives attention here. An expedition records the crowds and the junk on the mountain, the Japanese make gallant attempts in winter and the Indians fail on the route from the north. In between the crowds a climber claims a 'solo', perhaps an indication of how to use the crowds to be alone! These ideas are explored elsewhere to explain mountaineering's psychological utility and 'other experiences'.

There are dawdles in the Dibibokri and elsewhere, unsolved enigmas like Nilkanth's south face or climbing secret mountains like Gyala Peri. In short enough temptations to look forward to.

With the passing away of D.F.O. Dangar, the H.J. has lost a devoted supporter. He indexed H.J.s for many years and the systems set by him are still being followed. Himalayan literature was never better served by someone who never visited the Himalaya.

I hope readers will enjoy this 49th volume in the 65th year of the Club. With 17 articles, 24 notes.... Oops, we are back to the number game again! Sorry, it does not seem that we will escape from it.

Happy reading.

HARISH KAPADIA

1

THE PSYCHOLOGICAL UTILITY OF MOUNTAINEERING*

JOHN THACKRAY

THE MAGNIFICENT EDIFICE of mountaineering literature contains little material on the psychology of climbing. This is not for lack of curiosity about motive. To the contrary, those climbers I've known tend to be fascinated with the subject, though the older ones have grown a little tired of the unrewarding nature of these discussions. Most of the accepted ideas about the impulse to climb are couched in the romantic language of conquest, adventure, closeness with nature, character-building, etc. But today's climbers know how inadequate these explanations are; how little of the inner reality they embrace.

Mallory's obiter dicta — 'Because it is there!' — is in fact the climber's cry of despair at the impossibility of coming up with an explanation, persuasive to himself or the non-climbing community. This offhand response to a question following a lecture in Philadelphia during a money-raising tour, was, I imagine, spoken in a testy voice. A wire service reporter in that audience knew a good headline when he heard it. Ironically, but perhaps wisely, the world accepted this fatuous remark as something to fasten on to.

Mallory's mixture of prickliness and evasion is typical. Yet many of the better statements about why people climb seem to have at their centre a psychological void, a lacuna of defensiveness. As if there is a moat around the castle of the ego that the climber is scared to cross for fear of losing the enchantment.

Probably the most common psychological observation about climbing is that it strives for 'the overcoming of the self', Nietzsche's phrase originally, in which the self is divided; one part strong, winning over the weaker aspects of the self. This is in many respects a fair description. But to find out why self-overcoming is necessary, we should turn to the ideas of that Viennese doctor and occasional hill-walker,

---

* Based on a presentation at Montagna Avventura 2000, Florence, 15-17 November 1991.

Sigmund Freud. Though Freud himself wrote nothing directly on the subject, some of his disciples and interpreters have. They acknowledge what climbers know from experience is true: the thrill, the fantastic emotional charge, the sublime pleasure of climbing. These feelings are the core of our avocation. They are also corroborated by some direct research on climber's psychology. (See the *Himalayan Journal*, Vol (1972-73) 'Psychopathology in Alpinism' by Zdzislaw Ryn.)

The central question is, why climbers find this pleasure sometimes verging on ecstasy — in situations that in the average person inspires dread, panic, terror. At the point where most of the human race pulls back and runs, the climber rushes eagerly forward.

Freudians believe that the climber is not under-endowed with a capacity for fear. The difference lies in the psychological predisposition for coping with such feelings; a predisposition laid down in childhood. The helpless infant is awash with fears of inadequacy, fears of authority and punishment, terror at the animal world and ghouls and goblins, fear of hunger, of murderous rage — fears of every shade and stripe and in all directions. The sensations of fear are physically uncomfortable for any child, and emotionally stressful. For relief from this anxiety and discomfort, the child has three choices. One is simple avoidance of fearfilled situations and thoughts, and energetic suppression of such threats.

The second possibility is for the child to resolve the fear at its source and discover that it is groundless. Overcoming situations that formerly were overwhelmingly fearful is a keen source of pleasure. This pleasure comes from the sense of relief, the relief of never having to be so fearful in this context again. Whereupon the ego experiences the thrill of being liberated, and a surge of triumph. Every one of us enjoyed hundreds of these triumphs on the path to maturity. But in all of us, too, there were fears, phobias, that could not be successfully resolved and put behind us when we grew up.

So we come to the third possibility. Here the individual attempts to compensate for those unresolved fears in an unexpected manner. The professional terminology for this activity is 'counter phobia' and is synonymous with 'overcompensation against fear'. In these situations, the fear-filled person paradoxically believes that his or her underlying anxiety is more effectively warded off by seeking, not avoiding, situations that provoke it.

Thus the over-compensator against fear tries to conquer his anxiety anew by putting himself in the path of danger, with the hope that he will re-experience the wonderful sensation of a child vanquishing a fear for the first time. This overcompensator against fear has an impossible dream: to banish in maturity the residue of apprehension and panic that he could not resolve in childhood. And of course, he continually fails. True, he gets the sensation of overcoming fear, but not the substance. The sensation passes. The fear's source remains, dooming him to successive repetitions of the counter-phobic act. Otto Fenichel, the great codifier of Freudian thought, observed that: 'When we see that many people with counter-phobic attitudes nevertheless consciously feel a good deal of pleasure inspite of this failure, and avoid becoming aware of the anxiety still operative in them, we must admit that they are relatively well off.'

Everyone has counter-phobic possibilities. Life is impossible without it. No one entirely resolves and banishes all the fearcharged obstacles of childhood. Fenichel had a male patient who was an amateur authority on railroads. After some years of psychoanalysis it turned out that the origin of this enthusiasm and his knowledge lay in forgotten infantile fears of railway journeys. Another of Freud's disciples, Helena Deutsch, had a patient who crippled by phobias, was both isolated from others and sexually impotent. The only area where he was fear-free was in sports, which he pursued with a vengeance.

The climber-overcompensator against fear has a rich imagination. His mind vividly recreates terror-inducing images. In him, imagination is almost indistinguishable from reality, because like reality itself the fantasized dangers and enemies provoke unpleasant sensations of anxiety and discomfort. The only way to quell the imaginatively induced fear is to step out into the concrete environment and vanquish it by courting danger and assuming unnatural risks. Fortunately the objective world, most of the time, is not as terrifying as the fantasy — providing another source of relief and delight. What he cannot get is final proof that his imagination played him false. So the next time the imagination conjures up a fearful image, he must tolerate the anxiety, or go forth and risk again in the real world.

Many sports are counter-phobic rituals in which mature men and women can relive fear and relish its conquest. Says Fenichel: 'The essential joy in sport is that one actively brings about in play certain tensions which were formerly feared, so that one may enjoy the fact that now one can overcome them. People for whom sport, or at least, certain kinds of sport (for example mountaineering) which are not a mere occasional relaxation, but a matter of significance in their lives, are true counter-phobic subjects'.

There is not a strict correspondence between the origins of a particular fear and the counter-phobic reaction to it. As a child I was more afraid of snakes, of being abandoned by my mother and punished by my father, of catching leprosy in public transport than I was afraid of heights. Perhaps my summit euphorias have come from the sensation of vanquishing all those old suppressed terrors with a single blow. And with each 'success' — even when that involves no more than saving one's skin from rock fall at the base — my counter-phobic attitude becomes a stronger and a deeper part of my life.

Helena Deutsch believed that the underlying goal of counter-phobic behaviour is to free the psyche from its inner burden of apprehension, by displacing the inward knowledge of danger onto the outer world. In the climber's case, the fear of fear becomes transmuted into fear of the mountain. She wrote 'It is perfectly possible to convert neurotic into real anxiety and to create for oneself the pleasurable situation of a game instead of the painful situation of a phobia. Once the anxiety-object is located in the outside world, the need for mastery over it is directed either at some opponent in the game, or the element which has to be mastered, such as mountains, water, air.'

Overcompensation against fear is a tendency, not a fail-safe psychological technique. There is always uncertainty as to whether it will or won't make an appearance. When it does not, then primary dread crashes down upon the climber. Instead of running forward to vanquish it, he must flee. The mountain that he thought to invest with significance and the nobility of a worthy enemy is suddenly transformed. It becomes demonic, ugly, murderous.

The cyclicality of over-compensation against fear explains the times we and our companions are bold one day and timid the next, why we seem to go through phases of intense commitment followed by inexplicable periods of retirement. Why a good climbing friend can call up to suggest a great adventure and you suddenly feel irritated, cold, and turn him away. But most of the time, obviously, the hard cases have their over-compensation machinery in good shape. The proof is in the deed.

Climbers thus face a perpetual dilemma: either denying risk and danger, or exaggerating it — as phobia and counter-phobia contend for dominance. It is almost impossible for the climber to match so-called objective risk with just the right amount of apprehension — though that is what we all claim to be capable of.

If this theory is correct, there are some practical lessons to be drawn. First, a climber should try to be aware of the natural fluctuations in his capacity to over-compensate. Such awareness is an absolute pre-condition for a long career. It should not be taken for granted. Many years ago Rheinhold Messner travelled to one of the Himalayan peaks and after setting up base camp suddenly decided, without explanation, to pack up and return to Europe. This seemingly impulsive behaviour, squandering lots of money in the process, suggested to me a climber with great self-awareness.

Another danger is that the climber may become addicted to the thrill of over-compensation against fear. A good friend of mine, a reformed drug addict, depended on his counter-phobic 'highs' from hard climbing to drown feelings of anxiety and anguish from other sources — job, family, money etc. — and finding that a day's climbing sometimes did not have that effect, he'd slide into deep depression and a negligent attitude to safety on the rock. In exactly these circumstances, that climber fell to his death four years ago. The over-compensator against fear may be 'relatively well off', as Fenichel cheerfully remarked above, but he must not abuse the process.

When the counter-phobic tide is out, there is a risk that the climber will be harshly critical of himself and believe that the upswelling of fear and panic he feels is a weakness, a failure of will, a moral flaw — instead of a normal and transient event. My advice here is to go easy, in judging one's own and other climbers' lapses of keenness.

I suspect that over-compensation against fear was present at the dawn of climbing. The golden age of alpinism was also a time of the discovery of neurasthenia — an umbrella term for a wide range of complaints that today look distinctly psychosomatic. It was widely believed by doctors that the murky invalidism, mental alienation, hysteria, insomnia and apathy, lack of appetite of this syndrome were the product of industrial civilization. An oftprescribed remedy was vigorous outdoor exercise. Some of the early pioneers first visited the Alps for vague reasons of health and were cured when they discovered the thrill of over-compensation against fear.

The counter-phobe has an instrument that requires very careful handling. Remember, he knows no other method for coping with fear and anxiety. So he tirelessly hides from an awareness of what he is doing, sometimes cunningly, sometimes ingenuously. Climbers are creative when it comes to defending their obsession against interpretation.

This same defensiveness also explains why they often seem callous — or anyway ambiguous — about grieving for the loss of their friends. Such a death undermines the logic of counterphobia. So grief is difficult to feel without the accompaniment of a painful sense of guilt, which comes from the climber's refusal, ultimately, to draw the inferences that his friend's death calls for. At such moments climbing seems an affront to nature, an insult to life's preciousness, and it seems only right to break the chains, and leap out of the climbing obsession. I've many friends who've done just that. But for me those yearnings are transient. Sooner or later, my counter-phobia reasserts its control, and lures me with its rewards.

Is this over-compensation against fear the whole story? Far from it. Obviously climbers have a diversity of mental and emotional qualities that foster and motivate climbing. Yet I believe this concept offers one the better road maps to the climber's psyche.

SUMMARY

A psychological explanation for the motivation to climb.

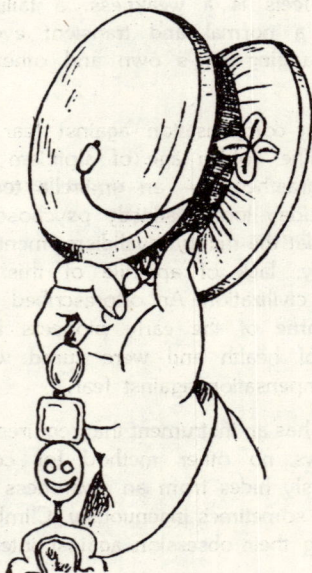

2

BASINGTHANG PEAKS —
EXPLORING IN THE HIDDEN KINGDOM*

PETER MOULD

MY SPECIAL INTEREST interest in Bhutan can be traced back to 1979 when I was introduced to Dago Tshering, now Home Minister but at that time Bhutan's first ambassador to Bangladesh, and had convinced him that Spencer Chapman really did ascend Chomolhari in 1937. It was not until seven years later that a consultancy assignment fortuitously took me to Bhutan. One part of the assignment involved assessing domestic grain production for which I needed detailed maps, and I gained access to the restricted Indian survey series. I had a hidden agenda : to look for modest, alpine-type peaks, accessible by a short trek from Thimphu the capital, in the hope of organising a trip at the end of my assignment. The Basingthang peaks seemed ideally located, being a three to four day's walk from Thimphu, just off the route to Lingshi which now forms part of the popular Chomolhari base camp tourist trek.

It soon became evident, however, that the Basingthang peaks were not accessible to a spur of the moment solo jaunt aided by a local porter! Movement of foreigners was, and still is, strictly controlled by the police/immigration authorities and by the army and district administrations. Tourists were welcomed (in limited numbers) on standard cultural or trekking package holidays organised by the Bhutan Tourism Corporation (BTC). Mountaineering was even more controlled, being restricted to two or three named peaks at any one time. Since 1983, when regular mountaineering was first permitted, the only 'open' peaks over 6000 m have been Jitchu Drake, Masakang, Kangbum and Gangkar Punsum, of which all but the last have been climbed.

Fortunately, on a subsequent consultancy assignment in 1988, I found myself sharing a tourist lodge with the Director of BTC, and over dinner I tackled him about an expedition to Basingthang. 'For

* Reprinted from the *The Alpine Journal* 1992/93 with the kind permission of the author and the editor.

Photo 1

7

you,' he said, 'I will grant permission. We will treat you as a tour operator visiting trekking peaks along the Chomolhari base camp trek.' Obviously I had to do something about such a concession, especially as Basingthang had not previously been visited by climbing parties.

Initially my idea was to invite a few climbing friends who had recently been on treks to Nepal, and to set aside October 1989 for the trip. Initial enthusiasm evaporated somewhat on counting the cost — BTC's daily rate charges for hotel and trekking nights, plus the air fare, being much higher than for a similar excursion to Nepal. The solution seemed to be to upgrade the idea of an active holiday into a fully-fledged expedition which might qualify for a grant. Thus an application was made to the Mount Everest Foundation for approval and a grant in 1990. Reflecting the growing ecological awareness of the times, the expedition acquired the unoriginal label of 'Green Expedition to Bhutan'. The 'green' image would fit in with my offer to the Director of BTC to prepare a report for his government, based on our experiences, about improving services while minimising the adverse environmental and cultural impacts of trekking and mountaineering. It might help in getting financial sponsorship, or so I thought, and it was an issue close to my heart. The MEF did offer us a grant but of the 13 members six withdrew, including the doctor, so the expedition had to be postponed.

The four 'hard core' members were determined that lift-off really would occur in 1991. The workings of the grapevine ensured that we had no shortage of interested persons and a successful reapplication was made to the MEF. As preparations advanced, there were further changes in composition, but both the membership and the itineraries eventually jelled. The option of an extended trek for non-mountaineers during the climbing phase of the expedition, and a bit of cultural sightseeing at the beginning and the end, had always been part of our plans. The trekkers split off at Lingshi, a day's walk before Basingthang, and continued along the strenuous, but spectacularly beautiful, Laya-Gaza trek to Punakha and Thimphu, arriving the same day as the mountaineers. The final line-up was :

Mountaineers: George Band, John Blacker, John Innerdale, Jonathan Innerdale, Eric Langmuir, Jerry Lovatt , Peter Mould (leader), John Nixon (doctor) and Steve Town.
Trekkers: Susan Band, John and Georgina Harding, Diana Innerdale, Peter Lowes (trek leader), Kristina Malmberg, Tim and Sue Powell and David Seddon (doctor).

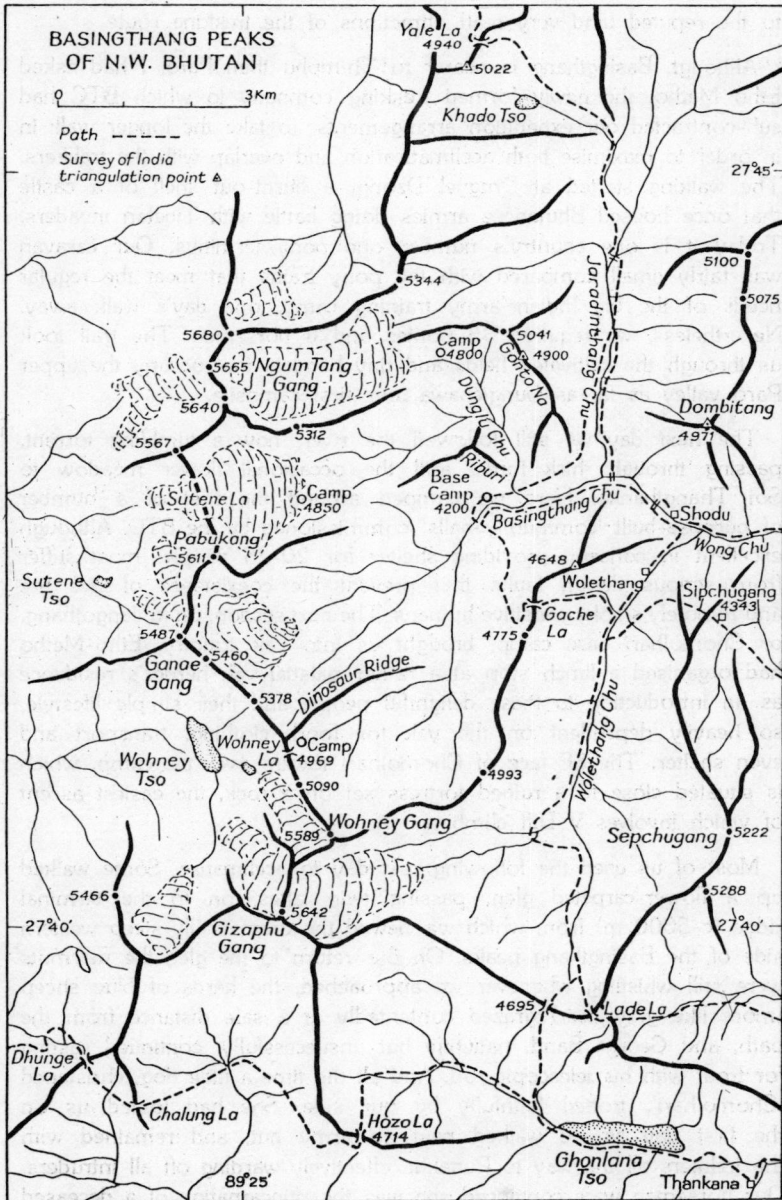

BASINGTHANG PEAKS
OF N.W. BHUTAN

0 _____ 3Km

Path - - - - -
Survey of India
triangulation point ▲

Yale La
4940
▲5022

Khado Tso

27°45'

5344

5100
5075

5680
5665 Ngum Tang
       Gang
5640
5567
5312

Camp
4800
5041
4900

Golto Na

Jaradingthang Chu

Dungji Chu

Dombitang
4971

Sutene La
Camp
4850

Ribur
Base
Camp
4200

Basingthang Chu

Shodu

Wong Chu

Pabukong
5611

4648

Wolethang

Sipchugang
4343

Sutene
Tso

5487
5460

Ganae
Gang

5378 Dinosaur Ridge

Gache
La
4775

Wolethang Chu

Wohney
Tso

Wohney
La
Camp
4969
5090

Wohney Gang
5589

4993

Sepchugang
5222

5288

5466

5642

Gizaphu
Gang

27°40'

4695

Lade La

Dhunge
La

Chalung La

Hozo La
4714

Ghonlana
Tso
Thankana

89°25'

It will be noted that even a hard man like John Harding succumbed to the reputed (and very real) attractions of the trekking route.

Although Basingthang is nearer to Thimphu than Paro, I had asked Etho Metho, the newly formed trekking company to which BTC had sub-contracted our expedition arrangements, to take the longer walk-in in order to maximise both acclimatisation and overlap with the trekkers. The walking started at Drugyel Dzong, a burnt-out shell of a castle that once housed Bhutanese armies doing battle with Tibetan invaders. Today it is one country's number one pony terminus. Our caravan was fairly small compared with the pony trains that meet the regular needs of the big Indian army training camp, one day's walk away. Nevertheless, we required 35 ponies and 6 horsemen. The trail took us through the cultivated fields and tiny hamlets that occupy the upper Paro valley as far as Gungichawa, our first campsite.

The next day we still followed the river, now a tumbling torrent, passing through thick forest and the occasional flower meadow to Soi Thangthanka. Here we camped around the first of a number of purpose-built 'community halls' commissioned by the BTC. Although excellent in concept, providing shelter for 20-25 people, most suffer from serious design faults that prevent the coexistence of live fire and remotely smoke-sensitive humans. The next section, on to Jangothang, or Chomolhari base camp, brought us into yak country. Etho-Metho had organised a lunch stop at a rather palatial yak herder's residence as an introduction to these delightful people and their simple lifestyle, so heavily dependent on the yak for food, clothing, transport and even shelter. The SE face of Chomolhari towers over the camp, which is situated close to a ruined fortress set on a rock, the easiest ascent of which involves V Diff climbing.

Most of us used the following rest day to acclimatise. Some walked up a flower-carpeted glen, passing twin lakes, on to the terminal ridge (c 5000 m) from which we viewed the dramatically steep western side of the Basingthang peaks. On our return to the glen the marmots were still whistling whenever we approached, the herds of blue sheep (more like grey deer) grazed contentedly at a safe distance from the path, and George Band, patiently but unsuccessfully, continued casting for trout with his telescopic rod. And all the time a little dog, christened 'Chomolhari', trotted faithfully by our side. She had joined us on the first day as we walked past an army hut, and remained with the trekkers all the way to Punakha effectively warding off all intruders. Our horsemen were convinced she was the reincarnation of a deceased trekker.

The next day took us to Lingshi over the barren Nile la pass (4700 m). Near the campsite were some yak herders' tents or *jha*. Courtesy callers were received with warm hospitality marked by offerings of tasteless, bullet-like cheese. Although seemingly totally dependent on their yaks, our hostess and her family looked healthy and well fed. She sported new trainers, and showed off a transistor radio.

On the following morning five of the nine climbers parted company from the trekkers and set off, over the Yale la (4940 m), to Shodu and Basingthang. Here we chose an idyllic flat grassy site between the river and two stone huts. Singye, our suave guide, and six assistants rapidly set up our 'village' of mess, cook, toilet and five sleeping tents. We really appreciated this happy team over the next ten days, not least because of their volunteer porterage duties. Especially memorable were Phunzo the imperturbable cook (the more adverse the circumstances the better the meal), Chime the cheerful kindly steward, and Chorten the minute young assistant — but mighty load-carrier.

With four climbers still en route at Lingshi, careful planning was needed to make the most of our seven or eight full days in Basingthang. The fine weather looked set to continue and we did not need to allow for being snowed in. Our strategy was to set up, in sequence, a two-tented camp for each group of mountains and arrange for as many members as possible to attempt routes over a one-or-two day period before moving on to the next group. This worked well.

We chose the Ngum Tang Gang, with the highest but relatively easy peaks, as the first group. Our route up the prominent Gonto Na ridge gave splendid views of the whole range and helped in locating all the higher campsites. As we neared the top of the ridge, it became clear that the 1 km horizontal section linking it to the glacial plateau was too serrated and rotten to 'go'. The alternative traverse across steep scree was exhausting but led to a good site in a rocky cwm from which an intricate line of ramps and gullies breached the 200 m wall below the glacier. The next morning Band, Blacker, Langmuir, Mould and Nixon quickly gained the gently-inclined glacier and snaked up its 3 km length to the foot of the snowy E ridge of Ngum Tang Gang III, the lowest of the three peaks. (The rocky E ridge of Ngum Tang Gang I, the highest peak, would, we judged, be dangerous and unpleasant.) Tackling the ridge in two ropes, we enjoyed pleasant straightforward climbing despite some steep sections up to 65°. The minuscule summit (5640 m), looking towards Chomolhari, Jitchu Drake and Tsheringang, gave the most magnificent mountain views that I had ever seen. A narrow, gently-inclined ridge led on from the summit to Ngum Tang Gang II (5665 m) but, sadly, it was too late in the day to go further, given the need to descend to base that night.

The next day we shifted our attention to the Wohney Gang group. The Innerdales and Lovatt set up a C 2 just below the Wohney la and reconnoitred routes for the following day. Rejecting the steep, rocky N ridge, they crossed the la and descended to and crossed the Wohney glacier in the hope of being able to find a way up the rocky buttress that bastioned the NW/W snow ridge. They ran out of time and returned to C 2 where Band, Blacker, Langmuir and Mould were waiting, ready to plan the next day. The Innerdales would immediately descend to base and take a rest day in preparation for an attack on Gange Gang. Band and Blacker would go to Point 5090 m on the N ridge and a 'strong' party of Langmuir, Lovatt and Mould would make a second attempt on the NW/W ridge of Wohney Gang.

On a cold clear morning we set out across the glacier towards the foot of the rock buttress but, through an unspoken consensus, we veered south and made for the least steep of the snow gully/ribs on the N face of the ridge at the head of the glacier. Our route gave us eleven rope-lengths of fine climbing up to the slightly corniced crest and on to the summit. An infinity of peaks and imagined valleys lay all around us. I had to pinch myself — was this real? I had gazed on the majesty of God's creation in the mountains many times, but this view surpassed all my memories. Yes, it was 2 p.m. on 15 October 1991 and we were on the summit of Wohney Gang (5589 m), the most prominent of some twelve peaks that form the western watershed of the Baisingthang Chu. Nearest, and to our south, were the fluted white peaks of Gizaphu Gang (5642 m) and its three outliers. To our north the rocky N ridge of Wohney Gange dropped sharply to the la we had crossed that morning, while beyond the col lay the NS band of peaks, clustered round three separate glaciers, that form the rest of the Basingthang chain. In an easterly direction we could glimpse our base camp at the head of the grassy levels of Basingthang ('hidden fields') and, beyond that, the jumble of the Lunana peaks punctuated by the snow dome of Kangbum and the isolated white towers of Masakang, Gangkar Punsum and Kula Kangri. To our west, the ridge we had just ascended fell away in sinuous undulations, curving NW and leading the eye on to Chomolhari, Jitchu Drake and distant giants beyond. We could clearly distinguish Kangchenjunga and, at 260 km distance, Everest.

The same day Nixon soloed the highest point (5487 m) of the next group to the north, which we nicknamed Saddle Peak ('Ganae Gang' in Bhutanese). It was the only one that merits the title 'trekking peak', being safely accessible to a guided party of mountain walkers. The day after, Band, the Innerdales, and Town repeated the route and bagged both Ganae Gang I and II.

1. Basingthang peaks. Wohney Gang (5589 m) and Gizaphu Gang (5642 m), centre right, seen from the south summit of Ganae Gang (5460 m).

(George Band)

Article 2

2. Dorje Lhakpa (6966 m): NW side, west ridge visible centre right.

(Carlos Buhler)

Article 3

There was just time to explore the last group of peaks clustered round the Pabukang snowfield and glacier. Access to a beautiful grassy campsite up the Riburi ridge was direct but steep. The prominent moraine, on the S side of the rapidly retreating glacier, ended close to C3 and turned out to be a veritable animal motorway. The post-monsoon sun had hardened the traces of the more recent passers-by into cleanly-cast footprints. We could clearly distinguish the hooves of blue sheep, the pugs of snow leopard with claw marks 'frozen' in the fine gravel, and the bigger imprints, with thicker claws, of bear. Then there was one line of marks, slightly bigger and broader than that of the bear, with toe rather than claw marks, and what seemed to be a biped gait. In response to our description, Singye's verdict was 'mountain gorilla, or yeti'.

The following morning we lethargically ascended the Pabukang glacier following the recent marks of snow leopard, mother and young, which had skilfully negotiated the crevasses. At the col (5220 m) we second-breakfasted in the sun while weighing up the planned routes. The snow/ice couloirs up the tooth of Pabukang (5611 m) to the snow summit ridge looked desperately steep. Closer inspection of the easily inclined scree-like S ridge of Peak 5567 m revealed that the rock step would be more formidable than we had thought. Lassitude won and we retraced our steps to C3 and returned to base.

As we bade farewell to Thinley Dorji and his family, his yaks thundered past like bison on the prairies. The long, hard two-day walk-out to the roadhead at Dodina took us through more beautiful country. Most dramatic was the 12 km gorge section, very similar to Verdon.

Reunited with the trekkers, our last week in Bhutan involved celebratory meals, shopping, visits to spectacular dzongs and monasteries, a drive half-way across the kingdom to Bumthang to witness traditional dancing at an annual festival, and Bhutanese hot rock baths. But all that is another story. In Thimphu we met Ronald Naar, a professional climber, and Bas Gresnigt of the Dutch-Bhutan Expedition 1991, who were about to set off to tackle 'unclimbed peaks up to 6000 m in NW Bhutan'. We told them about our experiences and lent them maps. On our return to the UK we learnt that they had made first ascents of Chatarake (5570 m) some distance to the SW of Basingthang, and two of the Gizaphu Gang peaks, which they propose to christen 'Victor Kangri' after Ronald's son.[1]

---

1. Such personal names must be avoided please. Anyway Survey of India will not accept them. — Ed. (HJ.)

A few days before our arrival the BTC was abolished; the newly-established Tourism Authority of Bhutan will regulate tourism in its place. Fortuitously, our expedition report coincided with their need to publish new trekking regulations, and should be of help to them in revising those for mountaineering and in preparing guidelines for cultural tourism. Our report also mentioned the scope for many more 'trekking peak' expeditions in other parts of Bhutan, especially the Lunan area. In Basingthang itself there is, of course, unfinished business on Gizaphu Gang, in the Pabukang group, and no Ngum Tang Gang; and there is ample scope for those (in limited numbers, please) who simply wish to absorb the beauty, peace and harmony of Basingthang; its peaks, the wildlife and its people.

SUMMARY

Green expedition to Bhutan. October 1991, from U.K. Nine climbers on this 18 member expedition explored the western watershed peaks (5000 m — 5700 m) of the scenic Basingthang valley some 25 km SE of Chomolhari. They made what are thought to be first ascents of Wohney Gang (5589 m), Ngum Tang Gang III (5640 m) and Ganae Gang I (5487 m) and II (5460 m).

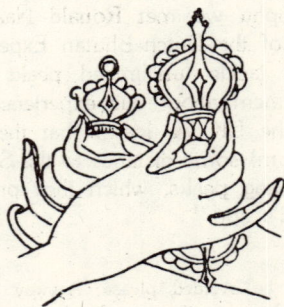

3

DORJE LHAKPA, 1992

CARLOS BUHLER

I AM STILL struggling with the choices I made that allowed me to continue climbing. The outcome was that I made a lone ascent of a relatively unexplored but beautiful peak in the Jugal Himal of Nepal, Dorje Lhakpa (6966 m).[1] This is the same group of mountains in the Himalaya that the well known peak, Xixabangma, is a part of. Dorje Lhakpa is located 55 km northeast of Kathmandu, near the eastern end of the Langshisa glacier. The Langshisa valley runs westward to join the Langtang valley near the grazing grounds known as Langshisa Kharka. It is the southern-most of the three principal peaks near the head of this glacier. The other two are Gur Karpo Ri (6874 m) and Lengpo Kang (7083 m). All three mountains are worthwhile objectives but Dorje Lhakpa is the most luring from this side and, therefore, the most often attempted.

Until 1981, Dorje Lhakpa was off limits to climbers by decree of Nepal's Ministry of Tourism. However, such are the difficulties of enforcing these rules, an ascent of the mountain by the west ridge is rumored to have taken place in the spring of 1980. Whether it was the first ascent, or followed in someone else's undisclosed foorsteps, is hard to verify. The first official and recognized ascent of the mountain took place in 1981, when the peak was opened to joint foreign/Nepali teams only. A Japanese/Nepali team reached the summit via the mountain's west ridge.[2] Over the following 10 years six teams attempted the peak with four of them achieving success. All of them climbed the same west ridge.

As permits to climb Dorje Lhakpa were unavailable until the spring of 1981, the peak's mountaineering possibilities were relatively unknown. In the sixties and seventies, much energy was devoted to exploring the big 8000ers. Since even nearby Xixabangma remained closed to

---

1. Spelling of the name of this peak is given a Dorje Lakhpa in previous literature. Height was stated as 6989 m. The present spelling and height are as per the list of Elizabeth Hawley, Kathmandu -Ed.
2. See Illustrated Note 3, H.J. Vol. 39, p.204 -Ed.

Photo 2

the outside world until 1979, there was little traffic near Dorje Lhakpa from which photographs emerged. Even after the first ascent in 1981, a factor keeping some climbers out was Nepal's issuance of permits to only joint foreign/Nepali teams. The mountain's whereabouts was certainly obvious, however, as it is visible from Kathmandu on a clear day. Although I saw photos of Dorje Lhakpa in the mid-eighties and was enticed by the vastly unvisited area, I was discouraged from going due to the added cost of the minimum of three Nepali members that must accompany any foreign/Nepali expedition.

I was inspired to apply for the peak in 1991 when the Ministry of Tourism explained to me the peculiarities of assembling a joint expedition. Since I had two experienced Sherpa friends who were interested in working with the expedition, the officials let me include our cook as the third Nepali of our team. To make matters simpler, my Sherpa friends were not interested in going to the summit. This simplified scenerio was the incentive I needed.

In keeping with my approach that the most enjoyment comes from climbing with the smallest groups, I decided to limit the number of climbers to three, not including the three Nepali members. Jon Aylward, from Yorkshire, England, one of the young generation of British alpinists, had written to me earlier about climbing in the Himalaya's less explored areas. A phone call to him was enough to arouse his interest. After a month's unsuccessful search for an additional partner, the two of us agreed to be the entire 'foreign' team.

I suspected that several unexplored ribs on Dorje Lhakpa would reveal brilliant climbs. But since we were unable to judge the true difficulties from our limited selection of photographs, we decided to take a wait and see approach to choosing a route. Our most promising line was the unclimbed buttress on the left side of the mountain's northwest face. Another possibility was a direct route up the central part of the face itself.

Though Dorje Lhakpa can be approached in five or six days from the village of Dhunche, a longer walk to base camp does wonders for getting one prepared for a Himalayan peak. We decided to extend the approach to four days by beginning from Sundarijal, a village 50 minutes from Kathmandu. This trail took us up a beautiful ridge to the Laurebinayak pass (4600 m) and led us through the famous Gosainkund lakes. From there we dropped down 2400 m to the village of Syabru, where the Dhunche trail joins from the west. Our route continued up the Langtang valley past Kyangin gompa (3800 m) to Langshisa Kharka. Here we entered the Langshisa valley and continued to a site on the Langshisha glacier (4780 m) directly beneath

the north side of Kanshurum (6078 m). The path was heavily used
until Kyangin gompa, but beyond this point we saw no one outside
of our party. We had some difficulty with the porters in placing
our base camp as high (east) on the glacier as we wanted. Some
expeditions have made a lower base camp, and only established their
C1 or ABC near the mountain. But with everyone carrying loads
and a team of seven porters willing to work for elevated wages,
in five days we managed to establish our base camp within a three
hour walk of the Kanshurum-Dorje Lhakpa col. It was 2 April. We
were in the middle of the Langshisha glacier in a fabulous spot which
gave us a full view of the northwest side of Dorje Lhakpa as well
as full-on views of Gur Karpo Ri and Lengpo Kang.

During the final days of hauling loads up the glacier to this BC,
Jon became fatigued and then somewhat ill. Although we suspected
that his loss of strength came from some sort of ·intestinal bug,
we could not cure him with any of the treatments we had. While
I had exhausted myself in Kathmandu and been sick during the walk
to Gosainkund lakes, I felt stronger by the time we reached base
camp. For several days after our arrival, Jon rested, trying to give
his body a chance to catch up. Meanwhile, I teamed up with Lhakpa
Dorje and made a quick day trip up the 5100 m col at the base
of the West Ridge. We found the remains of much fixed rope that
perhaps the Korean party had deployed in the previous December's
ascent of the mountain. After another day's rest, Jon was still not
feeling strong. The weather had not been stable during the past two
weeks and I was content to spend some time acclimatising and becoming
familiar with the lower section of the west ridge. We assumed that
no matter what route we ultimately ascended, we would descend the
west ridge. Time spent reconnoitering the lower part of this route
would aid us in coming down quickly and safely later on.

Lhakpa Dorje and I took two days of provisions and a tent and
camped on a low shoulder (5250 m) of the west ridge just before
the climbing steepens up. There was little snow and the terrain included
a good deal of hard blue ice on an exposed ridge. Though Lhakpa's
experience on Himalayan mountains is impressive (two routes, to the
summit, on Everest; Ama Dablam summit twice, etc.) he was not
comfortable on this hard, blue ice without fixed rope. He was happy
to remain in the tent the next day while I climbed up to have a
look around. Old ropes, which had originally been anchored with
snow stakes, were now dangling on top of the hard ice. To facilitate
a future descent, I reset some anchors to make use of the rope
that I could chip free from the ice. While clouds partially covered
the sky, I made good use of the day. I climbed on 35 to 45

degree ice, passing nervously over some large crevasses that criss-crossed the ice-ridge. My high point was 6050 m; about 100 m above another large shoulder 'where the Koreans, and others, had obviously put up a camp. From my position at 6050 m on an exposed, narrow ridge, the remaining 900 m to the top left many unanswered questions. The knife edge I was on leveled out for about 200 horizontal meters. It then curved upwards at about a 30 degree angle and ran into some unstable looking seracs at about 6250 m. Above these blocks, the ridge continued straight upwards until, at about 6400 m, it took a sharp turn to the left. From where I was, it looked as though one could follow the ridge to the left and eventually gain some easier looking slopes which led towards the summit cone. Though overall the ridge did not rise steeply, one would be forced to climb to the right of the crest on snow and ice of about 55 degrees. It would not be easy to move quickly on such terrain as one would be making a continual rising or descending traverse.

I climbed back down to the tent where Lhakpa was waiting for me and enjoyed a beautiful sunset. The next day, the 9th, we returned to base camp hoping that after these three days Jon would be over whatever had been ailing him. When we arrived he was enthusiastic but skeptical. I took a rest day on the 10th and on the 11th Jon and I set off for an acclimatisation hike towards the Dorje Lhakpa/Kanshurum col. Only an hour out of base camp however, Jon realized he was not feeling his normal strength yet. The disappointment was agonizing for him but we had no choice other than turning back.

That afternoon we agreed that the only course of action that made any sense for him was to descend to Kyangin gompa the following day for a period long enough to fully recover. Our delightful cook assistant, Minga, was willing to go down to help with any translating and generally keep him company.

Unsure of what I should do during his absence, I started thinking about whether the west ridge could be soloed. As luck would have it, the 11th dawned exceptionally clear and cold. We had not had a day like it so far. As Jon gathered up the few things that he would carry down with him to Kyangin I pondered what to do if the weather remained clear. Up until the 11th we had had a series of days that would start out clear and then cloud up around 1.00 p.m. Usually we had a few inches of snow by late afternoon in base camp which melted off the next morning when the sun came up. I suggested to Jon that in the event there was no snow throughout the day, and the 12th dawned clear, I would consider attempting the mountain by myself. After his 12 days of illness, there was no way for us to tell how long it would take before he felt strong enough to climb. Furthermore, he would have to acclimatise before we could do any sort of alpine style climbing.

When Jon left base camp, I sensed that I should try the ridge while the weather was steady. But I had a hard time committing myself to the idea. The biggest mental barrier was the unknown terrain around the seracs that barred the ridge at 6250 m. I knew that it would only take one uncrossable crevasse to stop me. In addition, I did not like the thought of downclimbing 2000 m of hard ice after an exhausting climb. There were a lot of fears I had to resolve before I could make the decision to try the route alone.

On 11 April I took a walk up the Langshisa glacier towards Lengpo Kang. All the way up the rock covered labryinth I struggled with the idea of whether or not to attempt the west ridge during this spell of terrific weather. Every twenty minutes or so I stopped on the glacier and studied the ridge. It lay parallel to the glacier I was walking along. By hiking up the valley, I had a slightly different perspective each time I stopped. Ultimately, I decided I should start early the next day.

I did not extend my walk too far up the glacier as I wanted to be completely fresh and hydrated in the morning. By the time I returned to base camp, my mind was whirring. I explained my plan to Lhakpa Dorje and Pemba and asked Pasang, our cook, to prepare a special meal for supper. My preparations were rather simple; I carried only what was absolutely essential. To reach the summit and descend in 55 hours implied a willingness to solo terrain that I normally use a rope on. The factor that would make that possible was travelling with practically nothing the day I pushed for the top.

Sleep came that night more peacefully than I expected. I wrote a few thoughts to my friend, Anne, and described my feelings. They weren't so much of impending disaster, although I admitted a disaster was possible. I looked forward to the episode concluding. I could then loosen up and not feel the need to put myself through such an ordeal. They were familiar feelings and I knew that the emotions were unique to mountaineering situations. [Even the intense anxiety of speaking to an important audience does not have the same impact on me. In situations before a difficult climb, my overriding emotion is a fear of being unable to handle every situation that might arise. The emotion includes a fear of dying. Yet it is more a fear of the 'What if's?' than the fear of being hit by a falling stone or a rappel anchor giving way. At any rate, I usually don't sleep before an important climb and on the night of the 11th I slept reasonably well.]

In my mind I broke the climb into two sections and allowed myself to consider turning back at my previous highpoint. In addition, I felt illogical assurance from Lhakpa Dorje's offer to accompany me for about an hour's walk from base camp. Having someone to begin the walk with was extremely comforting. I didn't like leaving base camp by myself. It was a significant act of companionship that allowed me to sleep deeply. Perhaps it was the camaraderie that I missed so much. In any event, by 7:30 a.m. I was on my way.

On any climb that I have attempted there are different battles that the team faces as a whole and that I face individually. Questions of strategy, team coordination, and maintaining equilibrium among members, are team problems. Personal drive, maintaining my health, and accepting the demands of others are a few of the individual challenges. When climbing alone all the battles become personal. Strategies and actions during a climb demand so much attention that personal doubts of the moment are quieted while the 'production' side takes over. Each difficulty requires quick analysis followed by decisive action. When time is of the essence, I think less about fear. This is not to say I don't fear the consequences of my actions. I'm always evaluating the risks from moment to moment. Yet my imagined fears are usually worse than confronting the true predicament. When I face a problem in reality, I'm much more comfortable with it than when I come upon the same problem in my imagination.

The Climb of Dorje Lhakpa

I lie in my tent with the radio bringing news of the outside world; the elections in Great Britain, the acquittal of a few Los Angeles policemen for beating up Rodney King, the death of a great Indian film director, the severe struggles for democracy in the streets of Kathmandu.... It all seems so incredibly intense. I am dulled by the exhaustion I have pushed myself through. I have dug deeply into my mental and physical reserves and I am living on each calorie that I swallow. Outside my tent stands the shimmering wall of the northwest face of Dorje Lhakpa. On its right hand border rises the ridge I have just climbed. I know this view is spectacular but I don't want to take it all in right now. I just page through *Newsweek* and let my mind flow in a stream of conscious state that is unobstructed. This is my reward for having pushed myself to the conclusion of this climb. It is an unfiltered, unprotected state of mind that flows like sparkling water gurgling out of a mountain spring on a summer day. I can feel the coolness on my tongue and lips. Its soothing gentleness kindles relaxation and the release of anxiety.

3. Chamlang seen from the Hongu side of Mera la. Route of ascent takes the right hand skyline ridge.

(Dr Andrew Pollard)

Article 4

4. Kusum Kanguru: Dick Renshaw near the summit.
Twin summits of Gonglha behind.

(Stephen Venables)

I was pretty maxed out at times. Descending the rock ridge at night, I was like a little child with no strength left. I tried to choke down a biscuit as I stood in the lonely darkness. I was so thirsty. Placing small bits of ice in my mouth gave faked momentary relief. I needed strength to go on. The ridge wound its way into the shadows. Over the cornices at its end lay the two rappels to the base of the triangular ice-face. My bivouac tent was there, offering safety and water. I lived for that arrival. I was wiped out but I could not let myself stop. Surrounded by the blue light of the moon, I faithfully followed the beam of my headlamp. I thought about Assiniboine (in the Canadian Rockies) where, during winter of 1976, I verbalized the same thoughts I was having now to my partner, Tom Breeze. Back then we had only to keep moving a while longer before reaching the hut. As I heard myself say the words sixteen years earlier, I kept moving on Dorje Lhakpa. I could make no mistakes. Employing both my hand tools, I negotiated short ice traverses between rock, clawing along until I reached a restful stance. I lavished the thought of lying in my bivi tent, safe from the verticality tugging at my heals. I negotiated one rappel and set off on the second, impatient with the clumsiness I displayed to the stars and moon. Then, as my weight came fully on the rope, I remembered the last 15 m and how precipitous they were. I had removed the ice screw that held this section of rope 17 hours earlier that day. It was also dark when the climb was just beginning. I thought I might need that ice screw higher on the mountain and, as it turned out, I had. Now it was time to replace it with another. It would be foolish to take a chance now. I reharnessed my tools and stepped up on my front points to unweight the rope. After chopping a small platform for footing on the 65 degree ice, I drove in a solid screw. As I fixed the rappel line, I felt a sense of satisfaction. I could still take precautions though my body weeped for rest. When I reached the tent a few minutes later it was 10 p.m. Barring a mistake, I would make it down the next day.

Twenty-four hours earlier I had set my alarm at 3 a.m. and set off from my 5950 m bivouac at 5 a.m. In my ultra light rucksack I carried a liter of water, 30 m of 6 mm line, some shortbread, sunscreen, film and a camera. I celebrated in the beauty of the sunrise, for it had taken me a full year to return to climbing after suffering severe frostbite on Dhaulagiri in 1990. I climbed along the long horizontal section of ridge staying to the right of the crest. I prayed that the seracs at 6250 m would allow me a safe passage. My pace was comfortable though rapid. As the daylight widened my world, I was surprised by the airiness of the ridge. It was much more exposed than the photos had revealed. Langtang Lirung caught the light of the sun before any of the other peaks. Its beauty left me dazzled. Alone, in a sea of peaks, I felt like a flea on the arm of a mighty giant.

As I approached the seracs, a yearning for the answer to my doubts made me impatient to reach them. A short, steep wall led me into a labyrinth of ice. Insecurity competed with my desire to go on. I climbed delicately up a shattered ice band and traversed right on a narrow ice ramp beneath an overhanging wall into a cluster of 30 m seracs. The ice underneath me was studded with crevasses and I stepped carefully to avoid them. After a tricky step over a bergschrund I climbed the wall to my left. In another 50 m I found remnants of a camp. It was 8 a.m. and my mind began recalculating the distance to the summit. Had the previous team begun from this point and not lower where I had bivouacked? It would mean many more hours of climbing than I had anticipated but there was no question of stopping here.

Beyond the seracs, I was barred by a horizontally running crevasse across the face of the ridge. I climbed delicately up, stepped onto the lip, and planted my tools in the soft snow above. But I could not make the move. Would the tools hold if the snow beneath my feet gave way? Losing precious time, I traversed along the edge of the crevasse searching for a place I could cross. After a fruitless 20 minute search, I returned to my initial spot. I dug the tools in again and pulled hard to step up. They held and I panted heavy sighs of relief. The thought of this and other obstacles on my descent preoccupied me though. I had rope to rappel these difficulties, but I had insufficient anchors for many of them.

Once across the crevasse I continued climbing the ridge's right hand face. Numerous smaller crevasses carved through the ice. In each case I found a point where the edges came close enough to stem across and continue upwards. I was making good progress when I front-pointed up a 55 degree sheet of ice levelling onto a shoulder at the point where the ridge made its sharp turn to the left. Three more hours had elapsed and I was feeling the weight of the numerous difficulties I would be forced to reverse before getting any rest.

I was completely unprepared for the view that awaited me when I stopped and surveyed the last 500 m. From the shoulder I was looking into a 200 m wide glacial amphitheater. The ridge I had hoped to continue on became a sheer-sided knife edge of crumbly rock circling around to form the left border of this bowl. It was bare of any snow for 200 gradually rising meters. A three meter wide, snow-covered bergschrund separated the snowshoulder I was standing on, from the basin I was looking into. Another open crevasse cut across the middle of the bowl barring access to the face beyond. Yet the real dilemma was above. As the walls swept up towards the base of the summit cone, a wide open, nasty bergschrund cut continuously across the entire breadth of the face. As I looked up I gave in. I could not find a route through the upper bergschrund. I ate and drank a bit as I stomped around in the cold trying to lace together a crazy string of manoeuvers that would bring me to a point above the gaping schrund. Without much confidence, I envisioned a complicated solution involving a long traverse and very steep ice climbing which, although extremely unlikely, might justify going a little bit further. To cross the 3 m bergschrund immediately in front of me I took out my 6mm line and tied it to a snow-stake that an earlier team had left behind. While remnants of ropes had been plainly visible up to this point, I could see no sign of progress beyond it. Slowly letting out line, I inched my way out across a stable looking snow-bridge. Whoosh! Instantly, I was up to my waist in a crevasse. My reaction was a call for sanity. A strong voice scolded me for pushing too far. I had no back-up system and only a slight injury would put me out of the game. But another voice answered the first, suggesting I ignore it. I chose which to listen to and led out and across the rest of the bridge. As I pulled my rope across I felt a strong sense of risk. I was amazed at the determination I had. If I stopped now, I was letting doubt and uncertainty make decisions for me instead of logic and planning.

Entering the bowl rewarded my decision. What appeared to be an unmanageable crevasse actually had a simple snow bridge to cross. I then had to deal with the wall in front of me. The ridge to the snow shoulder at 6400 m began to feel like the approach to an alpine climb in the Rockies. I felt cut off inside a huge amphitheater unable to see the ridge I had climbed to get there. Reaching the summit from here became a climb in itself, separated in my mind from the route below.

Refocusing my energy, I gained elevation rapidly. The complicated route I had chosen from the shoulder began to appear unfeasable, however. Rather than a traverse along the lower lip of the bergschrund, I could see that hundred meters of traversing on difficult ground would be necessary to cross the gap to the upper slopes. Again I searched for a way across. There was a second possibility where the 'schrund split into two veins. There were two points on the 50 degree face, about 40 m horizontally apart, where each vein narrowed to a manageable 1.5 break. Beneath them was a mass of broken seracs and crevasses which prevented me from considering the possibility earlier. From my new perspective, I could see a traverse along the lip of the 'schrund

would take me to the first narrowing of the lower vein. If I could
get over the first break, I could make a 40 m traverse left and
deal with the second. From there it looked like a clear 55 degree
slope to the base of the summit pyramid. Above, I knew I would
have one last bergschrund to cross. Unlike the bowl, the pyramid
was visible from base camp.

I thought it was worth one more try. After climbing up to the
lip of the enormous gap, I edged my way towards the veins fanning
out to my left. Huge holes lay beneath me as I traversed over.
I concentrated on climbing to avoid the exposure. When I reached
the point where the gap narrowed, I was in luck. I placed my axes
in the firm ice above hauled myself up. Like several earlier passages,
I knew I'd need to rappel this on the descent. Moving left was easy.
With another move over the second vein, I was perched above the
bergschrund. I almost could not believe it. The fifty five degree face
slowly eased back as I climbed upward and eventually I reached the
summit cone. The last crevasse did not pose such a problem for
me. I crossed a long, slender bridge of ice with my hands gripping
the top edge and my front points on the face. I was doing things
now that I would have been reluctant to do with a solid belay at
any other time. My desire to see this climb through was strong.

Fifteen minutes later, I was on top. There was little wind and
not such cold as on the summit of Dhaulagiri 18 months earlier.
Clouds drifted across the summit and obscured my view for a few
minutes. I was amazed at where I stood. My watch read a few
minutes after 2 p.m. I sat and ate more shortbread for strength.
The south face of Xixabangma came into view. I appreciated those
who had made quick ascents of it. It was only a short distance
away to the north. Gur Karpo Ri and Lengpo Kang became visible
through the clouds. I would have liked a clearer view from the summit
but I could make no complaints about the weather. It was stable
and unthreatening.

I didn't stay long. The downclimbing would take all the strength
I had left. If I made no mistakes route-finding through the nasty
bergschrund, I could reach the ice shoulder before dark. I knew front
pointing down the ridge would occupy me long into the moonlit
evening. It didn't matter though. I could go on all night. 'Slow and
steady' would become my mantra until I reached the safety of my
tent.

Descending the summit ice-slope, I got confused and crossed a
different snow-bridge over the first crevasse. This surprised me. How
easily I could become disoriented further down the slope when I
would be looking for the twin veins I needed to recross! Subsequently,

I followed my crampon indentations so as to come out in exactly the right spot above the 'schrund. The upper edge of the vein came up suddenly beneath my feet as I descended facing in. I had to climb up again and left, to a patch of hard ice to drive a good screw for the first rappel. After the traverse back right, the one snow-stake I was carrying drove in firmly. I was terribly relieved it felt solid. My second short rappel went quickly.

I reached the shoulder at 4 p.m.; it had taken me five hours to the summit and back. With only a few hours of light left and fatigue tugging on every muscle, I started down with quiet resolve. Over and over I repeated to myself that I could go on all night if need be. I reaped the benefit of some old fixed line in places but the condition of it was inferior. I could not trust it to hold much weight. The sun dropped behind the horizon while I descended in a trance of activity. One set of front points followed by another, two axe placements and a rest. Over and over into the darkness. I could eventually see the light from the cook shelter a mile beneath me on the glacier. I knew that the others had been watching me all day and were now worried. Thirst and hunger dominated my senses, however. I summoned forth the determination to continue without agonizing over my speed. Whatever it took, I was willing to accept the price. It seemed a journey without end.

By 9:45 p.m. I was descending the last few meters of the triangular ice-face. I stopped above the final, 10 m, vertical wall, only minutes from my bivouac tent. I replaced the screw, as I explained earlier, and rappelled down. It was a final act of cautiousness. At 10 p.m. I was at my bivouac tent.

The next morning I descended the ridge with the comfort of knowing I had negotiated this section earlier. I was familiar with the terrain and made use of the knowledge. To my utter surprise, in the notch where the West ridge ends in the col, Lhakpa Dorje stood waiting for me. He had come up from base camp early in the morning, knowing that I would descend and need a friend. It was one of those moments one never forgets. The coming together of two friends high on a Himalayan glacier. I hoped I would never climb a mountain by myself again.

SUMMARY

The solo ascent of Dorje Lhakpa (6966 m) by the west ridge on 13 April, 1992.

4

BIG BIRD FLAPPING WINGS

DR. ANDREW POLLARD

AT 12.30 P.M. on 1 August 1990, Andrew Knight and I met in the bar of the Ski Club in Eaton Square, London to plan an expedition. We spent the afternoon reading in the library of the Alpine Club about peaks and valleys in Nepal. After another week of almost continuous research one mountain, Chamlang, had caught my imagination.

Chamlang, (7319 m) which in the Sherpa dialect means 'Big Bird Flapping Wings', was first climbed in 1962 by a Japanese team on the south ridge, a route repeated by the Koreans in 1987. Our attempt at the south ridge was to be the first British attempt.

Thatcher resigned, Mr Hussain invaded Kuwait, Mr Major went to the Gulf and the might of the Allied forces fell upon Iraq. Meanwhile we received permission from the Nepal ministry of Tourism to climb Chamlang and our plans materialised. Finally, a team of 10 members formed consisting of 7 climbers (Andrew Knight, Andrew and Peter Pollard, Annette Carmichael, Angus Andrew, Neil Howells and Dave Gwynne-Jones), an expedition doctor (Andrew Knight's wife, Carolyn), an amateur botanist (Richard Hancock) and our scientific officer, David Collier, led by Andrew Knight and myself.

We arrived in Kathmandu in mid-September 1991, a year after the expedition's conception and immediately began the struggle against bureaucracy and corruption to get the necessary permits, and to extract our freighted equipment from Customs before we could set out for base camp.

The march to the base camp took two weeks and the variety was tremendous. We began our trek almost at sea level in the Arun valley with temperatures in the sun of over 45°C and 100% humidity. These days were sweaty and I remember one evening drinking 5 litres of tea!

On 21 September we left the Arun and headed west, gradually gaining height and cooler air. However, this brought a plague of leeches which seemed able to get into, through, up and down all articles of clothing for a feast.

Photo 3

During the trek David was conducting his experiments in a frenzy. The expedition members were enticed into his tent late at night, even invited into his sleeping bag to be connected up to a selection of gadgets measuring everything from arterial oxygen saturation to blood pressure. Our Nepali staff were fascinated by his flashing lights and rude mechanical noises and sat for hours watching.

From Naulekh at the head of the Hinku valley, we headed east, ascending to 5400 m and crossing the Mera la below which we made our base camp. From the eastern side of the pass we had our first view of Chamlang, an enormous sheer face of snow, ice and rock, 'the big bird'. It was breath-taking and wonderful and I was filled with doubt that we could climb it.

Because of a strike by some of our porters it took several days to ferry loads across this glaciated pass and I stayed behind to escort the porters while rest of the team set up base.

On 4 October I arrived at a deserted base camp, the others who had gone in two parties to reconnoitre a route to the south ridge of Chamlang were expected back on the next day. Base camp (4700 m), in the early morning sun was glorious. It was a grassy place strewn with large boulders beside a babbling brook from the banks of which hung cold fingers of ice. Camp was 100 m above the Hongu river, a wild torrent draining innumerable glaciers. Across the

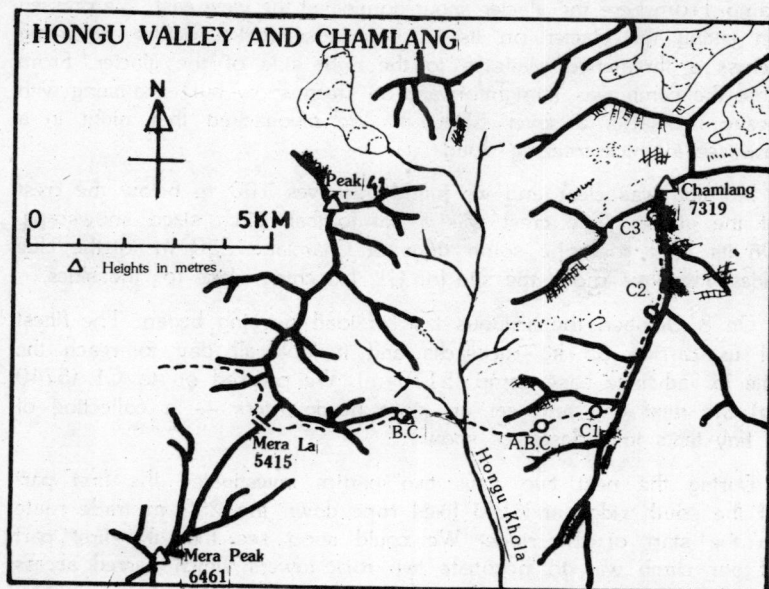

HONGU VALLEY AND CHAMLANG

river and now 2.5 km straight up above a tremendous face of rock and ice stood the snow-covered summit of Chamlang, golden in the sun. Beautiful and terrifying.

At lunchtime the two parties returned from their reconnaisance. Neither group had found a straightforward way to reach the south ridge of Chamlang and the mood was solemn during the afternoon. In 1962, the Japanese took nearly two weeks to find a route onto the south ridge, and we didn't have that amount of time.

6 October. Angus, Neil, Ngatemba and I left the base camp at 3.30 a.m. resolute in our determination to push a route onto the south ridge of Chamlang. First we descended with difficulty down to the river Hongu, following the brook from base in the dark. Then we headed steeply up the other bank of the river resting frequently, weighed down by ropes, stoves, gas, axes, crampons and gear for a bivouac. Initially, we followed a loose rocky ridge to the right of a glacier flowing west from the end of the south ridge of Chamlang. Soon as we approached steeply sloping snow-covered rocks it became clear that we didn't have the resources or the time to push this highly technical route.

Instead, we dropped down onto the moraine below the snout of the glacier, passing a meltwater stream amongst the loose unconsolidated boulders and noting the place as a possible site for advance base camp. From here the glacier snout dominated the view east. We pressed on taking the glacier on its left, up loose rocks, before traversing across a threatened platform to the right side of the glacier. From here the climb was straightforward on steep snow but exhausting with heavy rucksacks at over 5500 m. We bivouacked that night in a crevasse in thick freezing cloud.

Morning was clear and we found ourselves 100 m below the crest of the glacier. The crest was a flat football pitch sized snowscape. On its right rose the south ridge of Chamlang 250 m to the blue skies. Here we chose the site for C1, launching place for the skies.

On 8 October, the arduous task of load carrying began. The fittest of us carried 35 kg rucksacks and it took all day to reach the site for advance base camp (5170 m). We pressed on to C1 (5740 m) the next day and set up siege headquarters — a collection of 3 tiny tents in a desert of snow.

During the next two days two parties investigated the first part of the south ridge and laid fixed rope down the 250 m trade route to the start of the ridge. We could soon see that the first part of our climb was to negotiate two rock towers which barred access to the next part of the ridge. On the second day Angus arrived at camp in the dark, filled with anxiety. He had descended the fixed rope expecting Ngatemba (our Sirdar) to follow but he had not appeared. We discussed a plan of action and concluded that it was not safe to search in the dark. At first light Ngatemba appeared, he walked stiffly and silently into C1. He had spent the worst night of his career without shelter or bivouac equipment in high winds on the rocky ridge. The night before he had been unable to descend to warmth and safety as he didn't have a torch.

Demoralised, we talked all day about alternative routes, the danger, and giving up. Finally, we decided to push the ridge. However, Andrew who had only been married a few months made the brave decision to turn back. For him the danger was unacceptable.

Our next task was to make the first rock tower safe and we spent a day fixing rope in a rising traverse on loose rock.

Neil and Ngatemba pressed on to the second rock tower with more fixed rope, planning to bivouac that evening and go further in the morning. Meanwhile Dave and Annette carried loads on to the ridge above C1. The next day, we rose early and climbed the fixed rope along the first rock tower. At one point I turned round to see Angus sitting with his head bowed on his chest, emotion hidden behind his reflective goggles. Whilst unclipped from the fixed rope, he had stumbled and fallen onto his left shoulder, narrowly escaping an enormous fall to his death.

It was nearly midday and we spotted the other two already on the top of the second rock tower some 4 hours ahead of us but just within earshot. Neil shouted that they were going on.

That afternoon was the most glorious climbing for me. We descended from the first rock tower to take a line between the snow plastering the west face of the ridge and the second rock tower above. We were carrying heavy loads of climbing equipment and food to dump in preparation for the summit bid. Behind we could see C1 and ahead was the summit of Chamlang and in the distance to its left the black South West face of Everest looking most unfriendly.

Angus and I returned to C1 that night, while Neil and Ngatemba established C2 (6280 m) on a thin snow aréte on the crest of the south ridge of Chamlang — base camp visible as a collection of red dots far below.

That night I lay awake for a long time. The next problem was who to send for the summit. Neil and Ngatemba returned the next afternoon and Peter's arrival with buffalo fried rice and cooked potatoes decided our fate. We would rest for two days at C1 and then all 4 go for the top together.

On 18 October we set off for C2, fixing the last 100 m of the second rock tower and arriving to pitch tents in the afternoon mist.

The morning of the 19th was fine and we set off over the frozen snows northwards at 7.45 a.m. The morning was a long and terrific ridge bash with incredible exposure and hard work as the sun softened the snows. We climbed as two pairs, Neil and Ngatemba ahead breaking trail. By mid afternoon we reached the feared rock band which had dominated our conversation as we viewed the mountain from base camp. This had been the crux of the climb for the Japanese on the first ascent. Neil led the climbing on the rock band, 50 m of technical rock (VS) followed by a steep ice slope. Above this we roped together again as a four, Neil still leading. We were now on steep, unconsolidated snow, 3 m deep and we found ourselves almost swimming to stay on the mountain. Neil fell. Angus shouted, 'He's off.' There was nothing I could do, I was struggling to make any upward progress myself let alone arrest a fall. He whizzed past me and momentarily I realised that we were all about to plummet down the west face over the rock band, seven and a half thousand feet (2300 m) down, pulled by the rope. Then it was all over, he stopped just past me, incredibly held by Ngatemba, I don't know how.

As darkness fell we clambered into a crevasse and dug out places to sleep, brewed and spent a fitful night at 6800 m, short of air and desperately cold.

The morning of 20 October was again clear, but as we climbed out of our crevasse leaving behind all of our bivouac equipment the full force of a high altitude easterly wind hit us. Painful spin-drift struck all exposed flesh and dropped chilling flakes inside clothing. The slopes were straightforward now and at 10.50 a.m. we stood on the summit of Chamlang at 7319 m.

Ngatemba took out a Nepali flag and we all posed beside him for photographs. The wind was terrific, burning our faces and taking breath away. Neil took off his gloves to take some pictures and his fingers were frostbitten within seconds. We hurried down from that unpleasant spot to escape the cruel wind.

It was dark as we climbed along a knife edge of snow following our footsteps of the day before, back to C2. The wind was still roaring but with less ferocity than it had 7 hours previously when we had stood on the summit where, now, in the dim moonlight

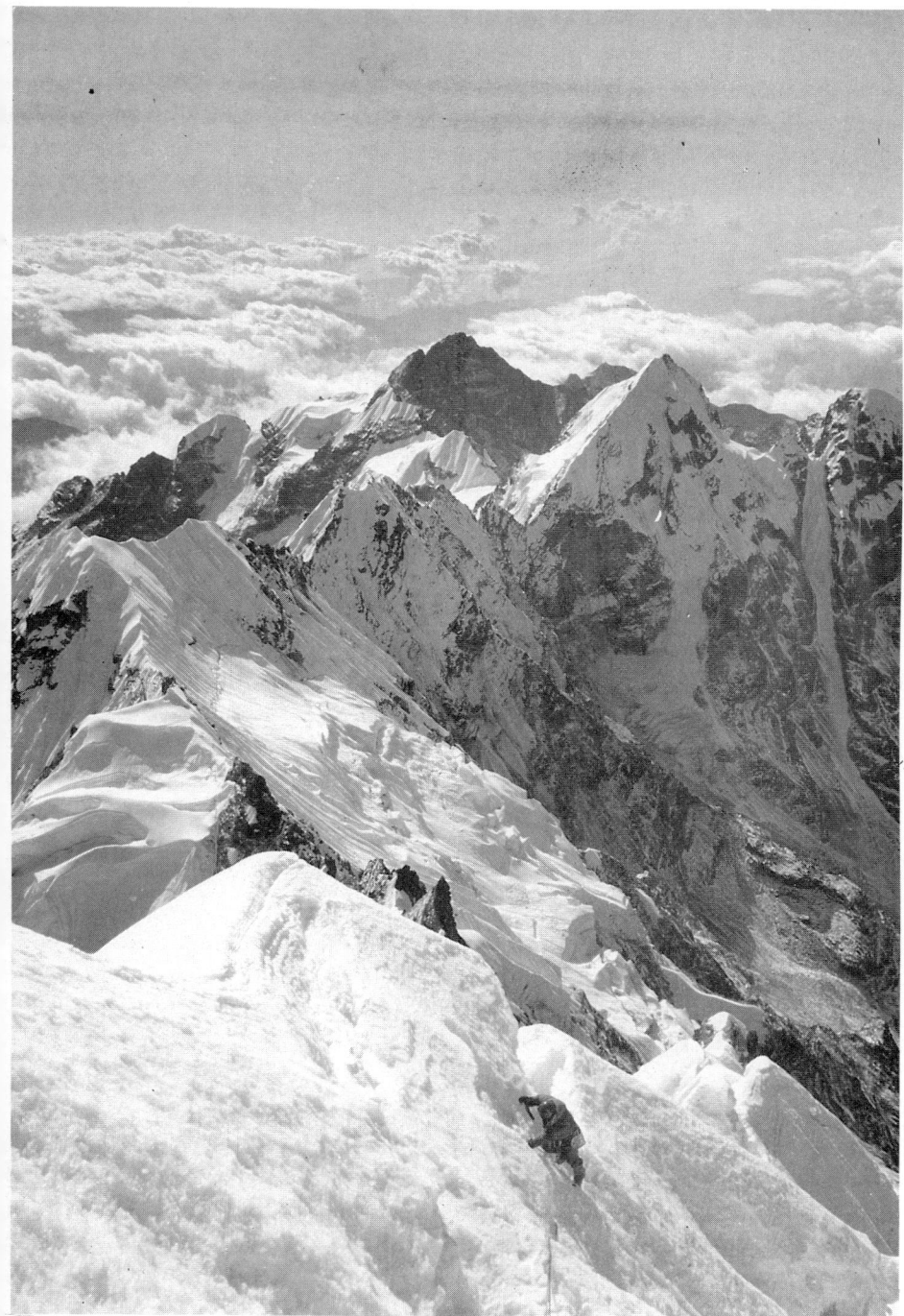

5. **Kusum Kanguru: Renshaw on summit ridge. Gonglha in background.**

(Stephen Venables)

6. Climbing on SW spur of Kusum Kanguru. Numbur on left,
Rolwaling peaks on right.

Article 5   (Stephen Venables)

a plume of snow was blowing unrelentingly east. I was staggering with exhaustion after 10 hours of climbing at high altitude. At 7 p.m. we collapsed into C2. Neil and Ngatemba Sherpa had been back an hour and had some hot orange ready and we sat rehydrating in silence and relief.

SUMMARY

The ascent of Chamlang (7319 m) by a British team, on 20 October 1991.

5

KUSUM KANGURU, 1991

STEPHEN VENABLES

IF THE KUSUM KANGURU expedition had a theme it was that excellent adage, 'any old fool can be uncomfortable'. Henry Day, Himalayan veteran of Annapurna, Everest and many other bumps, asked to join the trip as team manager. He offered generously to contribute to expedition funds on the condition that we walked into Solu Khumbu from Jiri, travelling in gentle stages, with suitable staff to ensure maximum ease and comfort. Neither he nor his wife, Sarah, had any need to prove themselves. There would be no unnecessary suffering.

I was delighted. Even the ascetic Dick Renshaw, now mellowing into middle age, accepted the idea; the third member of the climbing team, Brian Davison, although younger, was equally happy to travel in style. So we contacted Pasang Norbu.

Pasang runs his own trekking business based in Namche Bazar and Kathmandu. He had been our cook on the 1988 Everest Kangshung Face expedition. He makes arguably the best momoes in Asia and he has trained up a young apprentice, Jeta, to carry on the tradition. Dawa and Mingma made up the complement of domestic staff.

It was great to see Pasang again and he did a superb job of organising our approach to the mountain. After eight enjoyable days we arrived on 26 October 1991, keen and fit, at the entrance to the Kusum khola, which branches off from the main valley just north of Lukla. I had never climbed in Nepal before and this was my first experience of Solu Khumbu in the high season. Watching the rush hour traffic heading up to the airport at Lukla, we felt glad that in the morning we would be heading off into the jungle for a spot of peace and quiet.

I had picked on the southwest face of Kusum Kanguru after looking through John Cleare's and Bill O'Connor's photos. The mountain is

Frontispiece
Photos 4 to 9

32

stunning and as far as I could gather no-one had ever set foot
on the southwest face. We later heard a rumour that Peter Hillary
had once been to have a look but had never reached the head of
the valley. Pasang, who lives only a few miles away, was extremely
vague on the subject.

There was a path of sorts but it soon petered out. Brian, Dick
and I did a recce and started marking a route with cairns. Then
the following day the whole caravan started up the Kusum khola.
The first campsite was a delightful bed of moss in the forest. On
the second day we found ourselves in steep thick bamboo jungle,
slithering and hacking our way up with kukris. Evening came and
several porters asked for their pay but a few gallant volunteers promised
to return in the morning. Meanwhile Pasang set up kitchen on a
small rocky ledge while the rest of us used bamboo, rotten rhododendron
trunks and leaf mould to construct tent platforms. Only on the third
day did we finally emerge from the jungle. The final obstacle was
berberis — impenetrable, thorny thickets of the stuff, through which
we hacked a path to a sloping shelf of ground by a stream. While
Pasang performed a puja, producing delicious wafts of smoke from
the aromatic leaves of Rhododendron anthopogon, the rest of us started
terracing the mountainside. During all our time in the Kusum khola
and on the mountain we were never once able to pitch a single
tent without first building a platform.

Base camp was Sarah Day's Annapurna and after only one day
in residence she had to leave to return to England. However, Henry,
the team manager, had longer holidays and stayed on to provide
moral support for the three climbers. He helped us find a route
up to advance base, where we did some more inspired landscaping,
nicely complimented by Jeta's magnificent cairn which stood like a
beacon to guide us into camp on foggy nights.

All this time we had been pursuing a quiet debate about our precise
objective on the mountain. Renshaw, with his infuriating, persistent,
good sense, had pointed out that my proposed 'diretissima' up the
centre of the southwest face looked very dangerous. Davison reinforced
the argument by pointing out that my consolation alternative — a
subsidiary line on the right — led to the crest of the undimbed
south ridge which sported a magnificent great buttress of granite. Happy
hours were spent at the telescope, spying out cracks, corners and
other tempting features to exploit my weakness for high altitude rock
climbing. So the great Eigerish concave wall was left for 'other men,
less wise', and we set off to explore the sensible men's alternative.

The team leader accompanied us one fine dawn to the foot of the southwest spur and wished us good luck as we headed off towards a band of dark, loose, overhanging rock. Brian led us up the band and later that morning we established a cache of food and gear part of the way up the route, ready for our full attempt. A hundred yards to our left the central buttress — my diretissima — was bombarded by flying granite. Not for the first time I felt glad to be guided by such sensible companions.

Satisfied with our recce we returned to advance base. Descending the scree slopes, Dick suddenly found a rusty battered Camping Gaz cylinder, destroying in a moment my deep satisfaction at being in a valley where no man had trod before — a state of affairs that I had already boasted about in my despatches to the *Daily Telegraph*.

It was a terrible shock. I wondered what sort of bribe would be required for a promise of secrecy. Then I remembered that Dick was a man of principle, not the type to toe the party line for a few pieces of silver. My thoughts continued in this gloomy vein until I realized that the gas cylinder was not in fact any proof at all of a previous visit. When people dispose of gas cylinders they either burn, flatten and bury them properly or they just dump them as they are. This cylinder was only partially dented. Its dents were obviously not the work of a manic ecologist. No — they were the haphazard blows inflicted on a light object falling from a great height — in this case from the crest of the west ridge of Kusum Kanguru, 1500 m above us. All the debris from that part of the mountain ended up next to our advance base, including this gas cylinder which Tommy Curtiss must have thrown away from his bivouac at the top of the north face, years earlier. That was the nearest anyone had been to our virgin cwm.

I felt much better after concluding this thesis (later confirmed by Mr Curtiss) and returned to base camp next morning in high spirits. Satisified with our recce, we enjoyed two days of Pasang's catering, then said goodbye to Henry and returned to the mountain.

There is no point in describing the climb in detail. It was a magnificent route with steep climbing on snow, ice, rock and mixed terrain. It probably approximated to the French alpine grade of TD sup. Travelling as a threesome and delayed by unsettled weather, we took four days to climb the mixed spur leading to the south ridge.

On the fifth day we did a recce to the first steepening of the great buttress on the ridge. It was a glorious morning and for the first time we had a new view, out over the Hinku valley to Mera,

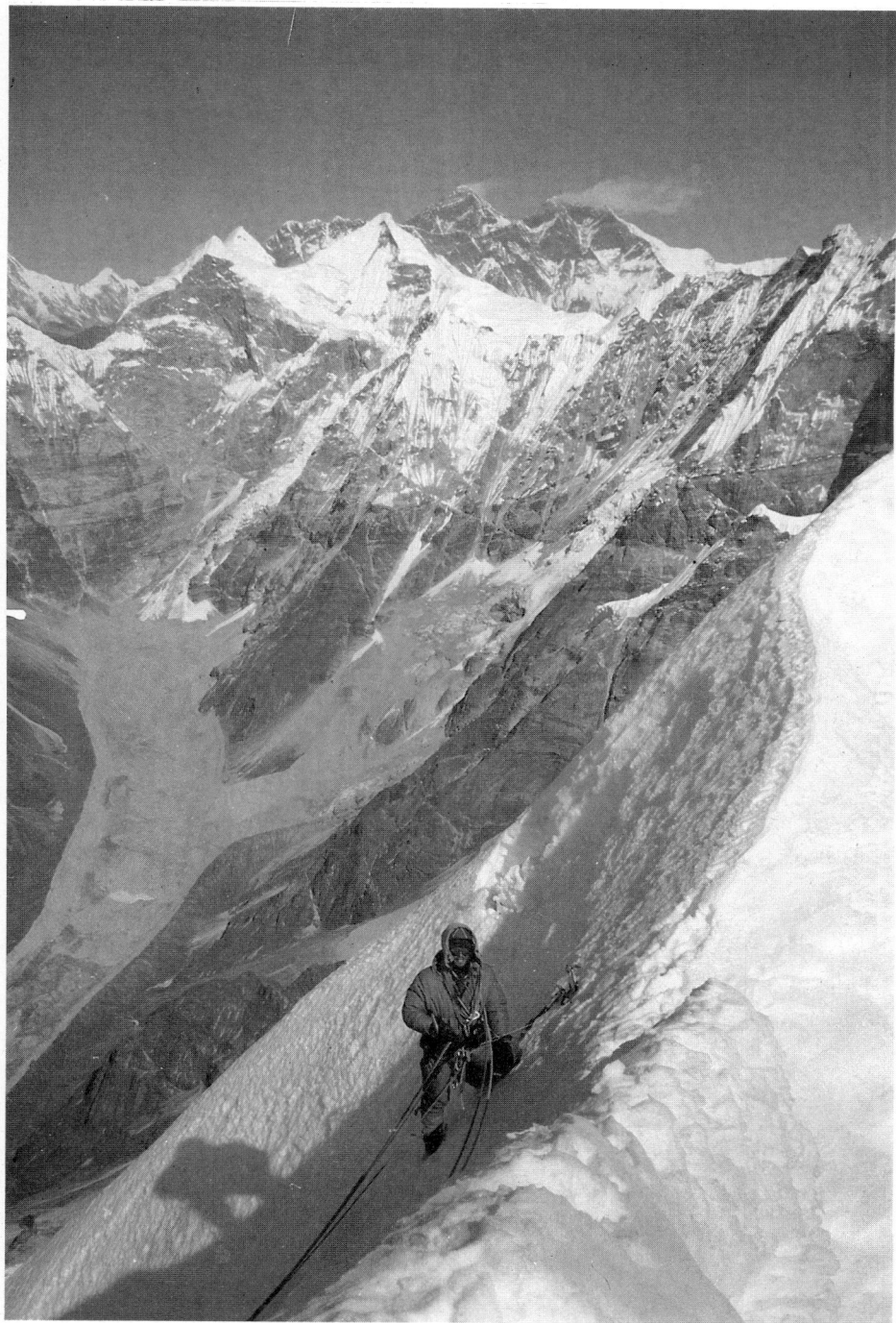

7. Dick Renshaw 15 m below the summit of Kusum Kanguru. Everest peaks behind.

Article 5 (Stephen Venables)

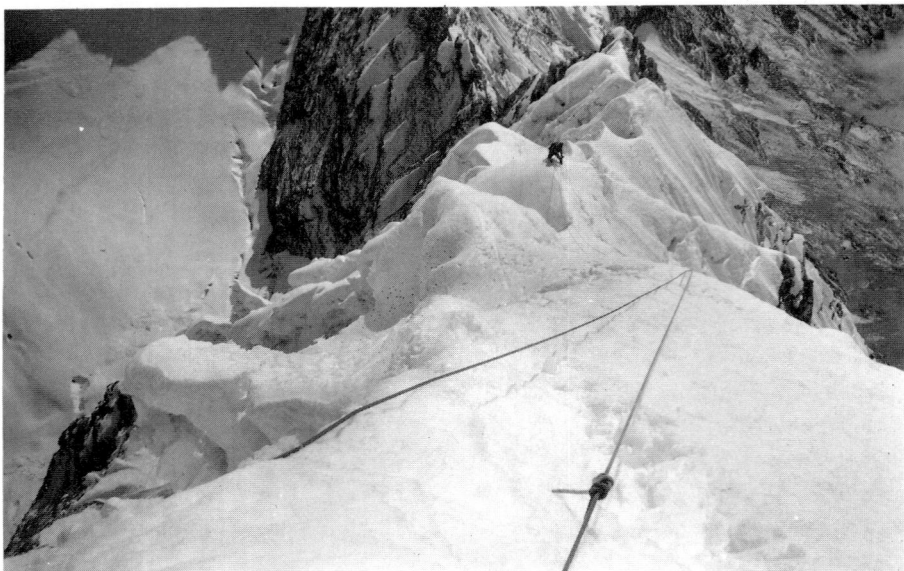

8. Snow-bollard abseil on south ridge of Kusum Kanguru.

Article 5   (Stephen Venables)

9. View from the summit of Kusum Kanguru, Peak 43 (centre) to
Everest and Lhotse.

Chamlang and the distant outline of Jannu and Kangchenjunga. The rock buttress looked wonderful and that evening Brian enthused about possible tactics on the steep pitches to come. In the morning, however, he was very lethargic. He had been developing steadily worse headaches and occasional vision problems. Only a few months earlier, on Broad Peak, he had suffered a retinal haemorrhage — a problem which he thought had cleared up completely. Now, obviously at risk again, he offered to wait while Dick and I attempted the summit, but Dick insisted rightly that descent was the only option. So, bitterly disappointed, we set off down, taking twenty abseils to get off the mountain.

Late that night we arrived back at base camp, to wake up a very surprised Pasang. Already Dick and I were talking about the possibility of another attempt and in the morning Brian offered generously to wait at base camp and man the telescope for five days while we had another attempt at the route.

This time we were much quicker, straightening out the line and reaching the previous highpoint in 1 1/2 days instead of 4 1/2. On the second afternoon we started up the granite buttress, following a huge square cut corner, formed by a giant pillar leaning against the buttress. We hoped to camp on top of the pillar, but after an hour of struggling in a vicious wind to build a platform with granite blocks all I had achieved was some very numb, bloody fingers. So, at Dick's suggestion, we climbed down into the chimney behind the pillar, where there was some shelter. We pitched the tent on a vague ledge of jammed blocks. Unfortunately a giant chockstone was suspended, like a pendulum, just where we needed to put our heads. Determined to stick to the principle of not suffering unnecessarily, I organised a winch, hauling up the lower end of the chockstone and belaying it to a Friend wedged higher up the chimney.

It worked like a treat, leaving just enough room for the two of us to sit upright in the tent. I could swear that the entire pillar, 70 m high, swayed in the wind that night; but my main problem was a desperate attack of claustrophobia. In the end Dick had to give me a sleeping pill to shut me up.

On the third morning we had to wait a while for the wind to die down. When we eventually left at 9.00 a.m. it was still very cold and I spent a lot of time talking to my fingers, willing them back to life after each skirmish with the ice-cold granite. But it was wonderful nevertheless — first a long steep corner pitch, then easier ground, then another long pitch up thin cracks, tiptoeing on the edge of a huge overhang. What with blowing on fingers and hauling sacks, we only did five pitches that day and it was dark by the time we had built accomodation for the night — a half metre wide ledge with just enough room for the two of us to half sit, half lie, with feet hanging over the edge.

In nearly twenty years climbing I had rarely had such an enjoyable day. The rock climbing had been a treat and Nepal in November really was everything that it was cracked up to be. The weather was perfect, with that brilliant blue clarity that you never get in summer and we had been enjoying ever more spacious views out to Rolwaling; in the morning, provided that we reached the summit, we would be able to look north to Everest.

We did reach the summit on the fourth day and we did see Everest. It was November 20th and a huge plume was blowing off the top of the world, eighteen miles away. Down on our summit, at 6369 m, it felt quite cold enough and I understood just what a miserable business it must be, climbing 8000 m peaks in winter. Our so-called 'trekking peak' had been quite demanding enough. It had given us four days of beautifully varied climbing and we still had a long descent to complete. We did four abseils and downclimbed back to the top bivouac that afternoon. The next day, everything, for once, went like clockwork. Many of the anchors were in place from the first attempt and we completed the 25 abseils in 7¼ hours. Even Brian, a far better climber than either of us, was impressed and complained when we arrived at base camp for supper that we were two hours early.

The direct line up Kusum Kanguru's southwest face remains untried, but in retrospect I think that the flanking route we climbed was actually a better one. Just reaching the foot of the face had been exciting and on our approach to base camp it had taken .three days to cover four miles. It was encouraging to discover that even in Solu Khumbu, on a famous trekking peak, you only have to walk a few hundred yards off the beaten track to find an adventure. With someone like Pasang Norbu in charge it can even be a comfortable adventure. It makes one hopeful for the future of Himalayan climbing.

SUMMARY

A three person British ascent of Kusum Kanguru (6367 m). The peak was climbed on 20 November 1991 via the south ridge.

6

PUTHA HIUNCHULI

ANDREW KERR

THE SCOTTISH/SWISS Putha Hiunchuli expedition 1992
was a small family expedition trying to climb the remote and
little visited Putha Hiunchuli. This is situated at the extreme west
of Dhaulagiri, and is the last 7000 m peak, to the west, in this
range. We wished to climb the summit alpine style, making a first
British/Swiss ascent from the south side, using a new route if possible.
Our climbing team consisted of my Swiss wife Bernadette, my brother
Gary and I, with my father James Kerr as base camp manager, and
a family friend Stewart Smith as a support member.

Putha Hiunchuli (7246 m) was first climbed by the reknowned British
expedition organiser and expedition leader Jimmy Roberts, the father
of trekking in Nepal. He climbed the peak from the Kaya valley
on the north side in 1954. The early seventies saw 2 ascents of
the south side using the traditional siege style tactics, by Japanese
teams. Since then the mountains have seen a handful of attempts.[1]

Leaving Kathmandu on 26 September 1992 we had our first night
under canvas outside Pokhara, and at the same time our first taste
of the torrential monsoon rains. After a 9 day trek through this
sparsely populated region, with the obligatory 'who's got the biggest
leech?' competition, we established base camp at 4100 m on 4
October. Fortified by 'ramburgers' provided by a reluctant ram who
had walked with us over a 4600 m pass, we made a recce the
next day to our C1 at 5200 m. Immediately it became apparent
that our proposed route to reach a large snow slope, giving access
low down on the east ridge, was barred by suicidal looking seracs.
We immediately decided to try a variant of the Japanese route on
the south ridge, following the glacier several kilometres to the west
before tackling the technical climbing. In effect this route traverses
underneath the long east ridge, and avoids serac danger, apart from
the occasional huge serac avalanches, one of which covered our tracks.

---

1. See H.J. XIX, p. 106 for Roberts' first ascent, H.J. Vol. XXXIII. p. 49 for
the Japanese ascent, H.J. Vol. 36, p. 192 for German attempt.— Ed.

We made 3 carries to C2 at 5800 m, which was established on a flat glacial plateau. On 11 October it began snowing heavily during the night. The next 3 days were spent at C1, digging out our tents, eating and sleeping. During the 3rd night my wife Bernadette had problems with her breathing. Gary, the expedition doctor, diagnosed a pulmonary oedema. Bernadette's condition seemed to be deteriorating rapidly so I got ready to escort her down to base camp. However, Gary gave her some Adalat, manufactured by the company Bayer, along with some Dexamethasone in case of cerebral oedema. The Adalat greatly improved the condition of Bernadette's pulmonary oedema. She was able to pass a comfortable night, and descend with help to base camp in the morning. This drug Adalat is little known in high altitude medicine, its use in this field being recent. Certainly our experience proved it to be highly efficient. Gary and a medical colleague have written a paper on this, which appeared in the British medical journal *Lancet* in December 1992. Future expedition doctors would be well advised to look at the high altitude qualities of this drug. Gary and his colleague hope to research this drug further, with the backing of Bayer, in the near future.

On 14 October Gary and I broke trail in thigh deep snow to reach C2 after 12 hours of effort (normally it took us 4 hours). Our Sirdar Moti Lal and Lhakpa Sherpa came up behind us in support. Throughout our expedition these Sherpas were extremely helpful, and very strong on the mountain.

After a recce on the 15th to a col, we moved up on the 16th, over a technical ice slope/serac, trying desperately to keep on the right side of the conspicuous serac crack line. Moti and Lhakpa followed behind us belayed on our 2nd rope. We made a rather cramped one tent C3 on a snow-shelf at 6400 m. We decided to try for the summit the next day, going as lightly laden as possible. This decision was influenced by our lack of gas and limited time for our trip. Immediately after C3 we climbed a 50° wall of rotten snow and ice which allowed minimal ice-screw protection. Again we were supported by Moti and Lhakpa. Arriving on a shoulder we traversed over a subsidiary summit at around 7050 m, to arrive at the foot of the final ridge. This is a variation of the Japanese route, as they dropped down from the shoulder to an upper glacier, and climbed a ridge further to the right, from a top camp established on this glacier. On climbing our final ridge, the afternoon cloud came swirling in to obscure our route. Given the late hour and the thought of a bivouac without a stove, we decided to retreat. Abseiling down the 300 m 50° wall in the dark, we arrived at C3 at 8.30 p.m.

In retrospect our summit attempt was too optimistic given the technical ground and height we still had to cover. We ruled out a 2nd attempt, not wishing to climb the 50° wall of rotten snow again. Had we been equipped to fix rope in this section, a 2nd attempt would have been undertaken. However, our 1st attempt could have been successful had we moved our C3 equipment with us, and established a C4 below the final ridge.

Disappointed yet happy with our progress with limited resources, we abseiled down the large serac to the col on the 18th, cleared C2, and descended to C1 before dusk. C1 was cleared on 19 October, before descending to base camp. Base camp was cleared the next day.

Being a mainly Scottish expedition, we celebrated the end of our climb with a good Scottish whisky. The Sherpas also seemed to appreciate our 16 year old Lagavulin Malt. However I wish I could say the same for the local rum.

We certainly appreciated our adventure in this beautiful part of the world, and hope to return for another expedition, and renew our contacts with the Sherpas who helped us so much to make our attempt. Must remember to bring more whisky though. They drink it almost as much as the Scots. Which whisky company will sponsor us?

SUMMARY

An attempt on Putha Hiunchuli (7246 m) by a Scottish/Swiss expedition in October 1992.

7

EVEREST SOLO

JONATHAN PRATT

IT WAS A cold, crystal clear night with the moon, now nearly full illuminating brilliantly the surrounding peaks. For once the air was still, disturbed only by the occasional swirl of snow bouncing down the slope beside me. I lay there amidst this silent world, an insignificant dot perched precariously on the side of this massive mountain. I was bivvying out on the small platform, carved out of the snow, on the steep Lhotse face, which is C3 (7400 m) on Everest. I was all alone, just one man, on this great mountain. This was during my solo climb of Everest; however, right from the start I had run into a number of minor difficulties: There were 100 other people climbing the mountain as well. To be alone was as hard as climbing the mountain itself. Before this I had climbed from one crowded camp to another, but now with the other teams resting in their base camps I finally found myself all alone in this white wasteland.

I had not intended to climb solo, I had not intended to climb Everest. I had arrived in Nepal for another climb when, at the last minute a permit for Everest became available. It was too good an opportunity to miss. Unfortunately my partner had not been able to arrive in time so if I was to go, it had to be solo. I pondered whether to take up the challenge. To climb Everest is a major undertaking; to climb it solo even more so. It had been done before but not often. I would have to climb without oxygen: that had been done before, but again, not often. And on my budget I could not afford any Sherpa support, making it even more demanding. Certainly large expeditions are still very much the norm; after all, the satellite dishes and direct phone links to Europe are standard equipment on Everest these days. It seemed audacious to be mounting an expedition along my modest lines, but I had solo'd on the big peaks before and besides, what about the 100 or so other climbers on the mountain? It did not take me long to make up my mind.

I spent the next few days in a mad whirl of activity rushing around Kathmandu, from one office here, to a shop there; completing some paperwork here, buying some equipment there, until out of apparent

41

chaos everything was assembled, and I was ready to fly up to Lukla on my way to the base camp. Unfortunately, the plane wasn't, due to bad weather, a common occurrence at this time of year, The planes were unable to fly. After my mad rush to get ready, I now had to spend three idle days waiting in Kathmandu. Nothing could be more frustrating.

Once in Lukla things seemed easy after the commotion of Kathmandu. While I quietly sipped coffee on the veranda of my hotel my porters were quickly and efficiently organised. I would have two porters, young lads about 18 years old, who had been working on a nearby building site, and had promptly stopped work for the more lucrative occupation of carrying loads. I commented that maybe they would not be strong enough, as I looked at their small, sparse bodies against my large, heavy packs. 'Don't worry', I was told, 'They may look small but they are so strong and fast you won't be able to keep up', They were right and I soon found myself hurrying along behind them.

An hour up the trail it started raining, reminding us that the monsoon had not yet ended. The boys stopped and in unison sang out 'plastic, plastic;' so I pulled out the plastic sheets I had brought for them, and now, suitably dressed, we continued on our way.

I was to discover that 'plastic' and 'oxygen' were the only two words of English they knew. They appeared a little cheated when I was unable to produce the latter.

That first night we arrived, tired and wet, in Namche Bazar, where I shared a hotel with some Italian scientists on their way up to study the effects of high altitude at their research station above Lobuche. One of their members had climbed Everest some years previously with what had been the largest expedition ever on Everest. They were clearly unimpressed by my modest expedition. However, they did give me some helpful advice for my climb, and a welcome glass of whisky, which, while apparently not necessary for good acclimatisation, certainly provided useful psychological benefits.

The next day my porters rushed on ahead to the base camp leaving me behind to continue at a more leisurely pace. I wanted to take my time on the hike up the Khumbu valley so I would arrive in the base camp well acclimatised. Unfortunately, in the haste to get to the base camp, my porters had left me embarrassingly underequipped, with only an umbrella to supplement my T-shirt and shorts.

The next few days the monsoon decided to go out in one final fling and several times I found myself completely lost in swirling mist and in driving rain, wondering if I would make it to the next little hamlet. After a few miserable days I stumbled into an inhospitable base camp in the process of being bombarded by a snow storm. It was not the most inviting welcome. The next day the clouds cleared, to reveal, for the first time, the magnificent scenery around me which would be my home for the next couple of months. With that final storm the monsoon bade us farewell and for the next couple of months I was blessed with good weather.

I pitched my tent on the outskirts of what had now become a sizable tent city. Across from me was the massive Spanish expedition with their 16 climbers, countless Sherpas, and 8 tons of equipment; behind me the Khumbu icefall, an impenetrable barrier to any solo expedition. However I would be able to use the ladders and ropes installed in the icefall by the Sherpa team a few weeks before.

While I would be climbing alone, I would still be dependent on the work and equipment put in by some of the teams, without which my climb would not be possible, especially the route through the icefall. Apart from that my expedition would be completely my own effort. I would be making all my own camps and carrying all my equipment, every kilogram of equipment I would have to, step by step, transport up the mountain on my own back. It would mean carrying heavy packs, not just through the icefall but all the way up to C4 (8000 m). Whereas most climbers could go to the South col with a minimal pack I would not only have to carry a full load but have to make the trip twice. I hoped all the extra work would not wear me down too soon.

My acclimatisation up to the base camp had gone well, and it did not take me long to ferry my loads up through the icefall. Soon I was able to establish my C2, (6500 m) at the end of the Western Cwm. Here, I took a few days rest to aclimatise before setting out to make a carry up to what would be my third camp at 7400 m on the Lhotse face. I did not get far. After just half an hour I had to give up, totally exhausted. I was struck down with a bad case of diarrhoea, which at this altitude leaves one completely drained of energy. With so many people at C2 there is always the risk of drinking contaminated water, and at some time I must have done so and was now suffering the consequences. I was now at a crucial stage in my climb. I would not be able to recover from my illness at this altitude but yet it was vitally important for me to make that carry to C3 before I went down to the base camp to rest.

When climbing Everest during the post monsoon season a short period, or 'window', of good weather appears above 8000 m between the end of the monsoon and the beginning of the winter winds. This window can be as short as a day or as long as couple of weeks. I had to be ready for my summit attempt when that window of calm weather arrived, and if I did not establish C3 now I would be too late.

This is where being on a solo climb really counts. There was nobody to take over for only I could get that load up the Lhotse face. I envied the bigger teams who in a similar situation could just send up some Sherpas instead. I cursed my luck at being ill at such an important time.

The next morning I set out on this major test. As I slowly advanced up the slope I would slump down, utterly exhausted, thinking I could go no further but after a brief rest I was able to move on a bit more until, once more, I would have to stop, completely tired. It seemed impossible I would make it to C3, as I climbed each section of the rope I prayed it would be the last, but there was always more climbing its way endlessly upwards. After an eternity I finally collapsed totally drained onto the shelf at C3. It was one in the morning and now, after some sleep, I too could go down and rest.

In the base camp I found myself in the queue outside the makeshift stone shelter that was the French doctor's clinic. Each day during 'open hours' she attended a small line of ailing climbers and Sherpas. She was well prepared for my sort of complaint and on her prescribed medication I was soon regaining my strength. To fully recover I decided to go down further and rest for a few days at a lower altitude, So I set off down to Lobuche at 4900 m. Unfortunately (or fortunately!) I fell in step with an attractive Australian trekker on her way down the Khumbu valley, and instead of only going to Lobuche I ended up in Thyangboche, 6 hours further down the trail.

Although I knew the rest at Thyangboche was doing good I found it impossible to relax. On a climb such as this you get immersed in achieving your goal, and I found it unbearable to just sit around. I was itching to get back to the mountain. My impatience did not improve as news of the other expeditions came. The news was not good. It appeared that they had all encountered very strong winds higher up the peak and that all the expeditions had abandoned their summit bids for the time being. I also heard some strange, and rather disturbing news — my tent had blown up. I had visions of all my equipment, which I had laboriously dragged up the mountain, scattered about as debris on the glacier. I could wait in Thyangboche no longer and hurried back to Everest as fast as I could.

Back at C2 I found out it was true, my tent really had blown up but luckily it had not resulted in the widespread destruction I had envisioned. One of my cooking gas cylinders had exploded; shot through the top of the tent; rocketed over the rest of C2, and landed 50 m further on down the glacier. Fortunately the only damage was to the top of the tent, which I was able to repair with the aid of a flysheet borrowed from the Australians. Maybe it was just as well I had gone to Thyangboche, I hate to think what would have happened if I had been in the tent at the time.

I made one trip to C4 but the weather was terrible so I quickly descended back to C2. Without oxygen, staying at C4 will quickly sap all your energy, so you cannot afford to spend one moment longer than necessary at this altitude. You cannot just wait up there for good weather to appear, instead you must wait much lower down the mountain, and when the good spell does come, rush up as fast as possible hoping you will get back up there in time. I decided to wait in C2 until I got news of better weather at the South Col. On the other hand, the Spanish team adopted a completely different approach, more befitting a large expedition. When they realised that the final climb to the summit was going to be so difficult they decided that one all out effort was called for, which would require most of their team to sacrifice their own summit aspirations for the good of the team as a whole. While I waited at C2 some of their members were able to stay at C4 using oxygen to stay fresh. When a small break in the weather came 3 days later, they were ready to go. With some members taking on a supporting role, four of their team managed to force their way to the summit. It was a fine accomplishment, but it was bad news for me, as it showed what sort of effort was required to make it to the top, and without any backup I realised I could not make that kind of assault on the mountain.

Although the Spanish succeeded, the weather was still not good and was probably getting worse; it seemed our window of calm weather was not coming this year. I realised I would have to go for the summit now regardless, so once again I set off for C4. As I climbed the final hundred metres to the South Col I met the French and Sherpa teams descending; they too having finally given up. They wished me well, but their failure did not bode well for my success.

When I reached C4, I found Mark Jennings, of the French expedition to be the sole occupant of that desolate campsite. He had stayed on for one last try and from what I know of Mark he was not the one to give up without a fight. We realised that the weather was not good enough, but this was our last chance; so together we decided to go for the summit the next day.

Conditions in the tent were miserable, and the noise of the wind was so deafening that even when we shouted in each others ears we could not hear. We could communicate by sign language only. We forced ourselves to drink a few cups of soup and eat some fruit bars, as we gathered ourselves around the hissing stove. Cooking a meal was much too arduous a task to contemplate. As the night wore on we made a futile effort to sleep, but to no avail. The strong winds continued to shake our tent all through the night and despite our hopes the condition seemed only worse in the morning. When we set off, we knew our chances of success were slim; but we had to try.

Soon it ceased to be a quest to conquer the mountain but more a struggle for survival. Pummelled by a hail of snow-pellets we clung to our ice axes, our faces hugging the ground, fighting for breath. When we moved it was in uncontrollable spurts at the whim of the wind. We could not survive in such conditions for long; desperately we clawed our way off the Col, back to the comparative shelter of the Lhotse face.

Back in the base camp most of the other expeditions were preparing to leave; everything was an uncoordinated bustle of activity as large portions of the tent city were dismantled and packed away. Every yak in the Khumbu valley was on hand to carry it all away, and little by little they drifted off down the glacier until by dusk they had all gone, leaving only the occasional tent behind for the few remaining climbers. It all seemed strangely quiet now that the familiar sounds of the base camp had gone. No longer the hum of generator, the chatter of 100 people sitting down to dinner. Now, just the silence of the mountains.

I resolved to make one final attempt, along with the German expedition who had also remained behind. However it was to be short lived: at C2 we met their Sherpas returning from the South Col. Their tents had been destroyed and they had a hard time getting down from the col. Clearly, things had not improved since I was there last. Reluctantly I had to admit it was over, and for the last time make my way back down through the icefall. It was disappointing after all the effort I had put in, especially as the mountain gave me no real chance. But failure is an integral part of mountaineering, and I am glad I still made the trip. If I retain just one of the friends I made on Everest it will be a success enough.

SUMMARY

A 'solo' attempt on Everest by a British climber in autumn 1991, amidst many other expeditions operating on the mountain.

8

THE WORKMANS :
TRAVELLERS EXTRAORDINARY[*]

MICHAEL PLINT

OR MUCH OF this century that formidable American couple, Dr William Hunter Workman and Mrs Fanny Bullock Workman, have exercised a certain fascination on the mountaineering world. My favourite picture of the Workmans shows them at lunch, or rather tiffin, at 14,000 ft on the Chogo Lungma glacier in the Karakoram. They are wearing pith helmets and sit formally at a little table, attended by a bearer wearing a puggaree of the correct design. They do not give the impression that, had you been passing, you would have been invited to take pot luck. In fact this picture encapsulates the strangeness of the Workmans. It is not only their achievement—the seven great Himalayan expeditions that they mounted between 1899 and 1912 — that is remarkable. It is also the extraordinary lengths to which they went to conceal every detail of their own personalities, feelings and indeed of their lives generally, except where these were concerned with marching across glaciers and up mountains.

During the past two years I have been fortunate enough to gain some access to this unknown region. I stumbled across what are, in effect, the Workman archives — a large collection of papers, photographs, newspaper articles and unpublished writings, together with the notebooks kept by both the Workmans during the expeditions. These papers had been in the possession of their daughter, the late Lady Rachel MacRobert.

Their background was patrician. She was the daughter of a governor of Massachusetts and he the son of a distinguished doctor. In both cases their education included polishing in Europe and their marriage, in a ceremony of almost royal splendour, was the social event of 1881 at Worcester, Massachusetts. After three years of marriage their daughter Rachel was born, and life as GP and fashionable wife continued until 1889 with no indication of the obsessive travel that was to be the most notable characteristic of their life together.

* Reprinted from *The Alpine Journal*, 1992/93 with kind permission of the author and the editor.

There were, however, subterranean rumblings. Some unpublished short stories by Fanny, dating from this period, bring her closer than any of her other writings. The heroine of 'A Vacation Episode' is a beautiful and aristocratic English girl who is bored with the Season, with her crowds of admirers, and with the restrictive attitude of her aunt. A determined young woman with plenty of money, she takes herself off to Grindelwald, where she rapidly becomes an experienced alpinist and infuriates her family by marrying an American. The dominant features of Fanny's life — restlessness, mountains, women's lib, and perhaps an awareness of her own plainness — are clear to see.

In the case of the Doctor, we may look for clues to his personality in the series of studio portraits, far more numerous than those of his less-than-beautiful wife, that start in 1881 and continue for more than 30 years. They show a handsome man, conscious of his good looks. The pose is a little theatrical, the mouth grim and set, the eyes betraying no interest in the observer but fixed fiercely on some distant horizon. A man not to be trifled with, not the life and soul of the party, but nevertheless a good man to be with in a tight spot.

After eight years, in 1889, the crunch came. Dr Hunter gave up work, allegedly on the grounds of ill health, and the Workmans left America, in her case for ever. In December of that year, in Dresden, the city that was to be the nearest thing to home that they were to recognise for the next 20 years, an event occurred which is, I believe, crucial to an understanding of the Workmans: their son, Siegfried, was born. The very existence of Siegfried seems to have been suppressed in all the published references.

Early in 1891 the Workmans discovered the so-called safety bicycle, which was to dominate their lives for the rest of the century. It is difficult, at this distance of time, to appreciate the immense impact of the advent of this new invention. It was made for the Workmans. The next year they almost achieved that state of perpetual motion that was to become normal. They cycled all over Italy, attended the Wagner festival at Bayreuth, and then went off to Switzerland. On 14 September Fanny climbed Mont Blanc, by the old route of the Grands Mulets and the Grand Plateau, and of course it was the guide, and not Fanny, who suffered from mountain sickness.

In 1893 they cycled around Italy again. On their return to Dresden disaster struck them. Siegfried, the little boy they had left at home, caught influenza. This developed into pneumonia and, at the age of $3^{1}/_{2}$, he died. There remain several photographs of him, a clinical account by the Doctor of his illness and death, a valedictory ·poem

by Fanny and a long-forgotten name given to a peak near the Biafo glacier in the Karakoram : the Siegfriedhorn. People deal with this kind of situation in different ways. It is possible that the Flying Dutchman life adopted by the Workmans after 1893 had something to do with this loss.

The following year they made their first excursion outside Europe, when they cycled round Algeria and first demonstrated their ability to cope with extreme discomfort. Next year they cycled round Spain. These trips resulted in their first two books. Their publisher, Thomas Fisher Unwin, had his knuckles rapped by the Doctor for putting a picture of the Workmans on the cover: 'We strongly object to any picture in which we appear.' Spain was followed by more cycling with Rachel, and Fanny climbed the Matterhorn with Peter Taugwalder, who had made the first ascent, with Whymper, in 1865.

On 7 November 1897 the Workmans left Marseilles for the still-mysterious East and 29 months of arduous travel. Their main object was to study the ancient architecture of India. A secondary objective, one suspects, was to engage in cycling on an even more colossal scale than was practicable in Europe and North Africa. It is surprising to realise that when they landed at Colombo it was their very first contact with the Indian subcontinent. He was then 50, she 38.

They made a serious initial mistake. They decided to employ an Englishman as valet cum cycling luggage carrier, and much of Fanny's account of their six week cycling tour deals with the shortcomings of this unfortunate individual. After a series of spectacular accidents, no doubt precipitated by the effect on his stability by the mass of luggage he was expected to carry on his handlebars, he finally cycled over a precipice in a rainstorm. He was observed standing, apparently unharmed, some 40 ft down, but his cycle was lying 'maimed' (as Fanny described it) beneath a waterfall.

After this incident the Workmans and valet parted company by mutual consent, and from then onwards they employed native servants, though these were not always to their liking either. The index to one of their books carried the following entries under 'coolies': greed and laziness of, helplessness of, mutiny of, trouble with (eight entries under the last heading).[1] There is no denying that their attitude to those unfortunate enough to labour for them in the high mountains was unattractive. It compares unfavourably with the accounts of such contemporary travellers as Sir Martin Conway, who wrote with understanding and affection of the mountain people.

Early in January 1898 the Workmans landed in India, at Tuticorin, and started on a two-year marathon. Stage one was a meandering journey of 4000 miles from the southern tip of India to Srinagar in Kashmir. *Through Town and Jungle*[2] describes the Indian travels of 1898 to 1900, which eventually extended to 16,000 miles on the cyclometer. They described the last leg of the journey, the 198 miles from Rawalpindi to Srinagar, as a pleasant cycle ride of five days!

---

1. W H Workman and F B Workman, *The Call of the Snowy Hispar*. London, Constable, 1910.
2. W H Workman and F B Workman, *Through Town and Jungle*. London, T Fisher Unwin, 1904.

It was on arrival in Srinagar that they seem quite suddenly to have heard the call of the Himalaya. Their first Himalayan journey would be considered a formidable undertaking, even today, by modern trekking companies. The 250-mile trip from Srinagar over the Zoji La to Leh, made of course long before this became a jeep road, they regarded as so commonplace as not to be worthy of description. At Leh, they immediately set to work to organise a journey along the southern branch of the Silk Road to the Karakoram Pass (now closed for political reasons), an even more formidable undertaking.

Returning to Srinagar, they hurried off to Darjeeling. Their attempt to organise a trek to the foot of Kangchenjunga was perhaps their only reported failure to achieve what they set out to do. With their usual Olympian disregard for expense, they had ordered tents and a mountain outfit from London and no less a guide than Rudolf Taugwalder from Zermatt. However, I suspect that they fell out in a big way with the political Officer in Sikkim. Certainly their account, brief and somewhat bitter, of their ten-day foray into the steaming forests below Darjeeling bears all the hallmarks of official obstruction.

The first six months of 1899 were spent cycling round Cambodia and Indonesia and by the end of June they were once more in Srinagar, poised for the start of the first of the seven great expeditions that were to be their life's work. They had engaged as guide the great Mattias Zurbriggen, the obvious choice since he had accompanied Sir Martin Conway on his great expedition of 1892. Almost immediately on arrival at Askole, Zurbriggen was called upon to show his mettle. There is a famous picture of him emerging from a crevasse having gone to the rescue of a sheep which, owing to 'some inadvertence' had slipped from the copious footholds visible in the foreground. At the Great Snow Lake there was a further encounter with a crevasse. Unfortunately the Doctor was too busy helping with the rescue to set up his cumbersome apparatus and we only have an artist's impression. Even when emerging from the ice, Fanny is portrayed as being completely in command of the situation.

They reached the Hispar pass, surely one of the world's greatest viewpoints, on a perfect morning and took a round of splendid photographs. They then devoted themselves to mountaineering in the area between Askole and the main Shigar valley. Here they christened two peaks: the Siegfriedhorn and Mount Bullock Workman, both names long forgotten. They also climbed a mountain they called Koser Gunge. The account of the ascent, made in a storm, and marked by the loss of Fanny's topi complete with its specially made *Touring Club de France* badge, is unusually dramatic. This adventure completed the 1899 expedition.

There followed a quick whizz round Sumatra, Siam and Burma and the Workmans finally sailed for Europe, where they landed at Marseilles two years and five months after their arrival in Ceylon. One would have expected their first priority to have been to see Rachel, now 16, who had been at school at Cheltenham during her parents' wanderings. There is no mention of any such meeting in the notebooks; it seems their immediate action on landing was to mount their beloved bicycles and have a brief spin to Nice and back before taking a train to Dresden. Rachel received a copy of *In the Ice World of Himalaya*[3] for Christmas.

Just two years after their return to Europe they pedalled into Srinagar again. The Chogo Lungma is one of the more difficult Karakoram glaciers, and it was a considerable achievement to fight their way as far as the upper basin in a season of exceptionally bad weather; they were, on occasion, stormbound for 60 hours on end. They also reached the Harmosh la and, thanks to Zurbriggen and good fortune, survived the ascent to what was clearly a hideously dangerous col at the head of one of the branch glaciers.

They returned to the Chogo Lungma the following summer, this time accompanied by the guide Cyprien Savoye of Courmayeur. They covered a great deal of ground around the head of the glacier and in the remote area between the Chogo Lungma, Hispar and Biafo glaciers. A problem with this expedition is to work out exactly where they went, as the map they produced differs in important respects from current interpretations. The surveying activities of the Workmans are wrapped in more dense obscurity than almost any other aspect of their lives.

They spent most of 1904-05 in Europe, and it was during this period that they developed their careers as lecturers — pursued with the same demonic energy as everything else they undertook. Hunter gave his first paper to the Royal Geographical Society in November 1904. Fanny offered to lecture in English, French or German, as required. An account of a triumphant lecture in Lyons mentions that 1000 people were crammed into the Palais des Beaux Arts and fully 700 were turned away. In November 1905 Fanny finally stormed the citadel of the Royal Geographical Society, and delivered a paper on the subject of the Hoh Lumba and Sosbon glaciers. Immediately afterwards they sailed for the East again.

3. F B Workman and W H Workman, *In the Ice World of Himalaya*. London, T Fisher Unwin, 1900.

The fourth expedition was something of a diversion from their usual areas of activity. They made a quick dash from Srinagar to Nun Kun and, displaying even less regard than usual for economy, they decided to overcome the problems presented by the 'natives' by employing no less than six porters from Courmayeur in addition to their guide Savoye. This expedition is notable for considerable mountaineering achievements on and around the great snow plateau, south of Leh, from which rise the twin peaks of Nun and Kun. It also became, in later years, the subject of a topographical dispute of exceptional bitterness even by Workman standards. The map accompanying their book *Peaks and Glaciers of Nun Kun*[4] is described as having been made by Dr W Hunter Workman from actual observation, with angles taken by prismatic compass. Years afterwards, the saintly Dr Arthur Neve, of the Mission Hospital, Srinagar, accompanied by no less a personage than the Lord Bishop of Lahore, carried out a considerable rearrangement of various features of this map.

The Call of the Snowy Hispar,[5] the account of the fifth expedition, in 1908, gives the impression that the Workmans had at last got the hang of organising these journeys; there is less of an atmosphere of perpetual irritation with their unfortunate companions and even, on rare occasions, a word of praise. Thanks to the efforts of Major Bruce, the Political Agent at Gilgit, they received VIP treatment from the Mir of Nagar, who was required to dislocate the lives of a considerable proportion of his subjects in order to meet the demands of the Workmans for food and transport. The Hispar is perhaps the most splendid of all the great Karakoram glaciers and some of the Workman photographs convey an overwhelming impression of the lonely magnificence of the region.

They were not the first explorers of the Hispar; in 1892 Sir Martin Conway had travelled the same route, discovered the Great Snow Lake beyond the Hispar pass and travelled down the Biafo to Askole and Skardu. The Workmans, however, visited many of the side glaciers and the map prepared by their Italian surveyors greatly increased the topographical knowledge of the region.

The final chapter of *The Call of the Snowy Hispar* is of startling irrelevance. It deals with perhaps the most famous of the Workman battles; the case of the height of Huascaran. The opponent was worthy of their steel. Miss Annie S Peck was an American mountaineer of

---

4. F B Workman and W H Workman, *Peaks and Glaciers of Nun Kun*. London, Constable, 1909.

5. W H Workman and F B Workman, *The Call of the Snowy Hispar*. London, Constable, 1910.

great distinction. In April 1908 she had ascended the lower summit of Huascaran in northern Peru, for which she claimed an altitude above 23,000 ft. This claim meant that she was in direct contention with Fanny for the female alpine championship of the world. The Workmans tackled this problem with their usual energy and disregard for expense. A team of surveyors from Paris spent four months carrying out a detailed triangulation which established the height of the upper summit of Huascaran as 22,182 ft. According to Fanny this confirmed her own claim to the title, based on her ascent of Pinnacle Peak in the Nun Kun massif, for which she claimed a height of 23,300 ft. This has since been reduced to 22,810 ft, which still gives her the edge on Annie by a few hundred feet.

It is generally accepted that the last two expeditions, of 1911 and 1912, were in a different category from the earlier Workman journeys, partly because they broke more new ground, partly because of the higher quality of the survey work. Their last great book *Two Summers in the Ice-Wilds of Eastern Karakoram*[6] was not published until 1917 and is perhaps a little more human in tone than the earlier volumes. They decided each to write one half of the book and, with a hitherto unheard of relaxation, to use the first person singular. Part one, describing the expedition of 1911, was written by the good Doctor who was always rather more relaxed, even in his personal notebooks, than was Fanny.

They started off as usual from Srinagar, crossed the Zoji la and on 4 July were half-way up to Kondus nala. I mention this date because on that day their daughter Rachel, now aged 27, married the 57-year-old Sir Alexander MacRobert in York. Fanny in fact remembered the occasion in her notebook, but two days late.

They went on to take a quick look at the Sherpi Gang glacier while Dr Calciati, one of the surveyors, and the guide Savoye continued on up the Kondus nala and made a survey of the Kondus and Kaberi glaciers. The Workmans then hurried back down to the Shyok and up the long Hushe valley to explore the glaciers on the south side of the Masherbrum-Chogolisa range. To complete what must have been a very strenuous summer they returned to the Shyok valley and travelled east to the Bilafond glacier, which they ascended to the Bilafond la for their first view of the Siachen.

The expedition of 1912 was undoubtedly the Workman's crowning achievement. They secured the services of Captain Grant Peterkin and Sarjan Singh of the Survey of India, who between them were responsible,

---

6. F B Workman and W H Workman, *Two Summers in the Ice-Wilds of Eastern Karakoram*. London, T Fisher Unwin, 1917.

during nine weeks of exceptionally good weather, for the triangulation of the Siachen glacier, which remains the basis of current maps. The two elderly Americans (Hunter was now 65 and Fanny 54) spent the two months in continuous strenuous travel, never below 15,000 ft and, on occasions, as high as 21,000 ft — a truly remarkable feat of physical endurance. The high point of the expedition was the ascent to the Indira Col, which they discovered and named. They were thus the first people ever to see that tremendous view northward towards the remote mountains of Chinese Turkestan. One cannot help envying them.

Their last book was extensively reviewed in the *Geographical Journal*, and it is sad that a considerable part of the review is devoted to criticism of the attacks made by both the Workmans on other explorers. The review ends with words that have to some extent become their epitaph: "If they fail to reap their natural reward in the cordial appreciation of their readers it will be because of the lamentable temper they show in regard both to the explorers who went before them and to the people of the country in which they were allowed to travel".[7]

7. Anon, 'Glaciers and Passes of the Karakoram'. *Geographical Journal 51 No 1, 38-42, 1918.*

This is a fair comment. Perhaps the only excuse must be the ultimate one : the Workmans were as the Lord made them, and in their case He chose a very odd mould. He then ensured that their peculiar characteristics were reinforced by bringing them together. There is no indication that they lived in anything but perfect harmony, despite a rather chill quotation in the Commonplace Book of the 17-year-old Fanny; 'Make no man your idol for the best man must have faults, and his faults will usually become yours, thus adding to your own.'

Quite simply, the company of their fellow men was, on the whole, disagreeble to the Workmans. This is made clear at numerous points in their writings, both published and unpublished, and extends throughout the range of the social hierachy, from the governer of an Indian province, described by Hunter as 'a d...... f......', to the sick inhabitants of poverty-stricken mountain villages who annoyed him by begging for medicine.

On the positive side, they were people driven to a quite exceptional degree, and another entry in the Commonplace Book may be seen as a programme for their lives. Fanny had pasted in a copy of one of the bleakest poems in the language, Matthew Arnold's 'Self Dependence':

> For alone they live, nor pine with noting
> All the fever of some differing soul.
> Bound by themselves and unobservant
> In what state God's other works may be,
> In their own tasks all their power pouring,
> These attain the mighty life you see.

There is little to add. They spent the years of the Great War in France where in 1917 Fanny became ill with heart trouble, finally dying in Cannes in 1925 at the age of 66. Hunter then returned to the United States, to Newton, Massachusetts, where he lived to be 91, still running a tight ship. The last entry in his meticulously kept personal account book is dated I October 1937, six days before his death. They remain a lonely, mysterious but essentially heroic couple. Let us hope they will not be entirely forgotten.

SUMMARY

An account of the travels and explorations of the American couple Dr William Hunter Workman and Mrs Fanny Bullock Workman.

9

FIRES ON THE MOUNTAIN

Ascents in the Panch Chuli Group

HARISH KAPADIA

'**A**MOUNTAINEER NEVER RETIRES. In a sense he never hangs his boots to call it a day. As he grows in years he continues with treks and loving the hills....'

'This is Chris certainly'.

'Yes'.

'Is he lecturing Graham so early in the morning?'

I peeped out of my tent and could hear Chris snoring loudly. It was the radio. BBC was broadcasting an interview with Chris Bonington. We were at ABC (4840 m). This must be surely a record of sorts, listening to an interview at this height, with the interviewee snoring in the next tent!

Our expedition had come a long way already. When Bonington and the others arrived at Bombay on 7 May 1992, we were ready with all the last minute preparations. A super fast train took us to Delhi ('British rail can learn a thing or two from this'). A two day bus ride with half a day's rest at Ranikhet followed. ('Solving the case of the missing "tempo" with our all expedition luggage'). Finally everything was in place at Munsiary, the roadhead.

By this time we were learning the diplomatic charms of Bonington. If he paid you a compliment, he wanted something done. His adaptability was amazing. In a jacket, so to speak, he was a great diplomat shaking hands and smiling for hours, enough to disarm a formidable bureaucrat. Once in a bus, or on the mountains, he was totally different.

'Now you know why he has reached, where he has', was the best comment on these amazing transformations.

Photos 10 to 20   Front Cover
Panoramas A to D

57

Starting on 15 May, we walked 3 days in an amazing virgin forest, halting at Domol, and Balati. Base camp (3200 m) was at the snout of the Uttari Balati glacier, one of the lowest BCs in the Himalaya. In fact, the height difference from BC to Panch Chuli II (6904 m) was 3700 m, more than on most high mountains, including Everest.

'Shit, how are we going to go through this?' It was exclaimed looking at the three icefalls of the glacier. The first one was by-passed and the Glacier Camp (3900 m) was established. Victor opened a route on the (true) left of the glacier. It was a maze of collapsing crevasses, and stones bombarded the fixed ropes after 7 a.m. We christened it 'Victor's Terror' and very reluctantly moved in.

'Surely the Pandavas did not go this way'.

'Why, this is the surest way to heaven'.

'But we have to reach the peak and cook a meal before that is ensured. These peaks symbolise their cooking fires on the mountain'.

'They are, figuratively speaking. It is the spirit that counts, isn't it?' We all certainly intended to return, let the Pandavas go their way.

'Forget the *Fires on the mountain, Run Run Run.*' Someone said reminding us of the childhood rhyme, warning us about the falling stones.

We were discussing the legend of the Panch Chuli peaks. Folklore has it that the five Pandava brothers cooked their last meal on these peaks and proceeded to heaven. These peaks were the hearths from which the sun-rays rose towards heaven, every morning and evening.

There was a loud sound. As we looked up Chris was hanging on a jummar on the fixed rope. The entire floor beneath him had collapsed.

'Chris do you still think we should follow this route with loaded porters.'

'If I were you, I would not follow this route,' he replied with perfect British understatement.

'I am certainly not you. We will try a route on the right hand edge'. I pointed to it and started descending. Chris and Graham continued upwards.

We found two gullies, leading up and by-passing the second and third icefall. This was the route followed by all the earlier teams. But it was highly exposed. All the difficulties we had faced on the

The third icefall, Uttari Balati glacier. Panch Chuli II rising behind.
(Monesh Devjani)

left route on snow and ice, were present here on scree and rocks.
We fixed a rope and on the first run I almost lost my rucksack.
After crossing it once, Victor got even with me.

'I heard all about it Harish. If the left route was "Victor's Terror"
this is "Harish's Horror".'

He almost proved right. Later on in the expedition Vijay slipped
in one of these gullies and almost fell down the rocks. Sundersingh
literally slid after him and stopped him at the last bump. Vijay broke
an ankle and that's when the helicopter flew for the first time, to
pick him up.

Above it we climbed another icy gully and reached ABC. Chris
and Graham were there, having just climbed Sahadev (5750 m).

Sahadev East (5750 m):
(Chris Bonington writes)

Graham Little and I had the Upper Balati glacier to ourselves. The
others had gone back down to help rejig the route round the second
icefall, one of three that blocked the Uttari Balati glacier. Our camp,
which was to become our advance base, nestled beneath a little rocky
buttress on the northern side of the glacier. On the other side towered
a tooth-like peak that had dominated the skyline both on our walk
up the Balati valley and even more dramatically during our ascent
of the glacier. It seemed a good objective for a first climb. A direct
ascent up the ridge facing us looked too challenging — steep rock
steps divided by snow-clad ice-slopes — but there appeared to be
an easier option up glaciated snow-slopes leading to a spur that
in turn led to the summit ridge.

We set out at three o'clock the following morning, picked our way
across the glacier and then made an endless-seeming plod, lit by
the small pools of light from our torches, up the slopes leading
to the spur. It was good moving without the weight of a heavy
rucksack. I could even keep up with Graham, taking my turn out
in front. One of the problems of climbing with people nearly twenty
years younger is that all too often they are tiny dots disappearing
over the horizon, or tugging insistently out in front on the rope.

Night changed to the grey of the pre-dawn and, as we gained
height, the skyline of the Balati glacier took shape, ridges and snow
slopes becoming defined, then etched in the golden light of the sun,
as it lit the tops of the peaks. Opposite and behind us was Rajrambha,
a big sprawling peak, whose steep crenellated face fell away sheer
to the glacier. At the head of the valley was unclimbed Nagalaphu,
with twin rocky peaks and steep walls.

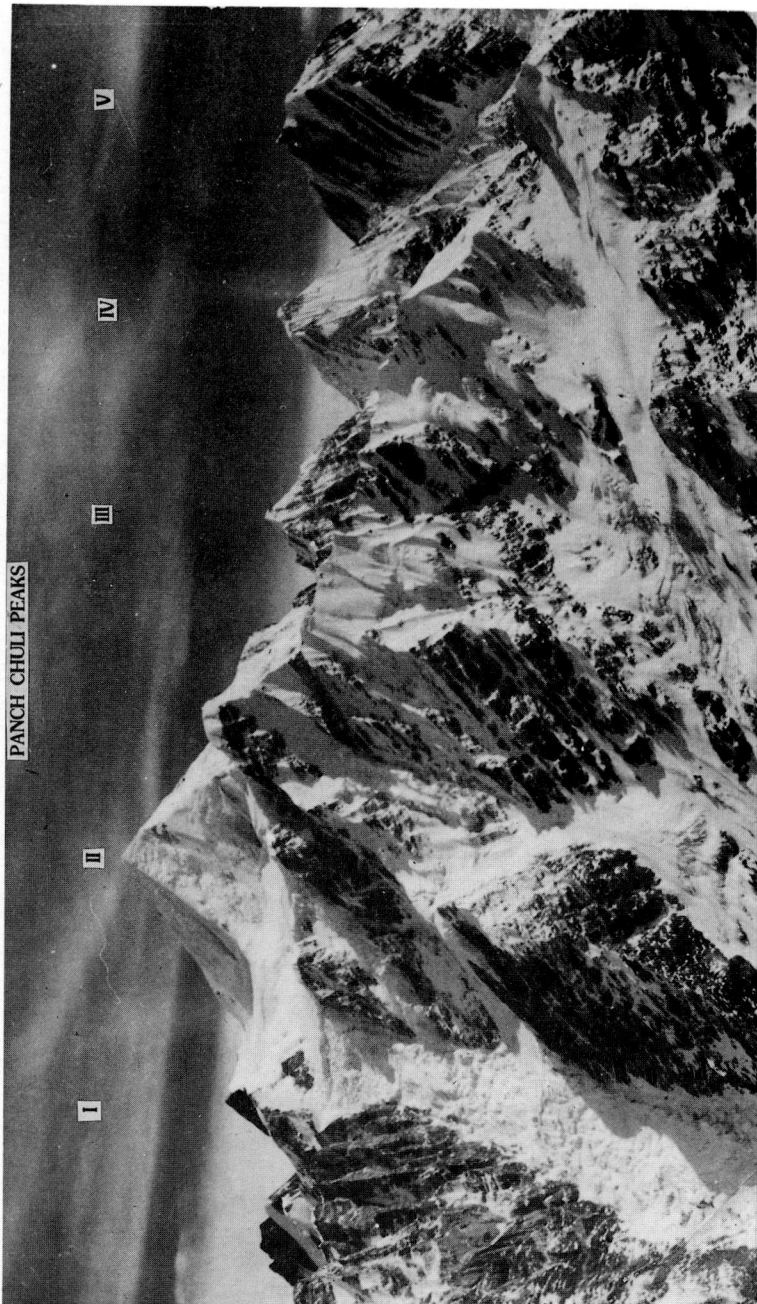

PANCH CHULI PEAKS

I   II   III   IV   V

10. Panch Chuli peaks, aeriel view. Dakhini Balati glacier on left foreground, Nagalaphu (6410 m) far left, the Balati Plateau in centre with west ridge rising up. Southwest ridge on right, north ridge on left.

(Capt. N. B. Gurung)

Article 9

PANCH CHULI II

THREE HUMPS

SW ridge

BALATI PLATEAU

West ridge

11. Panch Chuli II (6904 m) seen from Sahadev East (5750 m). West ridge on left, southwest ridge on right above the Balati Plateau. Three points on right were possibly climbed by 1964 I.M.F. expedition.

(Chris Bonington)

Article 9

We reached the bergschrund as the sun crept round to us. It was my turn to lead. The bergschrund was bigger than it had seemed from below, Snow crumbled away. I sank up to my thighs, edged further across, ice-tools thrust into bottomless soft snow, and heaved myself up into a praying position with everything sliding away around me. Panting hard, I was able to stand and kick into harder snow above. I kicked my way up, twenty metres or so, cleared a stance, buried my axe and brought Graham up.

Pitch followed pitch, about nine inches of softish snow lying on ice at an angle of around 50°. Not difficult, but nerve-wracking. It was around 9.00 a.m. by the time we reached the crest of the ridge. Looking across to what had seemed the summit from below, it now appeared lower than us and we were only just short of the top of what we named the East peak. It looked a long way to the West peak, so we unanimously declared our summit the higher. It was only after returning to advance base, when we examined the map that we had to admit the West peak was a few metres higher. We called the two peaks Sahadev East and West after the second and youngest brother of the Pandavas.

Graham and I next decided to attempt Nagalaphu (6410 m) by a bold traverse. We left advance base on the afternoon of 29 May, walked up the Uttari Balati glacier in thick cloud and stopped below what we judged to be the face we planned to climb that night to reach the crest of the ridge. It was snowing hard by the time we had put the tent up and a violent thunder storm quickly followed, hail drumming on the sides of the tent through most of the night. It stopped at last and we got away at 3.00 a.m., plodding past serac walls and part hidden crevasses in the dark. It was only as it dawned, just after I had stepped into a huge bell-bottomed crevasse, that we could discern the mountains around us in the faint grey light. The dreadful realisation came to me that in the dark we had started up the wrong mountain and were just short of the upper Balati Plateau instead of the big face we had planned to climb.

We were so shaken by our mistake that instead of continuing we retraced our steps and after a half-hearted probe up the glacier, returned to advanced base feeling very shamefaced, to find the entire team assembled there. We decided we needed a rest so continued on down to base camp that same day.

Panch Chuli II (6904 m), southwest ridge:
(Harish Kapadia writes)

'Mus, do you think the porters will make it to the next camp today? I was shouting from behind, plodding in deep snow. The route appeared too long.

'They will bloody well have a long day', is all that Muslim said as he continued plodding.

Cl (5750 m) was established at the edge of the Balati Plateau. We were to take on the southwest ridge, while Chris and Graham were to climb the west ridge. Both the ridges were separated by a little distance. We were to open a main route to the foot of the peak as four Britons were traversing Rajrambha (6537 m) from ABC[1]. On 3 June with Chris, Graham, and Monesh, I joined Muslim and Bhupesh who had already recceed the Balati Plateau. The next day we crossed the maze of crevasses to C2 (6120 m) on the col at the foot of the southwest ridge. Chris and Graham bifurcated off half way through for the west ridge.

'Pasang and myself will fix some rope ahead to move the camp. We will surely be up in 2 days', Monesh said with enthusiasm as we embraced wishing each other good luck. The next day as Bhupesh and myself returned to C2, Muslim, Monesh and Pasang were on the ridge, establishing C3.

7 June was a little cloudy. From C2 we could not see a thing at first.

'I can see three dots moving up the final ridge', I shouted at about 10 a.m. Slowly the dots moved up and disappeared from view. We could see two dots moving up the west ridge too from our ring-side seat.

Starting from C3 (6400 m) three of them had reached the foot of the upper rock band in 2 hours, at 6.45 a.m. This band was climbed with some difficulty in 45 minutes and in an hour they reached the point where the southwest and south ridges met at 6800 m. But the 'fun' started now. The cornices hanging on the east were very thin ('so thin that we could see sun shine through', Bill Murray had written about this ridge, observing it from the east). They carefully crept up, without any chance of fixing a protection. Finally they were on the top at 10.15 a.m. There was no time to waste. Descent was started immediately. A little below the top Monesh fell through the cornice almost up to his chest. As he pulled out he realised how close the heavens were. He left a scarf there to mark the spot. Losing their way in a white-out they abseiled the upper rock band and with difficulty reached C3. This was only the second ascent by this ridge. Whereas the earlier team had fixed the entire route, now

---

1. For details of the traverse of Rajrambha, climbs and accident on Panch Chuli V, see article 'Rajrambha and Panch Chuli V' in this issue. — Ed.

only about 60 m of fixed rope was used. Carefully they retreated
to C2 where Bhupesh and I were waiting with hot mugs of tea.

After about 2 hours, two other figures were reaching us for cups
of tea: Bonington and Graham after their ascent by the west ridge
and descent by the southwest ridge had reached our camp.

Panch Chuli II (6904 m), west ridge:
(Chris Bonington writes)

When we returned three days later on the afternoon of 2 June,
Victor Saunders, Stephen Sustad, Dick Renshaw and Stephen Venables
had already set out for a traverse of Rajrambha. Harish Kapadia
and the Indian members of the team were completing their build
up of supplies on the upper Balati Plateau for their attempt on the
southwest ridge of Panch Chuli II. Graham and I decided it was
high time we also concentrated on the main objective and chose
its unclimbed west ridge.

Starting out the next day with the Indian team, we carried heavy
loads to the head of the icefall guarding the Balati Plateau. The
camp was on the shoulder of the ridge between the Uttari Balati
and Dakhini Balati glaciers. From there, the following morning (4
June) we reconnoitred a route to the foot of the west ridge and
moved up the next day to pitch our little Gemini tent at 6120 m
within easy reach of the bottom of the ridge.

At 3.30 a.m. on 6 June we began ferrying all our tentage and
gear. It was a moonless but starlit night. A steep little bergschrund,
climbed by the light of head torches, led onto the ridge itself. It
was only 45° in angle but was hard ice with only the occasional
thin smear of neve, clinging to it. We were climbing one at a time
and, feeling the altitude, had slowed down. Dawn came and the sun
crept up and over the crest of the southwest ridge. The view was
magnificent; the two peaks of Sahadev were far below us, across
the valley sprawled Rajrambha, whose long serpentine ridges the other
four were climbing, while out to the west towered the steep pyramid
of Nanda Devi, surely one of the most beautiful mountains in the
world.

The angle steepened and the crest of the ridge was barred by
a serac, forcing us onto the west face up steep, poorly consolidated
snow. Our progress became even slower and the day was beginning
to slide away. We had been on the go for ten hours and reached
around 6500 m but there was no sign of a bivvy site. Graham
led up a steep ice-gully and pulled out on a little vertical ice-wall
leading back onto the crest of the ridge. I panted slowly up behind
him and was happy to let him lead the next pitch. He was hunting
for somewhere to camp, but to no avail. It was late afternoon and
the cloud was swirling around us. The occasional lump of ice or

slurry of snow came tumbling down, but he could find nowhere large
enough for our tent. The rope came tight between us. I abandoned

Upper Balati glacier and route to Panch Chuli II (right). Nagalaphu
on left.

(Stephen Venables)

the belay and started moving up behind him. At last, I heard a tired shout of triumph. He had found a camp site.

I joined him on the crest of the ridge. Just above was a small ledge below a serac wall. We were able to dig out a camp site with minimum of work and pitched our little Gemini at 6610 m. It feels very secure, can stand up to almost any weather, but it is small. It would make a reasonable one-man tent but is cramped for two, especially if one of the occupants (Graham) is six feet two inches tall. Fortunately I had had a modification made of a commodious sleeve entrance in one end. Graham was able to put either his head or feet into that extra space to stretch out.

It started snowing almost immediately, but what was more serious was that Graham had a savage headache, something that is always worrying at altitude. Inevitably I thought of cerebral oedema, but Graham told me that he had fractured his skull as a child and suffered from time to time with debilitating headaches. There was none of the puffiness associated with oedema around his eyes and they weren't unduly bloodshot, so I was slightly reassured.

We were slow in getting away the next morning. We were both tired from the previous long day, and anyway there was not too much urgency. We wanted to reach the summit very early in the morning to be sure of being rewarded with a view. We only had 400 m to go to reach the top, and therefore decided to push our camp a short way up and closer to the southwest ridge which we planned to descend once we had completed our climb.

Fortunately Graham's headache became more bearable once he started moving, and we took alternate leads, progressing slowly over the crevassed upper face in the direction of the southwest ridge. Just after midday we saw three small figures moving down the crest of the ridge. It was the Indian team descending after a successful ascent. We shouted, but got no reply.

By this time the cloud had rolled in once more and we stopped on the lip of a bergschrund at around 6730 m. It was snowing again by the time we pitched the tent and once Graham got into his sleeping bag, his headache returned with renewed fury. I could almost feel the pain he was obviously experiencing. Neither of us slept that night. The snow pressed in on the tent, making it even smaller. Had the weather finally broken? Would Graham be able to go for the summit if it was fine in the morning? Could I go for it on my own? Perfectly feasible, but how could I justify leaving Graham alone? The snow stopped just before dawn. I started melting some in the gas stove hanging from the roof of the tent, asked

Graham what he wanted to do, and to my immense relief he said
he'd have a go for the summit.

We left the tent in place, and cut across towards the crest of
the southwest ridge. It was easy-angled but hard ice. Just below the
summit we came across some red rag (Monesh's scarf) left by the
others the previous day. Graham had rallied once he got going, took
his turn in the lead, and suddenly we were almost there. Graham
led the last few feet towards the summit of Panch Chuli II. We
had our reward for our high camp and early start, for the sky was
still clear, the view magnificent, with fresh vistas to the north of
mountains in Tibet, of Gurla Mandhata, massive, majestic to the northeast,
and further to the north, a distant pyramid, Kailash, most holy of
all mountains in both Hindu and Buddist mythology. Looking to the
east we could see Api and the mountains of West Nepal, shapely
snow peaks in the distance, while in the immediate foreground, much
lower but still dramatic, were the peaks of Panch Chuli IV and V
(III was hidden by the lip of a huge cornice), Telkot and Nagling,
all of them unclimbed, all steep and challenging.

We spent half an hour on the summit before returning to our
camp, where we stuffed the frozen tent and all the gear into our
packs and started the long descent of the southwest ridge to rejoin
Harish and the others who were still encamped on the col at the
foot of it. It was wonderful to enjoy their hospitality, crammed three
to a two-man tent, to have endless cups of hot tea and to share
with each other the stories of our two ascents. It had been an immensely
satisfying climb snatched in the teeth of deteriorating weather.

To Pyunshani valley:
(Harish Kapadia continues)

'There is nothing more to do in the Balati valley. The others have
climbed Rajrambha also'.

'Venables and co. are coming up to climb Panch Chuli II'.

'We will talk to them'.

Chris and myself were discussing plans as we descended together
after ascents of Panch Chuli II. I was to see the master diplomat
in action. We met the others on the glacier below. Congratulations
to each other and lots of laughter followed.

'What are your plans', Chris inquired.

'We will try another ridge on Panch Chuli II'.

'Harish and I are going to the Pyunshani valley, a little to the
south'.

'Graham is up at ABC, waiting for us'.

'Good luck then. We will tell you about those unclimbed peaks. No one has been to the Pyunshani before us. It will be a wonderful exploration for us'. Chris started walking down.

The others looked alarmed. Graham was pulled down, camps wound up and the entire party was moving to the Pyunshani valley.

There was no record of any party visiting this valley which drained the Panch Chuli glaciers from Panch Chuli peaks III, IV and V. After some persuasion we found a guide, Dhansingh, who as we discovered later, had been up here years before. But he promised fresh meat from the shepherds in the valley. All went well to begin with. We retreated to Phunga Gair (2920 m) a gem of a place as the name implied. On 15 June we climbed a steep incline through dense forest to cross Bagarthora col (3800 m) and camped at Shyama Gwar (3600 m). Ahead the route traversed up and down numerous ridges. Dhansingh stopped every five minutes. Ultimately it was too much for Britain's best mountaineers.

'Harish, there is no meat here, Shall we eat Dhansingh?' They started descending to the river wanting to follow it to the base camp in the upper valley.

Dhansingh nodded his head in disapproval to say that no route was possible from there.

'We have a rebellion on hand. What shall we do Chris?' I asked helplessly.

'If I were you, I would follow Dhansingh', Chris replied in his characteristic style. He had dealt with many such restless climbers.

After a while as the others descended, Chris gave a shout.

'Follow the river, camp in the open and in rain. Remember we have the tents. See you at the base camp in 2-3 days'.

Four cursing Britons climbed back in line behind Dhansingh!

On 16 June we established our second base camp (3320 m). We had 5 days. Two plans were made. Muslim, Monesh and myself were to climb in a side valley and explore the adjoining Rula and Bainti glaciers. The five Britishers were to try one of the Panch Chulis and meet us back at Munsiary. We were to leave some food and three porters for them and go back early to wind up the expedition at Munsiary. Accordingly both teams left on 17 June.

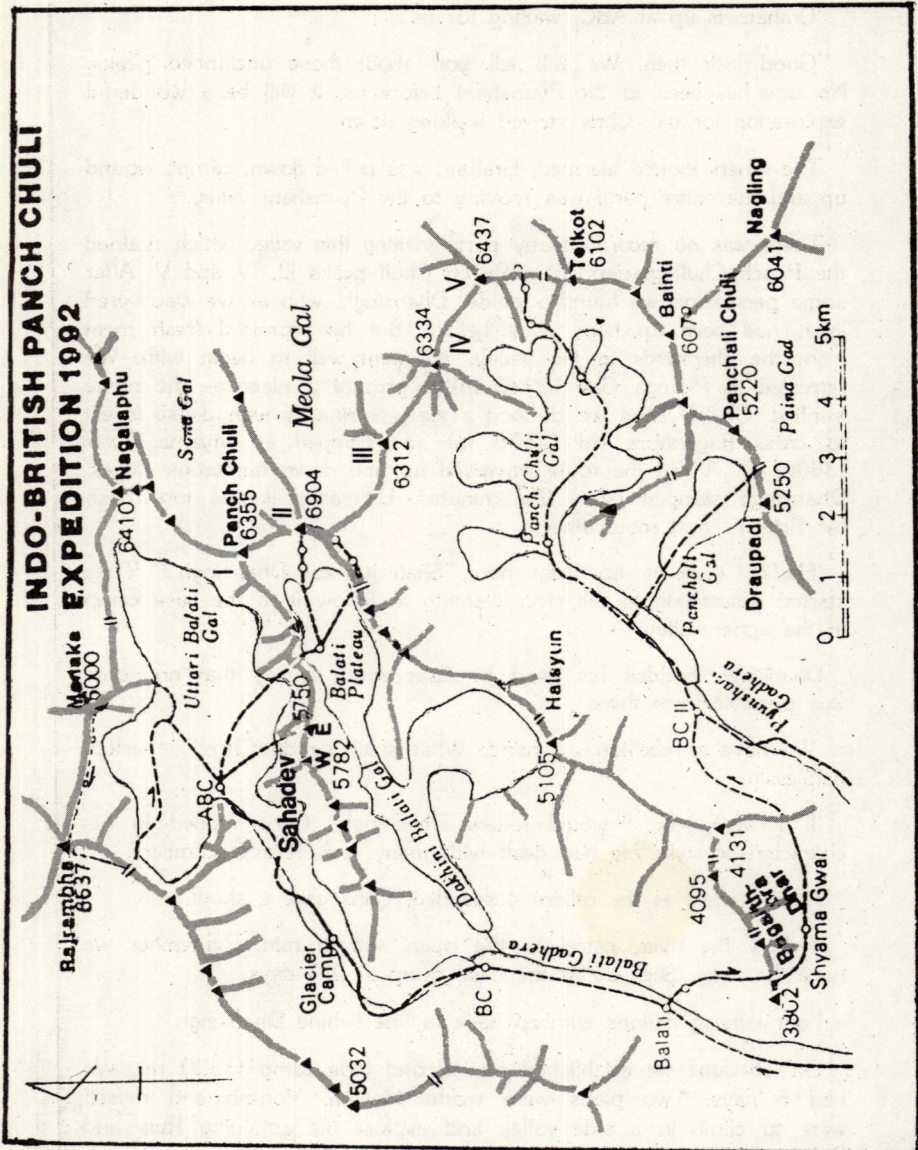

INDO-BRITISH PANCH CHULI
EXPEDITION 1992

12. Uttari Balati glacier icefalls. Final route proceeded on true right.

(Monesh Devjani)

13. Crevasses on 'Victor's Terror' in Uttari Balati icefall, on true left edge.

Article 9 (Graham Little)

14. Fixed ropes on true right of the Uttari Balati icefall: 'Harish's Horror'.

Article 9 (Harish Kapadia)

These were the most delightful days for us. We had already achieved the main objective, Panch Chuli II. Where most teams would have gone back, here we were in a valley never visited before. Totally relaxed we moved two camps to reach the Bainti Col (5100 m) on 20 June. Two peaks rose to the northeast and southwest of the col. We climbed both, Panchali Chuli (5220 m) and Draupadi (5250 m). The view to the east was of the Bainti and Rula glaciers, looking most fearsome. Many unclimbed peaks like Bainti (6072 m), Nagling (6041 m) and others rose above it. These icefalls would keep experts busy for sometime.

'Surely the Pandavas could not have gone this way', was the clear verdict as we saw Panch Chuli II rising in the north.

'Make sure, you have gone up that ridge', I said to Monesh and Muslim pointing to the southwest ridge, looking steep, and exposed with ice shining on it. Both of them looked at it with satisfaction.

We came down and in rain and clouds returned to Munsiary on 23 June leaving the Britishers to follow.

Little did we realize the drama that was being unfolded on Panch Chuli V.

The Rescue

We were finalising the expedition account on the afternoon of 23 June. We could hear someone running towards our room.

'There is a phone call for you. It is Chris from Madkot. He says there has been an accident'.

We ran down to the office below. 'Harish, Stephen Venables has fallen, breaking his right knee and left ankle'. Chris' voice was choked with emotion.

'The only way to rescue him is by helicopter. They could all perish. Their camp is in the line of avalanche slope'.

We exchanged grid references and other details. Action followed. Our most efficient liasion officer Wing Commander Anil K. Srivastava started flashing out messages. Muslim ran down to gather our porters scattered all over Munsiary, relaxing and celebrating. Monesh started hectic purchases for a ground party to start in a hour. We drove down to Madkot, 22 km away.

Looking at Chris was half the story. He was shaken, disturbed and choked with emotion as he narrated the details of the accident. With a big gash on his cheeks, due to his own fall, he looked ghastly.

An eight-strong party left for the base camp with lots of food and supplies. We came up to Munsiary, feeling cut off without much communication with the outside world. For the next 2 days and nights no one slept well, particularly Chris. He kept tossing about.

'Why did this have to happen on the last day? Why always on my expeditions? They are all happily married. What will I say to others' or sometimes in excitement he would say, 'I'll talk to the higher ups. Let's go by the ground route. We will get him out'. We were seeing the human side of Chris.

We waited two days on open ground, with binoculars scanning the skies. The helicopter went in twice and came out. The lack of communication was killing. We did not know what was happening. In fact as we learnt later, the chopper was flying the next morning, on 24 June itself. Due to clouds and the height the pilots could not locate the tent.

We prepared a complete ground plan. If the chopper was not able to pick up Venables on the third day we would go in with a 20 strong army party with a doctor and all the support required. We requested that the helicopter should land at Munsiary and take Chris with them to show them the exact spot.

On 26 June we were waiting at the helipad. Chris ready in full mountain gear to go aboard. We saw the helicopter going into Pyunshani valley and returning after half an hour. Chris was ready and we waved to the pilots. It came towards us, and turned to land. Suddenly we could see a red duvet jacket with Stephen Venables smiling in it! There was hugging and dancing — our joy knew no bounds. The pilots, Sqd. Ldr. P. Jaiswal and Flt. Lt. P.K. Sharma had done a magnificent job and picked up Venables on the last attempt at great risk to themselves. This view of the helicopter and the red duvet in it is a sight we will never forget.

'Harish, I did not put Mother's petals, given to me by Nawang on the summit. That's why I fell', Venables instantly said on being brought out on a stretcher.

He was referring to the votive petals from the Samadhi of Mother of Pondicherry. He had carried a similar packet to the summit of Everest in 1988 during his solo ascent. He had put it on the summit, photographed it and survived a night alone above the South Col.[2]

'You survived because you had the blessings with you', I consoled him.

2. For details of this earlier experience, see article 'The Climbing Partner — The Other Experience in the Himalaya' in the present issue. — Ed.

The helicopter flew off and we sent Muslim with the porters by taxi. All of them met at Bareilly hospital. Within the next 48 hours Venables was on a flight to London.

That evening Chris, Monesh and myself sat quietly at a small temple of Shiva, in a Hindu gesture of thanksgiving for Venables' rescue. It was peaceful and the feeling of gratitude total. I was surprised to receive a letter from Chris months later, recalling that sojourn and the strange peace we all experienced then.

On 27 June, tired and emotionally drained Renshaw, Saunders and Sustad returned. We had a lot to talk about. The narrow escape, the hard work by our porters, dangerous avalanches and of course the incredible rescue.

They were of full of praise for Harsinh jr. In boots four sizes too large, without any previous technical know-how, he had carried loads higher up the icefall to feed the stranded climbers. The British wanted to sponsor him for a training course at a mountaineering institute in India. I pointed out that these courses are generally undertaken by the educated and by army officers. Harsinh jr., a shepherd by profession, would be a misfit there.

'We will get him over to England. He can do the course at Plas y Brenin. Ask him if he would go'.

I translated the offer to Harsinh, jr. Pat came his reply.

'I just want to go back to my goats. My flock has been unattended for a long time now'.

We sat in a way-side hotel and Chris typed out the expedition report on a Laptop Apple McIntosh Computer, taking the place a generation ahead in technology. Around him there was no electricity and ladies were carrying wood as fuel for cooking. We were packing up for the final bus ride home after a most satisfying expedition.

'We are one up on the Pandavas. We came back from the Panch Chulis'.

'We lit enough fires on the mountain though'.

'Venables almost reached heaven, didn't he?

'In a way we all reached "heaven". It's the spirit that counts, isn't it?'

'I am in heaven now'. We turned back. Victor was sucking the first of the hundred mangoes we were to finish that evening.

History of the Panch Chuli Group of Peaks:

The Panch Chuli peaks lie in the eastern Kumaon area. They form the watershed between the Gori and Darma ganga valleys. The eastern approaches are through Sona and Meola glaciers. The Uttari and Dakhini Balati glaciers guard the western approaches. The peaks are numbered NW to SE. I (6355 m), II (6904 m), III (6312 m), IV (6334 m) and V (6437 m). It is not known how the highest peak came to be regarded as peak II, (and not peak I), but the nomenclature is too well established to change now.

Legend

As per the legend, these peaks are named after the five Pandava brothers from the Indian epic *Mahabharata*. These peaks represent their cooking hearths *(chulis)* as they cooked their last meal before proceeding to their heavenly abode. As one watches the group from the bungalow at Munsiary before sunrise, the rays directly reflect on these tops and throw the light upwards to the sky. The same scene is repeated in the evening, a little after sunset, for the people in the Darma valley. Thus the legend is firmly established in folklore.

Early Explorations from the East

The mountaineering history began with Hugh Ruttledge. He saw the group at close quarters reaching high up on the Sona glacier. He examined the routes and thought that the north arete may be possible. After 21 years two teams examined the eastern approaches again. W. H. Murray and his Scottish team followed the Ruttlege route. They intended to reach the north col and follow the northeast ridge. They found the terrain too difficult.

> North Col was ringed below by a bergschrund, from which 300 ft of bare ice swept up to the rocks and ice was everywhere raked by stonefall. We were beaten.

And about the upper ridge they opined that it '...... was so thin that we could see sun shine through.' Later Murray and Douglas Scott went up the Meola glacier. From its junction with the Sona glacier they climbed 'till 16,000 ft. by way of the central cliff and found the only way to Meola.'

Just 20 days after them came Kenneth Snelson and J.de V. Graaff. By early September they reached the upper Sona glacier and 'found that at its head was a cradle of 600 foot cliffs offering no route to the northeast summit ridge.'

They then followed Murray's route to upper Meola and reached the south col to examine the west side.

> The Goriganga side of the col falls precipitously, to the Panch Chuli glacier and the almost vertical face rises another thousand feet above the col making the lower part of the ridge razor edged. Hardly a route!

They thought of the south ridge but wrote; 'The ridge towards south col has a rather easier gradient but is very broken and heavily corniced'. They gave up the southeast face also after 400 ft.

With such verdicts, the eastern approaches were left alone. Only a team each in 1970 and 1988 tried them unsuccessfully.

Attempts from the West

The western approaches were tried one year after Murray, in 1951. Heinrich Harrer and Frank Thomas were joined by two Sherpas and a botanist. Though their account in the *Himalayan Journal* is not very explicit, their photographs in the archives clearly indicate that they pioneered the route through the Uttari Balati glacier, bypassing three icefalls. Harrer with Sherpas reached the Balati Plateau and examined the north and west ridges. They tried the west ridge but a Sherpa fell off on hard blue-ice. Harrer gave up. They had spent only 16 days on the mountains but pioneered the route which was followed by all subsequent expeditions from this side.

In 1952, P. N. Nikore followed the Harrer route and his attempt in June almost coincided with an attempt by another team led by D. D. Joshi which included Maj. John Dias. Both the teams reached the Balati Plateau. Nikore returned in 1953 and claimed a solo ascent of the peak without any conviction or proof to corroborate his claim. He was disbelieved and claim ignored.

Wrong Claims

Group Capt. A. K. Chowdhery led a team sponsored by the Indian Mountaineering Foundation to this group in 1964. Following the Uttari Balati glacier they reached the Balati Plateau. Their cursory attempt on peak II failed. They then claimed mistaken ascents of peaks III, IV and V in two days, in fact two peaks on the same day.

These peaks stand above the southern valley of Pyunshani and are completed unapproachable from the Balati Plateau at all. To climb these peaks, as claimed, the party would have to traverse and climb over very difficult terrain covering almost 10 km in one day, above

Panch Chuli II from summit of Chaudhara, looking at northwest face. Three small points on right background were possibly climbed in 1964. (S. N. Dhar)

6300 m and crossing low cols. The party had mistakenly climbed three distinct humps situated near their camps and running east-west from peak II instead of peaks III, IV, and V, which broadly run north-south. The mistake was ultimately accepted by the sponsors, after, at first, the so called summiters either refused to reply or were adamant in their claim. The records were corrected after 28 years, when the mistake was pointed out by the 1992 Indian-British expedition.[3]

First Ascents

The history of the group continued with two large expeditions from the Indo-Tibet Border Police teams. The first team in 1972, was led by Hukum Singh. They powered their way to the Balati Plateau via the Harrer route and made the first ascent of peak I. The first of Panch Chuli had fallen. Repeating their route, Mahendra Singh led another team in 1973. They fixed almost 3000 m of rope. The entire route on the final southwest ridge was fixed. On 26 May 1973 18 people summitted. The highest peak was climbed.

The mountain was left alone for 18 years. In 1991 two routes were climbed by the eastern approaches. Both teams were from the Indian army. The first team followed the Sona glacier, climbed the northeast slopes to reach above the north col and established a camp on the north ridge. The ridge was followed to the top. Thus the route suggested by Ruttledge in 1929 was completed after 61 years. The second army team followed Murray's route to the Upper Meola glacier. They pitched a high camp following the southeast slopes to the east ridge. The summit team broke the cornice to reach the top. Thus the route suggested by Snelson-Graaff was completed after 41 years.

Last Climbs

The scene finally shifted back to the west. The Indian-British expedition 1992 followed the route along the Uttari Balati glacier to the Balati Plateau. On the way the team divided into groups to climb Sahadev East (5750 m), Menaka (6000 m) and Rajrambha (6537 m). On peak II, a team of three climbed the southwest ridge. It was a hard climb on ice, keeping well away from the hanging cornices. Compared to the earlier ascent only 60 m of rope was fixed on the ridge. This was the second ascent of the southwest ridge, now after 19 years.

Another team of two, pioneered a new route up the steep and icy west ridge, with bivouacs. They descended the southwest ridge completing the traverse. Thus the route tried by Harrer was completed after 41 years.

---

3. See 'Correspondence' in this issue.

The 1992 expedition made the first ascent of peak V later. Peaks III, IV and the direct south ridge on peak II still remain unattempted.

EXPEDITIONS TO THE PANCH CHULI GROUP

(All the expeditions were to Panch Chuli II, 6904 m, the highest peak of the group, except in 1972 and 1992.)

Expeditions from the eastern approaches

1.	1929:	Hugh Ruttlege reached *c.* 5730 m on the Sona glacier. He thought that a route to the summit was possible via the north arete.	Book Ref. 5-6
2.	1950 :	W. H. Murray and the Scottish Himalayan expedition reached *c.* 5790 m via the Sona glacier. They tried to reach the north col.	H.J. XVI, p. 38 Book Ref. 1-2
3.	1950 :	K. E. Snelson and J. de V. Graaff reached *c.* 6100 m from the Meola glacier. They ruled out the south ridge, southeast face and northeast ridge from the Sona glacier.	H.J. XVII, p. 97
4.	1970 :	C. K. Mitra led an Indian team from the National Cadet Corps. They reached *c.* 5950 m, both on the Meola and Sona glaciers.	H.M.J. 6, p. 112 H.C.N.L. 28, p. 2
5.	1988 :	Aloke Surin and his team from Bomay attempted it via the Meola glacier and stopped before the south col.	H.J. 45, p. 196 H.C.N.L. 42 p. 29
6.	1991 :	Capt. N. B. Gurung led the Gorkha regiment (Indian army) team. They climbed via the Sona glacier to the northeast ridge to the summit in August.	H.J. 48, p. 48 H.C.N.L. 45, p. 18

Second ascent of peak II

7.	1991 :	Col. Suraj Bhan Dalal led a Kumaon-Naga regiment (Indian army) team in September. They climbed via the Meola glacier up the east face and east ridge to the summit.	H.J. 48, p. 54 H.C.N.L. 45 p. 18

Third ascent of the peak

15. Sahadev East (5750 m) rising above
advance base camp.

Article 9   (Chris Bonington)

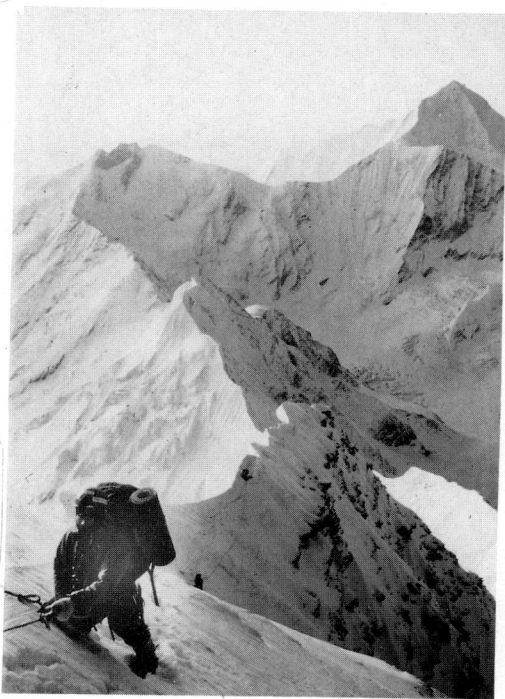

Climbing on Rajrambha, Panch Chuli
II behind.

Article 10   (Stephen Venables)

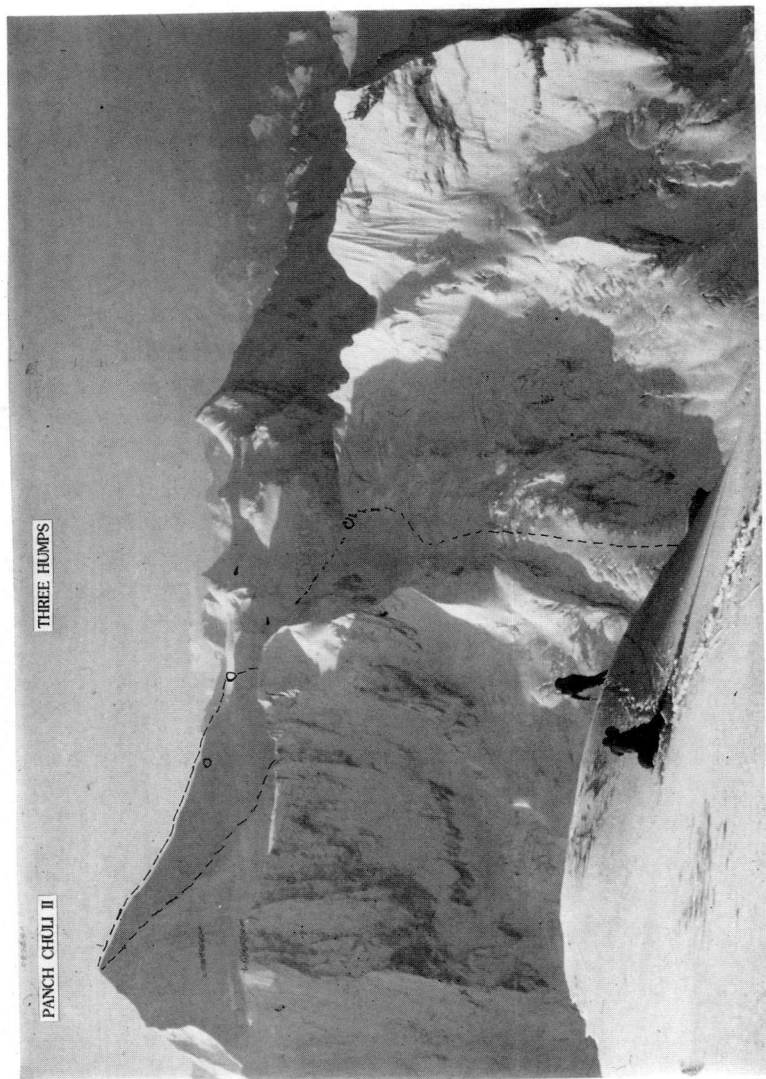

PANCH CHULI II

THREE HUMPS

17. View from the traverse to Rajrambha. Left to right: Panch Chuli II, the Balati Plateau, Sahadev West and East. Note three points on the edge in centre, possibly climbed by mistake in 1964.

(Stephen Venables)

Article 10

Expeditions from the western approaches

1. 1951 :   Heinrich Harrer and Frank Thomas   H.J. XVIII, p. 171
             pioneered the route via the Uttari Balati
             glacier. They reached c. 6100 m. on
             the Balati plateau, and attempted the
             west ridge. They found the north ridge
             in bad condition.

2. 1952 :   P. N. Nikore attempted via the Harrer
             route.

3. 1952 :   D. D. Joshi led an Indian team via the   Book Ref. 3
             Uttari Balati glacier to reach the Balati
             Plateau in June.

4. 1953 :   P. N. Nikore claimed a solo ascent, via
             the Uttari Balati glacier route. Claim not
             ·believed and not accepted.

5. 1964 :   Group Capt. A. K. Choudhary led   H.J. XXV, p. 207
             a team from the Indian Mountaineering   H.M.J. 3,
             Foundation. Reached the Balati plateau   No. 1, p. 53
             from the Harrer route. Tried the   H.C.N.L. 22, p. 5
             southwest ridge of peak II. Later claimed **Claim corrected:**
             mistaken ascents of peaks III, IV and   H.J. 49,
             V in two days. Now corrected.   H.C.N.L. 46, p. 19

6. 1972 :   Hukam Singh led the Indo-Tibet Border   I.T.B.P. Report.
             Police Team (I.T.B.P.) via the Uttari Balati H.C.N.L. 33, p. 26
             glacier. They climbed peak I.

First ascent of peak I

7. 1973 :   Mahendra Singh led an another I.T.B.P.   I.T.B.P. Nov.-Dec.
             team by the same route. They climbed   1973 and
             from the Balati Plateau and via the   Jan. 1974
             southwest ridge, to the summit.   H.C.N.L. 29, p.
                                                       23.

First ascent of peak II

8. 1992 :   Chris Bonington and Harish Kapadia led   H.J. 49
             the Indian British expedition via the Balati H.C.N.L. 46, p. 17
             Plateau. They climbed peak II via the
             southwest ridge and also the west ridge
             — a new route.

Fourth ascent of peak II

The expedition also made the first ascent
of peak V, from the Pyunshani valley.

Summary: 1929-1992: expeditions to Panch Chuli II.

From eastern approaches: 5 attempts and 2 climbs
From western approaches: 6 attempts and 2 climbs

Totally 11 attempts, 4 ascents; 15 expeditions in 64 years (not counting the heavenly journey of the Pandavas!).

H.J. = The Himalayan Journal
H.C.N.L. = The Himalayan Club Newsletter
H.M.J. = Himalayan Mountaineering Institute Journal
I.T.B.P. = Indo-Tibet Border Police Bulletins

Book References:

1. The Scottish Himalayan Expedition. By W. H. Murray.
2. Ultimate Mountains. By Tom Weir.
3. Panch Chuli Abhiyan (in Hindi). By D. D. Joshi.
   (Himalayan Publications, New Delhi — Bombay, October 1953)
4. Throne of Gods. By Arnold Heim and August Gansser.
5. Abode of Snow. By Kenneth Mason.
6. Exploring the Hidden Himalaya. By Soli Mehta and Harish Kapadia.

Nomenclature of western valleys of the Panch Chuli peaks:

Panch Chuli: Five (panch) cooking hearths (chulis) of Pandavas (of Indian epic Mahabharata)
Rajrambha: Apsara (celestial nymph) of Kings.
Menaka: A beautiful apsara.
Chaudhara: Four cornered peak.
Sahadev: Younger brother of Pandavas.
Draupadi: Wife of Pandavas.
Panchali: Another name for Draupadi.
Nagling: Peak of serpent.
Nagalaphu: Serpentine peak.
Halsyun: A plough
Balati: Strong (fearsome)
Madkot: Fort of devil 'Mad'.
Madkani: Wife of devil 'Mad'.
Munsiary: Place of snows.
Domol: Meeting place of two rivers.
Phunga Gair: A meadow of flowers.
Bagarthora: A place where shepherds stay.
Athansi: Staying alone.
Ringapani: A round (valley) containing water.
Kamrani: A nala at corner.
Kachautha: Place where crows die.
Pyunshani, Dhunakhan, Jauni, Shyama: Different types of grass.

SUMMARY

Details of climbs by the Indian British Panch Chuli Expedition, 1992.

Peaks Climbed	Date 1992	Summitters
1. **Sahadev East — 1st ascent** (5750 m) via north snow rib.	28 May	Chris Bonington Graham Little
2. **Rajrambha** (6537 m) Traversed via east ridge over Menaka peak — 1st ascent	5 June	Dick Renshaw Victor Saunders Stephen Sustad Stephen Venables
3. **Menaka — 1st ascent** (6000 m) Traversed on way to Rajrambha.	2 June	as above
4. **Panch Chuli II** (6904 m) via southwest ridge — 2nd ascent	7 June	Muslim Contractor Monesh Devjani Pasang Bodh
5. **Panch Chuli II** (6904 m) via west spur — 1st ascent	8 June	Chris Bonington Graham Little
6. **Panchali Chuli — 1st ascent** (5220 m) via Panchali glacier	20 June	Harish Kapadia Muslim Contractor Monesh Devjani Khubram Prakash Chand
7. **Draupadi — 1st ascent** (5250 m) via Panchali glacier	20 June	Harish Kapadia Muslim Contractor Monesh Devjani Khubram Prakash Chand
8. **Panch Chuli V — 1st ascent** (6437 m) via south ridge	20 June	Dick Renshaw Stephen Sustad Victor Saunders Stephen Venables

Cols Reached	Date	Persons
1. **Bagarthora col** (3800 m) crossed	15 June	By entire team
2. **Bainti col — 1st ascent** (5100 m) reached	20 June	Harish Kapadia Muslim Contractor Monesh Devjani Khubram Prakash Chand

RESCUED

A. Vijay Kothari: Air lifted by helicopter from Glacier Camp on the 8 June due to a broken ankle sustained in a fall on the way to advance base camp.

B. Stephen Venables: Air lifted by helicopter on 26 June from 5600 m below the south ridge of Panch Chuli V after an eighty metre fall on 21 June whilst returning from the summit. He severely damaged his right knee, broke his left ankle and injured his chest.

Period
10 May to 30 June 1992.

Members
Harish Kapadia (co-leader), Muslim Contractor, Monesh Devjani, Bhupesh Ashar, Vijay Kothari and Wing Cdr Anil Srivastava (liaison officer).

Chris Bonington (co-leader), Graham Little, Dick Renshaw, Victor Saunders, Stephen Sustad and Stephen Venables.

Supported by: Pasang Bodh (Sirdar), Yograj, Khubram, Prakash Chand, Suratram, Sundersingh, Revatram (cook), Harsinh Snr.. and Harsinh Jnr.

Sponsored by: Godrej, Bombay.

(Also refer to the article 'Rajrambha and Panch Chuli V', in the present issue covering other climbs on this expedition.)

10

RAJRAMBHA AND PANCH CHULI V

A. V. SAUNDERS

THE PANCH CHULI expedition was the third in a distinguished series, the Indo-British excursions organised largely by Harish Kapadia of Bombay. The first was the 1985 Rimo expedition, which accomplished a large number of firsts including that classic exploration, the first ascent of Rimo III (Fotheringham and Wilkinson). The second excursion, to Chong Kumdan, took place in 1991 and placed four climbers on the highest unclimbed massif in India, including Church, Porter, MacAdie and that Wilkinson person again. Both the above expeditions visited the Eastern Karakoram via Ladakh. For 1992 Kapadia chose the Kumaon Himalaya, that part of Uttar Pradesh just west of the Nepalese border, the general target being the Panch Chuli massif. This is a historically interesting area, with visits from Hugh Ruttledge in 1929, and Bill Murray and Heinrich Harrer in the early 50's. Several Indian expeditions have visited Panch Chuli, and the first ascent of Panch Chuli II was achieved in 1973 by the Indo Tibetan Border Police. All parties commented on the bad weather endemic to this region.

In recent years the border regions of India have been closed to foreigners, the dreaded 'inner line' marking off a corridor of some of the finest mountains in the Himalaya. The inner line was, of course, a British invention. For us, the way into this corridor is the joint Indo-British expedition. There is some sort of just Karma in that.

I was going to say that Bombay seemed an odd place for a concentration of Himalayan mountaineers, but on reflection, it seems no odder than London, Bath, Cardiff, Edinburgh or Calbeck, our homes. Bombay is much closer after all. Harish Kapadia, co-leader of our expedition, editor of the *Himalayan Journal*, and walking Himalayan encyclopedia, practices his family trade as a cloth merchant in what spare time he can muster from his duties to the journal and the Bombay Mountaineers. With him he brought Vijay Kothari, Monesh Devjani, Bhupesh Ashar, and Muslim Contractor. For our part, there was co-leader Chris Bonington, Graham Little, Stephen Venables, Dick Renshaw, Stephen Sustad and

Photos 16-17, 19-20

myself. We had then, Gujratis, a Sindhi, an American, a Scot, a token Welshman from Yorkshire, and a couple of English if you include me. Or to look at it another way, 3 Hindus of various castes, a Jain, a Muslim, a Lutheran, an athiest Catholic, and few agnostic Protestants. Looking over the lists from Harish early in the year, Chris commented on the name Muslim Contractor;

'That is a person, not a job, isn't it?'
'Yes Chris, he was with us on Rimo. Good company too.'
'Funny sort of name that, Muslim, don't you think?'
'Yes indeed..........Christian.'

On the mountain we were to split up into three teams working from the same ABC at 4840 m. Harish's team would attempt Panch Chuli II via the SW ridge, first climbed in 1973 by the ITBP. The original ascent involved fixing almost the entire route with fixed rope by a very large team. Harish was going to try a light weight ascent. With him he took his Manali porters, Pasang Bodh, our Sirdar, Prakash, Khubram and Yograj. Chris and Graham would try a new route on the same mountain, the west ridge, and the rest of us were going to kick off with Rajrambha.

Rajrambha

In Hindu mythology the fairy Rajrambha protects the Devas from the interfering mortals. Rajrambha was the most beautiful of the guardian fairies. The mountain which takes this name is correspondingly the most beautiful of the western outliers to the Panch Chuli, protecting the place of the last meal of the Pandavas. (Panch = five; chuli = cooking hearths). It's all in the Mahabharata, the Hindi version of which has been running on C4 for seemingly years.

Walking up the tortuous Uttari Balati glacier, the view was dominated by, and we had been originally attracted to, the undimbed south face of Rajrambha (6537 m). But exploratory excursions on the neighbouring peaks suggested that this would consist largely of sunsoaked deep snow on steep mixed ground, and it was Dick who first suggested the Intregral Traverse, a journey of some 10 kilometres, about half of which would be over 6.000 m. A sort of giant Peutery Ridge I suppose. (Note: Mt Blanc 4807, ABC 4840).

From ABC our western skyline formed the route. There was a low col at the head of the glacier due north of us, we'd start there, then follow the skyline from right to left. We could see a mixed entry buttress to the ridge, then a summit of about 600 m, (Menaka, yet another of those fairies, of course), then a long and possibly corniced ridge, three more mixed buttresses, the last of which was

undoubtedly very steep, more heavily corniced ridges, and a giant
summit cornice. The descent looked deceptively straightforward. Amble
down a sort of mixed buttress with bulging seracs, find a narrow
col and a final six hundred meters of front pointing down to the
glacier should see us walking home. No? Well almost. There were
a couple of cards that nature had played that were not in our favour.
First there was the weather. Violent storms clouds with towering black
anvils blossomed every day, usually by lunchtime. Thunder, lightning
and thrashing hailstorms followed in the afternoon. By early night
the energy driving these microcosms had been drained, and clear
skies would return for another twelve hours. The second card was
the sheer spiteful ferocity of the sun. By 8 a.m. every day the snow
had softened till it was thigh deep. Our window of opportunity was
midnight to 9 a.m.

Oh yes, and one more thing, nature had imbued us with the propensity
to underestimate almost everything. It was obvious, then, that we would
have to climb quite a lot of the ridge and all the lower buttresses
at night. We planned to stop by 8.30, perhaps 9 a.m. at the latest,
and somehow thought that, unacclimatised as we were, we would
still be able to do it inside three days. This would be a straightforward,
quick and above all, safe climb. Perhaps.

The idea was simplicity itself. Stephen Sustad and I would take
a tent and one rope, Dick and the other Stephen would do the
same. Each pair would take three days food. We'd be able to cut
down on hardware, and share ropes for the abseils.

It was a minor nuisance that when either Dick or I asked for
Steve, the answer always came back in stereo, and while packing
for the traverse, Harish or Muslim noticed that Venables with his
Young Fogey felt homberg bore an uncanny resemblence to Freddy
Kruger. The best bit was that Stephen had never heard of *Nightmare
on Elm Street*. With careful training we were able to get Venables
to answer to his new name. That only left Sustad to deal with,
and he's a Lutheran, though exactly what Martin Luther would have
made of him, I am not too sure.

The Hindu calendar, said Harish, predicted 10 days of good weather
from the beginning of the month, and so we set off during the
night of 1 June; Freddy and the Lutheran stomping across the expanse
of glacier to the start of the climb, preceded by small pools of
torchlight. Soon Dick would take over, leaving me plodding asthmatically
in their steps. Warnings floated out of the dark, 'slot here!' or 'Watch
the rope a second!' The back marker would take in a few coils.
Being extremely cowardly, we always took the utmost care with crevasses.

There was a moment, early in the approach, when the Lutheran said 'Stop Victor.... listen.' There was nothing to be heard. Not a breath of wind. No crunch of serac fall. No rumble of avalanche...nothing. It was silent as the night surrounding us was black. It was so still that the air, though well below freezing, felt warm. Later there was a slight breeze, enough to strip the layer of warmed air from the body. That's normal, the predawn breeze seems as much a feature of mountain meteorology as the katabatic wind. The breeze died away with the growing light. We crossed the schrund, where we unroped, and began soloing up the easy buttresses.

There was a small but beautiful coincidence, we reached the watershed at the same moment as the thin early morning sun. The view was new to us. The silver ridge unfolded above us in rolled volumes, serried ranks of pale ridges and peaks marched away into the Tibetan mists. We could clearly see Harrer's route to Peak II which Chris and Harish would be following. Not long afterwards, the sun grew stronger and the snow softer. Soon we were panting for air under the heavy press of the rucksacks and the sweltering heat, and looking for the first possible tent site.

That afternoon we lay exhausted, making desultory brews and trying to sleep. The biological clock makes this difficult. The Lutheran had surprised us by bringing a book, 'The Good Terrorist'. We tried to get him to read us passages, he wouldn't, but did give us a one line precis; 'It's about people with cockney accents, who start speaking BBC English when they get angry.' The tent poles froze solid the next morning and I broke one. Speaking gently to it in BBC English I packed it away leaving bits of pole sticking out. For the rest of the trip my sack sported a long whippy antennae. This was to become significant.

For the next two days Freddy, the Lutheran, Dick and I travelled slowly as snails over Menaka and down to the long col before the last steep buttress. Sometimes there were delightfully steep pitches on barely frozen shale, more often we were creeping sideways on ice, covered thinly with a faithless film of powder, and trying to stay below the cornice line; at the end of each day the sun deepening the snow. Usually the climbing was brittle and insecure and needed a lot of care and some pitching.

By late morning on day four we could look back with some satisfaction on the ridge, winding like a country road above the deep shadowed valleys. We'd had a couple of exhilarating sections of very Scottish climbing, 'tip toeing' in crampons, fist jams, rock-overs on snow covered rock and unbalanced bridging. The pro was interesting too. The cracks

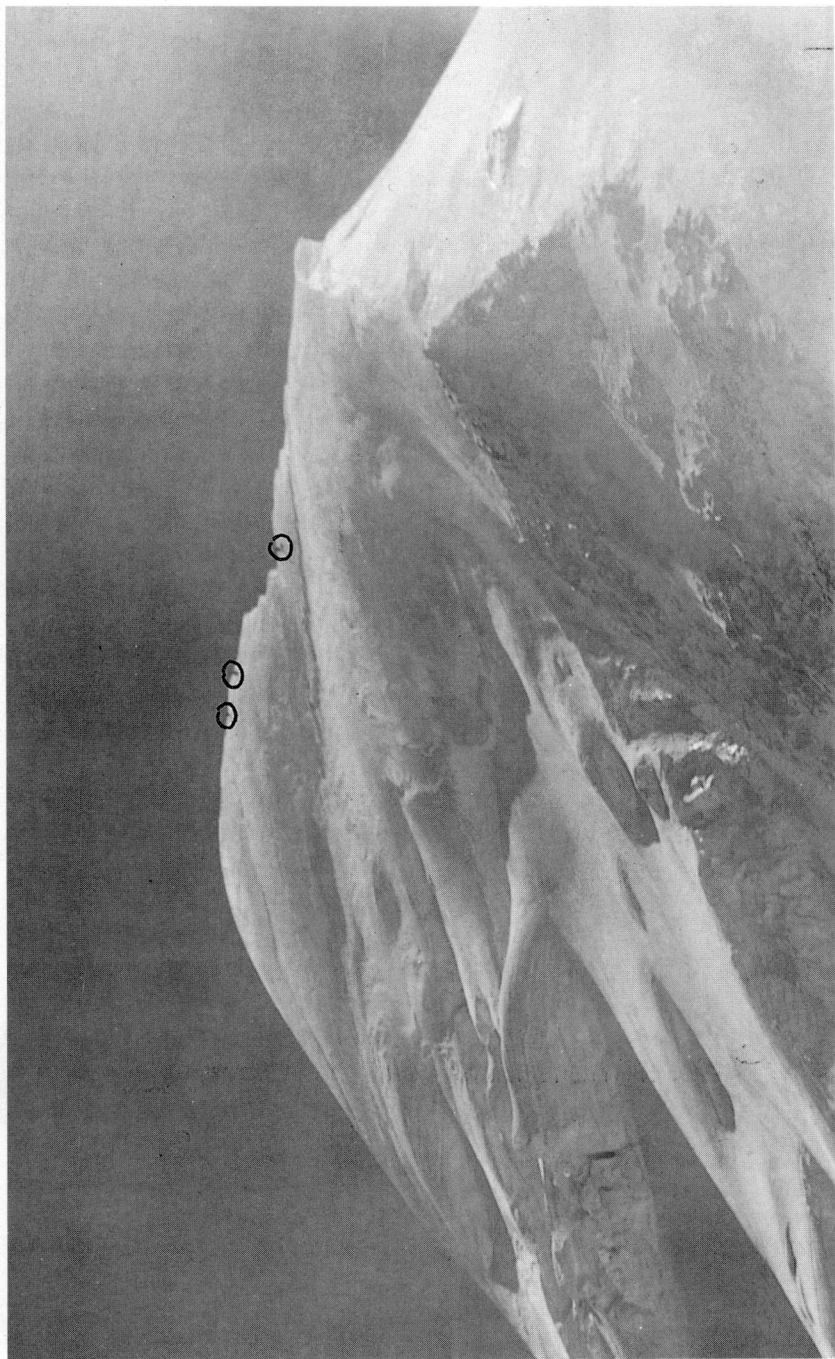

18. Southwest ridge of Panch Chuli II. Three climbers on the final cornice.

(Harish Kapadia)

Article 9

19. The huge summit cornice on Panch Chuli V (6437 m). Telkot on right.

Article 10 (Stephen Venables)

NAGLING TELKOT UNNAMMED PEAK BAINTI

20. Telkot (6102 m), foreground, from Panch Chuli V. Background: left to right: Nagling (6041 m), Unnamed peak (5800 m) and Bainti peak (6072 m)

Article 10 (Stephen Venables)

in the shale forced unusual nut placements. It was like chess; you
had to think. Almost as enjoyable as bouldering. Earlier Freddy had
had a pitch of the most unlikely laybacking up massive frozen-in
(we hoped) jugs.

'It's actually quite rare to get that sort of climbing on big mountains',
he enthused, even from 50 m we could see his grin, 'and look,
my first nuts in opposition belay!'

'Sounds painful', said the Lutheran. 'Better not fall off on them'.

The summit looked close, though how close we could not tell.
There was no scale to judge by. A narrow ridge ran up to a small
ice wall then a whale back to the apparent top. Large cornices on
the right, endless ice slopes to the left. The valleys had long since
filled with the diurnal mists, the wind blew wreaths from left to right
making a ghostly broken spectre of Freddy over the vast and empty
space over the east face. Dick and the Lutheran joined him, disappearing
intermittently in the mist.

The sky flickered over Panch Chuli II. Sheets of lightning etched
the outline of Naglaphu on the eyeball. The thunder exploded like
surf, all round us. I followed the rope up to the others wondering
about it all. I had already felt that familiar and dreadful itching at
the ears, the buzz of static, and knew the elemental forces were
building up for something unusual. I had almost reached the others
when the unusual happened.

The sky ignited overhead. A momentary, almost subliminal whitening
of the sky. I felt a sharp pain in my shoulder and side. Someone
was trying to electrocute me. Like with a cattle prod. I heard the
scream as the electrons tore the air apart over our heads. And I
still had those antennae sticking out. I tried to bury the sack in
the ice before me, but not before another banshee shrieked across
the sky, bringing on more fear and pain. The other three had been
quite unaffected, but then they weren't carrying lightning conductors.
The wind had risen, and we were now engulfed in a full storm.

There was no possibility of a bivouac on the ice, but the summit,
we thought, might be even more exciting. I feel that at this point
in the story I should explain something about lee slopes, cornices
and windslab formations, but I shan't. It's too complicated. I'll just
say that in the Himalaya they are often east facing, and the snow
is usually soft, and often unstable, and may form interestingly baroque
shapes. Somewhere behind us the cornice overhung several large blobs,
one of which looked like a tent sized ledge. Being on the lee side
of the slope it would be out of the wind. The problem was one

of access, how to bypass the cornice. The team moved down the ridge.

The storm ripped the words from our mouths, we had to communicate in gestures. Freddy, belayed to an ice screw, held the rope while I looked for a safe way down to the enticing ledge. There was a very clear line marking the danger zone, a plating of hard ice on the windward side and softer snow over the cornice. I chose a slight dip in the ridge, perhaps the cornice would be smaller here, and crossed the line. There was a small crevasse on the line. I stepped in the soft snow, nothing happened. I took another step, and leant over to see past the edge. There was a loud report, a thunderous clap, the world collapsed around me, and suddenly I found myself slowly spinning at the end of the rope looking down two thousand feet of fluted snow slopes down the east face. A crescent showed the break in the cornice above, and half our prospective ledge had been carried away too. Life really is a bitch, as they say in BBC English. We eventually excavated a platform on the windward side of the cornice. The storm blew itself out, as usual, by late evening.

The summit came on day 5, Freddy had formed the opinion that the easiest way to make progress was to follow the fracture line of the cornices, it was too hard and icy below the line. It was inevitable that he should eventually step through. When he did, he just appeared to slowly settle in a cloud of snow dust. Dick was holding his rope, and turned to me, 'he's fallen through the cornice' he said incredulously. Freddy reappeared at the edge mouthing impeccable BBC.

The summit came early in the morning, with tremendous views across to Api and Nampa under the sun. Turning west we gazed as the morning light picked out Nanda Devi, Changabang and Dunagiri. Dunagiri. The mountain where it all began. Dick and Joe Tasker. Hard alpine style climbing. 11 days. 15 years ago. It makes you feel rather humble. Freddy was still taking photographs when the Lutheran started down, and we reached our ABC, 33 m above Mont Blanc, in the drifting afternoon mists.

Panch Chuli II[1]

We'd been away five days. Chris and Graham had gone up Panch Chuli II with Harish's team. Two days later Muslim Contractor, Monesh Devjani and Pasang Bodh reached their summit having made the second

---

1. For full details of the climbs here and on other peaks on this expedition, see article 'Fires on the Mountain' in this issue. — Ed.

ascent of the south west ridge of Panch Chuli II. The next day
Chris and Graham completed their new route on the west ridge of
Panch Chuli II. Both teams had kicked off from a camp at 6000
m and had two bivouacs above the bergschrund.

There had been an accident while we were on Rajrambha, Vijay,
our Jain, had taken a monster fall in a snow gully, his crampons
must have balled up. He rolled and somersaulted about 300 m coming
to rest on a slight knoll above a deep schrund. I came to rest
by the help of.... Vijay pointed at the heavens. It may also have
had something to do with one of Harish's Manali men, Sundersingh,
who ran to Vijay and fielded him at the last moment. Then again
it may have been the Ganesh medallions which Geeta, Harish's wife
had given to all members of the expedition. Ganesh, the elephant
god, is also the deity of new enterprises. Venables had been given
one before his ascent of Everest, and still had that one. The medallions
seemed to work, so when Freddy sent the new one home to his
son Oliver, it may have been a mistake. Ganesh is, after all, the
guardian of new enterprises, and should be signified with new medallions.

It was already looking like a successful expedition when the others
returned safely to base. But we decided to push our luck. We'd have
a look at the unclimbed group of Panch Chulis. May be this was
a mistake too.

Panch Chuli V

From Madkot, the road head to the range, there is a spectacular
view of the Panch Chuli wall. The view is from southwest, and in
the evening the peaks catch the Alpenglow. The peaks are ranged
in numerical order from II to V , and though II is the highest at
6904 m, the other peaks attract the mountaineer's ambition. These
are steep mixed faces, falling some 2000 m to the south flowing
Panch Chuli glacier. This glacier had not been visited by mankind,
though the valley, the Pyunshani gadhera, had seen the occasional
hunter from Madkot. From this select group we hired a guide who
said he knew the Pyunshani valley, though he didn't tell us till much
later that his last visit was more than nine years earlier. The man's
name was Dhansinh.

Dhansinh had one property that was extremely disconcerting for
those of us following. The Lutheran summed it up neatly; If there's
a lone bush in the middle of an open field, he'll walk through it.
It was commonplace over the three days it took us to trek to Pyunshani
to find Dhansinh clambering into dense bamboo bushes, while everyone
else walked round to meet him.

The trek was also notable for the astronomic number of flowers that Freddy recognized, usually, with orgasmic enthusiasm. He saw dozens of species of Primula. 'This maxiflora, look at it, the tiniest Primula you'll ever see.' I couldn't; he appeared to be staring at a patch of dirt. He pointed out the megacarpea, which is a tall leafy plant with a taste like bitter chicory and pepper. 'It's edible....' I tried and had to spit it out. 'But first you have to boil it and throw away the water.' Oh thanks, now that I've poisoned myself, he tells me. There was wild garlic, two species of strawberries and a blood red potentilla which he described as being like strawberry, but not fruiting. 'Pretty useless then, isn't it?' said the Lutheran, which seemed to sum up something, but I am not sure what. And nobody got very excited by the evil looking Cobra Lilies lurking in the shade.

On the third day Dhansinh's route took us down a section of vertical jungle. With the rucksacks catching on every creeper and vine, we slid down wet cliffs, dangling from bamboo and climbing down a greasy scaffold of rhododendron. Then suddenly out into the open, and blinking in the light. Looking back we could see the canopy ripple as the rest of the team made their way down the vegetated cliff. Look! the Lutheran pointed. There was a particularly rapid green wave, a howl, (anguish?) and great deal of shouting in Hindi, BBC Hindi. Monesh had fallen out of the forest and landed on Harish. A little later the entire team was watching with interest as a lone ripple followed the peregrinations of Dhansinh as he looked for an alternative and bushier way out of the jungle.

The next day Chris and the four of us were surveying Panch Chuli V from a bivouac at 4200 m. We were tired, having brought up large loads 1000 m from the new BC. We were going to be short of time, we'd have to be back inside five days from base. We needed a straightforward route. Simple route finding, and moderate technical difficulties. Preferably with little traversing on brittle ice. And we could see our route. It was to be Panch Chuli V from the south col. There was an easy summit ridge, and below it a rock buttress that could obviously be turned; we couldn't quite see how, but that didn't worry us. Below the rock was an easy and pleasant looking cwm. High above the entrance to the cwm there was a lone serac. The Tower. We did not suppose it posed any great danger. The only niggling doubt was that below the cwm, all was hidden from view. We could only guess at what the dead ground might contain, but again chose not to fret about it.

24 hours later we knew we should have fretted. The two Stephens broke trail while Chris, Dick and I followed them across the icefall

we had not been able to see. It was ugly, tortured, ground. First
the tracks led across The Splits, an unstable arch of iceblocks, which
needed wide bridging to avoid overloading the central span. (Avert
eyes from chasm below). Next the footprints wandered very slowly
under the Venus Fly Trap, a weird overhang fringed with ice fangs,
Then there was the Long Jump, slightly downhill, we'd not be able
to reverse that. The Maze followed. In bad weather this section could
be impossible without millions of marker wands. Later there was the
Double Snowbridge, a traverse over that most unstable of structures,
two bridges holding each other up, then a final section under innocuous
looking ice ramparts, whose detritus belied their looks. That night
we bivouacked at 5200 m in the mouth of our cwm. Above us
the Tower began to look a little threatening. Fresh avalanche tracks
swept down from the slopes under it and through the cwm over
the ice cliffs below. Freddy and the Lutheran had chosen a site by
a wide mouthed crevasse where the avalanche tracks bifurcated. The
whole cwm was tilted at 30^0, perfect slab avalanche country. I was
beginning to get bad feelings about the valley. We all were.

The following day we pushed on through thigh deep snow, Dick
making a deep trench, and though he was breaking trail we found
it hard to keep up with the man. On this sort of ground he is
phenomenal. That night we excavated a platform from the side of
a cornice. We were on the south col at about 5850 m. That should
leave us with just 600 m for the day trip to the summit. We reckoned
we'd be back the next morning by 9 a.m. It was true that we'd
be out of food the next day, but that didn't matter, we'd be on
the way down. It was more worrying that the Tower had begun
to lose material. We were finishing our lunch, a soup brew and
a packet of instant mash, when the noise of an express train attracted
our attention. A spectacular climax avalanche was sweeping our tracks
out of the cwm. Another followed it five minutes later. 'There goes
last night's bivi.' said Freddy, wiping a minute blob of instant mash
from his beard and back into his mouth. I wondered who bought
the stuff in England. It's vile, I just could not imagine giving up
real potatoes for this. Perhaps people buy it for wall paper paste.
Tastes the same. Not only were we almost out of food, the two
vegetarians were also down to their last tobacco. The Lutheran said
'Dick, If we get up this mountain, can I have one of your Gitanes?'

'Hmmm, only got one left.'

What about a couple of drags? He was looking forward to the
next day. Two or three hundred metres of steep mixed climbing should
take us on to a gentle summit ridge. Given reasonable weather it
should be enjoyable. Short day.

He was wrong. When the alarm went off at 2 a.m. Chris announced his decision to stay put and wait for us. He was unusually tired, and felt he'd only hold us up. Perhaps though, there was more to this decision than rational explanation allows. Perhaps it was the survival instinct which has served Chris so well over the years. Always listen to your instinct. It's what keeps mountaineers alive. Back at base, Muslim watched Harsinh Sr making a pan of tea, which fell from the fire, dousing the flames. Harsinh looked up horrified. Bad sign.... he said, backing off. They are in great danger.

'It's going to be a long day.' said Dick. The steep mixed ground between the pillars had already taken us much longer than we'd allowed. It was now 10.30 a.m. That's not snow, it's ice. Where we hoped to stroll, we now knew we'd have to traverse on front points. It would be almost half a kilometre. A night descent began to seem increasingly likely as we slowly crept along the ice, staying well clear of the cornice. We reached the top at 3.00 p.m. on 20 June. The afternoon clouds shrouded us and the mountain. We knew Chris would have expected us back by now. It was not till midnight that he saw our head torches. He had been desperately worried, and now he was able to relax. He put on a giant brew.

Freddy and I watched the others go down. We'd had no food or water for the last 23 hours. It was 2.00 a.m., but after this abseil there would only be one more to the tent and that brew we felt sure Chris would be making. Freddy said;
'I am really pleased we pulled this one off, Victor.'
'We're not down yet.' Not intended as any kind of put down, more a form of neurosis on my part. Abseils have always terrified me. Gingerly I stepped off the ledge and loaded the ropes. The anchor was a good looking short angle, driven to the hilt in a horizontal crack. There were two back-up nuts. Nothing to worry about there. I turned the torch down into the void and began to dangle.

Freddy had seen two of us safely down, and began to remove the back-up while I was still on the rope. It was obviously safe. Dick and the Lutheran were not too sure about the next anchor, and were still adding to it when I arrived. Dick threaded a rope end through the abseil sling. The Lutheran was groping about in the dark for yet another nut placement. It was 2.30 a.m. Chris'd turned the gas off, he'd reheat the brew when we got down.

Freddy stepped off his ledge and began down. He'd been a little violent in loading the rope, but it was ok. for about twenty feet. Then he entered the dream sequence.

'Look!' Dick, Sustad and I turned towards the crashing sound. A large squarish black shadow skidded past trailing a shower of sparks. It looked like stonefall.

'His anchor's gone!' In that instant we all knew it was true. That was no stonefall, those sparks were made by crampons. Silence for a moment, for an eternity. The ropes! I grabbed the tangle of ropes before me just as they began to whip through in pursuit of Venables, they shredded trousers and my gloves, but it was Dick who stopped them leaving the belay. Dick held the 240 foot fall in his gloved hands, with just one turn of the rope through our anchor.

PANCH CHULI V (6437 m) STORY OF THE ACCIDENT: 20-26 JUNE 1992

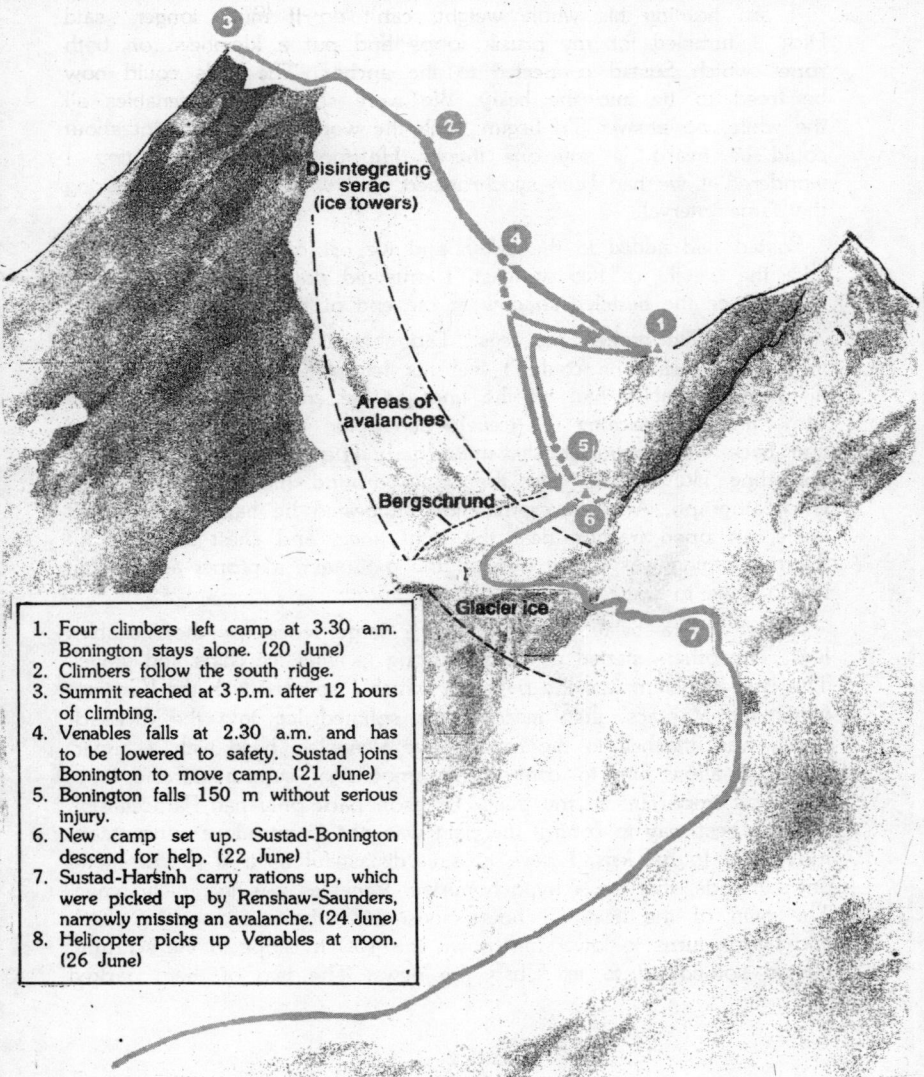

Disintegrating serac (ice towers)

Areas of avalanches

Bergschrund

Glacier ice

1. Four climbers left camp at 3.30 a.m. Bonington stays alone. (20 June)
2. Climbers follow the south ridge.
3. Summit reached at 3 p.m. after 12 hours of climbing.
4. Venables falls at 2.30 a.m. and has to be lowered to safety. Sustad joins Bonington to move camp. (21 June)
5. Bonington falls 150 m without serious injury.
6. New camp set up. Sustad-Bonington descend for help. (22 June)
7. Sustad-Harsinh carry rations up, which were picked up by Renshaw-Saunders, narrowly missing an avalanche. (24 June)
8. Helicopter picks up Venables at noon. (26 June)

Chris heard noise, and watched the falling head torch, as it bounced down to the glacier. Tears filled his eyes. One of them's gone, he thought. Venables thought so too;

I hadn't connected the dream sequence with the abseil. It was only afterwards I thought Ah Yes, the anchor's come out. I think that was on the way down. So many thoughts as I somersaulted and cartwheeled. I felt, Ah God, how can my body put up with this violence, so loud and crashing. He fell through a vertical 80 foot section, across a slab, and down another 80 foot wall.

'I am holding his whole weight, can't do it much longer.' said Dick. I fumbled for my prusik loops and put a klemheist on both ropes which Sustad connected to the anchor. The ends could now be freed to tie into the belay. We were shouting to Venables all the while, no answer. I'd begun think the worst when a distant shout could be heard. Is any one there? He too had been shouting. I wondered if we had been synchronised, and waiting for replies during the same interval.

Sustad had added to the belay, and we felt confident that it would take the weight of two at least. I prusiked down the tight rope till I could see the huddled shadow at the end of the rope.

'I think I've broken my legs.' Dick heard that, and wondered if that really meant he couldn't feel his legs, and had in fact broken his back. Venables had hit the knot at the end of the rope at the same time as reaching the icefield above the bergschrund. His head and back were, miraculously, untouched. There was a lot of blood, spreading like a halo into the snow around him. A sort of red chromatograph. A quick examination suggested he had a broken left ankle, an open fracture near the right knee, and chest injuries. But the main thing was to get him off the mountain, a proper assessment would have to wait.

I fixed up a belay and dug out a large ledge for the Venables legs. The others started down, showering us with ice chips and gravel. The chief problem was the right leg, which I splinted with the Karrimat from our Macsacs, then inserted the splinted leg into the rucksack which was attached to the rope above Venables' head with a jumar. It would allow him to control the amount of support to the limb. This was important as my trusty Gregson pack only had Paracetamol, and the best way to control the pain was not to introduce unnecessary movement to his legs. I have to say, distasteful as it is to commend one's friends, that for a hypochondriac, Venables was incredibly brave. The pain of the next 12 hours must have been excruciating. Dick and I took turns to lower him down the 400 m slope to the schrund. Sustad soloed off to tell Chris the news. The two of them packed

21. Nanda Devi peaks and unclimbed Changuch *(foreground)* from
summit of Nandabhanar.

(Divyesh Muni)

22. Nanda Kot from summit of Nandakhani.

Article 11 (Divyesh Muni)

up the tents and started climbing down. About 150 m above the
schrund Chris chose to cartwheel. His crampons must have balled
up, he slid, tried to brake, caught his frontpoints in the ice and
lost it completely. He shot over the schrund trying to curl up into
a ball, with the idea that he'd less likely to break his limbs if they
weren't sticking out.

Dick saw it all. Chris coming to rest, sitting up, and holding his
head in his hands for ages. When Dick joined me he was looking
pale and climbing very very carefully. Sustad reached the cwm and
helped Chris cut out a platform and erected the tents. Chris tried
again with the waiting brew scenario. This time it worked, though
we were not to reach the tents till 3 p.m. Almost 36 hours after
we'd left our bivi on the south col.

The next morning Chris and Sustad went down leaving us three
and a half cylinders of gas, three packets of the dreaded instant
mash and a few packets of soup. They reached base the same afternoon.
Chris went on the next day, and using kukris to cut their way out
of the jungle, walked out with Harsinh Sr (who now knew his tea
pan had not lied) in a blistering 9 hours. It would normally have
been a three day effort. At Munsiary, Chris and Harish would telephone
for the helicopter. The Lutheran rested a day, then with Harsinh
Jr carried a load of food and gas 1800 m up to a broad ridge
at c 5000 m. This operation took 2 days. My friend was exhausted,
and had to solo the last 400 m gully at night. But he was driven
by an intolerable round of fears and anxieties. Dick and I collected
the food four days after the accident. We had shared the last dreadful
little packet of dehydrated potato, and were down to a quarter cylinder
of gas. Although we only had to climb 600 m back to the tent,
we thought we might not have the strength to do this without food.

In addition to the vertical interval there was the sheer fright we
felt everytime we passed under the Tower. Some instinct had made
us go down for the food a few hours earlier than seemed sensible.
This meant that we'd be climbing back up to the tent at 3 a.m.
rather than 7 a.m. The whole operation would have to take place
in the dark. But some small voice had told us to go, and go soon.
On the way back, Dick had broken trail at heartbursting pace in
order to pass through the danger zone under the Tower, when the
whole face of the serac began to break up. With a roar the avalanche
swept across the cwm, up the other side of the valley, and on into
the glacier beyond. Horrified I looked at how much of our track
was left. About five minutes worth. The Tower continued to disintegrate
for the next four hours. As I followed Dick up the rest of the cwm,
I fancied I could hear him muttering to himself, something about
always listening to your instincts....

The helicopter flew in that afternoon. We were at 5600 m, which is pretty damn close to the flying ceiling for Alouettes. There was no winch, presumably to save weight, and and so the pilots had to attempt a half landing. They hovered twenty feet from us and motioned their requirements. It was like trying to communicate with gods in a maelstrom. Dick lay on the collapsed tents to stop them blowing away. I clutched at Freddy to stop him tobagganing down the cwm in his sleeping bag. Now THAT would have been embarrassing. The chopper put one skid down on the outside edge of the tent platform. The rotor tips inches from the snow, and not much more above our heads. One mistake from the pilots, and Venables and I would be salamied. A door opened, the co-pilot motioned, I pushed and Venables pulled, he landed his torso on the floor behind the pilots. The aircraft wandered slightly, the co-pilot gestured violently. In desperation Venables put his broken ankle on the skid and pushed off on it, I heaved the other leg. With a howl of pain he was in. The door wouldn't close, but he was mostly inside the bubble. I collapsed exhausted. The chopper wobbled uncertainly and moved off. The leg withdrew, the perspex door shut. The pilots waved and turned for home.

At home, Freddy underwent operations in Bath Hospital. His left ankle had been pinned, I think he had a fracture of the lateral maleolus. The right tibia had a bit knocked off its head; that was the open fracture producing all the blood. The knee cap was shattered, and was wired together again, and they said that his chest was undamaged, just bruised. The Lutheran is back at his carpentry workshop in Shropshire and Dick will be supporting his vocation as a sculptor with abseil work again. Chris had planned to take up canoeing in France with Wendy. Unfortunately the lorry drivers had blocked all major routes through the country. Judging by the television coverage, France was one enormous stationary traffic jam then. I think their best hope of using the canoe was to put it on the top of the Volvo and sit in it, admiring the French countryside from the peaceful silence of the motionless motorway.

SUMMARY

A personal account of the Indian British Panch Chuli expedition, May-June 1992. Peak Menaka (6000 m) was traversed, second ascent of Rajrambha (6537 m) by a new route, the first ascent of Panch Chuli V (6437 m) and the accident and rescue of Stephen Venables after a fall, were achieved. (Further details in article 'Fires on the Mountain' in the present issue).

11

AROUND DANU DHURA

DIVYESH MUNI

AFTER DISCUSSING VARIOUS ideas, we were keen on a visit to the Shalang gad in the Kumaon Himalaya. The *Himalayan Journal* XIII, p. 134 carried an article on 'Possible Alternative to Traill's Pass'. We studied this in detail. In August 1926, after an expedition to Kailas in Tibet, H. Ruttledge and Colonel Wilson crossed Traill's pass from the Johar side to Phurkia. They had with them a party of four Bhotias from Martoli village in Johar, headed by Diwan Singh Martolia who was well known as a guide. These four were dismissed at Phurkia to return to their village, and advised to go by the safe Namik route. They had ropes and some equipment with them. Instead they struck up east from Phurkia, slept the first night below the snow-line, and keeping south of Nanda Kot found themselves by midday the next day in the Shalang gad, and were in their village Martoli the same evening. This information was gathered by J. C. Donaldson in June 1945.

Harish Kapadia and his team had attempted to cross over this pass from the Shalang gad in 1988 but bad weather forced them to retreat from a high camp just below the ridge between Nandakhani and Laspa Dhura. We also studied pictures of the Nandakot, Nandakhani, Nandbanhar peaks taken from Shalang Dhura by Vinay Hegde in 1991. It showed a possibility to cross over the connecting ridge between Nandakhani and Laspa Dhura. Geoff Hornby had visited the area in 1987 with an Indo-British expedition in which they had scaled Laspa Dhura, Nandakhani and Nandabhanar from the Pindari valley. His article describes a route from the Pindari which matches with observations of J.C. Donaldson. They had in fact reached the Danu Dhura from the Pindari glacier.

We were very excited with the idea of crossing the Danu Dhura from Shalang gad and attempting peaks Nandabhanar, Nandabhanhar and if time permitted Nanda Kot. Once we reached the Danu Dhura, attempting the first two peaks would not be much of a problem

Photos 21 to 26

96

Dangthal (6050 m) from Nandakhani.   (Divyesh Muni)

but Nanda Kot was another question. Except for Geoff Hornby's comments on the possibility of attempting the south face of Nanda Kot, discussion with most people who had viewed the face was discouraging. A detailed study of the map however gave us some hope on the possibility of the attempt. With this in mind we set about planning and organising our expedition.[1]

Our final team consisted of Mrs Immai Hu, Ms. Chetna Rana, Mrs Vineeta Muni and myself. We had hired two H.A.P.'s from Manali to assist us. Yograj Thakur and Koylu Ram became two more members of the team.

Approach

The three ladies left Bombay on 10 September 1992. They trekked from Munsiari to Lilam, Bugdiar and on the third day to village Martoli. The trek is along the true right of the Ghori ganga through thick forest. The gorge narrows down at many places to a few hundred metres with towering granite walls on both sides. A paradise for the rock climber. As the winter was setting in the shepherds and residents of the valley were moving down with their flocks to the lower regions. At Martoli our team stayed in one of the houses in the village. They now had to move into the Shalang gad.

---

1. For earlier expeditions see, H.J. Vol. 45, p. 53 (Kapadia), H.J. Vol. 44, p. 76 (Hornby) and H.J. Vol. 48, p. 174 (Hegde). — Ed.

The Shalang gad is formed between two high ridges. From northeast to southwest, on the right lie the peaks Martoli (4586 m), Shella Dhura (5264 m), Tamkhani (5218 m), Shalang Dhura (5678 m) and Dangthal (6050 m). From southwest to northeast, on the left lie the peaks Laspa Dhura (5913 m), Nandakhani (6029 m), Nanda Kot (6861m) and Kuchela (6294 m).

As you move up from Martoli, the track stays close to the right of the valley. After about a two hour walk, one has to climb up steeply to high alps. You come to Talla Shalang (lower Shalang). Two stone shelters have been made by the shepherds where they camped. Further ahead is Malla Shalang (higher Shalang) and Karbaciya. A little after Karbaciya they had to climb down to the glacier and cross over to the left. A short climb up the lateral moraine and they came upto Bhadeli Gwar and the base camp site was below the north-east ridge of Nandakhani at 4800 m on 20 September.

Shalang Dhura (5678 m)

One night was spent at Karbaciya and they moved up the scree and grass slopes for 500 m. They had decided to put up a camp at about 5100 m. Next day they went up deep snow to the top. The climb was exhausting due to the deep snow. They soon made

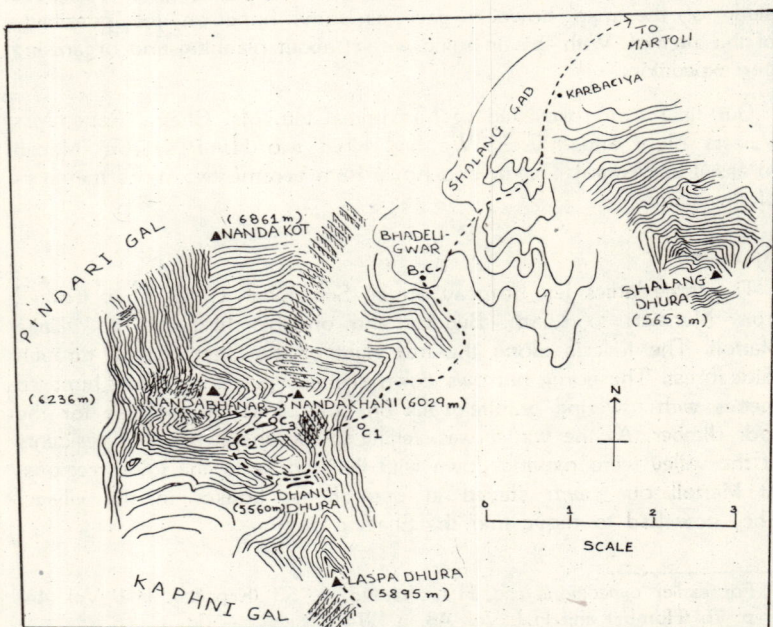

their way back to the camp and next day down to Karbaciya and base camp.

Travelling alone I reached Munsiari in 3 days from Bombay, and two days to base camp. I received a great welcome at base camp. Every one was very eager to go ahead to Danu Dhura. Since they had already spotted a good route to the pass, we would go up with loads.

Camp 1

We left early. The cold was biting. We moved southwest from base camp, skirting the Nandakhani massif keeping the glacier on our left. We continued gradually gaining height in a broad gully till we reached a small basin. A small icefall came down from Nandakhani. Crossing it was tricky, since stones came down with the melting. Once across, a short climb of about half an hour brought us level with a plateau which we could skirt to reach the base of Danu Dhura. To reach Danu Dhura would take many more hours, judging from the terrain we decided to pitch C1 (5200 m) on the edge of the plateau at the east end of Nandakhani.

Camp two and Danu Dhura

From C1 we had to skirt the plateau and climb up to the depression between Nandakhani and Laspa Dhura. The terrain was broken with crevasses. We made our way close to the slopes of Nandakhani and started climbing the snow slopes diagonally towards Danu Dhura. Rope had to be fixed at one point to cross the slope along a crevasse line. We fixed markers throughout. The last traverse was below the corniced ridge of Nandakhani. We reached the depression on the ridge with mixed feelings. We were happy to be there, but across, things didn't look too good. We would have to traverse down a steep gully to reach the plateau on the other side. The route towards Pindari was badly broken and we would have to climb down an icefall. There was no suitable spot for a camp at the pass and the route to the camp between Nandakhani and Nandabhanhar was not clear. Since the weather was packing up we found a suitable spot to dump our loads and made our way down.

Next day we reached the pass in clear weather. We had a good look at the terrain now. To attempt Nandakhani from the south ridge which connects Laspa Dhura would be difficult since it was badly broken and huge gendarmes blocked the way. We would have to find some other way towards our summit camp.

We decided to shift camp now. From the pass we traversed down a steep gully and reached a plateau. A little ahead we set up camp. It was evening by the time we pitched out tents and brought down the loads from the dump. Sunset was a riot of colours. The tiredness of the day was forgotten.

Camp three

A snow ramp climbed towards an icefall coming down from Nandabhanar. We hoped that we would be able to skirt the icefall and find a way to put up C3, which we had planned to locate between Nandakhani and Nandabhanar. Our attempt to find a way proved futile since huge seracs blocked the way. We looked for an alternative route. There is a rock ridge coming down to the southwest. From a distance this looked reasonable. Only, we were not sure how it ended. It was our best bet so we went to the base of it and dumped our loads. We would come up next day and go up the ridge. We would take up seven day's rations to the last camp, to attempt all three peaks.

Next day we started off early. From the base of the ridge we had to fix a rope since the rock was very steep. At the end of the first rope length we roped up to climb the rest of the ridge. I suggested that we fix two more rope lengths, though we may take some more time, but movement would be much safer. After that the angle of the slope eased and we roped up and belayed each other to the top of the ridge. The last pitch was steep but with

Nandakhani from Camp 3.   (Divyesh Muni)

23. Danu Dhura *(left corner)* viewed from Shalang Dhura peak. Nandakhani *(centre)* and Nandabhanar.

Article 11

(Vineeta Muni)

24. Lamchir (right) and the slopes leading to Kafni glacier.

Article 11

(Divyesh Muni)

25. Panch Chuli II (extreme right), Rajrambha and Chaudhara viewed from Danu Dhura.

Article 11   (Divyesh Muni)

26. View from summit camp of Shalang Dhura: right to left: Suli Top, Burphu Dhura, Chiring We, Bamba Dhura and Kalabaland Dhura.

Article 11   (Vineeta Muni)

firm snow. The most wonderful sight greeted us as we crossed the last slope to the plateau. Straight ahead stood Nanda Kot. The south face dominating the view. On the left was Nandabhanar and to the right was Nandakhani. We dumped our loads near the base of Nandakhani. We were sure the next few days would be very rewarding. However the Gods had something else in store for us — a storm. We all had to withdraw to base camp.

Our fortunes had taken an unfortunate turn. We would have to wait for the snow to settle before moving up. This would mean another two days at base camp. It was 13th October. We were nearly into the beginning of winter and it was time to start winding up. We came to a consensus that if the weather remained settled, Yograj, Koylu and I would go up to retrieve the equipment and if possible attempt the peaks. It would have to be a quick attempt.

We waited for two days. On 15 October, Yograj, Koylu and I left for C2. The slopes below the Danu Dhura had avalanched. We had come down in time. On the 16th we left early for C3, reaching by 12.30 p.m.

Nandakhani (6029 m)

We pitched camp and had a hot drink. Considering the unstable weather and shortage of time, we decided to attempt Nandakhani that evening. We left by 1.45 p.m. The route went through deep powder snow. The snow slope meets a rock patch below the summit ridge. The snow was so unstable that I felt as if I was swimming

Nandabhanar from Camp 3.

(Divyesh Muni)

in the snow. The rock was steep but with good holds. A short overhang was negotiated before reaching the rocky summit ridge. By 3.20 p.m. we were at the top. Due to clouds the view was obscured. We were back at the camp by 4.30 p.m.

Nandabhanar (6236 m)

That night we spent cramped in a single tent. The cold was intense. We had planned to leave very early so we were up by 4 a.m. but it was so cold that we decided to leave after sunrise. At 7.30 a.m. we came out of the tent shivering. We started walking across the plateau quickly in order to generate some warmth. We went to the southeast face of Nandabhanar. The snow was deep so we felt no need to put on our crampons. Higher up the slope, the snow was harder. We came to a point where we had to put on our crampons. We made our way diagonally from here till we reached the southwest ridge of the peak. We front pointed our way to the summit by 10.45 a.m. From the top we were rewarded with views of Nanda Devi peaks. The lower altitudes were covered in clouds but we could see the peaks of the Pindari and Sunderdhunga valleys. To the north of us was Nanda Kot. Unfortunately we could not attempt the peak now. We discussed possible routes to attempt Nanda Kot from the south. It would be possible to put up a camp or bivi at 6400 m below the south ridge of the peak. From here it would be a 400 m climb to the peak. To our south we had a look at the south ridge of Nandabhanar. To get across to Pindari valley one would have to cross this lower down at about 5600 m from where Geoff Hornby and his team had come up in 1987.

We came down the east ridge and were back at our camp by 12.30 p.m. It had started snowing by the time we were in camp. Fearing another spell of bad weather we decided to move down immediately. It took us four hours to make our way down the ridge and remove the ropes fixed earlier.

It was the fourth day since we had left base camp. Moving two camps at a time we had managed to scale Nandakhani and Nandabhanar and retrieve all the equipment from the mountain. This was the second ascent of the peaks. We were satisfied with the climb. It was unfortunate we could not attempt Nanda Kot. It would have been a good climb. Maybe some time in future. Maybe we could try to come up from Kafni glacier or Pindari glacier. Maybe!

───────────────── SUMMARY ─────────────────

An Indian team from Bombay reached the elusive Danu Dhura (5560 m) from the east. Shalang Dhura, Nandakhani and Nandabhanar peaks were climbed in October 1993.

12

MANA NORTWEST EXPEDITION, 1992

ARUN SAMANT

WE HAD VISITED Amrit Ganga valley in 1988 and were fascinated by the grandeur of the various mighty peaks like Kamet, Abi Gamin and Mana, all seven thousanders. While studying the map, we realised that there was one more seven-thousander, Mana Northwest (7092 m). We made plans to attempt this peak during May-June 1992.

Mana Northwest (7092 m) lies on a ridge connecting Mana and Kamet. We approached it from Purvi Kamet glacier, which lies east of Kamet in the district of Chamoli in Uttar Pradesh.

Mana Northwest has no record of being attempted by any party, though adjoining peaks Kamet (7756 m), Abi Gamin (7355 m) and Mana (7272 m) have received many ascents from various directions. The notable attempt on Mana by a team from Bombay led by Prajapati Bodhane in 1985 and the successful climb of Mana by I.T.B.P. team led by Harbhajan Singh (from the east) were important for us as we had to share a part of their routes.

We left Bombay on 16 May, obtained inner-line permits in Joshimath and reached Malari, the roadhead by a local bus on 21 May.

We engaged five local porters and goats to carry our loads to the base camp near Vasudhara tal. Though we had packed our food in Bombay in small cotton bags suitable for goats to carry, a lot of readjustment of loads had to be done on the spot. The trek to the base camp from Malari commenced on 23 May. All of us reached the base camp (4795 m) on 27 May with night halts at Gamsali, Niti and Shepu Kharak. Three loads were left behind at Malari and hence we lost one day in fetching up these loads by sending down three porters from Gamsali. At Shepu Kharak, Ganesh ganga was crossed by all of us including goats over a wooden log placed across the river by P.W.D. workers, of course, with a charge of 'bridge toll tax'. We crossed Raikana nala above Nand Kharak

Photos 27-28-29

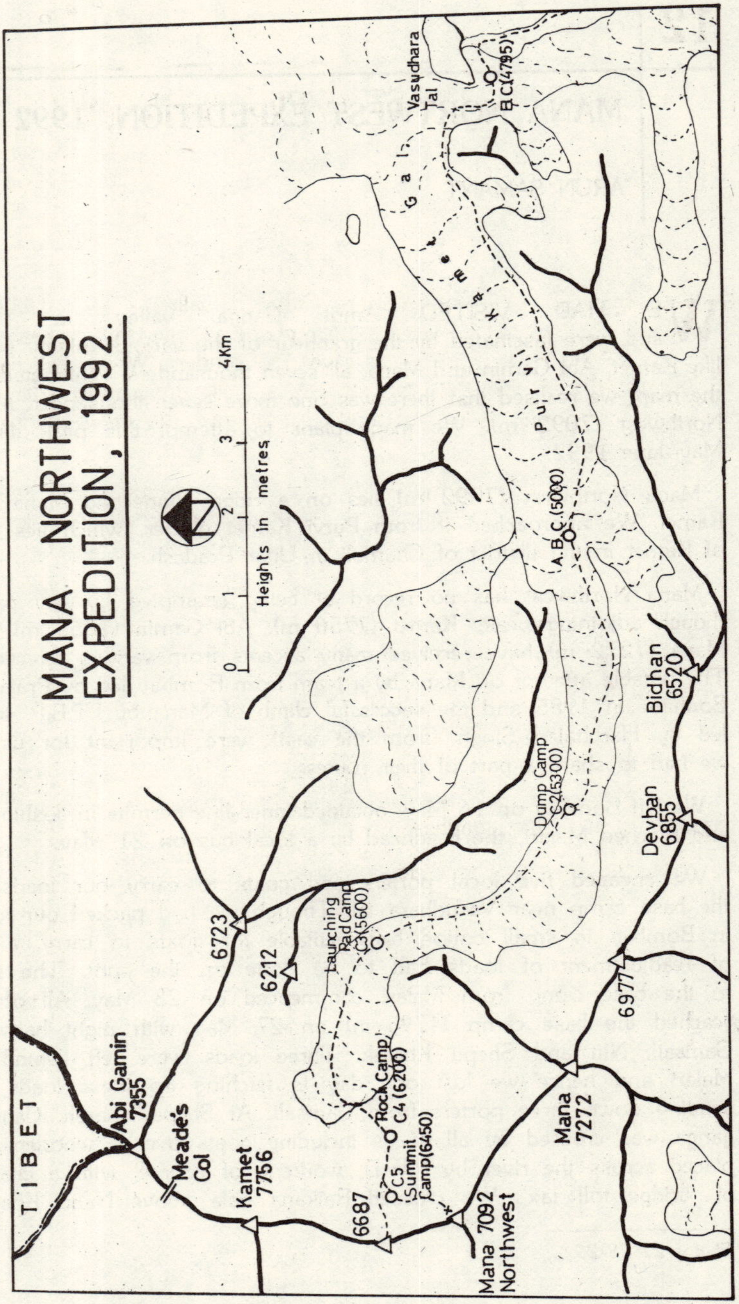

MANA NORTHWEST EXPEDITION, 1992.

Heights in metres

0 1 2 3 4Km

TIBET

Abi Gamin 7355

Meade's Col

Kamet 7756

6687

6723

6212

C5 'Summit Camp'(6450)

Rock Camp C4 (6200)

Mana 7092 Northwest

Launching Pad Camp C3(5600)

Dump Camp C2(5300)

Mana 7272

A.B.C. (5000)

6977

Devban 6855

Bidhan 6520

Vasudhara Tal

B.C.(4795)

G a n g o t r i

over a snow-bridge without any difficulties. Vasudhara tal has been breached recently and Raikana nala is uncrossable at this place making the old base camp site now unapproachable. For the last few years expeditions have been establishing their base camps at a new site on the west of Raikana nala, where we were also headed.

Prajapati Bodhane, the deputy leader, fell ill at the base camp and had to go down to Niti. Unfortunately, even after staying for three days at Niti, he could not recover and had to return to Bombay, leaving us depleted.

On Purvi Kamet glacier

Purvi Kamet glacier is a 19 km long tortuous glacier similar to the letter 'S' and hence heavily crevasse-ridden. It has a lateral moraine ridge along its left bank, which has been the obvious traditional route for all these years. However, due to the new position of our base camp we had to go along the right bank of the glacier initially, then cross it and join the old route near the position of C2. The new part of the route was quite easy when we went up as it was a gradually rising snow-plod. Later, while returning to the base camp it had become totally unfamiliar and difficult due to melting of snow and one had to jump from boulder to boulder most of the way.

Three camps were placed on this glacier at 5000 m, 5300 m and 5600 m. The last camp was fully stocked and occupied by

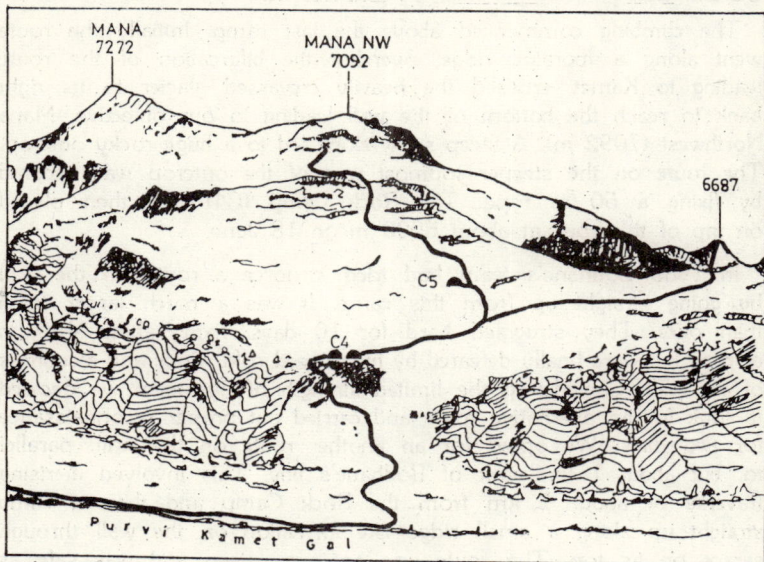

MANA NW WALL from northeast.

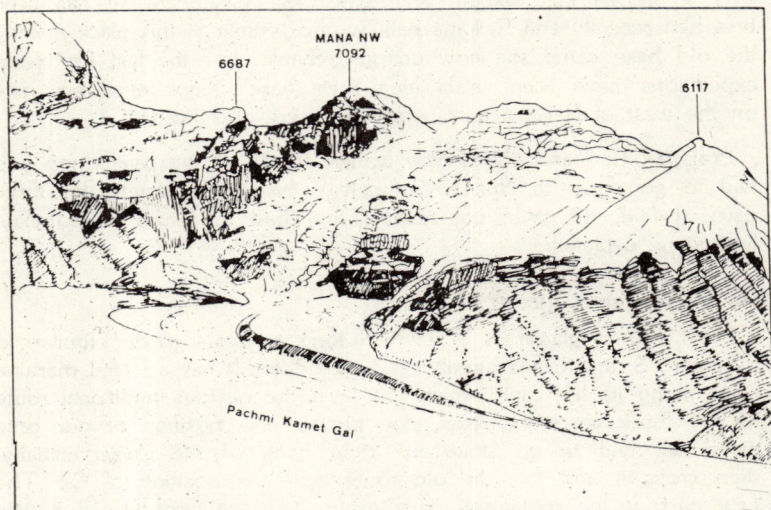

MANA NORTH WEST from west

three remaining members of the group and two permanent porters on 15 June. Except for some help from one local porter initially, for a week we ferried all loads and established camps.

On the wall

The climbing commenced above the last camp. Initially the route went along a moraine ridge, overshot the bifurcation of the route leading to Kamet, crossed the heavily crevassed glacier to its right bank to reach the bottom of the wall leading to our objective, Mana Northwest (7092 m). A steep snow-slope led to a huge rocky outcrop. The route on the steeper topmost part of the outcrop was secured by fixing a 50 m rope. The Rock Camp (C4) was then placed on top of this rock at about 6200 m on 18 June.

In 1985 Bodhane's team had tried to force a route on the wall by going straight up from this camp. It was a much larger team than ours. They struggled hard for 10 days, fixing about 450 m of rope but were finally defeated by high speed cold winds and steepness of the wall. Considering the limited strength of our team we decided to look for an alternative route and carried out proper reconnaissance for two days. We opted for an another route on the wall, parallel to, but about 1 km west of Bodhane's line. This involved a rising traverse of about 1 km from the Rock Camp and then a climb straight up along a small ridge like formation on the wall through seracs on its top. The route was not very steep and was safe as

Unclimbed south face of Kamet (7756 m).   (Arun Samant)

falling debris would have fallen on both sides of the ridge. Beyond
the seracs was the corniced, summit pyramid of Mana Northwest.

On 21 June, Suhas and Jagat Singh, H.A.P., launched the summit
attempt directly from the Rock Camp. They climbed upto the seracs

and slightly beyond them for about eight hours. However, they had to return from 6900 m as Suhas started feeling giddy due to dehydration, fatigue and lack of acclimatisation. On the same day Summit Camp (C5) (6450 m) was established and occupied by Arun and Anil. On 22 June both of them started at 2 a.m. but could not make much progress due to intense cold and biting strong winds. At 4 a.m. they made a hasty retreat as Anil's toes started going numb. The next day they started from the Summit Camp at 6 a.m. The snow was in good condition due to the cold night and they climbed very quickly. However, at about 9 a.m. a snow storm started. They struggled for two more hours and reached about 6800 m, at which point they had to give up, as Arun was exhausted. In the late afternoon they withdrew to the Rock Camp.

On 25 June Arun, Suhas and Jagat Singh started from the Rock Camp at 7.30 a.m. to attempt an unnamed peak (6687 m) at the foot of Kamet on its south side. Arun was slow, lagged behind and returned to the Rock Camp. Suhas and Jagat Singh reached the bottom of the summit pyramid by 2 p.m. after crossing a snowfield beyond the rising traverse. They climbed up along the rocky portion of the pyramid over loose scree to reach the summit at 4 p.m. They raced down to the Rock Camp in two hours, happy and jubilant with the success. Though it was a consolation prize, it was the first ascent of a high peak made after a hard struggle during four weeks spent above the base camp by a small five-man team and elation of all the members was amply justified.

The Rock Camp was wound up on 26 June and the team quickly descended. All loads were withdrawn to the Base Camp by 30 June and the team reached Malari on 2 July and Bombay on 7 July.

On 23 June the team members were surprised at the Rock Camp by a visit of their so called mail runner, Jay Singh. He had collected one letter from Niti post office and travelled all the way alone and later with our porters to the Rock Camp (6200 m) to deliver it — unparalleled postal service.

SUMMARY

An attempt on Mana Northwest (7092 m) by a small team from Bombay in June 1992.

Members: Arun Samant (leader), P. B. Bodhane (deputy leader), Anil Chavan, Suhas Kharde

Sponsored by: Holiday Hikers' Club, Bombay.

27-28. Mana (7272 m), (above) and peak 6977 m (below): close ups from Purvi Kamet glacier.

Article 12

(Arun Samant)

29. Deoban (6855 m), close up from Purvi Kamet glacier.

Article 12   (Arun Samant)

30. Ice Sail (c. 6250 m). Route of first ascent was up extreme left of the icefal
and up the north ridge in profile.

Article 13   (Aloke Surin)

13

A DAWDLE IN THE DIBI

ALOKE SURIN

Prologue, or The Death of an Expedition

IT ALL STARTED very respectably: five climbers to attempt a second ascent of Kulu Makalu (6350 m) in the Dibibokri basin of the Parvati valley. Our confidence, however, was shaken when three of them pulled out for various reasons. Which left only Harsha and me to climb while Franklyn said he would be happy to mind the base camp, thank you very much. So we scaled down our ambitions to a suitably vague concept of 'looking around,' without fixing any objective.

Franklyn and I were outmanoeuvred in the opening set which saw us travel overland with all the expedition gear to Manali, which we reached on 30 August. Harsha, with Anita in tow, would fly in directly to Bhuntar and the two would rendezvous with us in Kullu. To recover from the *joys* of bus travel, we went up to (or at least that was the intention!) Bhrigu lake the next day from Vashisht. Our sea-level systems collapsed a little below the nearly 4300 m where the tarn was located, so we camped on lush green meadows. After a night of rain, which threatened to create a lake all around us, it cleared in the morning and we tasted sweet trekker's revenge when the peaks above Beas Kund and near Rohtang pass appeared freshly laundered. Later, shepherd Tarachand Thakur led us in ninety minutes to Bhrigu Lake, which was so exquisite that we did not grudge our friends their air tickets.

To the Dibi

After another foray up the Alaini nala and two commuter shuttles to Kullu for our permits, the four of us set off at last on 9 September from Manikaran for the Dibi nala. Night halts at Rudra Nag, Tunda Bhuj and a shepherd's stone shelter in the Dibi, saw us reach the

Photos 30 to 34

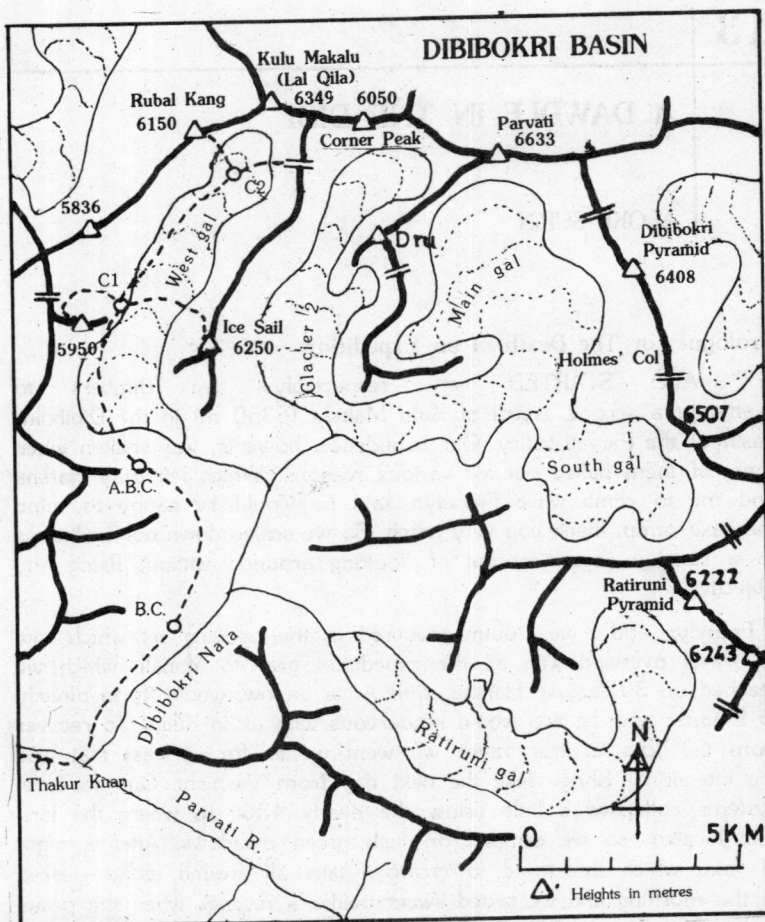

DIBIBOKRI BASIN

Heights in metres

base camp 4020 m on the 12th, just in time to bid farewell to a large contingent from Bengal which had been in the area. Which left us the sole inhabitants in an area of 200 sq kms drained by four glaciers. All the porters left us here, except for Ramlal, who helped us with two loads to an advance base camp (4630 m) at the snout of the west glacier. When, four days later, he and Anita left, Franklyn, Harsha and I moved up to this camp, arriving in a snow-shower.

After two days of ferrying loads up this glacier, Harsha and I decided to climb the icefall at our doorstep (it took ten minutes from the tent to reach its bottom!) as a diversion.

Diverting and devious it certainly proved to be, providing us with about seven hours of very enjoyable ice-climbing, well within our humble powers, and some grand views of the peaks above the main Dibi glacier.

Glacier Lassitude

Having run out of excuses to remain at ABC, the two of us camped up on the glacier, below the fourth tributary icefall on the right bank. On 24 September we climbed a minor peak above the icefall. It was a very easy and simple climb and roping up was necessary only when we came to cross the bergschrund giving access to the ridge. The summit was a rocky jumble of boulders with fabulous views all around. On the way down we visited the col leading into the Tichu glacier which Snelson had crossed in 1952, and were rewarded with good views of the peaks in the Tichu nala.

However, the highlight of the day were some tracks in the snowfield below the peak which we hoped in our excitement to have been made by a snow leopard, but had to reconcile ourselves to the view that they probably belonged to some other animal.

Ice Sail

In all our to-ing and fro-ing up and down the glacier, an elegant pyramid, shown as Ice Sail in Tremonti's excellent sketch, had always drawn our eyes upwards to its summit and we had harboured a secret hope to climb it. The obvious line up its north ridge, accessed via an icefall on the opposite (left) side of the glacier from where we were camped, seemed to be within our capability.

On the 27th having set the alarm for 0230 hrs, we were out of the tent at four o'clock and crunching across on the hard glacier ice to the foot of the icefall, a large moon illuminating the way. The lower part was fairly simple and the rope came out only an hour below the ridge when crevasses loomed beneath the undulating snowfields. The rocky triangle of the west face was in shadow even as we crested on to the sunlight at the foot of the north ridge at about 8 o'clock. A tea break was called here and then we started up the ridge. At first the snow was quite firm, but became deeper and softer the higher we climbed. A deep bergschrund, cleverly camouflaged, split the face below the summit block and after a couple of futile attempts, I managed to cross over from the extreme left, which brought us directly over the no. 2 glacier. An hour and a half of some very enjoyable climbing with the splendid backdrop of Parvati and the Dibibokri Pyramid behind us and the glistening tangle

Dru, on No. 2 Glacier from the col at 5550 m.   (Aloke Surin)

of the Parahio system ahead, brought us to the rocky summit at 3 p.m. just as a fine mist began to creep up the mountain. Our timing, and, more important, our luck, had been perfect — and there was a bonus: a first ascent on my birthday! What better icing on a cake could one hope for?

Not carrying any sort of flag or banner, we showed our gratitude by donating a red rope sling to the summit rocks, clicked a few pictures, washed down a few almonds with some powder-juice and carefully made our way down. At 7 p.m. we located our tent by the light of our headlamps.

Shakkar Kang (6050 m) from the slopes of Rubal Kang. (Aloke Surin)

Rubal Kang and the Col

Twenty four hours later I was drying my boot inners over the stove at our camp two, around 5370 m, at the head of the west glacier. We had arrived there the previous evening, and in my enthusiasm to get water from a deep ice-runnel near camp, had slipped and

Peak 5836 m on the Tichu-West glacier (Dibibokri) divide, seen from camp 2. (H. Subba Rao)

Parvati (6633 m) from col. White top is the true summit.   (Aloke Surin)

fallen upto my waist. Anyway, this seemed as good a way as any to kill time as the next day was dull and wintry.

On 30 September we again woke up early but could move only at 0545 hrs because it was cold and windy; in fact so windy that our jaws thawed only when the sun came out from behind Parvati and we could speak the first words of the day. The lower slopes leading to Rubal Kang were icy but easy. Soon we began to enjoy the cold, sunny day, especially as we crossed the bergschrund at the foot of the middle of the south face and began to climb its steepening ice. A protrusion of rocks halfway up the face provided some aesthetically satisfying runner and belay ledges. After about 300 m, the face sloped onto the gentle west ridge. However, the wind which slammed into us as we crested onto it was far from gentle. For an hour or so we struggled up towards the summit before deciding that the whole thing about reaching the top (which now lay a few hundred metres away and maybe 90 to 150 metres higher) was quite futile under these conditions. Crouched in the wind, with the windblown snow stinging our faces, we shouted our decision to go down.

To complete our stay in the area, the next day we visited the 5550 m col leading into the No. 2 glacier and revelled in the fabulous views of Parvati, Corner Peak, Kulu Makalu, the Dru and another formidable rock monolith next to it. On 2 October, we staggered into advance base with heavy loads to be received by a visibly overjoyed Franklyn who had been alone for eleven days. He told us the dismal news of the civil war in Yugoslavia (we had left the radio behind with him) but this hardly dampened our spirits. That evening we celebrated our reunion and our modest success with a feast: corned beef fried up with a few remaining onions and a bewildering array of seasoning, including garlic paste, veg puree, tomato puree, a few dried herbs, pepper and chilli powder; a big helping of 'khichri', mugs of hot chocolate; and everything topped off with Harsha's private hoard of cognac!

BIBLIOGRAPHY

1. 'The Dibibokri Basin...and beyond'. By Kenneth Snelson, H.J. Vol. XVIII p. 110.
2. 'Italian expedition to the Punjab Himalayas, 1961'. By Paolo Consiglio, H.J. Vol. XXIV p. 86.
3. 'Expeditions to the Ratang and Parbati regions, 1955 and 1956'. By P. F. Holmes, H.J. Vol. XX p. 78.
4. 'The first ascent of Mt. Parvati'. By Tremonti M., H.J. Vol. XXX p. 201.
5. 'South Parbati 1970'. By Charles Ainger. H.J. Vol. XXX p. 228.
6. 'South Parbati 1973'. By R. Collister, H.J. Vol. XXXIII p. 151.
7. 'The first ascent of Dibibokri Pyramid, Kulu, 1978'. By Nick Hewitt Alpine Journal 1979, p. 115.
8. Mountains and a Monastery, P. F. Holmes, London 1958.

A Note on Pt. 5836 m

This peak on the Tichu/West Glacier divides often mistaken been climbed as Rubal Kang by many Indian teams in the past. HAPs, who have guided climbs on this false 'Rubal Kang' confirm this. However, in Snelson's article (H.J., Vol. XVIII, p. 110), it is clearly evident that Rubal Kang (Tibetan for Turtle), 6150 m, is the peak which is adjacent to the unmistakable tower of (Kulu Makaluo Lal Qila) 6350 m, shown in P. Conciglio's article (H.J. Vol. XXIV, photo opposite p. 88) and also in the photo accompaning this article.

SUMMARY

Small climbs in the west glacier of the Dibibokri basin, Parvati valley-Kullu Himalaya, in September 1991, including the first ascent of 'Ice Sail' (estimated at 6250 m) via north ridge. The Indian team was from Bombay.

Members: Harshavardhan Subba Rao, Franklyn Silveira and Aloke Surin.

14

INDIAN EVEREST EXPEDITION: NORTH FACE, 1991

Group Captain A. K. BHATTACHARYYA

AN INDIAN EXPEDITION TO EVEREST (8848 m) from the north face was launched by the West Bengal Mountaineering and Adventure Foundation alongwith the Bhoruka Mountaineering Trust. Initially, the expedition was planned for three months from June 1991 to August 1991. However the schedule was revised to 60 days only from base camp to the mountain and back to base camp. Pranesh Chakraborty of West Bengal was the leader of the expedition and Samir Roy was the manager of the team. The team left Calcutta on 1 August 1991 and after an abortive attempt returned on 8 October 1991.

In December 1990. I was asked by the organising committee to conduct a selection camp in Sikkim and recommend names of probable candidates to the committee for final selection of the team. However, one of the members succumbed to high altitude sickness (pulmonary oedema) at the base camp and the selection camp had to be called off. The organising committee announced the team on 26 July 1991 and I was to be the climbing leader. In all, there were 21 members including the manager and two doctors.

The team left Calcutta on 1 August 1991 and picked up equipment purchased earlier from Kathmandu. On 3 August, we crossed over to Tibet from Kodari village. The Chinese Mountaineering Association (C.M.A.) detailed a liaison officer and an interpreter to be with us till the expedition was over. The first halt was a forced one at Zangmu hotel due to landslides enroute. After employing nearly 200 porters the loads were transhipped to the waiting trucks across the landslide area. The next halt was at Xegar (4375 m) on 4 August where the team spent two nights acclimatising. The CMA does not allow enroute camping and all expedition parties have to stay in the so called five star hotels in Tibet which can be compared to a most ordinary hotel in India. Since the tariff rate was $68 US dollars per head per day, it was rather difficult for the team to stay en route any longer and we moved to the base camp (5780 m) on

31. Parvati (6633 m) left, and Dibibokri Pyramid (6408 m) from the summit of Ice Sail.

(H. Subba Rao)

Article 13

32. Upper West glacier from an unnammed peak. Kulu Makalu (6349 m) in centre with Rubal Kang (6150 m) abutting against it on left. Corner peak (6050 m) is the sharp rocky aiguille at extreme right.
Article 13
(H. Subba Rao)

33. Rubal Kang (6150 m), left, and Kulu Makalu (6349 m) at the head of West glacier of Dibibokri basin.
Article 13
(H. Subba Rao)

6 August using two trucks and a land cruiser. Three members stayed back at Xegar for one extra day for better acclimatisation.

At the base camp, we took about two hours to establish camp and get organised for the first night. The weather was windy with partial cloud. The following day while some members stayed back organising and sorting out loads, some of us went up to reconnoitre our route and advanced base camp (ABC). The Belgian team had earlier gone ahead and they were planning to climb Everest along the Hornbein Couloir. Thus our camp sites were destined to be almost at the same locations.

On 8 August, we climbed a small rocky knob at 5940 m on the west bank of Rongbuk glacier. In the afternoon, Subhas was unwell and his condition deteriorated at night. The two doctors diagnosed a pulmonary oedema and Subhash had to be evacuated the very next morning to safer height at Zangmu. Earlier, it was planned to hire high altitude porters from Rongbuk village. But on arrival at Rongbuk we discovered that we could not hire porters directly and we had to go through the CMA and pay $ 26 US dollars per head per day to the CMA. This factor was never brought out by the CMA and thus there was no mention of high altitude porters in the contract. We could manage only four porters for about 5 days and that too these porters were not willing to go beyond the moraine level into snow and ice covered areas.

Now that we were stuck with such a problem, I had to reschedule my overall plan. The yaks arrived at base camp a day late and our first load ferry to ABC started on 11 August alongwith the yaks and by the 12th we established our ABC at 5600 m on the eastern lateral moraine of Rongbuk glacier. The yaks ferried loads to a dumping point 2 km away from the ABC on the glacier and we pitched tents to keep the stores inside.

On 15 August after ferrying most of the loads to ABC, we moved to occupy ABC while Pranesh Chakraborty and doctor Indranil Sen remained at base camp. From ABC, we started ferrying loads to C1 which was planned at 6100 m between Changtse and Lhola peak. The 4 HAPs ferried LPG and Oxygen cylinders to C1 and left after 5 days. Thereafter, we all had to switch over to the roles of porters cum climbers.

The weather was mixed with bad spells of 2-3 days coming in between. From 16 to 24 August we ferried most of our loads to C1. We had to follow a zigzag route along the glacier avoiding crevasses to reach the snowfield 1.5 km short of the camp site. The route along the lateral moraine was unsafe due to continuous rock fall.

We had to rope up at the snowfield due to covered crevasses. The Australian team in 1984 had camped short of the snowfield and used skis to reach the base of north face.

The first group to occupy C1 on 26 August were Sonam Sangbu, Gautam, Bibhujit and Shyamal. They were to open the route on the north face for two days and to be replaced subsequently by the other members. On 27 August, the team could open the route beyond the bergschrund and fix a length of rope on the north face. The second group comprising of Pasang, Ranveer, Sushanta and Raj Shekhar moved to C1 for support and replacement. But, from the early hours of 28 August, it started snowing and continued throughout the day and I recalled the team to ABC since the north face would be avalanche-prone for the next couple of days. It continued snowing till 30 August. The cloud started breaking up only by late afternoon.

On 31 August the weather turned foul again and it snowed throughout the day and I had to postpone our move again by a day. Finally on 1 September, I moved to C1 with Sangbu, Pasang, Rattan, Ranveer, Utpal and Shyamal with other members ferrying loads to C1 and back to ABC.

On 2 September, I went to the base of the north face alongwith Sangbu and Rattan for a recce of the slope and noticed that the ropes fixed earlier from the lower lip of the bergshrund to the north face were not traceable and buried under snow. These ropes could not be retrieved for use and we had to start all over again. Meanwhile the technical equipment was dumped at the Cwm. This equipment was kept in a nylon bivvy sack sheet and anchored there.

On 4 September, Rattan, Sangbu, Pasang and Ranveer were on the slope opening route. Rattan was in the lead from the bergschrund and in four hours he fixed nine lengths of ropes. The slope was of 45°-50° gradient with a layer of rotten snow on ice. By 1600 hrs the weather started packing up and the team withdrew from the slope and returned to C1 at 2000 hrs. While ferrying loads to the lead party, I sustained an injury on my spinal cord and could not lift loads thereafter. On the way back it started snowing heavily and by 2230 hrs. there was more than 18" of snow. The wind was strong and huge avalanches started rolling down the Changtse face and the north face. Our campsite was shaken up by the air blast of these avalanches. On the 5th and 6th no work was possible due to avalanches and deep snow condition and we sorted out tentage and other stores for higher camps.

The Belgians lost some stores in the avalanches and after making 3 attempts on the Hornbein Couloir and spending one night on the slope at 7000 m without shelter, called off their expedition on 7 September. Fortunately our stores were intact, though scattered by the avalanches and we could retrieve most of them.

On 8 September, at about 0430 hrs there was a huge avalanche which rolled down the great couloir. The noise was deafening and the entire Cwm was vibrating for about 10 minutes. A strong air blast brought in a snow cloud and covered the campsite. It was dark and the visibility was poor. For some time there was no sense of orientation. As the day broke and the weather cleared, I noticed that a huge portion of ice-shelf was dislodged from the hanging ice above the great couloir and had avalanched down. I was worried about our stores dumped at the Cwm.

After breakfast, Rattan, Utpal and myself, went up to survey the area and the condition of stores while others got busy in clearing the camp site. At the Cwm, there lay the massive debris of avalanched ice mass and our orange bivvy sack with the equipment in it was missing! We started scanning the area and noticed the tip of the bivvy sack about 35 ft. down the line of avalanche. We dug 3½ ft. into the ice mass and after nearly 2½ hrs. managed to retrieve the stores.

Fortunately for us, we found all the stores except one pair of crampons belonging to Rattan and one pair of ski sticks. The bivvy sack was shred into pieces yet held on to the stores. We ferried the stores 50 m down the slope towards the Changtse face and returned to C1 at 1730 hrs. It started snowing at dusk and continued through the night till about 0030 hrs in the morning.

Sangbu, Rattan, Pasang and Ranveer left C1 at 0230 and after picking up equipment from the Cwm started climbing by 0500 hrs. Ranveer took the lead today and using head lamps, the climbers inched their way up the north face clearing the fixed ropes which were again buried under one foot of snow. Sangbu took over from Ranveer at the last anchor point. Sangbu opened the route upto the western edge of the Great Couloir skirting the rocky knob from the west. The gradient became shallower thereafter for the next 300 m or so and the snow was soft and knee deep. The first ray of sunlight hits the north face only at about 0930 hrs. It was cold and windy, but the weather was clear and the first ray of sunlight hit Lhola at 0910 hrs. From this point Ranveer was in the lead again with Rattan in the belay. While the 1984 Australian team followed the route close to the Couloir, Ranveer moved away from the Couloir and took a mid course. After about 1½ hrs., Pasang took over from Ranveer and fixed one length of rope. Ranveer took over lead for the third time and fixed a couple of ropes upto the base of the rock gully at 6900 m. Atanu and Bibhu went up the slope carrying stores and dumped stores at the base of the gully. By 1600 hrs clouds appeared from Lhola and covered the north face and it started snowing dropping the visibility. The team had to withdraw and return to C1 at 1930 hrs. It was a long day of nearly 17 hours on the mountain but good progress was made.

Bad weather continued through the night accompanied by strong winds which persisted throughout the next day.

At 1500 hrs, a huge avalanche rolled down the Hornbien Couloir and went past 500 m short of the camp site. We were forced to stay back in the tents. There was no sign of any let up in the weather. It snowed through the night of 10 September till the early hours of the 11th. The snowfall stopped by 0900 hrs but the weather was dull. With 40 hours of nonstop snowfall, we couldn't move on the north face for at least the next two days. By afternoon it started avalanching from all sides.

On 14 September, all of us except Utpal and Sushanta moved to C1 again. Meanwhile I was given 5 more days to remain on the mountain. But we had already lost valuable days. The same evening I worked out the programme for the next day and decided that Chandra Prabha, Atanu, Bibhu and Raj Sekhar were to ferry loads moving behind the lead team.

On 15 September, the lead team of 4 members left as planned but after an hour I received a message over the radio that the bivvy sack had been swept away again and this time equipment was scattered and buried all over. The sack was probably blown away by the avalanche of 10th or 11th.

The next day, Rattan and Ranveer were in the lead and they were on the rock gully by 1300 hrs. After negotiating the rock gully, Rattan appeared on the steep snow slope at 1400 hrs followed by Ranveer, Sangbu and Pasang. This patch of 200 m of slope was of 70° gradient with knee deep soft snow. Rattan traversed to the west and hit the ridge and moved east-southeast followed by a right turn along the sharp arete. Beyond the arete the slope was not considered safe for camping as avalanches could come down along the path which the Australians had experienced. It was, therefore, decided to make a snow bivouac at the end of the arete. The height of the spot was 7200 m. It was indeed a tough climb and the lead group did a commendable job as this portion of the north face along the Great Couloir was the technically most difficult stretch. While Atanu and Gautam could reach upto the last point, Bibhu, Shyamal and Raj Shekhar left their loads half way up the slope. Meanwhile Utpal and Sushanta reached C1 from base camp and they brought some rice and fresh meat alongwith them.

On 17 September, Utpal, Sushanta and Soumitra left C1 for load ferry to C2 location and Shyamal and Raj Shekhar had to be sent back to ABC since they were not keeping well. By late afternoon the ferry party returned to C1 after dumping loads. On the 18th, Rattan, Sangbu and Ranveer and Pasang reached C2 site by 1230 hrs and tunnelled a snow cave in about 3 hours time while others including Chandra Prabha ferried loads upto the snow tunnel and returned to C1 by 1800 hrs. Utpal, Soumitra and Sushanta did not go up.

20 September was a clear day with a sharp drop in temperature and strong western upper winds at 6500 m and above. Chandra Prabha was the first one to leave for load ferry to C2 at 0230 hrs. Rattan, Ranveer, Atanu and Gautam left to occupy C2 and Sangbu, Pasang, Soumitra, and Ang Nima followed with loads for ferry. Soumitra returned with cold hands from the bergschrund. Sangbu and Pasang were the first to reach C2 snow tunnel at 1340 hrs. followed by Rattan, Ranveer, Chandra Prabha and Ang Nima at 1400 hrs. C2 was thus established at 7200 m in a snow bivouac on the exposed north face.

Ranveer took the lead in opening route beyond C2 a patch of which the Australians named as 'White Limbo'. The initial patch was good for crampon walk with easy gradient and the team made a satisfactory progress on 'White Limbo' and returned to the snow tunnel by 1945 hrs.

On 22 September the wind velocity attained the proportion of a severe storm exceeding 100 km/per hour, blowing in from the west on the north face. But the weather was clear and extremely cold. The 4 members on C2 carried tents and 10 lengths of rope with a view to establish C3 at 7800 m. Rattan was in the lead followed by Ranveer, Atanu, and Gautam. As they crossed the half way mark on the 'White Limbo', Rattan came across dry powdery snow which was loose and the snow started sliding down under slight pressure. Rattan tried a snow stake anchor but it wouldn't stay. He placed the stake horizontally, deep into the snow, but the stake would not hold. A desperate Rattan then dug a six feet deep hole and discovered that the entire mass of snow was loose, dry and powdery. He attempted to place an anchor 2 m deep and asked Ranveer to pull the rope to test. With a slight pull, the stake was dislodged! As Rattan tried in vain to fix rope on the snow patch, a huge powder snow-avalanche was released from the western side of 'White Limbo' barely 300 m away from the four members. The avalanche rolled down the north face and over Hornbien Couloir to the Cwm and shot up the Changtse face upto the North Col.

Without a fixed rope it was not feasible to move up the remaining portion of 'White Limbo' and there was no way to fix an anchor on the surface. To the east lay the Great Couloir with a huge hanging ice-shelf above and to the west was the exposed and highly avalanche-prone face of the 'White Limbo'. The wind velocity was strong as ever and it was difficult for a person to stand upright on the face. The team had to return to the snow-tunnel at C2. The tunnel entrance was filled with snow-drift.

The howling wind swept the north face throughout the night and the following morning. By day break avalanches were released frequently from the northeast ridge and the west ridge. It was not possible to move through the Cwm or up the north face. The four members at C2 spent the third difficult night inside the tunnel and confirmed in the morning that the condition of the slope remained unchanged and at such high wind velocity it was not possible to move up the avalanche-prone slope without fixed ropes. Further stay in the tunnel was also becoming difficult.

Thus with barely 8 days in hand and with very little support due to non availability of HAPs, it was realised that it was not possible to make any further progress in such wind condition on the face. I decided to call off the expedition and informed Pranesh Chakraborty at the base camp about my decision and asked the four members to return to C1.

The expedition thus abruptly ended by the afternoon of 23 September. The team returned to the base camp on 3 October after winding up C1 and the ABC and left for Kathmandu on 5 October. The Canadians also abandoned their expedition due to high wind which swept their stores away at 7700 m.

Members: Pranesh Chakraborty (leader), Gp. Capt. A. K. Bhattacharyya (climbing leader), Ms. Chandra Prabha Aitwal, Ms. Rita Chakraborty, Sonam Sangbu, Rattan Singh Chauhan, Pasang Namgyal, Ranveer Singh Negi, Gautam Datta, Atanu Chatterjee, Sushanta Majumdar, Bibhujit Behary Mukhoty, Shyamal Sarkar, Subhas Das, Rajshekhar Ghose, Soumitra Ganguly, Utpal Sarkar (photographer), Capt Dr. Niloy Sinha Roy and Dr. Indranil Sen.

SUMMARY

The attempt on Everest (8848 m) from the north by an Indian expedition from Calcutta, in August-September 1991.

15

MONGOLIA — THE GREAT ESCAPE

LINDSAY GRIFFIN

IT WAS IN 1990 that an exuberant John Blashford-Snell first brought up the prospect of a Raleigh International expedition to northwest Mongolia. John, who has all the attributes of the traditional intrepid explorer, not least the characteristic pith helmet which he still insists on wearing to all corners of the globe, seemed to be offering Julian Freeman-Attwood and myself the opportunity to climb in one of the most remote mountain regions of Central Asia. Of course there was a catch! We would spend the greater part of our time acting as guides and instructors to a small group of aspirant mountaineers. 'Well motivated though' John told us, then almost as an afterthought added that most of the 'students' would be unattached girls in their early twenties! We thought for maybe half-a-second before giving our answer.

The mystical mountains of the Altai span almost fifteen hundred kilometres, yet for most of their length there is little about which to get excited. However, where they pass through the triple border point of Russia, China and Mongolia, only a short distance from the frontiers of Kazakhstan, a compact isolated range rises to over 4000 m. This massif — the Tabun Bogdo — lies in the dead heart of Asia and was rumoured to hold the most spectacular mountains in the country. Not surprisingly, no information was forthcoming from the Mongolian authorities, and I spent the next two years trying to follow-up vague leads in various Eastern Block and Soviet states, always drawing a blank until, two days before our departure, a package arrived from Barcelona containing a sketch map and an incomprehensible report of the 1967 Polish expedition. I packed it in my baggage in the vain hope that we might bump into an itinerant Pole somewhere in Mongolia. When we left the UK, fortunately well in advance of our charges, we still had little idea as to how we should even approach the massif!

There were to be three 'instructors'. Julian is a wily Shropshire aristocrat with a power to weight ratio the rival of any Olympic

Photos 35-36-37

gymnast. He had come into high standard mountaineering later than most, yet his background, which included almost being blown into several hundred pieces by land mines whilst making the first crossing of Mauritania's Empty Quarter, stood him in good stead. On the other hand our partner in crime, Ed Webster from Colorado, started climbing when barely out of nappies. This would be his first expedition to the mountains since shortening his digits when climbing to the South Summit of Everest, four years ago. Now for a few basic statistics: Mongolia has an area equivalent to Denmark, Holland, Belgium, Germany, France, Spain and Portugal all rolled into one — yet with a population of only two and a half million! As half of these are nomads, who live on nothing but mutton and milk, and sleep in large circular felt tents called Gers, the number of permanent settlements is, understandably, small. Although an independent country for many years, it had been heavily reliant on the Soviet Union for its basic needs. After 1990 these quickly disappeared: on our arrival in May 1992 the economy had reached rock-bottom, ration books were being issued in an increasingly foodless capital — Ulaan Baatar — and aviation fuel had become very scarce.

We were forced to wait nearly a week in Hovd, the hub of several Raleigh medical and community programmes, but it would be untrue to say that the time was wasted. Across the far side of the river from our camp lay a 60 m high cliff of decomposing granite which sent Ed, and to a lesser extent Julian, into a frenzy of enthusiasm. Although not so sharp on the open walls, where the use of small finger holds is mandatory, Webster is still a demon when it comes to his old specialty — the crack. On our first day he took this esoteric part of Central Asia into modern times by leading us up the awkward 'Amarsana' (E2 5c), named after a popular folk hero.

Our first stroke of luck came the next afternoon. Two of the staff had just returned from Ger city, as Hovd was becoming affectionately known. To our surprise they had bumped into another foreigner. 'Well, he spoke to us in English but I think he might have said he was Polish' said the Yorkshire lass. Our eyes widened in disbelief. 'Anyway we've invited him along for tea.' I raced to my tent and pulled out the Polish article — surely this was a good omen; with the article even vaguely translated, we might have our first insight into this enigmatic range.

When Ryszard Palczewski stepped inside the Ger an hour later, and announced in perfect English that he ought to make a reasonable translation as it was he who had written the article nearly 25 years ago, we were—well—simply lost for words. More so when he informed

34. Peak 'White' (5950 m), left, and 'Black' from the slopes of Rubal
Kang, West glacier of Dibibokri basin.

Article 13   (Aloke Surin)

35. Upper Merandror glacier, looking SE.

Article 15   (Lindsay Griffin)

Article 15   36.   The Tabun Bogdo. The centre peak is Snow Church.   (Lindsay Griffin)

us that, subsequent to the 1967 expedition, he had met his future English wife while working in Afghanistan and now lived in Brighton — making regular trips three times a year to attend to his farming project in Eastern Mongolia! It's a perverse world that allows you to spend years making unsuccessful enquiries all over Europe, only to find that the best information lay right at your doorstep!

A few more granite gems succumbed to Ed's stumpy hands before we left in a high-wheeled military truck, armed with our newly acquired wealth of knowledge, and carrying our imported food, gaz and equipment for the next one and a half months. There are no roads in western Mongolia, only directions, and after three days of travel across a rocky arid wilderness we reached a small Kazakh encampment. A further 20 km on foot, with camels carrying the luggage, took us to a base camp site.

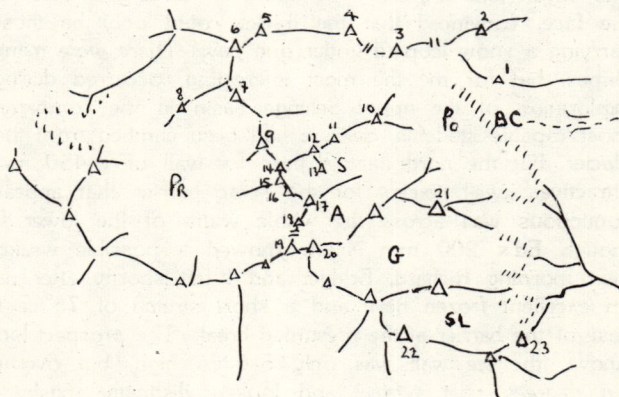

TABUN BOGDO

PEAKS

3 HERDSMAN
4 SHEPHERDESS
5 RUSSIAN MINER
6 TRIPLE BOLDER
7 HUITEN
9 4200m
10 HADAT
17 SELENGE
19 SNOW CHURCH

GLACIERS

Po : POTANINA
S : SELENGE
A : ALEXANDROV
G : GRANO
SL : SNOW LEOPARD
Pr : PRJEVALSKI

During the next five weeks we explored most corners of the range, feeling privileged to be the first western climbers outside the Eastern Block allowed a mountaineering permit. True the scale was no more than the Bernese Oberland, to which there was a close resemblance, but the ambience was distinctly Himalayan! The main peaks had been climbed by their easiest lines, but little, if any, technical climbing had yet been achieved. We were lucky to have students that were talented, and their enthusiasm meant that interesting new routes, rather than straightforward ascents, could be tackled.

Then there were the tracks — snow leopard, bear and... the other! We were crossing the head of the remote Alexandrov glacier, en route to climb a superb diamond shaped face of blue water-ice, on a peak that Ryszard had named Snow Church. A set of curious fresh prints crossed the glacier, heading towards China over a high col. They were large, showed a definite toe-shaped formation, and, inexplicably, were in sets of three. We had a choice; should we follow the tracks over the pass in an attempt to discover the origins of this mysterious triped; or should we climb the face? We climbed the face, convinced that the tracks could only be those of a Yeti carrying a snow leopard under one paw! There were many memorable climbs, but for me the most interesting, occurred during a five-day exploration of the upper Selenge basin in the company of our six most capable students. Selenge had been climbed from the Alexandrov glacier, but the north face a pure ice wall of c 450 m-looked most attractive......well, except for the serac barrier that appeared to be a continuous wall across the whole width of the lower face. A peer though Ed's 200 mm Nikon showed a possible weakness, so the next morning Richard, Bridget and I left shortly after dawn, moving up excellent frozen neve and a short stretch of 75°ice to reach the base of the barrier at the presumed break. The prospect looked gloomy. Above, the ice wall was only 5-6 m high, but overhung a good ten degrees past vertical and looked distinctly mushy towards the top. I moved first left then back right across the slope, peering upwards and then shaking my head in a manner bound to discourage even the most confident of clients. I then scanned the horizon for some ominous build-up of cloud, but none came to my rescue: in fact the weather — damn it was as perfect as one could wish! There was nothing for it but to try directly above the belay, where at least the wall was at its lowest. I climbed a metre or so and placed a screw. Not encouraged, I returned with a snow-stake and an additional hammer kindly donated by Bridget. At full stretch the stake was driven horizontally, then with wild flailing, that might have been misconstrued as front-pointing, I graunched my right foot on top of the protruding stake and hastily embedded a hammer over the lip. Maintaining the classic five points of contact at all times, I somehow arrived — too exhausted to be a jabbering wreck on the slope above, placed my four remaining screws and sagged onto the lot. Richard, who was considerably heavier, made a valiant effort before becoming airbone with the stake. With the main problem — extracting the runners — now solved, he felt it his duty to test the security of the belay screws and a fixed rope was arranged. Bridget was less fortunate. One of her many attributes is her weight — or lack of it; she looks somewhat less than four stones. 'How about giving me a little pull' came the almost casual remark from below. Richard and I took hold of the rope; a second later Bridget flew past the stance like a rag doll, a blur of gyrating arms and legs. Richard grabbed one of these and with great dexterity fielded her onto the belay. As I led up into more amenable terrain I caught snatches of conversation about the finer points of wicket keeping and whether Bridget's hair had come out of place.

Towards the top of the face another fine yet decidedly easier pitch led up past a smooth rocky rib. 30 m of hard water ice at 65° terminated at a precarious exit over a curl of snow. By continually slanting away from my companions I just avoided destroying both their helmets and a growing friendship. The summit attained, a fine traverse at AD standard concluded the day and we reached camp shortly before dark, tired but happy with our new route.

Towards the end of our stay, with the main group having returned to Hovd, there was just time to attempt Huiten (4356 m), Mongolia's highest peak, by the unclimbed south face. Although we had seen several more impressive virgin faces this was unquestionably the biggest, with over 1000 m of vertical height. Unfortunately it meant a tricky two-day crossing of the range via the heavily crevassed Alexandrov glacier, 'Yeti Col', and an appalling wade across the remote Prjevalski glacier — the latter named after the nineteenth century Russian explorer who also gave his name to the wild Siberian horse. We sat out the next day in bad weather but by 11 a.m. the sky was clear and the snow crisp. After a quick cup of tea we started our proposed line, a prominent ridge bordering the left side of the face, and climbed through the night of the 11-12 July 1992 in order to take advantage of the frozen conditions.

The weather was perfect — as good as any day in the high mountains and the summit views were intriguing. To the north lay the vast uninhabited nothingness of the Siberian Steppe. To the south and west a myriad of unclimbed and mostly unnamed peaks ran away into China. East the long gentle glaciers on the Mongolian side of the range flowed towards wide grassy glens and barren rounded tops that were strangely reminiscent of the Scottish Highlands. It was a mountaineers dream; but a dream that was, unfortunately, soon to be shattered.

At about 2 p.m. I had just started to descend a vast boulder slope near the base of the ridge. Prior to this we had kept more or less together, but I took a good rest whilst packing away the climbing rope, and the other two made their own ways down to the glacier. It was a slope typical of those found all over the lower reaches of Asian mountains; large angular blocks that, now and again, wobbled underfoot. Only this one triggered something above! Suddenly I was knocked rudely forward, landing on my side in a slight hollow with a large granite boulder across my left leg. At first I couldn't believe it! Not now; not here in one of the most inaccessible corners of the range!

I must have passed out for a while because when I came to, the lower part of the leg had lost all sensation. Miraculously the boulder had trapped it in a slot just wide enough to stop the full crushing power but, alas, not wide enough to avoid a serious double compound fracture. I knew immediately that I had to relieve the pressure and restore some circulation before it was too late. My basic first-aid kit contained Temgesic — perhaps the strongest oral painkiller. I put two under my tongue and set to work.

Pushing, heaving or even cursing the block proved useless. I tried to reduce the size of the leg by cutting away at the various layers of clothing with an annoyingly blunt penknife; but as fast as the material came away the uncooperative leg would swell to fill the gap. Using my axe and hammer I tried to chisel away at the granite constriction below. Whatever I did appeared to be futile.

I then remembered the climbing rope. Above my head and slightly set back from hollow lay another large boulder. After a couple of attempts I managed to lasso it and, by passing a loop of rope under the near end of the offending block, set up a pulley system with the few karabiners that I was carrying. Although unsuccessful at first, by increasing to a six to one mechanical advantage, I just succeeded in shifting it, not enough to withdraw the leg, but enough that a minute or so later a tingling sensation moved down towards my toes. I kept up the battle, pausing occasionally to let out a loud yell. At first it was 'Ed!!' 'Julian!!', as if there was a dozen or so people from which to chose. Then once or twice I tried 'Help!', but it sounded so ridiculous that I quickly reverted to a high-pitched wail which I guessed would be just as effective. At round 7 p.m.

I was greatly relieved to hear shouts from below; yet it took a further three hours for Julian and Ed to move the boulder sufficiently to free the leg and construct a temporary splint with ice-axes and the climbing rope. With Ed doing an outstanding job of supporting the leg and navigating a route in the dark, I bum-shuffled down for 14 hours, leaving a trail of red spots like painted waymarks on the boulders. In the meantime Julian had returned to the foot of the face and collected a tent, sleeping bag etc.

Finally we reached a flat spot on the moraine, where a clear cold stream, fresh from a melting snowpatch, had created a small, grassy oasis. After removing my splint, the components of which would be essential for the climb back over the range, the lads left hastily. By moving at night (their third consecutive night out) they hoped to reach base camp the following day and radio Hovd. In the Alps a rescue helicopter would be alerted and, often within hours, the patient would be receiving treatment in a well-equipped hospital. But this was Mongolia and by July there was, officially, no aviation fuel!

The days were hot; but with the tent entrance within arm's length of the stream, drinking water was plentiful. The first day was spent brushing up on my tourniquet technique. It had to be Ed's suggestion; Americans know all about snake bites! It was easy to convince myself that a friendly face was unlikely to reappear within three days: but what if something were to happen to the lads on the way out? Sloppy snow, rockfall in the couloir; I could imagine a number of depressing scenarios. What if I was still alone on the sixth? Should I try crawling down the glacier? It flowed in completely the wrong direction and as far as I knew led into a valley that was entirely uninhabited. Of course there might just be an adventurous shepherd.....
At the time I couldn't crawl out of the sleeping bag so the question seemed rather academic. I resolved not to dwell on the matter too much until nearer the time. Instead I either day-dreamed or dozed — rituals, so my friends say, that I usually perform well! Occasionally odd statistics, read somewhere in the dim and distant past, would enter my mind — like '70% of all victims with untreated compound fractures die after ten days'. Ignorance can be a splendid attribute sometimes!

Fortunately I was never put to the test. On the evening of the fourth day after the accident I heard the distinctive sound of rotor blades. Wild with excitement I twisted round to peer through the tent entrance and saw, coming over the range from the north, a large, old and unwieldy Russian helicopter.

As soon as the Raleigh base in Hovd received the radio message preparations were made for the evacuation. London was informed and SOS International alerted. The military felt they were unable to help; but the civilian airlines had a twenty year old cargo helicopter and a pilot who, despite having no experience of operating in mountainous terrain, was willing to fly if fuel could be found. After complex negotiation and diplomatic intervention sufficient fuel materialized to fly the 1200 km from the capital — Ulaan Baatar — to Hovd, where the state released the last remains of emergency fuel left in the west of the country, as a gesture of thanks for the work done by the various Raleigh projects. Unfortunately, it would not be enough to complete the round trip.

Having completely written off any possibility of air rescue, I was baffled, for one brief and bizarre moment, as to why the Russians should want to check-out this section of their border with China! Then I saw the letters MIAT that signify Mongolia's airline and the rest of my life suddenly began to look a whole lot more promising. If at that moment the chopper had turned around and crept back over the range I think I would have still felt elated because I now realized that other people knew!

Instead it circled crazily above the tent then, operating beyond its ceiling, made two attempts to land. On the second I got a distinct impression that things were going out of control but the pilot managed to pull out, and the chopper spun to the left, then disappeared south over the moraine. Feeling fairly confident that help was—well—at least close at hand, I settled down to wait.

More than an hour later Ed popped over the moraine carrying an old, green, military stretcher. He was closely followed by George Baber — an RAF pilot seconded to Raleigh and the third of my rescuers the Belgian doctor Jan Kennis. They were all visibly depressed! Three bewildered passengers, unable to communicate with their Mongolian-speaking pilot, dumped in the middle of one of the most remote glaciers in Asia with no equipment, and in the case of George, who had been flown direct from the desert climate of Hovd, virtually no clothes! Fuel was very low they told me, probably only enough for one attempt. Unable to see the direction in which the helicopter had flown, they had to assume that it must have escaped back over the range. Nevertheless the campsite was dismantled and I was strapped into the stretcher.

Time passed. Just to add to their anxiety the clear skies of the last four days rapidly clouded over and the tent was soon unpacked to give shelter from a violent thunderstorm. Ed, Jan and George huddled miserably around the stretcher, shivering, realizing that one or more nights out with no food were becoming increasingly likely. They cursed the folly of being off-loaded from the helicopter without any equipment. By contrast, I was over the moon! While base camp, having lost sight of the aircraft for nearly three hours, now feared the worst, and Hovd, in constant radio contact, slipped into despondency. I was ecstatic!

In fact Jamaldorj, the pilot, had made a bold and daring decision. Flying down valley towards Chinese Zungaria he lost just enough altitude to make a comfortable landing. Cutting out the engines to conserve precious fuel, he waited patiently, allowing ample time for us to complete our preparations and the weather to clear. Restarting the engines he disconnected then off-loaded the very heavy batteries, together with all non-essential equipment (including Jan's medical box!) and trusting to God that the craft would not stall, flew in for the pick-up.

George heard him first and ran to the centre of the grassy swathe, beckoning him forward with appropriate hand signals onto what seemed to him an almost perfect helipad. Obviously it wasn't! Jamaldorj finally elected to put it down on a large snowpatch in amongst the granite boulders, waving frantically for us to move as the slightest change in conditions might make it difficult for him to get airborne with our extra weight. The engines roared and I felt the cold turbulence buffet my face. We raced — well, rather they raced, I just yelled with pain — bumping and crashing across giant blocks. Bits of bone were moving in all directions. I saw the co-pilot jump and moments later struggle across the snow patch to help, flip-flops clenched tightly between his teeth!

By the time we reached the helicopter I thought I was past caring but I was wrong. Lifting the foot of the stretcher up to the door, Ed fell into a hollow and I crashed to the ground ('You do a nice line in screaming', George confessed a few minutes later!). I was successfully bundled inside on the second attempt, the co-pilot fighting with the door as the helicopter lurched forward over the moraine and skimmed across the glacier, struggling to gain height.

I lay back, propped on one arm, gasping with relief. Jan had both arms around me, his head buried in my shoulders, crying. I looked down the length of the stretcher to Ed who was hunched over, still gripping my legs firmly, also crying. Out of the corner of my eye I caught sight of George, collapsing into a seat, tears wetting both cheeks. In a sudden release of emotion I joined them and, there we were, four grown men all crying our eyes out! Then someone realised the chopper was flying in completely the wrong direction. It was only on landing to collect the batteries that the reason became clear.

After a brief stop at base camp in the gathering gloom, we flew 150 km to a small aerodrome, barely reaching it before the fuel cut out. I was taken to the local 'hospital' but it was on the manager's desk that Jan cleaned the wound under local anaesthetic. They didn't have splints but he improvised with long strips of wood, kindly ripped from the surrounding shelves and cupboards by the manager himself!

Although the chances of further fuel were less than slim, there seemed nothing else to do but try. Yet it was here that we had, perhaps, our best stroke of luck. Northwest Mongolia is largely populated by Kazakhs; crafty, tribal folk who hold no allegiance to the Republic, and who for the last few months had been desperately attempting to escape from a country rapidly approaching economic ruin. That morning there was an unscheduled and somewhat illegal landing of an aircraft, sent on an evacuation mission from Kazakhstan. After five bottles of Vodka had changed hands, fuel syphoned from the plane with an old hosepipe gave the chopper just enough flying time to reach Hovd where I was able to take my first bite of food for five days.

Meanwhile SOS International had obtained clearance from the Mongolian ministry to land their Singapore based Lear jet. Prior to this date no foreign aircraft had been allowed to enter western Mongolia, nor did Hovd appear on any aeronautical chart. At one stage there was even concern that the runway would not be suitable. However, the following day the Swiss pilot made a perfect visual landing and I was swiftly transferred to a modern casualty bag and flown to Hong Kong. Even here our run of luck held, allowing the pilot to break the curfew and make an emergency night landing just one hour before the airport was hit by a typhoon. I reached hospital at 4 a.m. and the same morning was lying in an operating theatre, having three metal plates internally fixed across the fracture sites.

The success of this rescue was due to the immense cooperation and strong 'bonding' between all those concerned; but their efforts would have been doomed had it not been for a spirited helicopter pilot who, against all odds, was prepared to have a go.

SUMMARY

The party made 23 ascents of peaks and lesser summits as marked on the map. Several were previously untrodden and more than half were climbed by new routes of varying standard up to alpine TD-/TD. The main ascents were made in the company of Richard Bruton, Vanessa Carter, Bridget Cowen, Claire Gosney, Tom Nichols and Colonel Tsanjid the Mongolian representative. There is still much scope for ice/mixed routes of great quality in one of the decreasing number of unspoilt wilderness areas left on the planet. Lindsay Griffin was injured and rescued by helicopter after many difficulties. The British, led by John Blashford Snell, were climbing in northwest Mongolia, May 1992.

Article 15 **37. NE face of Snow Church.** (Lindsay Griffin)

38. Gyala Peri.

Note 2

16

THE CLIMBING PARTNER — THE OTHER EXPERIENCE IN THE HIMALAYA

CHAMPAK CHATTERJI

ARE THEY HYPOXIA induced hallucinations? Derangements brought on by stress and fatigue when the human frame is stretched to the ultimate degree? Or are they real —'frontier' experiences as I would like to call them? Paranormal experiences in the Himalaya amongst mountaineers as chronicled stretch over since decades and there is sure to be a considerable corpus which has not been set down for fear of ridicule or worse.

The 1933 expedition to the North Face of Everest was remarkable in many aspects. For one thing it had men like Eric Shipton and Frank Smythe in the party. It was during this expedition that Wyn Harris discovered the ice axe belonging to either Mallory and Irvine who disappeared in 1924 on Everest on their way to the summit. The expedition also equalled the oxygen-less altitude record on Everest set up by Norton in 1924 — 28,200 ft which was broken more than 50 years later by Messner and Habeler. On 1 June 1933 Shipton and Smythe had set out for the summit of Everest from C6 at 27,200 ft and then when Shipton had collapsed Smythe had gone on alone until he was forced to turn back at about 28,200 ft, a thousand feet short of the summit. It was when he was nearing C6 on his return journey that he had the experience which is best related in his own words.

I was still some 200 feet above C6 and a considerable distance horizontally from it when, chancing to glance in the direction of the north ridge, I saw two curious looking objects floating in the sky. They strongly resembled kite balloons in shape, but one possessed what appeared to be squat underdeveloped wings, and the other a protuberance suggestive of a beak. They hovered motionless but seemed slowly to pulsate, a pulsation much slower than my own heart-beats, which is of interest supposing that it was an optical illusion. The two objects were very dark in colour and were silhouetted sharply against the sky, or possibly a background of cloud. So interested was I that I stopped to

133

observe them. My brain appeared to be working normally and I deliberately put myself through a series of tests. First of all I glanced away. The objects did not follow my vision but they were still there when I looked back again. Then I looked away again and this time identified by name a number of peaks, valleys and glaciers by way of a mental test. But when I looked back again, the objects confronted me. At this I gave them up as a bad job, but just as I was starting to move again a mist suddenly drifted across. Gradually they disappeared behind it; and when a minute or two later it had drifted clear, exposing the whole of the north ridge once more, they had vanished as mysteriously as they came.

Was this the first chronicled UFO sighting on the Himalaya? Did Smythe have extra-sensory perception or was it just stress that produced what a climbing colleague gently derided as 'Frank's pulsating teapots'? We shall not know.

More than forty years later something more eerie happened to Nick Estcourt when he was part of the team that was attempting the difficult Southwest face of Everest under Chris Bonington's leadership. Logistics dictated that on 26 September 1975 four bottles of oxygen had to be supplied to C6 high up on the mountain and to do this Nick Estcourt volunteered to leave C4 with the bottles early in the morning. In doing so Estcourt had an experience straight out of the bizarre world of M. R. James. This is the story in his own words.

I set off on my own at about 3.30 in the morning (from Camp IV) pulling up the fixed ropes leading upto Camp 5. It was a moonlit night and the shapes of the rocks were etched clearly against the brightness of the snow. I was about two hundred feet above the camp when I turned around. I can't remember why but perhaps I had a feeling that someone was following me. Anyway I turned around and saw this figure behind me. He looked like an ordinary climber, far enough behind, so that I could not feel him moving up the fixed rope, but not all that far below. I could see his arms and legs and assumed that it was someone trying to catch me up. I stopped and waited for him. He then seemed to stop or to be moving very, very slowly, he made no effort to signal or wave — I shouted down, but got no reply and so in the end I thought, 'Sod it, I might as well press on!' .... I carried on and turned round three or four times .... and this figure was still behind me. It was definitely a human figure with arms and legs and at one stage I can remember seeing him behind a slight undulation in the slope, from the waist upwards as you would expect with the lower part of his body hidden in the slight dip. I turned again as I reached the old site of Camp 4 (six hundred above Camp IV in the current expedition) and there was no one there at all. It seemed very eerie. I wasn't sure if anyone had fallen off or what. He couldn't possibly have had time to have turned back and drop down the ropes out of sight, since I could see almost all the way back to Camp 4. The whole thing seemed very peculiar.

Later discussing his experience with others it was clearly established that the figure could not have been a member of the team.

Once again there is no satisfactory explanation. Nick Estcourt was well acclimatised and in any case the altitude at which he had the experience was around 7300 m low enough to discount any hallucinatory factor. Was it then a psychic phenomenon, an ectoplasmic emanation of Jangbo the Sherpa who was killed in an avalanche in the area in 1973 and who had been closely associated with Estcourt in 1972? A pre-sentiment of death? Mick Burke a member of the team was to die later that day on his lonely plough back from the summit and a few years later Estcourt himself would die in a tragic avalanche on K2. Could this possibly be the Abominable Snowman plagued by loneliness following Estcourt in its desperate hunger for company?

Reinhold Messner arguably the greatest mountaineer of the modern age has had several paranormal experiences. In 1970 along with his brother Gunther, Messner made the first ascent of the famous Rupal face of Nanga Parbat. Their descent without ropes down the Diamir face is now mountaineering history. Part of the descent meant climbing down a chute of smooth polished ice at an angle of fifty degrees without ropes or any other aid using only the front points of crampons. It was here that Messner felt the presence of a third person climbing down with him as he and Gunther went down to the Mummery Rib in the darkness. Later Gunther was killed by an avalanche as the two fought their way through extreme exhaustion down to base camp.

Inspite of personal tragedy, Messner was back to the Nanga Parbat in 1978 to do his first 8000 m solo bid up the Diamir face. This time up the presence of the other person was even more vivid, guiding him and telling him to go left or right to find the best route as he made his way through the glacier at the foot of the mountain. Higher on the face, at around 7500 m, he was once again aware of a presence, this time a woman at the edge of his vision with whom he talked and who assured him of the success of his summit bid. Messner's successful solo ascent and descent of Nanga Parbat is now part of adventure history.

Once again the questions raised defy straight answers. The first time on Diamir with Gunther, Messner was not alone. Why then a third person? Supposing this was a result of mountain loneliness? On his solo bid, he felt the presence of a benevolent entity on the glacier itself which could not have been caused by altitude. It is possible though that the 'woman' he saw and talked with at 7500 m was born out of physical and emotional exhaustion. In 1977 Messner had been separated from Uschi his wife and he was emotionally drained by the experience.

In 1980 Messner mounted his remarkable solo bid on Everest up the North Face. Here also at the higher altitudes Messner felt a guiding hand and above 8000 m he could sense the mystical presence of Mallory.

In 1988 Stephen Venables as part of a team of four climbers took on the hitherto 'unclimbable' Kangshung Face of Everest. It was an ascent of epic proportions and ultimately it was Venables alone who climbed from the South to the top of Everest. During the descent from the summit to the South Col battling appalling weather and extreme exhaustion he found companionship in an 'old man' who appeared in moments of great danger guiding his way and nursed him to safety. Forced to bivouac in the open, above South Col as he was benighted, Venables had the 'old man' as his companion throughout the night, who disappeared only when the dawn came and his safety was assured.

What was this phenomenon — hallucination induced by lack of oxygen above 8000 m and extreme exhaustion or the guardian spirit of Everest or the shades of dead and gone mountaineers? Could it have been the protective aura of the ashram from Pondicherry from where Venables had taken votive petals to the top of Everest? The questions remain.[1]

It is not that paranormal experiences are confined to the Himalaya. Modern mountaineering began a century ago in July 1865 with the first ascent of the Matterhorn by Edward Whymper. In July on their descent from the Matterhorn, four of Whymper's climbing companions fell 1200 m to their death. Speechless and numb with horror the rest of the party climbed down to safety toward Zermatt when at 6 p.m. a strange thing happened. As Whymper reported

1. See article 'Fires on the Mountain', in the present issue on this subject about another accident to Venables in 1992. — Ed.

in his book, *Scrambles Among the Alps* .... a mighty arch appeared, rising above the Lyskanum high into the sky. Pale, colourless and noiseless but perfectly sharp and defined .... this unearthly apparition seemed like a vision from another world; and almost appalled we watched with amazement the gradual development of two vast crosses, one on either side .... The spectral forms remained motionless. It was fearful and wonderful sight; unique in my experience and impressive beyond description, coming at such a moment'.

Yet again the above 'fog-bow' appearance can perhaps be explained by natural causes but its curious occurrence immediately after the accident makes us wonder like Whymper nearly a century and a half ago. There are mysteries yet on earth and in heaven and in mountains that bridge them.

References :

1. *Everest,* by Walt Unsworth, (p. 182).
2. *Everest the Hard Way,* by Chris Bonington. (Pp. 191-192).
3. *Quest for Adventure,* by Chris Bonington.
4. *Everest Kangshung Face,* by Stephen Venables.
5. *Scrambles Amongst the Alps,* by Edward Whymper.

SUMMARY

A look at paranormal experiences in the Himalaya to different climbers over the years.

HIMALAYAN JOURNAL VOLUME II (1930)

AAMIR ALI

THE FIRST ISSUE of the *Himalayan Journal*, 1929, had been received very well, reported the editor, Major Kenneth Mason, M.C., R.E., 'not only in this country but in Europe and America; and we have to thank many contemporary clubs and societies for their flattering reviews.'

Perhaps Mason had now decided that there would not be more than one issue a year; while the first had been called Vol. I, No. 1, the second is called simply Vol. II. Like the first, it was published by Thacker, Spink and Co., Calcutta, and cost Rs 5 or 8 shillings. It consisted of 206 pages, with three maps and a dozen photographs. Sections I to XIII are articles; XIV is a section on Expeditions; XV-XX consists of Obituaries, Notes, Reviews, Correspondence, etc.

Mountaineering

While articles on climbing had been conspicuously absent from the first volume, Vol. II seems to be turning its focus in that direction and has rather less on scientific matters. Somewhat strangely, pride of place is given to a German expedition. Paul Bauer, the leader, himself contributes an account of 'The German Attack on Kangchenjunga'.

The expedition consisted of nine members of the German and Austrian Alpine Clubs, including Peter Aufschnaiter, who later escaped from an internment camp in Dehra Dun with Heinrich Harrer. 'The objective of the expedition was not fully determined but our scruples against an immediate attack on this tremendous mountain (Kangchenjunga) were lessened by the Indian Press calling us from the very beginning the Kangchenjunga Expedition'. (Interesting that even in those days, it was the press that decided many aspects of our lives!)

With Teutonic efficiency, they had prepared loads for porters before leaving, so with the help of officials and the HC, they were able to leave Darjeeling after only three days. They had 90 native porters, of whom 15 had been on Everest. To Bauer's great satisfaction,

Lieut. Col. H.W. Tobin, the local secretary of the HC, travelled with the second column to base camp.

Days of reconnaissance, of trying to open routes, setting up camps. On 3 September six sahibs and four porters were ready at Camp X, at 7100 m. But there was a heavy snowstorm. On the 6th, two porters, Keddar and Pasang, tried to move up to establish another camp but could not get far in the deep snow. The attempt had to be given up.

The descent was in deep snow with 80 lb loads for the porters and 30-40 lb loads for the sahibs. They marched through a lane of snow the height of a man. Two days later, they packed half their loads in two large bags and threw them over the cliff to the glacier 1500 m below. Did they recover them or was this just an attempt to keep the mountain clean and set an example to future climbers?[1] At the mouth of the glacier, there were severe storms, and the careful editor of the HJ notes that for those three days in October there were the fiercest storms of the year in Sikkim, with severe damage inflicted on roads and railways.

The section on 'Club Proceedings' tells us that on 30 October, a local dinner of the HC was held in Calcutta to honour the expedition. Seven members of the expedition were present, including Peter Aufschnaiter. Major Kenneth Mason was in the chair and proposed toasts to HM the King Emperor and to the President of the Reich. 'There is one great attribute possessed by the Himalaya', he said. 'There is room for all the climbers of all nations of the world. (He could not have said that today; on one day alone, 12 May 1992, 32 climbers queued up to stand on Everest. No room at the top.[2]) And Mason went on, 'The HC is a young club, the youngest mountain club, I believe, in the world. It has already been our privilege to meet and welcome to India mountaineers from Italy, Holland and America, and I have for many years been in touch with your compatriot,

1. In 'Climbing Bhrigu's Stone', Vol. 48, 1990-91, Martin Moran writes, 'Ian (Dring) packed all spare ropes and non-essential items into our larger haul bag, abseiled to the brink of the big white wall, and cast it gleefully into the void......At 1.30 we touched the grass at the bottom, cast off all ropes and hardware for collection another day and fled the scene. The jettisoned haul bag was visible across the slope, so that too could be salvaged. There was quiet satisfaction in leaving the route completely clean save for the abseil anchors'.
2. Trevor Braham's article 'Himalaya — The Next Twenty-Five Years', in Vol. 48, 1990-91, tells us '...how unconsciously we have lapsed into an era in which the normal annual incursion into the Karakoram could be up to 65 climbing expeditions comprising 700 climbers, with Nepal accounting for a further 100 expeditions, and India opening its doors to over 150'.

Dr. Emil Trinkler. I think we may, as mountaineers, claim that the thing lesser and lower men call "the Spirit of Locarno" was known to us long before it reached the valleys and plains.

'Everest, the highest mountain, has been assaulted three times,' Mason said. 'K2, the second highest, has been assaulted once. And now Kangchenjunga has been attacked for the first time in earnest.....We are almost justified in saying that it would have fallen, but for foul weather when all the hard work had been accomplished.'

Paul Bauer, in his reply, paid graceful tribute to his British predecessors. 'Whatever we may have accomplished is certainly not to our own credit. We could not have done it without the pioneer work of Freshfield and Kellas and with the experience gained by those Britishers who tried to climb Everest.' He paid special tribute to Kellas, Mallory and Irvine.

After the German Vice-Consul had, also spoken, the company adjourned to the drawing room 'where Herr Bauer explained the various features of the climb and illustrated his route by means of Freshfield's map and photographs... These were thrown on the screen by means of a Zeiss Epidiascope kindly lent by the Agents of the firm of Zeiss.'

E. F. Norton who was with the Everest expedition of 1924, had read a rough translation of Bauer's account, and wrote to the HJ comparing it to the attack on Everest, 1924. 'On the face of it.', he concludes, 'Kangchenjunga appears to me a more formidable and more dangerous proposition than Mount Everest.'

In the section on 'Expeditions', there is a record of a tragedy on Kangchenjunga in May 1929, a few months before the Germans arrived. Edgar Francis Farmer, of the Standard Oil Company of New York, lost his life on or about 27 May 1929 in a plucky but misguided attempt to reach the summit of Kangchenjunga alone. Farmer's only climbing experience was in the Rockies but he had studied his subject thoroughly. He kept his plans secret and went off from Darjeeling ostensibly to explore the Guicha la region. He had Sherpa and Bhotia porters; Lieut.-Col. Tobin interviewed them when they finally returned and wrote an account of Farmer's ill-fated attempt.

Farmer had signed an undertaking not to enter Tibet or Nepal, but nevertheless he crossed the Kang la into Nepal and came below the southwest cliffs of Kangchenjunga, at the camp site of Raeburn and Crawford in 1920.

On 26 May, with three ex-Everest porters, he started up the icefall below the Talung saddle. He was warmly clad and equipped but his porters were not; they had no crampons. As the going became worse, a porter slipped and was unable to proceed. Farmer told them to stop while he went on to take photographs, promising to return shortly. The porters tried to dissuade him but he was determined. He went on and on into the mist, the porters waving to him to descend when the mist cleared at intervals.

He was still climbing at five o'clock after which the mist obscured him. The porters remained on the lookout till dusk, when they descended to camp and prepared food for him. From here they signalled at intervals with a torch and meta fuel. Next morning they climbed to a spot where his route could be seen and they caught a glimpse of him far above them on a steep snow slope, but he soon disappeared to be seen no more. The porters described him as moving wildly with arms outstretched. Was it snow blindness? They continued their vigil till 9 next morning, when hunger forced them down.

Tobin checked the accounts of the porters and declared their conduct to have been unexceptionable. 'The greatest sympathy was with his mother whose only son he was', he added.

Ironically, while writing this, news was received of another solo death on Kangchenjunga, but in very different circumstances, that of the remarkable Polish woman climber, Wanda Rutkiewicz. In 17 years she had made 22 expeditions to the Himalaya, and had climbed eight of the world's 14 peaks over 8000 m. She was making her third attempt on Kangchenjunga; she had been the third woman on Everest and the first on K2. She joined up with a Mexican expedition; the leader Carlos and Wanda set off for the summit but separated because she was going much more slowly. Carlos reached the summit; on the way down he met her, 600 m below the summit. She had drunk all her water, had no gas, no stove, no food and no sleeping bag — nothing except will power, it would seem. She refused to go down with Carlos, was pleased she would have his tracks to follow and was very excited and determined. She was not seen again; perhaps she reached the top and died on the way down.

Wanda's decision is not too difficult to understand; she was an experienced mountaineer and at the age of 49, knew that this was her last chance. She knew the dangers and took a calculated risk (though it wouldn't have needed much calculation to conclude that her chances were infinitesimal). But Farmer's folly is more difficult to understand. With little experience, what drove him to undertake an attempt that was outright lunacy? He was akin to Wilson who made on equally foolhardy solo attempt on Everest, with similar results. Solo climbing is a special experience of its own, but such climbing by a Reinhold Messner, a Jerzy Kukuczka, a Herman Buhl or a Walter Bonatti bears no relation to the follies of a Farmer or a Wilson.

Vol. II had not yet done with Kangchenjunga. In a 'Note' by HTM, it is recommended that the spelling Kangchen Dzo-nga be used; the Survey of India used the spelling Kinchinjunga. Obviously Mason did not follow HTM's learned suggestion because the Journal continued to use the familiar form Kangchenjunga, and I believe it still does. Names and their transliteration still cause much fun and confusion. Thus we learn from E. Theophilus, 'Beneath the Shroud' Vol. 48, 1990-1991, that the mountain we have always known as Leo Pargial is really Reo Purgyil.[3]

Lieut.-Col. Tobin provides a historical account of 'Exploration and Climbing in the Sikkim Himalaya'. Three names stand pre-eminent, he writes; Sir Joseph Hooker, the great botanist; Douglas Freshfield, distinguished Alpine and Caucasian climber; and Dr A.M. Kellas, who conquered a number of peaks in the eastern Himalaya.

Hooker spent most of 1848-49 among Sikkim's wonderful mountains and has left vivid pictures in his *Himalayan Journals* (not to be confused with our own HJ).[4] In 1849, Hooker and his companion Dr Campbell, Superintendent of Darjeeling, were seized and detained as prisoners at Tumlong, under the orders of Namgay, Prime Minister of Sikkim. They were released after protracted negotiations. As retribution for this outrage, the portion of Sikkim south of the Great Rangit, now covered by valuable tea gardens, was annexed by the British Government. Ah, happy days, when there was no United Nations, no Security Council, to make an unseemly fuss about such righteous retribution!

In 1899, Douglas Freshfield, accompanied by Prof Garwood and the brothers, Sella and Rinzin Namgyal, made the high level tour narrated in *Round Kangchenjunga*

Tobin chronicles various climbing expeditions. W.W. Graham who claimed to have climbed Kabru in 1893; this led to much controversy. He climbed with two Swiss guides. In 1905, Dr Guillarmod and four

<hr/>

3. Harish Kapadia's article on *'Lots in a Name'*, Vol. 48, is a fascinating study of the origins of names in the East Karakoram. How enchanting to learn that the Sia of the embattled Siachen glacier means a rose; are the Indians and Pakistanis re-enacting the War of the Roses? And who would have thought that Indira col was not named after our late Prime Minister? Is it absurdly fanciful to think that one day the Siachen might become a joint Indo-Pakistan Nature Park, demilitarized, and left to roses and climbers?
4. A.D. Moddie contributed a most interesting article on 'The Himalayan Journals of Sir Joseph Hooker' to Vol. 47, 1989-1990.

others tackled the ice slopes below the SW cliffs of Kangchenjunga. While six of them were traversing a snow slope, two porters slipped and the whole party was dragged down. Pache and three porters were buried and their bodies not recovered till three days later.

In 1907, two Norwegians, Rubenson and Aas, made an attempt on Kabru. At 22,000 ft they discarded their nailed boots as the nails made their feet colder (they presumably had alternative footwear and did not continue in their socks). The attempt was abandoned; on the way down, Rubenson slipped in his non-nail boots; Aas checked him but four of the five strands of the Swiss rope parted.

A. M. Kellas climbed a number of peaks in 1907 and made three attempts on Simvu with European guides. In 1920, he was back again and climbed Narsing, 5832 m. He got back to Darjeeling only a few days before setting off with the first expedition to Everest. Unluckily he died on the way through Tibet and 'that indefatigable but extremely modest and reticent climber......lies in a lonely grave at Kampa Dzong.'

Also in 1920, Harold Raeburn carried out two tours south of Kangchenjunga; on the first he was accompanied by Tobin himself.

Tobin, and later E.O. Shebbeare, after leaving the German Kangchenjunga Expedition, explored the little known route over what is wrongly shown on the map as the Yumtso la (Blue Water pass) to the Tulung monastery, the Talung gorge and the Tista.

In the section on 'Club Proceedings', the editor tells us, 'Among those who have been fortunate enough to combine their duties with Himalayan travels are Messrs. Wakefield, Gunn, Ludlow, Todd and Burn'. From outside India, there were the Duke of Spoleto, Mr and Mrs Visser, Lieut.-Col. Reginald Schomberg, while the Roosevelts had a most successful expedition on behalf of the Field Museum of Chicago, and were fortunate to obtain the first complete specimen of the Giant Panda, the "Spectacled Bear" of the dense bamboo forests of Szechwan. (What would Peter Scott, who designed the now famous panda logo for the World Wildlife Fund for Nature, have said to that? Or George Schaller, who studied the endangered panda to recommend conservation measures?)

While the climbing expeditions and accounts seem to have focused on Sikkim and the area round Kangchenjunga or Kinchinjunga or Kangchen Dzo-nga — the western Himalaya is not ignored. Dr. E. F. Neve contributes a delightful article on 'Sonamarg as a Climbing Centre'. He sketches 'a few delights of travelling from a base at Sonamarg. With favourable weather a fortnight is sufficient to enable one to follow any of these routes and to climb one or more of

the peaks to which I have referred. Whatever the peaks may lack
in magnitude or mystery, compared with those north of the Indus,
is fully compensated for by their technical interest and beauty.'

Neve brings out well the flavour of a small expedition, enjoying
not only the climbs but the views, the forests, the flowers, the birds,
the rocks, the fossils, and finding that inner peace that is often lost
in those hairy expeditions hell-bent on a major climb, replete with
ironmongery and derring do. At least one of his climbs was with
Kenneth Mason himself, and it is not surprising that the article is
dotted with interesting footnotes from the editor.

Some of Neve's descriptions are worth quoting. 'Even the approach
to Sonamarg by the Sind valley is most impressive..... Right and
left the grey cliffs tower up, in tiers, to a height of five to eight
thousand feet, above the river, which, during the melting of the snows,
is a mighty torrent, descending in foaming rapids, intensified by the
rocky walls between which it is pent.' And the marg itself, 'Between
the curved ridges there are now grassy meadows, spangled with Alpine
flowers. Sonamarg may have derived its name from the sheets of
golden ragwort, the widespread orange-coloured weil wall-flower, or
the troops of yellow mullein. But many of the slopes are brilliant
with pink balsam, or gloriously blue with forget-me-nots and other
varieties of *boraginae*.... At the entrance of the glacier valley....is
one of the most impressive pieces of mountain scenery, not only
in Kashmir, but in the world.'

And the Kolahoi peak. 'Between Baltal and Sonamarg, and on the
left side of the Sind river, is the Saribal Nala, a beautiful, narrow,
steep little valley....The snow extends southwards to a pass which
leads to the wonderful little glacier cirque of Katar Nag, with its
seven little emerald lakes, a mile and a half below. From the pass
the snow extends to the great snow-field which stretches around Kolahoi
from south to east, and covers an area of four square miles at
an altitude of about 15,500 ft. It was from this snow-field that the
first ascent of the peak was made in 1912 by Major Kenneth Mason
and the writer.'

Neve refers to a score of peaks within easy reach of Sonamarg
which have never been ascended and upon which attempts should
afford real pleasure. How many of these still remain unascended?[5]

---

5. I note, wryly, that Neve says 'With favourable weather' In July 1972, I spent
some days in Sonamarg with Gurdial Singh, Nalni Dhar Jayal and assorted
family members. It rained shamelessly all the time and we could see nothing
of the beauties so lovingly described by Dr Neve. We finally set off in a commandeered
jeep towards the Zoji la hoping to get out of the rain zone; in two hours
we were back again. The road had been washed away and would take weeks

Central Asia

Vol. I No. 1 had seemed to give over the exploration of Central Asia to the Germans — Emil Trinkler and Wm. Filchner; Vol. II redresses the balance and has two long reviews of books by Sir Aurel Stein, K.C.I.E., Ph.D., D. Litt., D.Sc., still the Scientific and Technical Correspondent of the HC for archaeology.

In the Notes on Expeditions, there is an interesting account, presumably written up by Mason, of a journey in the summer of 1929 by E. B. Wakefield of the ICS, British Trade Agent for the year. He left Simla on 4 June on the Hindustan-Tibet road and reached Pooh (Is there really such a name outside Gilbert and Sullivan?) on the 20th. They split up and eight men followed the route commonly taken by Bashahri traders, who use sheep and goats. They crossed the Bodopo la 19,412 ft;[6] the conditions were bad and several members collapsed. One of the Gurkhas failed to recover and died.

They crossed the Indus below Demchok; four days later Wakefield was 'fortunate in finding an enlightened, well educated and most hospitable dzong-pon who had been educated at Rugby School in England and and spoke excellent English.'

There were 150 miles more to Gartok; the Indus was recrossed with great difficulty opposite the monastery of Tashigong. Wakefield himself swam the flooded river four times with loads. They joined the main Lhasa-Leh route at Barkha. They were back in Simla on 2 November.

Lieut.-Col. Schomberg had written about his trip to the Urta Saryk valley in the Tien Shan in Vol I; Vol. II contains an account compiled by Mason, of his two years in the Tien Shan and Altai, 1927-29. In the autumn of 1927, he went to Kashgar, on to Urumchi in early February 1928, and then to the Great Altai mountains, and to the Urta Saryk valley about which we read in Vol. I. He reached Ili in July 1928, 'Schomberg observes that travellers in the Tien Shan are much handicapped by what he calls the shortness of the exploring season. Winter stays long and goes late; it is only from the end of June to mid-September that any travel in high altitudes can be

___

to repair. Return to Nedou's in Srinagar where the sight of a scurrying cockroach in the bathroom was compensated for by a hoopoe's nest just under our balcony.

6. In the 'Notes on Expeditions', a member of the HC anonymously contributed a note on a journey carried out by him and his wife. Samlakar is 16,550 ft, he said, and the Bodpo-la is 19,810. (The meticulous editor notes that Wakefield gave its height as 19,412 ft.) Samlakar is very good for game, noted the anonymous writer. 'There are a few ammon, but burrhel abound, sometimes as many as half a dozen herds being visible at one time. The herds are magnificent and nothing under twenty-five inches is worth shooting.'

carried out.' Schomberg himself had great difficulty in getting to Manas in 1928, and Captain Sheriff, a month later, but much further south, lost all his caravan and nearly his life in crossing the lower passes of the Tien Shan, north of Kuchar.

Schomberg reached Yarkand in January 1929; left Kashgar in March and crossed in the Muz-art pass early in April; and finally left Kashgar for India on 19 September.

The Russo-German Alai-Pamir Expedition, 1928, consisted of 40 European members, and carried out scientific investigations with the utmost thoroughness. The members were divided into two sections, German and Russian, working in cooperation.

Kenneth Mason wrote a review of Sir Aurel Stein's book *Innermost Asia; Detailed Report of Explorations in Central Asia, Kan-su, and Eastern Iran,* Oxford 1928, four volumes, £ 26 5s. for The Statesman, and this is reprinted in Vol. II. 'The beautiful production reflects the greatest credit on the distinguished author and the Government of India', wrote Mason.

The expedition began in July 1913 and ended in March 1916. Stein went from Kashmir by the Barai pass to Chilas, explored the tribal states of Darel and Tangir south of Gilgit, under the Raja Pakhtun Wali. Darel had been visited by Fa-Hsien and Huang-tsang.[7] He explored the Tarim basin, including the pre-historic dried up Lop sea-bed, dead settlements and oases by the dying rivers. He traced the ancient route through the desert to Maral-bashi. His attempt to cross the Takla-makan desert was baffled by terrific sand ridges, but his observations have been supplemented by Dr Emil Trinkler, as reported in HJ, Vol. I. From Khotan he marched 700 miles to the Lop desert, examining ruined sites on the way. Perhaps 'the most remarkable finds' were the fine specimens of figured silks and woollen tapestries from grave-pits, showing clear evidence of Hellenistic art-influence.

Stein followed the route which the early Chinese traders had used across the forbidding salt-encrusted bed of the pre-historic Lop sea. Again and again, lucky finds of 630 early Chinese copper coins, small metal objects, stone ornaments and the like assured him that he was on the right track. 'On one occasion when the last traces of vegetation had long been left behind, he suddenly found the ancient track plainly marked for about thirty yards by two hundred and eleven *Wu-shu* (Chinese) copper coins. They lay in a well-defined line, no

---

7. Fa-Hsien travelled to India through Yarkand and down the Indus valley. He spent about ten years in India, c. AD 401-412, in the reign of Chandragupta II. He studied Buddhism, mainly at Pataliputra. Huang-tsang, similarly motivated, came to India in AD 630.

more than three or four feet wide, running north-east to south-west, and must have dropped unobserved from some leaky money bag or case. The swaying camel would account for the width of the track thus marked. What a romantic story could be based upon those copper coins carried by the last caravan that used his awful route, so full of peril and hardship! It was by such "lucky" finds as these, a chance coin, a scattered heap of bronze arrow-heads, an iron snaffle-bit, a broken copper buckle, and by his amazing ability to pick up and piece together his clues that Sir Aurel was enabled to trace this route right up to its eastern end, near an old terminal basin in the Tun-huang desert.' Stein could not resist the temptation to revisit the famous temples of the 'Thousand Buddhas' that he had first explored in 1907. In Mongolia, he set out for the high ranges of the Nan-shan where he met a serious accident. His Badakshi horse reared and fell backwards on him, crushing the muscles of his thigh.

Rai Bahadur Lal Singh of the Survey of India, Sir Aurel's most energetic and devoted assistant on two long journeys, accomplished important work in the Kuruk-tagh. 'Amidst icy gales and with the temperature falling well below zero Fahrenheit, he was at last able to view above the desert loess-haze the high snowy peaks of the Kun-lun, 150 miles to the south.'

Having despatched a hundred and eighty cases of antiques from Kashgar, Sir Aurel started across the Russian Pamirs for the valleys of the upper Oxus. At Samarkand, he took the Trans-Caspian railway and spent three weeks on the Perso-Afghan border.

He had covered nearly 11,000 miles in two years and eight months; perhaps his survey assistants had covered even more. 'It must be with intense satisfaction that Sir Aurel Stein looks back over his three great expeditions into Central Asia. Whatever has been accomplished since his first fruitful journey in 1900-01, by members of whatever nation we choose to name, has been directly due to the stimulation of Sir Aurel Stein, though he himself would be the last to lay such a claim. Little by little he has penetrated unexplored Asia; the Lop sea and the Turfan depression have yielded up their secrets; the sand-buried cities have been uncovered; the Emperor Wu-ti's ancient wall, with its watch towers and fortified posts have been traced for seven degrees of longtitude and surveyed; the whole civilization seems to have been laid bare. The four parallel ranges of the Central Nan-shan, previously visited only by Potanin, Obruchev and Kozlov, have been explored and mapped in detail; the headwaters of the Huang-ho have been reached and the Esting-gol and Su-lo-ho traversed; in the north, the southern ranges of the Tien Shan, the arid Kuruktagh, and even the moist upland pastures of Dzungaria have been surveyed. Is it too much to hope that Sir Aurel Stein has not completed his journeys of exploration in "Innermost Asia"?'

Vol. II has not yet finished with Sir Aurel Stein. H. L. Haughton reviews another book by the great explorer and archaeologist, *On Alexander's Track to the Indus, 1928.* The reviewer's enthusiasm is contagious. 'Alexander! Aurel Stein! Are not these both names to conjure with and the two together a combination which immediately commands our attention and guarantees that we shall not be disappointed?'

This is a personal narrative in which Aurel Stein tells us that throughout his many years of study, travel and exploration in India, Chinese Turkistan and North China, his real interest and hopes had ever been centred in Alexander and the elucidation of his campaign. From Chakdara, in the vicinity of which Alexander probably crossed the Swat river, he worked his way up the valley, spending four happy days among the extensive ruins round Birkot.

As an example of the accuracy of ancient historians and travellers, 'one may mention the Great Stupa, raised by the pious King Kanishka over the relics of Gautama Buddha, described by Huang-tsang as being south east of Peshawar city, where a few years ago, it was located and excavated, the relics being found intact in their beautiful bronze casket'.

H.T. Morshead reviews a reprint of Hazlitt's English translation of the classic *Travels in Tartary, Thibet and China, 1844-46,* by Abbe Huc and Gabet. In his introduction, Prof. Pelliot says, 'The lasting success of the Souvenirs is due above all to the literary gifts of their author. Huc had eyes to see, and the power to recall what he had seen; but these very gifts have their counterpart in a somewhat ardent imagination, which led him on occasion to invent what he supposed himself to be merely reporting.'

Morshead also reviews three books on Tibet, including *The people of Tibet,* by Sir C.A. Bell, and *We Tibetans,* by Rinchen Lhamo, a Tibetan lady married to Louis King, formerly British Consul at Tachienlu. The authoress explains that she knows very little English and her husband less Tibetan. Before one can jump to the conclusion that they had found the ideal recipe for living happily ever after, however, we are told that they both spoke fluent Chinese.

In her chapter 'Your Civilisation and Ours', she takes a gentle dig or two at her husband, upholding the merits of Tibetan culture against the materialism of the Western World. 'Civilisation is not bound up in material things. A civilised people must have a sufficiency of them and that is all. We have it. You have more than it. You have a great many things we have not. Wonderful things. Your electricity and the various uses to which it is put, your steamers and trains and motor cars and aeroplanes..... But there is another aspect of the matter. People can do without these things, but if they are there naturally everybody wants them.... So wealth becomes the goal of endeavour, and men's minds are taken off other things we consider more important.'

A lesson that many wise men and women have repeated in our times as well, but alas, there are none so poor to do them reverence. While agreeing fully with them, we continue to battle furiously for the wealth we purport to despise.

And what would the good Rinchen Lhamo — or Sir Aurel — have said if they learnt that 1992 saw a motor car rally from Paris to Beijing? That at Kashgar, they passed caravans from the Pamirs and Central Asia. Then it's north through the foothills of the Tien Shan mountains along the Mongolian border? The rally consisted of some 1600 persons through country that had survived invasions by Persians, Russians, Turks; one can derive some perverted pleasure from reading that the rally had to be interrupted as drivers stalled in heavy mud in Xinjiang province.[8] Perhaps they should be reminded of Kipling's warning, 'And the end of the fight is a tombstone white/With the name of the late deceased/And the epitaph dear "A Fool lies here/Who tried to hustle the East".'

Kenneth Mason himself reviews a translation in English from the German, *Buried Treasures of Chinese Turkestan,* by Albert von Le Coq, based on three expeditions between 1904 and 1914. The book gives a concise and accurate historical sketch from the conquests of Alexander and shows how Buddhism and its art reached the nations of Chinese Turkestan from Bactria.

RJW reviews China to Chelsea: *A Modern Pilgrimage Along Ancient Highways,* by Capt Duncan McCallum MC. From Peking, the McCallums drove to Tientsin, embarked for Haiphong, took rail and road to Singapore, a ship to Calcutta, then the road again to the Dardanelles and Calais. That the McCallums did succeed, in spite of mud, rain, snow, water, sand, rock and earthquakes, to say nothing of various forms of opposition, is a matter for pride."

The reviewer points out some errors. McCallum describes a previous motor journey across the desert from Damascus to Baghdad in 1923 as a pioneer journey. 'This is hardly accurate, as the same route was traversed by Major Kenneth Mason with three officers by car early in 1919.

---

8. *International Herald Tribune,* 3 and 19 September 1992.

And finally, there is a review, by Kenneth Mason of course, of a novel *Dainra*, by 'Ganpat' aka Major M.L.A. Gompertz. We had met Maj. Gompertz in Vol. I and wondered how he had acquired the name of 'Ganpat'; we continue to wonder. 'In *Dainra*, "Ganpat" has infused an immense amount of "kick" into the ashes of two thousands years ago', writes Mason. 'The scene is laid in the little mountain state of Asmaka......over which Queen Dainra rules with a cruelty hard to beat. Members of the HC will be puzzled to identify Asmaka, for "Ganpat" has set a problem in topography which even the genius of Sir Aurel Stein could never solve.' (Or of Kenneth Mason, we might add.)

Greeks, Bactrians and petty chiefs from all over keep the pot — and the plot — boiling. 'All these essences frothed and bubbled in the Indus Kohistan for the space of a hectic year or two. Long odds, forced marches, amazing archery, loyalty, treachery, malice and other forms of uncharitableness all come into the day's work, and are the natural result of mingling such incompatible temperaments. "Ganpat" is rapidly becoming the Rider Haggard of our Indian hills.' Or perhaps we should say today, the John Le Carre.

The Shyok Flood

Vol. I was much preoccupied with the Chong Kumdan dam across the Shyok and the impending flood when it burst, as burst it would. Vol. II completes the story with three articles on the flood.[9]

J. P. Gunn was sent by the Punjab Government and realised that the dam had burst. He pitched his tent three miles below the dam. 'Ice-blocks up to twenty feet cube were scattered about the banks of the river, sometimes seventy feet and more above the river bed, while occasionally there was a gigantic block about fifty feet cube by way of variety.' He was able to see clearly what had occurred. 'In only one particular was my anticipation of the bursting of this dam correct. I predicted that when the dam broke, there would be a big flood, in all probability larger than that of 1926. And it was so.'

H. J. Todd, the Political Agent in Gilgit, was returning from Kashmir on 17 August and arrived at the Partab Pul across the Indus at 5.30 a.m. Something was wrong for the clearance of the bridge was much less than usual. 'The water was coming down in a dark chocolate-coloured flood, carrying quantities of drift-wood, as if the river had just succeeded in washing its banks of the deposits of

---

9. The dam seems to be still going strong. Harish Kapadia, in 'Chong Kumdan' Vol. 48, 1990-1991, mentions their expedition's observations of the old glacier dam.

previous floods.....Later boards and roofing material began to arrive, clearly indicating the fate of some unfortunate village in Baltistan......A levy was sent galloping in to Bunji to wire the news to Kashmir, and Bunji and Chilas were warned to take all precautions.'

The river continued to rise, beating against the abutments of the 330 ft suspension bridge, the only link with Gilgit. But happily, by 9.30 a.m. the worst was over; no loss of life was recorded. Todd was chagrined that he could take no photographs. 'I always make it a practice to carry a camera with me on trek, but this morning of all mornings, my bearer had noticed that the sling was becoming unstitched so had packed the camera in my yakdan and sent it ahead! I thus lost the unique opportunity.'

Kenneth Mason adds a commentary, pointing out that it was lucky that the dam burst on 15 August and not the 25th, because on the latter date, the liberated waters would have arrived at Attock at the same time as the higher flood caused by an unprecedented rainfall in the Kabul river basin, and the combined floods would have caused an appalling amount of damage in the plains. 'The Shyok burst was a blessing in disguise, for it caused little damage, scoured out the bed of the Indus and so gave a better "runoff" for the rain flood.'

As we have by now learnt to expect, Mason gives an excellent scientific summary of various reports on the flood, and several photographs by Ludlow and Gunn.

The 'Notes on Expeditions' gives an account of the Netherlands Karakoram Expedition, 1929-30, the third expedition of Mr. and Mrs. Visser. (We learn later in the Journal that the Council of the Royal Geographical Society awarded the Back Grant for 1929 to Mr Visser for his exploration of the Hunza Karakoram glaciers. Mrs Visser was vice-president of the Ladies' Alpine Club.) On 26 July they crossed the Saser la and went on to Daulat Beg Oldi. In their camp on 15 August, at 5 a.m. they heard the bursting of the Chong Kumdan dam 19 miles away 'with reports like cannon-shots.' Mrs Visser wrote that a week earlier they would have been caught, as they were marching in the river bed for several hours.[10]

Natural History

Ornithology had received a great deal of attention in Vol. I; it receives rather less in Vol. II but is by no means ignored. L. R.

---

10. In September 1992, there were devastating floods in Pakistan, and India, because of exceptionally heavy rains that flooded the Indus. Some two hundred tourists were blocked at Karimabad near Gilgit because the road was washed away. Lower down, many villages were destroyed and an estimated 1400 lives were lost.

Fawcus contributes 'Bird Notes on a Journey to Gyantse', resulting from a trip he made in August-September 1929. He was required by the Government (of Tibet, presumably) to sign an undertaking not to shoot in Tibetan territory, and he took this rather more seriously than Edgar Francis Farmer had taken his undertaking not to enter Nepal. 'This prevented any collecting being done on the trip,' wrote Fawcus, 'but sufficient bird-life was observed during our somewhat slow marches to make it worth while putting something on record about what we saw[11].'

Fawcus crossed the Natu la into Tibet from Sikkim and descended into the Chumbi valley, a well-watered temperate zone, as different 'from the arid upland plains of Tibet as chalk is from cheese.' The Red-billed Chough was ubiquitous on the Tibetan plains but he never saw the Yellow-billed Chough (the common 'Chouka' of the Alps). In the bed of the Amo Chu, he constantly met the Himalayan Whistling Thrush, the White-capped Redstart (is there any more attractive bird of the hills?) and the Plumbeous Redstart. Among 'strong flyers', he saw the Lammergayer, the Black-eared Kite and the Great Himalayan Griffon. Around Gyantse, the Tibetan Tree-sparrow gave way to the more striking Cinnamon Sparrow.

On the Phari plain, 'the trees are left behind and the traveller sits nightly over the evanescent blue flame of a yak-dung fire, eked out by the hard turves which also serve for house-building purposes.......the grazing ground of countless yaks.........conjures to the mind what the plains of Kansas and Missouri must have looked like before the steam tractor replaced the herds of buffalo.' On two occasions, he 'saw wolves emerge from the ravines apparently on the look-out for straggling calves. Here we first met the strange little Ground Chough.'

Beyond the Phari plain, the road crossed the main Himalayan range by the Tang la, and the plain there was the home of many Kiang, 'whose curiosity sufficiently masters their fear of man to impel them to approach within some eighty yards and gaze at motionless travellers.' The fertile Gyantse plain and the torrent of the Nyang chu was haunted by the Ibis-bill, but we failed to see one. The plain was the home of Burrhel, the Blue Poppy and the Snowcock, the Tibetan Twite and the Wall-creeper.

---

11. Just after World War II, Salim Ali, the Indian ornithologist, went on a birding expedition to Tibet. He undertook not to carry a collecting gun or firearms of any sort. However, he spent months practising with a catapult, having convinced himself that collecting birds by this noiseless weapon would not violate the beliefs or the laws of Tibet, and endanger neither his person nor his soul. In the event, no great moral danger was faced as his success was limited to one specimen.

Blue poppies also entranced W.E. Buchanan, when he was following 'In the Footsteps of the Gerrards.' In the Baspa valley, he met a coolie with some very beautiful blue flowers. The coolie agreed to take Buchanan to where these had been found. They went up to a height of about 14,000 ft. 'Snow lay about in masses; and here I came across blue poppies in a profusion I had never seen before, and among them the flowers I was seeking. They were, I think, some species of delphinium, but I have been unable to indentify them in any botanical book'. (The editor of the HJ wonders if they were Kashmir Larkspur, Delphinium Cashmerianum?)

H.M. Glover, in his 'Round the Kanawar Kailas', records that 'On one occasion, when I was traversing a ledge, a snow-cock fluttered in front of me, apparently with a broken wing and behaving just like a mother partridge with young near by. Sure enough, a search revealed a nest with the prettiest little downy grey chicks.'

If we put together a note on Kingdon Ward's Journey from Burma to Annam, compiled from letters and personal information by Kenneth Mason, and a review of *Trailing the Giant Panda*, by Theodore and Kermit Roosevelt, 1929, also by Mason, we get a full account of a remarkable expedition. Its gloss is somewhat dimmed because the object of the exercise was hunting.

As Mason tells us, 'When the Roosevelt brothers and their companion Suydam Cutting, passed through Calcutta early in December 1928, they expressively remarked that the main object of their forthcoming expedition was "to knock the P out of Panda". Expressive, perhaps, but hardly endearing, and we have to keep reminding ourselves that this is 1929 and not 1993.'

They went from Bhamo in Burma through Yunnan, past the 20,000 ft Mount Satseto into the little kingdom of Muli in Szechuan. Then past Mt Koonka, about which Kermit remarks, 'The altitude of this mighty peak is unknown, but there are those who claim it rises more than thirty thousand ft and is the highest in the world'. And in the map included in the book, it is marked 30,000. Mason wasn't going to let the Panda hunters get away with this, but his admonishment is gentle. 'Until its height has been determined', he says, 'it is a little rash and not a little unfair to Everest to enter the altitude 30,000 ft upon the map as has been done on the one at the end of this volume, even though it is qualified in the text'[12].

---

12. In 1992, a Franco Italian Expedition, laden with hi-tech apparatus, went to Everest to measure with absolute accuracy the height of Everest and end the murmurings about K2 being higher. The expedition was sponsored by Baume et Mercier, the Swiss watch company, and led by the Savoyard guide Benoit

The Roosevelts got their Panda; also much other game, including 'a fine group of the Golden Monkey' for the Field Museum of Chicago.

In his review, Mason writes, 'Bandits seem to be as common as dacoits were in India before British rule, and the return journey through Lolo country was not unattended with danger. Possibly in no other country in the world are idols and gods treated with such scant veneration. Frequently they were found neglected and broken. And where else in the world is a god punished for not answering a prayer? "People ask god for something. Kill chicken for him. God not do it. Break his arm off." 'As Richard III might have said: 'Off with his head — so much for Buckingham'.[13]

So where does Kingdon Ward, the botanist we met in Vol. I, come into this? Starting from Mandalay, he was to work eastwards and join the Panda trailers somewhere in the French protectorate of Laos about May. Then they would all proceed together to the coast of Annam.

Kingdon Ward left Rangoon in March, and climbed the highest hill in the Southern Shan States, not much over 8000 ft. 'Using Kaw guides,' writes Mason, 'he ascended the hill in April, collecting a number of interesting orchids and other plants. Near the summit he found a fine white-flowered epiphytic rhododendron in full bloom and two other species — one almost certainly new — out of bloom.'

On 1 May he crossed the Mekong into French territory, finding more beautiful orchids. He was laid low with fever and held up for five weeks during which time he heard that the Roosevelts had reached Yunnan-fu and gone to Saigon by sea. Kingdon Ward crossed the mountains to the Namtha river; the rains had set in and travel was possible only by boat. Embarking in a canoe, he went down the Namtha for five days. 'The scenery was beautiful, and many of the forest trees and giant climbers were in flower.' When the Namtha joined the Mekong, he transferred to a raft and five days later reached Luang-Prabang. He took the post raft and completed the 290 miles to Savanakhet rapidly as the river was navigable. By this time he had travelled about 700 miles on the Mekong and 200 on the Namtha. This was restful but not very good for a botanist.

Chamoux, famous for his rapid ascensions; he had already climbed nine peaks of over 8000 m., three of them in less than 24 hours each. The Italians have already built a research laboratory at 5000 m. on Everest, EVK2, and propose to build an incinerator to take care of the more than 50 tons of garbage and junk left by expeditions. In Vol. 48, 1990-1991, Ardito Desio describes the Italian scientific expeditions of 1988, 1989 and 1990 to Shaksgam and the Everest area.

13. In the 'refined' version of Shakespeare's play, popular in the eighteenth century.

From Savanakhet, by car and rail to Hué and then the Tourane. Two days later he was in Saigon where he finally joined up with the Roosevelt party. Kermit had already returned to America; Theodore followed and Kingdon Ward continued his voyage to Singapore and Rangoon.

Among the book reviews is one of *Sterndale's Mammalia of India*, by Frank Finn, 1929, being an abridged and revised edition of the original. 'Himalayan mammals are there in force....though perhaps one would have preferred a little more and later information about Ovis karelini and the Ovis poli.' There are descriptions of 13 species of Langur, and 29 of Squirrels and Flying Squirrels. It includes the Dugong, but the picture of this last, alas, 'is nothing like the Mermaid of our dreams!'

The Bombay Natural History Society was not directly mentioned in Vol. I, but Vol. II has a special note about it. It outlines its aims and activities and states, 'Of particular interest to members of the HC are the wide and varied range of articles which have appeared in its Journal dealing with the Fauna and Flora of the Himalayan Region.' It also has a word for shikaris 'The Society's Taxidermy Department is at the service of members who wish to have their trophies mounted.'

The early determination to give due place to science has not been lost in Vol. II, and Dr A.M. Heron contributes an interesting article on 'The Gem-Stones of the Himalaya' (one might have thought that his name would have better fitted the author to write about birds rather than gems).

'The Himalayan region is strikingly poor in minerals of economic value,' he writes. 'The best place to search for gems is not in their matrix, but amongst the gravels, moraine and scree.'. Sapphires were first brought to Simla in 1882 from Lahul, where a landslide laid bare the rocks. The Maharajah of Kashmir wisely posted guards; the gems were sold in Simla at 'absurdly low prices such as a rupee a seer.'

In 1887, 'the largest weighed about 6 oz. and was partly of a very brilliant colour.' In 1906 the output was valued at £ 1327, in 1907 £ 3144; one stone sold for £ 2000. There were beryls, aquamarines, rubies, spinels and garnets. 'Great tracts of the Himalaya are yet unprospected, and though the HC would be the last to foster among its members that gambling instinct which characterises the true prospector, and would deprecate the idea that a fortune is to be picked up as an accompaniment to a mountaineering tour, nevertheless a search for beautiful minerals lends an interest and perhaps even a mild excitement to wanderings over the stony pastures and bare rock which come between the forest and the snow.' Alas, he tells us that 'the chances of finding anything of value are remote.'

Shikar

There is much about shikar in Vol. II, as there was in the first volume, and we have to remind ourselves yet again that we are in 1929 when shikar was a very respectable sport and a primary reason for visiting the Himalaya.

The shikaris of Vol. I had concentrated on the numbers they had bagged and the size of the horns; even the indomitable Mrs Lethbridge had not told us how she managed to get her ovis ammon and her burrhel. In 'Nine Days' Sport on the Pamirs' consisting of extracts from the diary of a journey to Chinese Turkistan in 1927, Capt. A.A. Russell gives us some of the excitement of the chase. Had he carried a camera instead of a rifle (and a tape measure), our sympathies would have been with him all the way.

19 July 1927. Way above the camp. Abu Khan, a local man from Kara-su, spotted a herd of poli[14] in the distance. 'As the wind was favourable and the poli were in a fairly get-at-able place, I determined to try and stalk them.' It was a long and difficult stalk of five hours, but he had to give up as the wind turned and blew towards the

---

14. In HJ Vol. I, No. 1, Mrs. Lethbridge and other shikaris had referred to Ovis ammon; I assumed this was o.a. poli, or the Marco Polo Sheep. Gurdial Singh wrote to me saying no, it was o.a. hodgsoni. Capt. Russell refers to poli, tout court. This is what the *Encyclopedia of Indian Natural History*, ed. by R.E. Hawkins, tell us. 'Wild sheep are found in a great arc from Turkey and Iran through Central and Northeastern Asia through western North America. Over most of their range they inhabit high mountains — preferring flat or rolling plateau country, not precipitous country like goats — but at either end of it they approach sea level. Of the five species, two occur in South Asia: the Urial (Ovis orientials) about 80-90 cm hight, and the heavily built Argali (Ovis ammon), 110-130... cm high. Argali in this region are of two races. The larger Tibetan Argali (Ovis ammon hodgsoni) with its very heavy horns which curve forward along the sides of the head, is found on the outer plateau of Tibet from Nepal and Bhutan west to the Karakoram pass in Ladakh; ....The Marco Polo sheep (o.a. poli) comes from the Pamirs to the Tagdumbash pass in Ladakh, but its range is separated from that of the Tibetan Argali by a 300 km gap; its horns are thinner, but they spiral outwards dramatically.'

The name, Marco Polo sheep, carries a strong flavour of romance, of Venice holding the gorgeous east in fee, of Xanadu where Kubla Khan did a pleasure dome decree, and where Alph the sacred river ran, (or polii). They once ranged in large herds through much of the Karakoram range in Pakistan, Afghanistan and China, but are now in danger of extinction. Even within the Khunjerab National Park, they are subject to illegal hunting, and the Karakoram Highway has made the area easily accessible. Live stock and yaks compete for grazing. If Capt. Russell were alive today, he would no doubt have been a fervent conservationist.

quarry. 'One phase of the stalk was most exciting. I was working my way down the edge of the stream when two ewes appeared about 200 yards on my right. There was no cover ahead and I had to pass them. If they spotted me where I was they would run straight down and alarm the big fellows. I crawled on my stomach inch by inch for what seemed an eternity, but was really about an hour. Every time one of them raised her head I lay like a rock, till after satisfying herself that I was a rock, she went on grazing.'

Next day, he saw the herd again and stalked them once more. It was a simple matter to get within 200 yards but impossible to get nearer, 'so I collected my wind, took careful aim at the biggest, fired and had the mortification to see my bullet strike the snow a foot short. I seized the bolt to reload and the cartridge jammed. I struggled with it and in about thirty seconds got it out, bent nearly double. The poli had disappeared, so I hastened to the spot where I saw them last and found them collected in the nullah below. I fired four more shots at the biggest and brought him down at 400 yards.......Within about three minutes of the death, the birds of prey appeared circling high above us, watching and waiting. We only took the head and skin, as the yaks were too feeble to reach this spot. It was not much of a head, 44 inches, but it was a beginning.' Next morning, he spent skinning and dressing the head. Later, he saw several poli on the way 'but my rifle was with the baggage some way behind.'

He had many more encounters with poli, some too small to bother about, some made his mouth water but were too far. His diary for 26 July is worth quoting at length. 'I rose at 2.30 a.m. and set off alone at 3 o'clock. It was difficult picking one's way amongst the boulders in the pitch darkness and I had to be particularly careful not to knock my rifle. I reached the place in the dry bed of the burn that I had fixed on the evening before just as the first grey light turned the world into ghost-land. I crouched breathlessly peering into the half-light, imagining every rock was a poli, a leopard or a bear. Suddenly I saw a shadowy object on the hill-side about 200 yards above me and up wind begin to move. It came down the sky-line, a poli. Then followed a procession, sometimes a single one, sometimes three or four — every one silhouetted against the sky as he passed. It was too dark to distinguish the big fellow and I waited until they had all passed — about a quarter of an hour — then crept down and across to a little spur overlooking the nullah where I heard stones rattling about."

'Knowing that there was good grass there I felt I really had the old man this time. On peering over I found that instead of feeding on the rich grass they had gone a little way up the opposite hill-side and were already out of safe range. At the same time I was horrified to see a black figure stalking along the same hill-side, straight towards them! It was that prince of fools, Aibash, who had come out to see the fun. I was powerless to warn him and I knew that if they did not spot him they were bound to get his wind. So I just waited and watched the tragedy. Aibash got to within about 80 yards of them before they got his wind. He never saw them till they were about three-quarters of a mile away, when he waved to me frantically to inform me of his great discovery! (Shahbash, Aibash, you saved their lives !)'

'When he eventually came down I told him in mixed Persian, Pushtu, Hindustani and English what I thought of him. But as he only speaks Turki, in which language I don't know a single swear word, I'm afraid a great deal of it was lost on him. Poor old man! He may have been a famous shikari once — which I can scarcely believe — but since he married three wives, I am afraid he has lost his prowess on the hill. I think the cold last night may have numbed his brain. He dithered all morning, left my camera in one place and my waterproof in another, and jolly nearly set my tent on fire fooling about with the candle-lamp.'

Capt D.G. Lowndes of the Royal Garhwal Rifles undertook a shooting expedition to Lahul in 1929, over the Rohtang and the Baralacha, and spent a month looking for game. But game was scarce, 'particularly ibex, and only two burrhel (Ovis nahura) were shot. Large numbers of snow-cock were seen and a few teal were shot on the Unan river.'

Among the reviews, is one of *Big Game Shooting in the Indian Empire,* by C.H. Stockley, DSO, OBE, MC, FRGS, FZS. The impressive titles of the author leave the reviewer, A.M. David, no option but to use the reviewer's well-worn standby 'This book fills a long-felt want among sportsmen.'

Native Dwellers of the Hills

Sherpas were not mentioned in Vol. I. Col. Tobin, writing his account in Vol. II of climbing in the Sikkim Himalaya, was obviously upset by Douglas Freshfield's comments on his porters, made in 1899. 'Freshfield hardly seems to appreciate properly the Sherpa and Bhutia porter', he remarks acidly, 'but it must be remembered that he wrote in 'pre-Everest' days.'

Freshfield's criticisms, whatever they happened to be, were counterbalanced by the comments of the two Norwegians Rubenson and Aas, in 1907, about whom Tobin was able to say, 'Another source of satisfaction was the capability and reliability of the Sherpa porter, especially when properly equipped and well-treated.' Could it be that Freshfield's porters were not properly equipped or well treated?

Tobin adds a footnote to Bauer's account of the attack on Kangchenjunga. He said, 'It is only fair to the Tibetan porter to remark that on this expedition he had little chance of showing his qualities. Two of the best of the Bhutias, Lobsang and Sonam Tobgay, had only returned two months earlier from Farmer's ill-fated expedition, on which they had suffered severely, and these two crocked up at the end of the first month. Another, Namgyal, who had been severely frost-bitten on Everest, also fell out early. It was no doubt largely on account of these failures that Sherpas were entirely selected for the high work, while to the Bhutia was allotted the arduous but less spectacular task of humping the stores up the glacier, where there was little room for initiative. The experience of other expeditions employing a mixed force of Sherpas and Bhutias has been that there is little to choose between these two splendid races, either in courage or endurance.'

When W.E. Buchanan reached Sangla in the Baspa valley in October 1917, after crossing the Rupin pass in deep snow, he paid off the coolies and 'gave them cigarettes. They immediately started back for the pass, singing and cheerful. I had found all the Bashahris in the Pabar and Rupin valleys most pleasant to deal with. Few Europeans seem to visit them and at first I often found them running off to hide when they caught sight of us. But it was easy to gain their confidence by means of a few simple medicines, and their faith in a tabloid administered by a European was most touching. It was however amusing to note how the inhabitants of each village on the way to a particular pass would assure me that the pass was the worst in Asia, while the one in the neighbouring valley, which would entail using other coolies, was ridiculously easy.'

On a subsequent visit in 1926, Buchanan noted that conditions had changed because the *begar* system of coolies had been abolished. 'Delay in collecting coolies is therefore inevitable and it is more economical in time and money to employ mules.'[15]

H. M. Glover, making the circuit of Kanawar Kailas, noted that the population was increasing and there was less food. The problem was met by polyandry and surplus girls were devoted to celibacy. All of them worked in the fields and were as cheerful a set of maidens as can be found anywhere in the world.

---

15. Philip Manson, who served in Garhwal, has described the end of the begar system in his very readable novel *The Wild Sweet Witch*.

Capt. A. A. Russell, on his shikar trip to the Pamirs, finally taught his men to pitch his tent correctly. 'The men have at last learned to pitch my tent properly. They never seemed able to get the pegs in the proper alignment.' When he pointed out to Nadir (who had previously been with the Roosevelt and Morden expeditions) that the canvas would certainly tear with the pegs as he had put them, Nadir protested that his life would be forfeit if it did. 'My remark that my tent was infinitely. more valuable than his paltry life 'filled him with admiration.'

Lt.-Col. Reginald Schomberg crossed the Muz-art pass in the Central Tien Shan in October 1929, after a heavy snowfall. 'The summit had 8-10 ft of snow, and if an animal or man stepped a few inches off this beaten track, the snow engulfed him at once and it was a hard task to dig him out again...No Turki has ever any thought for anyone except himself, and consequently caravans were always meeting here, with resulting head-on collision, followed by a panic among the animals which floundered and plunged, as they sank deeper into the fine dry snow. Victory went to the strong.'

Mrs Visser, writing of their expedition to the Karakorams, praised the admirable way the Ladakhi porters had behaved throughout.

Lieut. D. M. Burn, who undertook some triangulation on the northern slopes of Tirich Mir, writes about some Chitrali superstitions of the horse-shoe of peaks over 24,000 ft called the Istor-O-Nal. The coolies of the previous year refused to move on the glacier, so he called up some Chitralis of the Tirich area. At one point, they also refused to go further. 'Like all hill people who only touch the fringe of civilization, the Chitrali is steeped in superstition. He peoples the mountains with malevolent fairies and the glaciers with strange monsters. Ruined houses and graveyards are the abode of jins and spirits. The home of the fairies is Tirich Mir and on first seeing this great mountain it is easy to understand the strange fears and imaginings of this child-like people. High up on the slopes of Tirich Mir exists a marble-lined tank in which the fairies bathe and it would be certain death for anyone foolhardy enough to approach it. But lower down a pool where the fairies washed their clothes was all right.'

'After some months in the country, we were told by our *jemadar* that we were extremely foolish to keep so many dirty coolies at high camps if we wanted fine weather. The dirty clothes incensed the fairies. I personally took the *jemadar's* advice and after four days the weather changed the day after the coolies were sent down and the work was soon completed.'

There was a quaint superstition about the Thui pass. If anyone was killed while attempting to cross it, there would be clouds on the pass for three days, giving his spirit time to reach heaven. The year before, a Gilgiti fell into a crevasse and lost his life, and sure enough, for three days there were clouds. There was also a legend about a dragon about 20 ft in length living in the crevasses, with very hard scales which no bullet could penetrate. Unlike European dragons, this one had no wings and didn't breathe fire.

There were also the jins who chose old deserted dwellings to live in. They sometimes assumed the guise of a dog or a cow until they came upon an unsuspecting traveller.

Glover, on his way round Kanawar Kailas, noted some local legends. Kailas was reputed to be the abode of the souls of the dead. The death of the Rajah was said to be heralded by a cascade of water bursting from the centre of a precipice high above Shongtong and visible from Chini. Kali the terrible inhabited the heights and the villages, deotas were worshipped. A road was built by the Forest Department through the cliffs at the base of Kailas; man after man was killed, and after each death, goats had to be sacrificed to appease the evil spirits. At last an avalanche carried away the subordinate in charge and two of his assistants. The village of Mehbar was partially destroyed and the workers bolted. More goats were sacrificed and this allowed the work to be finished to peace.[16] As William McKay Aitken says in his article on Burha Pinat, Vol. 48, 1990-1991, 'Actually one does come across some spooky happenings in the wild'.

Some General Notes

The membership of the Himalayan Club had risen from 250 to 302. The Annual General Meeting was held on 24 February 1930 in H.E. the Commander-in-Chief's room in New Delhi with Field-Marshal Sir William Birdwood, Bart. in the chair.

The library, established in Simla, had bought 119 books. There was a total of 298 books, of which 155 had been presented and 143 purchased. Issues of books had not been many, amounting to 44.

There is an account of the first air journey to Gilgit. Four Wapiti planes went from Risalpur to Gilgit, via Chakdara where they refuelled, on 28 March 1929: over four hours. We can imagine the excitement at Gilgit. All the Mirs and chiefs of the Agency were collected to

16. It would be pleasant to think that the peoples of the hills are somehow free of the prejudices and bigotry that reign at lower levels, that they are imbued with the 'spirit of Lacarno' that Mason referred to. Alas, they seem to be as human as any other. So, at present, the pleasant Shangrila of Bhutan is undergoing some ethnic problems; Nepali-speaking people (45% of the country's population, many settled there for generations) of southern Bhutan, the Lhotshampas, are fleeing. Some 100,000 of them have already fled and truckloads are reported to be pouring into Nepal every day. (International Herald Tribune, 17 September 1992.)

see the wonderful "flying carpet" of the Sirkar....None had ever set
eyes upon on aeroplane....Gilgit, our nothernmost outpost, has been
linked up with India. The raiders of Tangir, Darel, and of the other
little republican States and unadministered independent territory enclosed
by Gilgit, Swat, Chitral and Hazara, will have realized that they are
no longer immune from punishment; and already the gentle suggestion
of an aerial visit by the Political Officer at Gilgit has settled with
blood money an account opened by certain Darelis.[17]

There is an obituary of Colonel Sir Thomas Hungerford Holdich,
1843-1929, an authority on the NW Frontier and an officer of the
Survey of India. He had accompanied Roberts on the famous march
to Kandahar. The obituary is 7 pages long and records an exciting
life. There is also an obituary of H. H. Maharaja Sir Chandra Shamsher
Jang Bahadur Rana, GCB, GCSI, GCMG, GCVO, Prime Minister and
Marshal of Nepal, 1863-1929. He was keenly interested in Himalayan
travel and exploration, and though Government policy did not allow
him to permit Everest expeditions in his territory, he contributed generously
to them. 'Had he lived, he would certainly have become a member
of the HC.' And what would he have said about the degradation
brought about by mass tourism?

Among the advertisements, it is interesting to see that Carew &
Co., Rosa UP, advertise Rosa XXX Rum matured for ten years in
wood, and Shahjahanpur Rum for coolies. The publishers, Thacker,
Spink & Co. advertise 'Binding cases in full art vellum, gilt lettered,
for each volume from the publishers.' Does our library have a collection
of Journals bound in art vellum?

The editor, Kenneth Mason, remained the main-spring of the Journal.[18]
Besides contributing articles and many footnotes, he seems to have
been mainly responsible for writing 'Notes on Expeditions' and 'Book
Reviews', and we can imagine him spending many precious hours
pressing his authors to write their accounts and submit them on time....

SUMMARY

A browse through the Himalayan Journal, Vol. II, and its relevance
to the present day.

---

17. In 1956, returning from the Har-ki-Doon, we engaged some porters from the
village of Osla. They were accustomed to seeing planes flying overhead, but
had never seen a car. The buses at Chakrata caused much alarm and wonderment.
18. A curious fact: Mason seems to favour the American z to the English s in
words like civilization, organization and so on. In our day, the z seems more
or less to have taken over.

EXPEDITIONS AND NOTES

1

TOWARDS GORICHEN

An exploratory visit to Gorichen and Nyegyi Kangsang's Portals

BIMAL CHANDRA GOSWAMI

THE PEAK GORICHEN (6488 m)[1] is one of the rarely seen peaks in the Panchakshiri range of the eastern Himalayan range in the NE of Tawang district of Arunachal Pradesh. Nyegyi Kangsang (7047 m) is the highest peak of the Panchakshiri range, and Kangto (7090 m), which towers nearby, is the highest peak of the Kangto range. On the 22 October 1992 five members from Assam Mountaineering Association left Guwahati for Tawang to get the inner line permits to go to Gorichen's base camp. The deputy commissioner was very helpful and not only did he give us our permits but sent wireless messages to Assam Rifles posts, gave us a jeep to take us back to Jang, and also sent an assistant to help us get porters, known as LCs (load carriers) here. We reached Jang on the 28th, but inspite of the *Gaon Bura* (village headman) trying to help us we could not get porters till the 30th. According to local practice LCs can take parties only till the next village, from where another lot of porters have to be hired. Their rates were Rs. 25 per day. The people of Tawang district are Monpas — a tribe of Buddhists, whose dress and life style is very Tibetan. Many of them inhabit the northeastern part of Bhutan contiguous with Arunachal. The airport and rail head closest to Tawang is 460 km away in Tezpur, Assam. The inner line starts from Balukpong about 50 km away. The river Tawang chu which starts from Gorichen and its neighbours enters Bhutan near Zumla, and later enters Assam as the Manas.

---

1. See H.J. Vol. 47 p. 156. — Ed.

Four of our LCs were women, and they were tough and fast. We left Jano at 9 a.m. for Rhobasti, a distance of 10 km, and reached it at about 12.30 p.m. after crossing the river Mang chu. There we were welcomed by *Mukha* (mask) dancers. Dancing and drinking continued for a long time and the *Gaon Bura* kept assuring us that LCs will be provided for us the next day. The next day he did not even recognise us! On 1 November we got five, 3 men and 2 women. The next day's march is a long and hard slog of about 28 km to Thingbu (3350 m). It is a quaint, attractive and sparsely populated village of just 20 persons. Radishes and cabbages are in abundance here, and we procured some. We could not get any porters from here, but on 3 November we hired two horses, and were accompanied by the *Gaon Bura* till half the distance to Mago. The route to Mago is risky with steep gorges and cliff-hanging narrow tracks. Mago is 18 km away, and is at 3380 m. From Mago a route goes directly north to Lungar near the Indo-Tibet border, which is just a 4-5 hours' march away. That night we stayed at an Assam Rifles camp. The *Gaon Bura* arranged for two horses and a young LC called Dorji, who had gone upto C1 with the successful Assam Rifles' expedition. (Incidentally, according to him and others only two expeditions to Gorichen have been successful, Assam Rifles and Assam Regiment), We reached our next camp at Jithang 11 km away, and at 4020 m.

Next day we started trekking to Merethang by covering a distance of 11 km to an altitude of 4270 m. It was the first foggy, wind-swept day of the trek, and so we had to cook in a rock house meant for a yak keeper. Here there are no sheep, only yaks. From here Merethang is a four day difficult trek to Munna near Dirang between Bomdi la and Se la.

Next day was once again spotlessly clear, and we started at crack of dawn to reach the Gorichen base camp at Chekrasom (5030 m). Nearby is the confluence of two rivers. One comes from the northeast from what appears to be the Takpa Shiri peaks picking up water enroute from the Kangto and Nyegyi Kangsang glaciers. The other one comes from the northwest draining the big glacier on the flanks of Gorichen I and II. We could make out a thin track along the true left bank of the river coming from the Takpa Shiri peaks. That track petered out after a while. There are rumours that every three years some Tibetans circuit Nyegyi Kangsang from the north. May be these tracks have something to do with that. We climbed another 300 m towards the ABC site to get a better look at Gorichen II, which we intend to get up, on a trip later this year. We spent about two hours there in a sharp freezing wind, and then rushed down to the base camp. By several forced marches we reached Jang on the 10th, and on 12 November 1992 we were back in Guwahati, having at last found out what we could not learn from any army account of Gorichen; that this is not a difficult climb, and has a comparatively easy approach.

The best season to attempt these peaks will be from the third week of October. Between ABC and C1 climbers will have to carry water with them, as it is not available at all till beyond C1.

This trip also helped us realise that in the northeast we have so many fantastic untapped climbing and exploratory opportunities that we can spend our life time here without ever thinking of visiting the crowded mountains of Garhwal, Kumaon and Himachal.

Members : Bimal Chandra Goswami (leader), Kishore Kumar Baruan, Nilu Talukdar, Madhuja Mahanta and Kami Cherin, a Sherpa from Darjeeling.

Summary: An exploratory trek to the base of Gorichen (6488 m) in Arunachal Pradesh, in October-November 1992.

2

A SECRET MOUNTAIN

Haj Gyala Peri Expedition 1986

YOSHIO OGATA

Prologue

YARLUNG TSANGPO JIANG (river) takes its source from western Tibet, runs to the east for 1500 km in Tibet plateau. After leaving the plateau it crashes through an immense gorge, beneath the high Himalayan peaks and comes down to the south. Then, this river is called the Brahmaputra in Assam. This was a river in riddle, for this has a very deep gorge which is called 'Great Bend' and nobody could approach it.

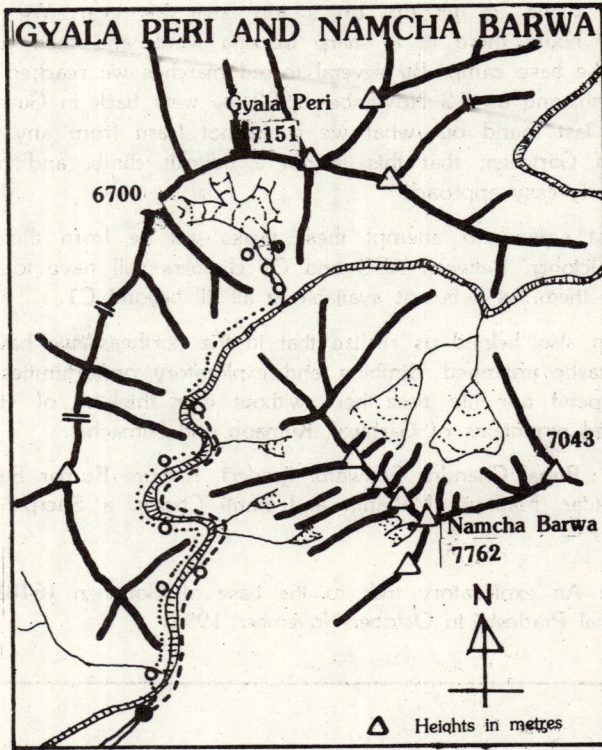

GYALA PERI AND NAMCHA BARWA

Gyala Peri 7151

6700

7043

Namcha Barwa 7762

N

△ Heights in metres

The Great Bend area has two high peaks, Namcha Barwa (7782 m) to the south and Gyala Peri (7151 m) to the north.

We had deep interest in some peaks in eastern Tibet, and we applied for climbing permission for the peaks to the Chinese Mountaineering Association (CMA) since 1983. Gyala Peri is also one mountain of great interest to us.

We, at last, got the permission to climb Gyala Peri through the good offices of CMA and Tibet Mountaineering Association (TMA) and we dispatched a reconnaissance party to the Gyala Peri in 1985.

After one year, our 6 members started for an expedition to the secret mountain by the side of the river in riddle.

Approach

We left Japan on 1 September 1986 with other three HAJ's Tibet expeditions and arrived at Lhasa on the 4th.

On the 8th we left Lhasa in 2 jeeps with a liaison officer, a translator and an assistant liaison officer. We drove about 400 km to the east and arrived at Bayizhen.

On the 9th, we met Yarlung Tsangpo Jiang and proceeded along the river. We crossed a log bridge and we called on the chief officer of Mainling Xian at his office. The chief officer told us that 100 porters were already arranged and a manager would be joining us.

We left Pe for the base camp at Gyala Peri on the 11th. We crossed the river at Pe. We were now introduced to a weird looking craft call a 'tru' which consisted of two conifer dug-outs, each about 12 m long, lashed together. It was a most unwieldy craft, but carried a big cargo. The first day we crossed the river, after which we went along the Tsangpo and arrived at the Susong. It had rained hard in the night.

On the 12th, we marched in a drizzle and the next day in rain. The second day, we camped at the Chube. Chube is the last Tibetan village on the left bank of the Tsangpo.

On the 13th, we marched for 6 hours and came to the place which is opposite the Gyala village. This place is called Gyala gompa. It is said that Tibetan people make a pilgrimage once in their lives to this gompa. On the 15th, we traversed along the right bank of Gyala Peri river with porters. The current seemed threatening and we judged it would be impossible to cross the river on foot. So we allowed porters to return home and we camped next to the ford. On the next day, however, some porters came with logs to make a bridge. We tied up with them to set a bridge. This bridge is called 'China-Japan friendship bridge.' And then, the place of base camp was decided.

Climbing

Staying in base camp for 2 days, we went scouting for advance base camp (ABC). We climbed on a moraine ridge to the end and decided to set up ABC there at 4200 m.

The unloading began from 22 September. Then we began climbing from the 26th.

On the 26th, 2 team members, Ohta and myself left ABC for route making to C2. As we climbed through the complicated glacier a big avalanche swept the west wall of Gyala Peri. We had a narrow escape. Avalanches occurred many times on the west wall afterwards. We changed our climbing route.

We climbed up on a ridge on the right corner of the west wall. And C1 was set up on a thin snow ridge on 3 October.

We had to climb in deep snow, a pinnacle-like gate, and knife edges. Moreover we climbed on a snow wall which we called 'Zebra Rock'. And at last we set up C2 at 5650 m.

We stood on the south ridge at 5800 m on the 12th. We could see the flow of Yarlung Tsangpo river right beneath. On the south ridge, the steep snow wall seemed to be leading up to the summit. But the bad weather continued.

We could see the blue sky at last on the 16th. Our party began route making for the upper part. We had a hard time marching in the deep snow which reached up to our waists. The route-making party set up C3 at 6300 m on the 19th. Ogata, Ohta and Hasimoto stayed in C3.

The next day, we set up 4 fixed ropes in the blizzard and came back to C2. On 21st, Tobita, Imamura and Fujiwara set up C4 at 6700 m and we were ready for the attack.

Attack

We took a short rest at 3200 m and we were refreshed. Then we began the attack.

The first party which consisted of Ogata, Hashimoto and Imamura left BC for C1 on the 25th. And reached at C4 on the 28th.

The 3 members left at 4:50 a.m. on the 29th. The snow wall was getting steeper and we had to put some fixed-ropes. Then, we gave up the climbing because of the lack of time and got back to C3.

The second party which consisted of Tobita, Ohta and Fujiwara left C4 at 7.10 a.m. on the 29th. But the weather continued to be bad. They, too, had to give up the climbing.

Hashimoto, Imamura and myself were charged with the attack again. We left C3 at 6.15 a.m. on the 30th. We had a hard time marching in the deep snow, and arrived at the beginning of the summit wall. It was 3 p.m. But we advanced without any hesitation. It took 3 pitches of climbing. Moreover we climbed into a very steep couloir with very acrobatic movements. In all, it took 11 hours for us to reach the summit since we had left C3. We left the summit in the violent wind at 5.15 p.m. and we descended to C3.

We could set foot on the summit due to the last-minute effort. The long climbing concluded on 1 November.

Epilogue

We left precious footprints on a page of the history of eastern Tibet. The height of the Gyala Peri officially is announced at 7151 m. But we felt it was higher, for we measured it by our altimeter.

Members: Kazuo Tobita (leader), Yoshio Ogata (climbing leader), Takeshi Ohta, Yasuhiro Hashmoto, Hirotaka Imamura, Takuo Fujiwara.

Summary: The Himalayan Association of Japan (HAJ): Gyala Peri expedition 1986, which made the first ascent of Gyala Peri (7151 m) from September to November 1986.

Photos 38-39-40

3

ON TOP OF THE WORLD!

ERIC SIMONSON

THE EXPEDITION WAS composed of twenty-two members. These included: Eric Simonson (leader); George Dunn (assistant leader) and others. Fourteen of the members were mountain guides who had nineteen previous attempts on Everest between them.

Two different groups reached Xegar, Tibet on 10 March. Ten members travelled via Lhasa, Tibet and accompanied 5500 kg of food and equipment that had been shipped to China in November, 1990.

The rest of the team came via Kathmandu, Nepal where they met the 13 Nepalese members (two cooks and 11 Sherpas). Propane fuel, oxygen and additional food were also brought in from Nepal.

Base camp was established 13 March at 5150 m.... the end of the road. It took 50 yak loads to establish C3 (advanced base camp) a week later at 6520 m. Severe weather and heavy snow made it impossible to reach the North Col (C4) at 7000 m until 30 March. The route to the Col was fixed with ropes and eventually 130 yak loads reached ABC.

C4 consisted of eight tents, walled in and held down by nets. Extremely high winds, often exceeding 70 mph for days on end, prevented C5 at 7800 m from being established until 21 April. Without the ropes, which were fixed on this part of the route, there would have been many days where we could not have climbed due to the extreme wind across the North Ridge.

C5 was again an extremely windy site. Only our four China-Everest tents were able to withstand the beating. C6 at 8230 m was established on 7 May after a long hard push that forced Wilson, Whetu, Okita,

Edwards and Van Hoy to all spend the night in a tiny two-person tent.

Every member of the team who was healthy got a summit bid. This was the plan from the beginning. On 15 May the top was reached by Simonson, Dunn, Politz, Sloezen, Lhakpa Dorge Sherpa and Ang Dawa Sherpa. An attempt the next day by Hahn, Rheinberger, Perry, Huntington, Ang Jangbo Sherpa and Pasang Kami Sherpa was turned back by high winds. Perry stayed at C6 while the rest descended and made the top solo on 7 May. An attempt on 21 May by Wilson, Edwards, Van Hoy, Frantz, Whetu and Okita was also partially stopped by the wind. Only Whetu and Okita were able to push on and reach the summit. Okita was forced to bivouac on the descent at 8530 m when he couldn't find the fixed ropes in the 'Yellow Band' above C6 in the dark. Fortunately, he suffered no ill effect from his adventure. Wilson remained at C6 for three more days and was joined by Mann for another attempt on 24 May. On the previous day, Peck had been stopped below C6. Ultimately, Mann was forced to turn back, but Wilson reached the summit.

All summiters used oxygen, though Wilson and Perry tried initally without. Van Hoy and Hahn also tried without, but were unable to stay warm enough. The team left base camp on 28 May and all members returned home via Kathmandu.

Rongbuk Research

Dr Daniel Mann of Fairbanks, Alaska, joined the expedition to study the extent and age of glacial moraines in the Rongbuk valley at elevations between 4500 m — 6400 m. His work consisted of examining different glacial moraines looking at the condition of weathering pits, the degree of soil development, and the diameters of lichens on surface boulders. The lichens help in estimating the age of the geological formations and as such were absent from the youngest moraine but were up to 30 cm in diameter on the older moraines. Lichens of this size in polar regions are known to be more than 5,000 years old.

Dr Mann's preliminary results show that the Tibetan ice caps assumed by previous geologists to have covered Tibet during the last Ice Age in fact never existed. Instead, the Rongbuk valley has been glaciated intermittently over the last 100,000 years by ice originating locally on the north side of Everest. The field research also showed that moraines of four different ages are preserved in the Rongbuk valley.

One of the difficulties encountered by Dr Mann was locating organic materials suitable for radio carbon dating. Nonetheless, he brought back two peat samples which will be analyzed in the laboratory to determine more precise dates from some of the younger moraines.

After this work is complete, Dr Mann's results will be utilized through a process of correlation to provide similar information for some of the better vegetated valleys to the east and south of Everest.

Ohmeda's Results

Oxygen saturation research sponsored by the Ohmeda Corporation was conducted by expedition member Jonas Pologe during the 74 days on Everest. The purpose of this research was to add to our knowledge of how people adjust to and compensate for the effects of high altitude.

The climbers were connected to an Ohmeda 3740 Pulse Oximeter, a device which reads the oxygen saturation of the arterial blood continuously and non-invasively. Arterial oxygen saturation (SaO_2) is the percent of hemoglobin that is bound to oxygen divided by the total amount of hemoglobin available. At sea level the normal SaO_2 is about 95% whether at rest or during exercise. The resting SaO_2 of the climbers, on the first two days of the climb, averaged about 83% while the average SaO_2 at the end of exercise was roughly 69%. Over the course of the climb the resting SaO_2 levels increased only slightly while the average end of exercise saturations increased significantly to just over 80%.

This rather dramatic improvement in oxygen saturation during exercise in the acclimatised climber had not been noted before and certainly helps to explain the improvement in performance one achieves with a long stay at high altitudes. Further analysis is expected to explain the physiology behind the improved SaO_2 readings observed.

The Video

Participating in the expedition was Markus Hutnak of Pullman, Washington, who was responsible for the expedition's video work. Markus operated two Ricoh video cameras, one of which went all the way to the summit, courtesy of Brent Okita. Based on this and additional footage from Mark Whetu and Charlie Peck, Markus is currently preparing an in-depth video account of the climb. A CBS affiliate, KIRO-TV in Seattle, Washington, is helping with the project.

Markus' 30 hours of Hi-band 8 mm videotape includes dramatic footage of a climber being blown down the glacier during a windstorm, climbers on the summit, a yak trapped in a crevasse, a tent burning, and an actual recording of the radio broadcast from the highest point on earth.

A Clean Climb

The American North Face Everest Expedition made a commitment from the beginning to minimize its impact on the environment of

Mt Everest. At considerable expense we removed dozens of yak loads of trash from Advanced Base Camp at 21,400 feet. This included picking up after previous expeditions. At Base Camp we worked with the Swedish and British groups that were there and collected close to 8,000 pounds of garbage. This was trucked out to the village of Xegar for proper disposal. We challenge and encourage future expeditions to do the same and preserve Everest's unique and fragile environment.

Summary: The climb of Everest (8848 m) by the North Face by an American team in summer 1991.

4

INDIAN (ITBP) EVEREST EXPEDITION, 1992

HUKAM SINGH

CLIMBING EVEREST IN the early days was quite different to what it is today. Ours was the 8th expedition reaching the Everest base camp on 29 March, 1992. Thereafter, Dutch, Chilian, Spanish and French expeditions followed taking the tally to a full one dozen plus male and female climbers wanting to make a solo attempt. In fact there was a strong feeling that the base camp may not be able to accommodate so many expeditions. This resulted in some kind of race to reach the base camp but it was not a mad race. With so many expeditions together the base camp had assumed the status of a high international camp, a mini form of earth summit! While we missed the peaceful atmosphere and solitude that our predecessors enjoyed at the base camp it was a new experience and also good fun for so many climbers to be together. Our initial efforts to generate good-will, healthy understanding and promoting mountaineering fraternity greatly helped us in warding off negative factors and we were able to maintain not only the route through hazardous Khumbu icefall, Western Cwm, Lhotse face and beyond to the summit but were able to create a healthy understanding and friendship. The route through Khumbu icefall, initially opened by the British expedition was subsequently maintained by other expeditions turn by turn. Since ours was one of the well organised teams with adequate means, the leading part played by our team was greatly appreciated by others.

On 1st April, when we had just commenced load ferry from BC to C1 at about 8 a.m., one Sherpa of the New Zealand expedition fell into the crevasse sustaining a serious head injury and bleeding profusely. While his Sherpa companions were dazed, hesistant to rescue him, members of our expedition not only rescued him from the deep crevasse but also evacuated him down to the BC safely on an improvised stretcher. The victim was given medical treatment by the doctors available at the BC and the next morning he was evacuated to Kathmandu by helicopter.

The climbing activities beyond the base camp even when so many members and Sherpas were moving up and down always remained a pleasant sight without any evidence of ill-will inspite of some limitations of space for C1. Our C1 was rather ahead of others The stones and big boulders generally falling at night from the Lho la side, did frighten us, although our tent remained well protected throughout. C2 at the foot of Everest massif on the upper limit of Western Cwm was safe. A huge quantum of garbage and filth are lying near this camp site. Not much effort has been made by any expedition, including ours, to fully clean the litter and garbage. Setting up C1 on 2 April, and C2 on 6 April, we moved to tackle the steep icy Lhotse face. Among the one dozen expeditions there were two commercial expeditions having members from different countries and they were very conscious about safety and success for obvious reasons. There were also expeditions who were supposed to climb by the Southwest face and South Pillar but ultimately followed the traditional South Col route. This caused some heart burn and animosity. Because of these human factors, we decided to move ahead to attempt the summit, assuming as if we were all by ourselves to do the task. We set up C3 (7400 m) on the terrace of icy formation of the Lhotse face on 14 April. The weather was so far quite favourable and our efforts continued to open route to South Col. We succeeded to set up C4 at South Col on 21 April and thereafter geared up our efforts to stock C4. At this stage while other team members went down to BC and even down to Lobuche for rest and recuperation, our team continued spearheading the climbing activity. Our effort to make the summit attempt on 30 April was aborted when a 6 member summit party had to return from the South Col due to hostile weather. Thereafter our subsequent attempt to make the summit bid on 2 May was also foiled, again due to bad weather and our summit party had to return from the South Col. In fact the weather was so dicey that on the night of 1 and 2 May, Dr Kulkarni the leader and Raymond Jacob member of the civilian Pune expedition breathed their last close to the South Col. We learnt about their tragic death only on the morning of 2 May when Ms Santosh Yadav spotted them and informed us on walkie-talkie. The rescue efforts made by Ms Santosh and party with oxygen and glucose water were of no avail since they had already frozen to death.

After the death of Dr Kulkarni and Raymond Jacob the weather on 2 May became worse, rendering any effort beyond the South Col suicidal. While climbing a tall mountain like Everest, it is always wise to lie low and preserve one's energy when the weather is hostile. This is exactly what we did after 2 May and resumed further attempts for the summit only after a week when there was slight improvement in the weather. Leaving BC on 7 May the 6 member summit team under S.D. Shrama reached the South Col on 9 May and on 10 May even though the weather was not favourable they set out for the summit leaving C4 at 4 a.m. 3 members, Papta, Sunder and Tajwar returned midway because of one reason or the other, while Sunil, Prem and Kanhaya Lal continued, reaching the South Summit at 11.45 a.m. and made contact on the walkie-talkie. At 2.30 p.m. they came on air again and said that they have just reached the Hillary Step. At this point some other expeditions had also switched on to our frequency and were monitoring our walkie-talkie communication. Normally the climbing to the summit from Hillary Step takes about 40 minutes and we expected the trio to reach the summit latest by 3.30 p.m. but there was no contact, causing us further worry and anxiety. Finally at 4.15 p.m. they came on air giving us the most eagerly awaited news of their success. They had finally made it.

First success on Everest for 1992 on 10 May opened the flood gates and on 12 May a record number of 32 members including 5 members of our team with Ms Santosh Yadav reached the summit, creating history. Other summiters were Mohan, Lopsang, Sange and Wangchuk. Santosh, Sange and Lopsang spent $1^1/2$ hrs on the summit waiting for Mohan who had finished his oxygen to join them on the summit. After doing the normal rituals on the summit, four of them started climbing down together, with Santosh giving her oxygen intermittently to Mohan till he could retrieve his cylinder from below the South Summit. Around 6 p.m. all of them returned to the South Col safely. Ms Santosh Yadav became 10th woman to reach the summit and the youngest to do so. Khem Raj had to abandon the summit attempt from the South Summit because of some fault in his oxygen system.

Our final summit attempt in which we had 7 members plus 2 Sherpas spent two nights on the Lhotse face and one night on the South Col. They woke up at midnight for the summit on 20 May but the weather created havoc with gushing wind making life miserable.

All the members came down safely from the South Col alongwith tents and oxygen cylinders, but what we could not avoid was frostbite on 3 fingers of Papta. With this we had to finally call off the expedition. Our proposed plan to have the summit meet with the two British climbers climbing along the West Ridge on 20 May was foiled by the hostile weather. When we had thought that everything was over, at the last minute at 4 p.m. on 22 May, when the last load was being brought down to the BC, our popular cook-cum-porter Sher Singh fell into a creavasse very close to the BC and died, making our last experience a bitter one. Our expedition left BC on 24 May with members carrying his dead body. His body was cremated near Lobuche the same day with full honour.

Besides climbing the mountain, we made an effort to also clean the BC and C1 and about 500 kg of garbage and litter were loaded back to Namche Bazar from BC. Some expedition should pay special attention to take care of a number of dead bodies lying at the South Col making it the highest junkyard and also the highest open graveyard on the earth. The dead bodies lying there is a horrifying sight and no religion in the world permits disposal of dead bodies in such a manner. It would be quite desirable to send a special expedition to bring down all the dead bodies from the South Col and give them proper burial or cremation. The base camp of Everest is not so dirty, it is the C2 and the South Col which needs a special cleaning effort.

Summary: The ascent of Everest (8848 m) by an Indian team in May 1992, 8 members reached the summit with many from other teams.

5

TWO SPANISH CLIMBS

FRANCISCO SONA CIRUJEDA

A. SHISHA PANGMA EXPEDITION, 1990

IN 1989 The High Mountain Army Group tried to climb Everest by the North ridge. It was impossible to reach the summit due to the weather and snow conditions, To reach 8530 m wasn't enough for members of our group.

Waiting for another permission for Everest in 1992 our group chose the Shishapangma for 1990 for the following reasons: First, because it is a great mountain, one of the fourteen 8000 ers, second, this mountain hasn't been climbed by any Spaniard and, third, the easy approach route can be made by trucks up to the base camp.

Through our Military Attache in Peking we obtained the permit for this mountain for October. The bureaucracy and the approach to the base camp took eight days. We arrived on 23 September 1990 at the base camp.

Reaching the base camp by vehicles, we had some acclimatisation problems and some members of the group had to descend to Qo-Chiang (3200 m) for better adaptation. On 28 September, nine members of the group were well acclimatised and began setting up advanced base camp (5500 m).

From 1 to 9 October the expedition team was divided in groups which set up C1 (5750 m), C2 (6400 m) and C3 (6900 m) after this work all the groups returned to the advanced base camp to rest and prepare the final plan to reach the summit. It was discussed whether it would be advisable to install another camp near the ridge and all the members agreed that it was possible to reach the summit without this camp, depending on the weather and the physical conditions.

On 11 October with very low temperatures the first group of six people started from the advanced base camp and reached C2 after a long hard day. The following day they climbed till C3 with no problems and had very good acclimatisation. It was decided not to install another camp and to go forward to the summit. Simultaneously another group started from the advanced base camp and reached C1. in order to make a second attempt or support the first group if need be.

Very early in the morning 13 October the first group started from C3 on way to the summit. At 17.30 all the group: Major Santaeufemia, Captain Gan, Warrant Officer Exposito and Staff Sergeant Arellano and the civilian climbers Martinez Selles and Vidal, reached the main summit. After a short rest they returned to C3 reaching it at 22.30 after a long and hard journey.

The following day, 14 October, the weather turned bad and the first group decided to descend to C2 and divided into two groups. Due to the bad weather conditions and the poor visibility one of the groups couldn't find C2 and decided to make a bivouac in the extreme conditions (-35^0 C and 100 Km/h wind). At 01.30 Joan Martinez Selles died due to exhaustion and hypothermia. The other two members of the group who had local frost bites attempted to reach C2, reaching there in very bad conditions.

Joan Martinez Selles was born in Barcelona on 9 July 1957. He was married and worked as a medical doctor. He was one of the best Spanish climbers and he had been to many other expeditions. and on many difficult climbs in the Alps and the Spanish Pyrenees.

Today his body lies on the north Shisha Pangma glacier, the place he chose for his last climb.

B. SATOPANTH, 1991

Satopanth (7075 m) is located in the Garhwal Himalaya and it was the goal of the High Mountain Army Group in the spring of 1991.

The route to the base camp goes along the Ganga river, at the end of the Gangotri glacier, at Gaumukh we continued over the glacier to the base camp which was located at Nandanvan (4400 m). Our base camp was located lower than originally planned due to the great amount of snow which prevented our 70 porters from going any further.

Therefore the 13 members of our expedition had to carry all the equipment by themselves to C1 at Vasukital (4900 m), subsequently we set up C2 (5100 m) and C3 (5950 m), the last one was set up close to the NE ridge which leads to the summit. This ridge is the key to the mountain. It is 800 m long and very steep on both sides.

We needed three days to prepare the ridge with four hundred metres of fixed rope, essential for the security of the climbers on the way to the summit. In addition to the technical difficulties of the ridge (over 65° slope on hard ice), there was a lot of powder snow on top of it making the climbing very dangerous.

On 17 May, four members of the group Major Juez, Warrant Officer Exposito and Staff Sergeant Fernandez and Mora, at dawn, crossed the difficult ridge; it took them two hours. Four hours later they reached the summit at 14.15 hrs. Until then the weather was good but a strong storm caught the successful climbers returning to C2.

The expedition was carried out from 24 April to 30 May 1991 in traditional style, setting up three camps.

Summary: Ascents of Shisha Pangma (8046 m), October 1990 and Satopanth (7075 m), May 1991, by a Spanish army team.

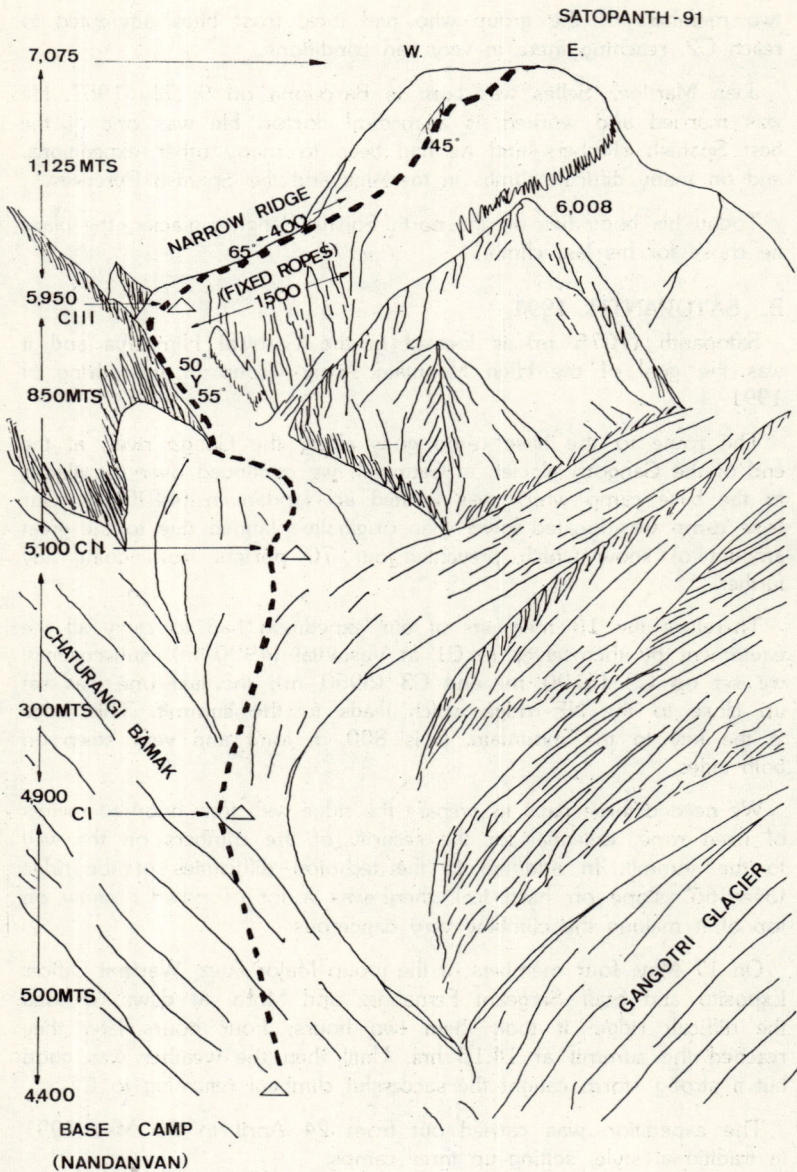

SATOPANTH - 91

7,075

1,125 MTS

W.   E.

NARROW RIDGE

45°

6,008

65°-400

(FIXED ROPES)
1500

5,950
CIII

850MTS

50°
Y
55°

5,100 CN

CHATURANGI BAMAK

300MTS

4,900
CI

GANGOTRI GLACIER

500MTS

4,400

BASE   CAMP
(NANDANVAN)

6

SAGARMATHA SOUTHWEST FACE EXPEDITION, 1991-1992

YOSHIO OGATA

SINCE SIR EDMUND HILLARY AND TENZING NORGAY first scaled Everest, in 1953, 453 people have climbed its summit till now in about forty years. Many kinds of attempts like variation of climbing routes, traversing, climbing without oxygen, climbing in winter or climbing in record time, have been done on the peak because it is highest in the world.

The Everest Southwest Face, which rises straight from the Western Cwm to the top, has attracted many ambitious climbers for a long time. In the autumn of 1969, the Japan Alpine Club went and observed the face, After that, five expedition teams bravely tried to climb it, but all failed. On the 24 September 1975, the British party led by Chris Bonington at last succeeded in climbing the Southwest face to the top. Since then, the Southwest face has been attacked several times by other teams and two of them also succeeded. One was the Russian team in 1982 and another was Czechoslovakian in 1988. But no climbers had tried it in winter.

Gunma Mountaineering Association planed to climb the Southwest face of Everest in winter from December 1991 to February 1992, as the commemoration event of its fiftieth year. In Japan, there are 47 prefectures and each of them has a mountaineering association, Gunma Mountaineering Association is also one of them. Since the expedition to Dhaulagiri IV in 1971, Gunma Mountaineering Association has sent seven expeditions to the Himalayan area and made some good climbs. For example, the first ascent of the southeast ridge of Dhaulagiri I in 1978, first winter ascent of the south face of Annapurna I. Noboru Yamada, who was called Japanese Reinhold Messner because of having scaled many 8000 m peaks, was also the member of this association.

In the spring of 1991, we went to Kangchenjunga as the pre-expedition for the Southwest face of Everest in winter. This expedition was supported by the Government of India, and we could get the permission to climb Kangchenjunga from the Sikkim side. In that Kangchenjunga expedition, three Indians and three Japanese scaled the top and most of the members could reach 8000 m. We successfully finished the

SAGARMATHA

Summit 8.848m

South Peak

South-East Ridge

C5 8,350 m

South Col

C4 7,600 m

West Ridge

South-West Face

C3 6,900 m

C2 6,500 m

C1 6,020 m

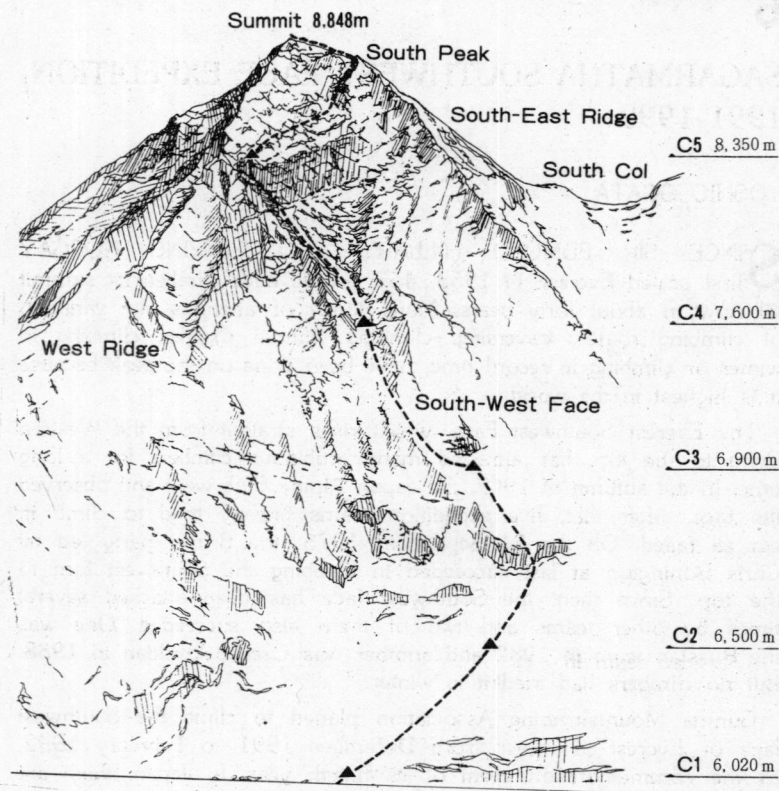

pre-expedition training. Some other members separately trained on Broad Peak in Pakistan, Nun in Kashmir and Korzhenevskaya, Lenina, Kommunizma in the Pamir in summer.

Our team divided into four parties and landed in Kathmandu from 3 October to 21 October 1991. After that, we trained for acclimatisation on a 5099 m peak behind Pheriche, and on Pokalde peak (5806 m) opposite Lobuche. We established the base camp on the Khumbu glacier (5350 m) on 11 November. We started route-making through the icefall, together with two Korean expedition teams attempting the South Pillar and the South Col routes. We had finished route making by 16 November. We trained for the acclimatisation for 6000 m and started ferrying loads to the C1 from 20 to 27 November.

After three days rest, we started climbing the Southwest face of Everest in December. We established C1 situated on top of the icefall at 6020 m on the same day.

The next day, we pitched the C2 on the Western Cwm (6500 m). We found a big schrund at the base of the Southwest face at 6700 m which had to be negotiated and one could cross it through a narrow gap. The upper part of the schrund was an easy ice-snow slope, the average gradient of the slope was 35 degrees approximately.

We established the C3 below the big rock (6900 m) on 5 December.

We stretched 23.5 pitches of fixed rope from C3 to C4, the average gradient of the slope was 40 degrees approximately. C4 was pitched on a slope at 7600 m on 11 December.

On 11 December, we started route-making for C5. We extended the route 18 pitches up toward the left couloir cutting into rock band from 11 to 14 December.

On 15 December, we reached the entrance of the couloir. We went up some 1.5 pitches of narrow gully to the amphitheater at the top. The couloir has a width of three or four meters, and is full of small chockstone almost covered with snow. The average gradient of the couloir was 50 degrees approximately. We reached just below the ramp at 8300 m. We had found old fixed rope on the very steep rock face presumably belonging to the 1975 British expedition.

On 16 December, we succeeded in overcoming a key point of the rock band. We took over and led up the rock face, turning slightly right onto a ramp. We went up the ramp and took care not to drop stones. The ramp was covered with loose and brittle rock. We extended the route one more pitch up on the ramp.

On 18 December, we stretched for another short pitch, until we were almost sure that the way was clear to reach the site for C5 (8350 m). We had found remains of the British C6 in that place.

On 21 December, we attempted to put up C5 but failed, the tent poles were broken by the cold and strong wind. Then the real winter cold descended on the mountain. On 25 December, we were compelled to evacuate from C2 to the base camp. After five days, we started climbing again, but we were troubled with strong wind almost everyday in January, and we went up to the upper camp and again went down to C2 without result.

On 8 January, we established C5 (8350 m), and two members stayed the first night at C5. Next morning, they went down to C2 due to the severe cold at C5.

We decided to continue the expedition until 15 February, then on the 25 January began to climb up again for the last try. As the expedition extended over a period of two months, we had to remake the route in the icefall area. The crevasses between C1 and C2 became large, and the Southwest face became rocky because the snow on it was blown away day by day.

On the 29th, two members reached C5 again but from the next day a terrible storm began to disturb them so they had to go back to C2.

In February the violent wind still didn't stop roaring on the West Ridge and South Col. We could do nothing but wait for good weather.

The endless strong wind made Sherpas depressed in spirits and they refused to support us to C5. After discussing all the problems on the 9 February we decided to give up.

On the Southwest face in winter season, we climbed 50 pitches on the ice and snow wall from the foot to the rock band which is one of the most difficult points. There is no need to climb the slab as there is in spring or no danger of avalanches like in autumn, so the condition of the face, we think, is best in winter. Due to the good condition of the face, we took only sixteen days from the base camp to the rock band. In spite of that good process, we couldn't scale the summit. There were several causes for the failure but the most serious one was the wind. Whenever the strong wind began to roar we could do nothing.

Of course we were prepared for the cold, the strong wind and the rock-fall before attacking the face, but the power of nature was mightier then we expected. Since we settled at the base camp, 83 days had been spent but on most days we did nothing but wait for the violent wind to stop.

We would like to attempt to climb the Southwest face against next winter season, and we hope to succeed next time.

Summary: A Japanese attempt on the Southwest face of Everest (8848 m) in winter, 1991-92.

7

SAIPAL, 1992

CHUCK EVANS

THE SIX OF us left riotous Kathmandu with two climbing Sherpas, cook, general factotum, liaison officer and 63 porters in two buses on 7 April. 24 weary hours later we arrived in Surkhet — a hot dry town on the edge of the Terai; north of Nepal Ganj in far west Nepal.

Our 18 day journey to base camp commences with a ludicrously hot 1520 m ascent. Pleasant rhododendron forests follow as we walk through the foothills to reach the major jungle-covered range of hills south west of Jumla. The Haudi Lagna at 3050 m affords us our first hazy view of Saipal (7031 m), miles to the north. Having descended to the Sinja Khola (which runs west from Jumla into the Karnali) another hot climb takes us to Manma, the local district capital, at the end of our first week.

From Manma we follow the Karnali river northwards for five days. The gorge is arid cactus country, and whilst of high caste Hindu origin, the people of the very poor villages here adopt Tibetan style flat roofed houses. In this season the river thunders by, a wonderful turquoise colour, and from far above is like a golden ribbon leading us onwards.

Finally we reach the Kuwari Khola, our secret backdoor to Saipal and Humla. We leave behind the Karnali zone and enter fragrant pine forests, and deep in the river valley, a wet and wonderful jungle of walnut and bamboo. This constricts to a narrower gorge before opening out into a parkland of Alpine meadows with one or two small Bhotia settlements. Here the goats which we have previously seen laden with bags of rice, kicking up dust further down trail, are grazing on green grass. Potatoes, chang and curd are available. There is a freshness in the air and for me a sense of home coming.

Base camp is established in front of the east face of Saipal on 26 April at the foot of the terminal morraine of a short flattish glacier which leads to broad open meadows. Trees cover the hills on either side — it is very low (3650 m) but very beautiful.

The Mountain

We make advance base at 3850 m in the middle of the glacier directly below two large icefalls separated by a rock buttress. A continuous barrage of serac avalanches from both sides and stonefall on the buttress renders any direct assault on the face unadvisable.

We therefore turn our attention to circumventing the right hand icefall to the north, and climb a gully and bowl to reach C1 (4800 m) on a hitherto uncrossed pass into Humla. From here attempts to reach the main north ridge along its northeast spur prove unfruitful, and so we decide to push round on the north side of the mountain.

We descend into Humla, and climb avalanche-prone slopes to C2 (5200 m) which is situated on a ridge running north from the northeast spur. Progress from here is blocked by an arete running between the mountain and Kerang Tse (an unattempted 6000 m satellite peak of Saipal). We push towards this, but retreat at the prospect of another descent and re-ascent under an unpleasant icefall. Our final effort is to climb to a high point of 5700 m on the northeast spur.

We meant to turn our attentions to the approaches to the east ridge, south of base camp, but unfortunately, descending from C2 on 16 May, Nuru Sherpa and I were involved in separate falls, sliding on unstable snow down the same gully. I was relatively unscathed but Nuru broke his ankle and hurt his back. John Holland and Roshan made a marathon journey over the Chote Lagna (4700 m) to Simikot to order a helicopter (possibly the first Westerner to cross this pass also). Nuru was evacuated on 21 May from the north side of the mountain. His ankle was operated on and pinned in Kathmandu, but he now seems to be making a reasonable recovery.

Humla

When we left Kuwari Khola base camp on 26 May it was covered in spring flowers. Yaks from the nearby Humla village of Chala were grazing in the summer pastures at Sain. However the north side of the 4560 m Sankha Lagna pass into Humla was still deep in snow. We struggled down through mist into a canyon and next day crossed the Kerang Khola to reach Chala — a primitive collection of flat roofed houses huddled together below a broad ridge separating the Humla Karnali and Kerang Khola rivers.

Next, we travelled north west into Humla, rejoining the Karnali at Muchu on the Tibetan trade route. The region was much more Alpine and less arid than expected. We had panoramic views of several unnamed 6700 m peaks to the north of the Karnali as well as exceptional views back to Saipal and of the south side of Gurla Mandhata in Tibet.

Humla was also less poor than we had been led to believe. Whilst the people clearly led a subsistence life-style, the Bhotia villages we passed through as we followed the Karnali back east to Simikot, were well ordered and prosperous in comparison to those further down river. The Thakuri villages neared Simikot were dirtier and seemed poorer through a lack of organisation, despite superior natural resources.

Members: Chuck Evans (leader), Frank Evans, Matthew Heffer, John Holland, Caroline Purkhardt and Julia Wood.

Summary: An attempt on Saipal (7031 m) in summer 1992 by a British team.

Photo 41

8

ANNAPURNA SOUTH FACE

TONE SKARJA

A QUICK AND unhindered journey from home to base camp; establishing C1, and C2 and C3 according to plan; reaching a height of 6700 on the south face; reaching the Tent Peak, 5587 (as a trekking aim); shooting a film in the valley (by Hrovat) and on the south face (by Bozic). However, none of the main aims was reached, nor the summit.

September 1992

19-24th: Departure from Ljubljana to Kathmandu, and covering additional 200 km to Pokhra.

25-29th: March from Dampus Pedhi near Pokhra (1000 m) to base camp, which was put up behind the eastern moraine of the Modi (or Annapurna) glacier at 4050 m.

29th: Establishing base camp (4050 m) on a fine grassy plain.

30th: Establishing C1 (5050 m) on top of a rocky promontory.

2 October 1992: Fixing ropes in a rocky couloir and establishing a relay tent (for deposit or as a temporary camp) at 5600 m.

4th: Establishing C2 (5900 m) on the ridge, which further up develops into a pillar leaning against the upper sections of the south face 1000 m higher.

6-10th: Gradual advancing towards the ridge and along the ridge. The ascent straight through the gully running parallel to the ridge was not considered prudent on account of the falling ice. It might have been negotiated only in the alpine style of climbing. The only remaining possible route of ascent led via extremely tiresome cauliflower-like formations of ice and snow on the sharp ridge, and via vertical and overhanging mushrooms of rotten ice and snow. The height 6400 m.

11-14th: Heavy snowfall stopped any progress on the mountain. Furlan and Supin were caught at C2 and pinned down by avalanches for four days, but they saved the camp by continually shovelling away the snow. Fresh snow reached 80 cm at 5600 m, and 150 cm at 6000 m. The snow also stopped the alpine style French rope, just below the top of the dierdre which we also had in mind. They were forced to retreat, and on the way down Pierre Beghin was killed. His rope mate Jean Christoph Lafille managed a three-day solo descent, and found refuge in our base camp.

15-17th: Continuing the ascent along the ridge, which, owing to the masses of fresh snow, was hardly suitable for climbing. The height reached by climbers was 6600 m.

18th: Levelling out a platform for deposit, later used for C3, at 6600 m.

19th: Soon above C3 Groselj and Bozic gave up their attempt to advance, and so did Jamnik and Ravnik, finding the ice and snow conditions unmanageable.

20-21st: After extreme strain Tomazin and Bence reached 6700 m, which was to be the highest point, and decided that at that speed of advancement the summit was out of the question.

21st: At 14 hours the decision was taken that the attempt on the British route should be given up. Instead, one or two ropes should try climbing via the extreme right wing of the south face and reaching the east ridge, which, though long, is not considered to be technically very demanding. The first to try this second choice were Groselj and Bozic, with the assistance of Sherpas.

23-25th: Groselj and Bozic found the orientation hard, but finally found a passage to the foot of the ice-slope leading up to the ridge. However, they had been delayed so much that they were forced to return. Moreover, a heavy snowfall set in. During the afternoon of the 25th and before the morning of 26 October base camp had 15 — 30 cm of fresh snow; at 5000 m the amount was 60 cm, and at 6000 m more than 100 cm, without, in fact, anyone of us knowing it at that time. Groselj and Tomazin were supposed to undertake another attempt, as Bozic had given priority to official duties.

In the meantime we began to clear up the former route. Bence and Supin had been taken ill and left the expedition on 24 October. On 26 October Kajzelj, Ravnik, Jamnik, Rupar and Bozic decided to leave the expedition, since, as they declared, they found any further attempt futile. Furlan joined them on account of a frostbitten finger. In the morning of 27 October they left base camp.

Only while clearing up C2 in the afternoon of the same day did we notice the enormous amounts of fresh snow which had fallen in higher parts. At least one week of fine weather would have been needed to let the snow on the gently sloped glacier settle and make walking possible. Until then the climbing on the steep slopes leading up towards the ridge was not safe either. Now the last chance of reaching the top was gone, as we had no more time left. So the remaining members left base camp on 28 October. Groselj, however, remained there until 1 November to supervise the transport of the equipment back to the valley.

On Annapurna, less than 30% of the expeditions are successful, and the death toll is one third, which means that out of three successful climbers who reach the top only two survive. Unfortunately, successes stand in no clear relation to fatalities. We did not succeed and we all returned home, but our safe return is nothing but a gilded pill. Our intention was to climb Annapurna, as well as to return safe and sound. We returned with the necessary experience, which will make it easier for us to accomplish the great adventure after two years when we hope to come again.

Summary: An attempt on the south face of Annapurna I (8091 m) by a team from Slovenia in October 1992.

9

ITALIAN KANG GURU EXPEDITION, 1991

GIANCARLO CONTALBRIGO

K ANG GURU (6981 m) lies to the NE of Annapurna Himal, to the west of Pisang peak, near the Tibetan border. It is placed in an area still closed to tourism and virtually unexplored.

That zone is bounded on the west by the river Nar Phu and on the south by the Marsyangdi river. Between the Kang Guru and the Tibetan border there are a lot of unnamed peaks, about 7000 m high, not easy and still to be climbed.

The expedition was mounted, equipped and put into execution by five people who had preceding experiences of alpinism in the Himalaya, Karakoram or Andes:

Contalbrigo Giancarlo (leader), Bidese Domenico, Dal Santo Imerio, Ghitti Paolo, Pagiusco Fiorenzo.

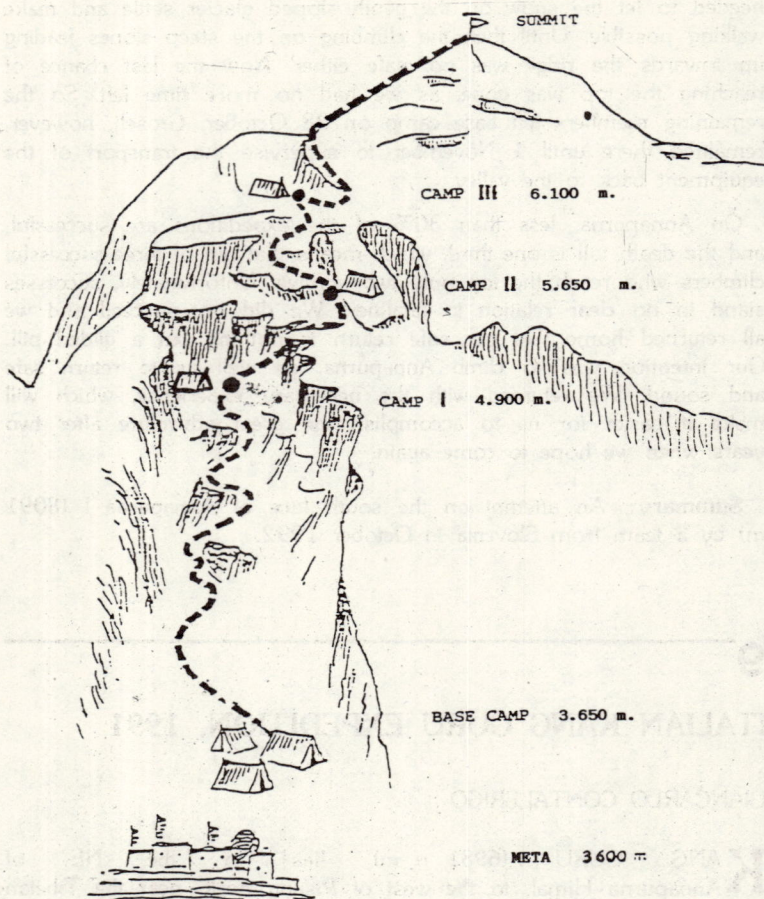

24 September: We leave Milano.

27th: From Kathmandu to Dumre, 160 km, by bus in 9 hours.

28th: Arrival at Phalesangu (670 m) by truck in 5 hours.

29th: We begin the trip on foot towards the north along the Marsyangdi valley.

2 October: We reached Kodo (2600 m) a village near Chame, where a police station blocks the entrance into the Nar Phu valley, which goes up straight until Tibet, on the west side of Kang Guru.

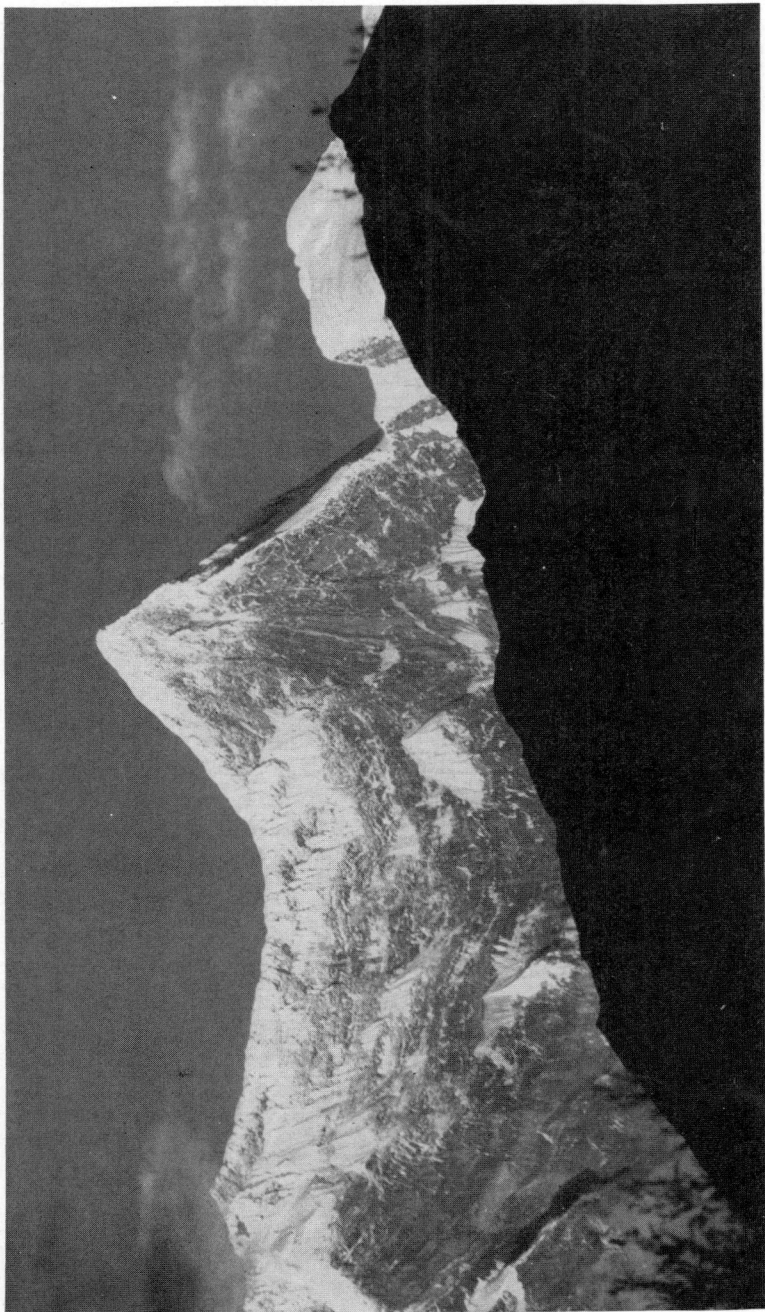

39. Namcha Barwa.

Note 2

Note 2   40. Namcha Barwa.

Note 7   41. Saipal.   (Chuck Evans)

4th: We established BC at Mera (3600 m), a deserted village, left after the invasion of Tibet by China in 1959. Now there are still a lot of terrace cultivations. It is situated at the foot of the mountain, at the point where a great ravine strikes up into its west flanks.

7th: After ascending the ravine, at first going up on steep grassy slopes and then on gravel with danger of injury from stones, we established C1 (4900 m) under the big rock barrier which seals off the upper end of the ravine.

11th: Second ferry from BC to C1.

12th: From C1 we climbed a steep and frozen canal, about 400 m high, very dangerous because of the stones. After a difficult passage through the rock curtain, where we fixed 50 m of rope, we arrived above the rock wall (5300 m). Then we climbed up on moraine until a prominent rock rib between the hanging glaciers. Under that rib, in a very safe place, we sited C2 (5600 m).

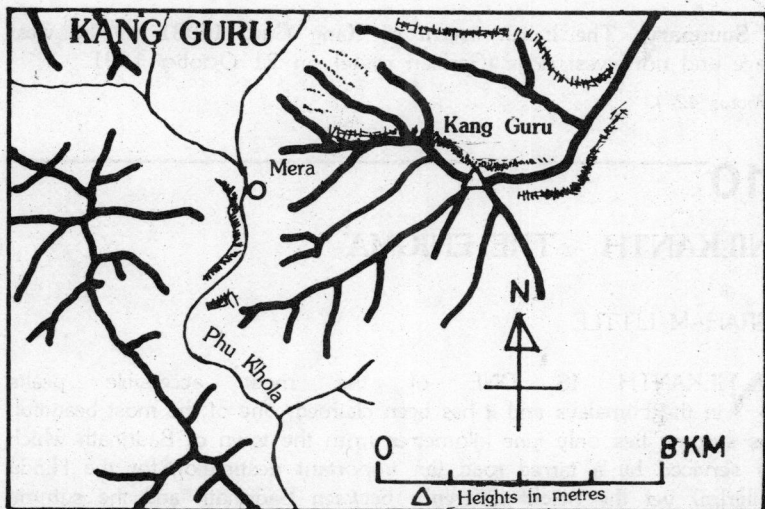

13th: Exploration to find the route to C3.

14th/17th: Rest at BC.

20th: Climbing the glacier with small crevasses, we arrived at the upper side of the west face. We established C3 at 6100 m in a spacious and safe plateau under the NW ridge. The west spur which joined the W face to the NW ridge protected the place from the wind. We pitched 3 tents: two for us, one for two Sherpas who accompanied us to the summit.

21st: Departure from C3 at 4 o'clock. We climbed the spur consisting of good ice (gradient 40°-45°) for about 400 m and we arrived at the very long and sharpened NW ridge. It ascended to the top by a lesser gradient but with a lot of big cornices.

At 10.15 a.m. the summit was reached by G. Contalbrigo, D. Bidese, P. Ghitti, F. Pagiusco and the two Sherpas.

It was windy and very cold (–30°).

At 11 a.m. we began a fast descent to C3. We closed the camp and went to C2 where pitched the tents to sleep.

22nd: Arrival at BC.
24th: Departure from BC.
30th: Arrival at Kathmandu.

This was the first Italian ascent of the peak and the fourth ascent of the peak.

Summary: The Italian ascent of Kang Guru (6981 m) by west face and northwest ridge (German route) on 21 October 1991.

Photos 42-43

10

NILKANTH - THE ENIGMA

GRAHAM LITTLE

NILKANTH IS ONE of the most accessible peaks in the Himalaya and it has been claimed, one of the most beautiful. Its summit lies only nine kilometres from the town of Badrinath which is serviced by a tarred road (an important destination for the Hindu pilgrim) yet the height difference between Badrinath and the summit of Nilkanth is 3500 m! Since it was first seriously attempted by Frank Smythe in 1937 it has received around a dozen attempts yet only two claimed ascents; the first of which (1961) is now widely discredited. So what is it about this mountain, named after Shiva the destroyer, that has attracted so much interest yet has proved so difficult a challenge? It is without doubt a striking, relatively isolated peak and one that has 'climb me' written all over it! However, for

TOPOGRAPHY OF THE
SOUTH-EAST RIDGE
OF NILKANTH.
By G.E. Little

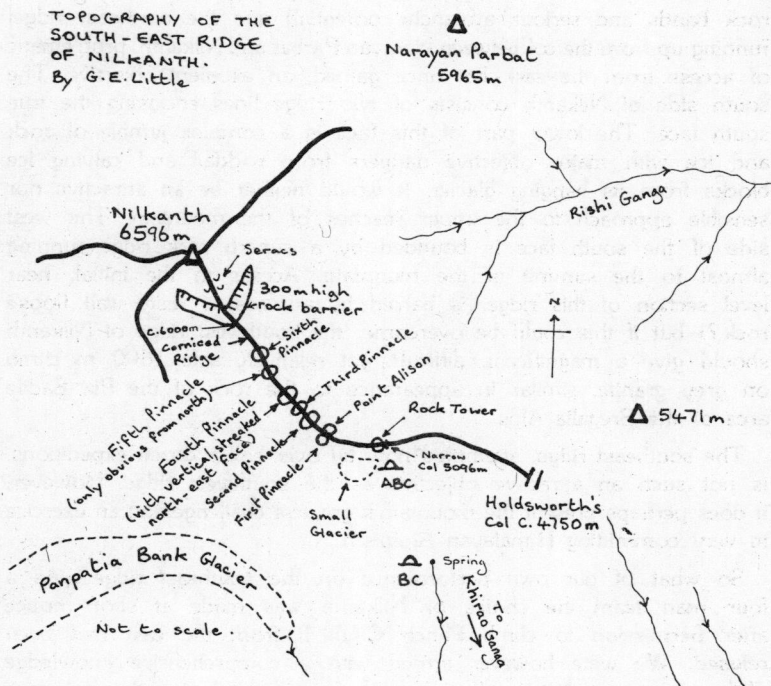

△
Narayan Parbat
5965m

Nilkanth
6596m

Seracs

300m high
rock barrier

c.6000m
Corniced
Ridge

Sixth
Pinnacle

Third Pinnacle

Point Allison

Rock Tower

△ 5471m

Fifth Pinnacle
(only obvious from north)

Fourth Pinnacle
(with vertical streaked
north-east face)

Second Pinnacle

First Pinnacle

Narrow
Col 5096m

△
ABC

Small
Glacier

Holdsworth's
Col C.4750m

Rishi Ganga

N

△
BC Spring

Panpatia Bank Glacier

Not to scale.

To Khiroa Ganga

all its accessibility and relatively modest altitude, Nilkanth is a mountain
with formidable defences. Its ridges are long, often pinnacled and loose,
its faces steep, seracced and avalanche prone and it's isolated position
encouraging a localised weather system. In recent years it has been
designated a restricted peak, with access by non-Indian expeditions
limited to a southerly approach and that only after payment of hefty
not to say unreasonable peak fee of 3000 US $!

The one accepted ascent of Nilkanth (although details of this event
are sparse) was by an Indo-Tibetan Border Police team in 1974.
Approaching from the Satopanth Bank, they ascended the north face
encountering difficult and dangerous snow conditions en route. Since
this expedition, all subsequent attempts on Nilkanth have been from
the south.

Nilkanth has four main ridges and four main faces but as my
detailed knowledge is confined to the southerly approach, I will restrict
my comments to this, other than to say that from distant inspection

the east face looks vast and dangerous (primarily snow and ice with rock bands and serious avalanche potential) and the northeast ridge, running up from the col between Narayan Parbat and Nilkanth, problematic of access from the east, but once gained, an excellent objective. The south side of Nilkanth consists of two ridge lines enclosing the true south face. The lower part of this face is a complex jumble of rock and ice with major objective dangers from rockfall and calving ice blocks from its hanging glacier. It would neither be an attractive nor sensible approach to the upper reaches of the mountain. The west side of the south face is bounded by a superb rock ridge running almost to the summit of the mountain. Access to the initial, near level section of this ridge, is barred by a massive, rusty wall (loose rock?) but if this could be overcome, the southwest ridge of Nilkanth should give a magnificent, difficult, yet relatively safe 1600 m climb on grey granite, similar in appearance to the rock of the Piz Badile area of the Bregalia Alps.

The southeast ridge, attempted now by over half a dozen expeditions, is not such an attractive objective as the southwest ridge. However, it does perhaps present the mountain's greatest challenge and an exercise in very committing Himalayan Alpinism.

So what of our own performance on the southeast ridge? As a four man team the choice of Nilkanth was made at short notice after permission to climb Panch Chuli II from the east had been refused. We were however armed with a comprehensive knowledge of previous expedition activity on the ridge thanks to the generous help of Roy Lindsey whose team had attempted it in 1990.[1]

Approaching via the Khirao ganga, base camp, sited on a level shelf to the east of an area of huge boulders and pinnacles at 4400 m, was established on 11 October in a snowstorm. The ascent of steep grass and a boulder field took us to an advanced base camp (on snow) at a height of 5000 m, below the steep rusty wall which flanks the southwest side of the initial section of the southeast ridge. The remains of a small glacier lay west of the camp (presumably the one mentioned by Smythe). Above this mini glacier lies an obvious pointed rock tower (with gullies either side of it). To the northwest of this feature a very shattered rock wall holding much unstable scree gave access to the ridge by following the general line of a pale band of rock until a short snow gully cut up onto the crest. From a large spike of pale rock, where the gully meets the ridge crest, three easy mixed pitches along a classic Alpine ridge led to its abutment with the foot of the 1st Pinnacle. To the east of the abutment lies

---

1. See H.J., Vol. 47, p. 79. — Ed.

a monolithic buttress with a steep open gully on its left. We climbed the left side of the open gully via cracks and ledges (50 m IV, old fixed rope) as the right side, although appearing easier, was very loose. A further pitch on mixed ground led to a rightwards traverse along a snow covered shelf. Another one and half pitches of broken snow covered ground led to the base of a steep rock barrier.

This barrier has two lines of weakness, the left, a formidable hanging groove, the right, an easier angled shattered groove. The left hand groove proved to be the safer line and easier than appearances would suggest (40 m IV, old fixed rope). The right hand groove is the outfall of a scree scoop above. 60 m of scrambling over very unstable ground took us to a small col between the rock towers of the 1st Pinnacle on the left and Point Alison on the right. The steep ice gully dropping from the col was abseiled for 40 m (old fixed rope) then a mixed traverse was made to gain a small snow col directly below Point Alison. After some snow levelling this provided a perfect site for one bivi tent.

A short level section of ridge ran up into a wide area of shattered rock which was climbed by a wide scree filled groove on the right to gain a little saddle. From this point a traverse right on steep soft snow linked into another wide, loose groove leading via short rock steps to two in-situ pegs at the top (old fixed rope). Moving out of the groove we gained a small snow basin flanked by a rock edge on the left and a snow arete on the right. The snow in this basin proved desperately unconsolidated and it took over an hour to climb a 60 m section close to the rock edge, swimming up thigh deep snow lying on rock slabs to a 'thank god' belay and ledge. One tent was later pitched at this point. Thankfully firmer snow led up on the right to the steepening of the summit tower of the 2nd Pinnacle. A tricky rightward traverse, (Scottish II/III) allowed an exposed descent down the arete to gain a big tablet of rock at the small col between the 2nd and 3rd Pinnacles.

In search of Smythe's by-pass ledge a line was first attempted on the west flank of the 3rd Pinnacle. This involved a promising start on steep sound rock to gain a descending, narrowing, slab ramp ending in a cul-de-sac of overhanging loose flakes. These were surmounted in a breath holding mode but the ground beyond did not give cause for optimism and a dignified retreat was made. The second foray up a short wide crack left of the arete gave some encouragement, leading to a ledge running out onto the more wintry east flank of the pinnacle. Needless to say this also proved to be bad news but in frustration a route was forced across it by dint of climbing more in keeping with a Scottish grade VI than the Himalaya. The most memorable sequence involved torquing off two axe tips, mantleshelving onto the same and then dynoing for a flat hold! The crest regained, an easy traverse led to a short descent onto the commodious snow col between the 3rd and 4th Pinnacles. The lower flank of the 4th Pinnacle looked slabby but fairly broken and not a major obstacle. However this proved to be our high point (C 5600 m). The following day another line was climbed on 3rd Pinnacle, on the left of the arete, up a wall, a chimney then a suicidal zig-zag traverse under, around and over evil piles of balanced blocks, 65 m V+, following roughly the line of the abseil descent of the previous day.

Whilst sitting, firmly lashed to a big flake on the top of the 3rd Pinnacle the early afternoon cloud drew aside like a stage curtain to reveal my first really good view of the summit ice pyramid of Nilkanth, defended by a continuous slabby 300 m high rock barrier with a base at 6000 m. I gazed in awe! It looked massive even at a distance of nearly two kilometres.

I've been mountaineering for over twenty five years and if I've learnt anything during this time it is to listen attentively to my inner voice. On the top of the 3rd Pinnacle it spoke to me very clearly. It said 'get down'. I abseiled the pitch and voiced this message to Dave and Matt. They didn't argue. We went down, stripping the mountain the following day in a snowstorm.

No article about Nilkanth would be complete without a reappraisal of the achievement of Frank Smythe and the enigmatic Peter on the southeast ridge in 1937 (see chapter 22 in *The Valley of Flowers*.) Was it a piece of very bold and futuristic climbing or, as some subsequent expeditions to the mountain maintain, a flight of fancy? Although Smythes' description of the climb is, at times, difficult to relate to the topography of the southeast ridge, there are enough identifiable references to confirm that he had a fair knowledge of this complex feature. However, he dismisses the technical difficulty and looseness of much of the ridge, makes no mention of extensive snow covered sections (surely there would have been a lot of snow about high on the ridge in late August) and doesn't mention any abseil descents. On the positive side Smythe's description of 'a thin and elegant pinnacle with sheer sides falling into unknown depths.... which proved to be more a step on the ridge than an isolated point' perfectly fits the 3rd Pinnacle, although if this was his idea of perfect granite ('the best that Chamonix can muster') I wouldn't like to climb on what he would consider to be poor rock!

If Frank and Peter did indeed reach the crest of the 4th Pinnacle as can be inferred from his narrative and his description of their final view towards the great rock barrier and the summit snow and ice slopes of Nilkanth, then one can only marvel at their route finding, the speed of their ascent, their relative indifference to loose rock and their technical proficiency. Truly mountaineers well ahead of their time!

The veracity of Smythe's attempt will probably never be absolutely confirmed and indeed fits in well with the general mountaineering history of Nilkanth, with much doubt being cast on other expedition claims. I prefer to believe that Smythe did indeed reach the 4th Pinnacle, further than any other expedition has yet reached and that seismic activity has since altered the character of the ridge (there was a magnitude 7 earthquake in 1991 in this region).

The mysteries surrounding Nilkanth will perhaps never be dispelled but it is certain that the 'Queen of the Garhwal' will continue to attract the admiring gaze of pilgrim and tourist alike, will continue to tempt the mountaineer with its great ridges and faces and will forever be regarded as one of the Himalaya's most beautiful and challenging mountains.

Members: Graham Little (leader), Dave Saddler, Matt and Gareth Yardley.

Summary: An attempt on the southeast ridge of Nilkanth (6596 m), by a team of Scottish mountaineers in October 1992.

Photo 44

11

ASCENT OF CHAUKHAMBA I

Col. AMIT C. ROY

THE MASSIF OF CHAUKHAMBA (4 pillars) lies between the Gangotri glacier in the west, the Bhagirathi glacier in the north and the Satopanth glacier in the east. The four peaks constituting the Chaukhamba massif, situated in the Garhwal Himalaya, are challenging requiring technical skill.

The magnificent, 30 km long ridge has 6 summits Pt. 6763 m, Chaukhamba I, 7318 m, Chaukhamba II 7068 m, Chaukhamba III

6974 m, Chaukhamba IV 6854 m, Pt. 6638 m. The summit of Chaukhamba I was scaled by a French expedition, led by E Frendo in 1952. An Air Force expedition, led by Air Vice Marshal S. N. Goyal put four members on the summit in 1967.[1] Our team of the Indian army Signallers decided to climb from the hazardous northeast approach in May-June 1992. The expedition was flagged off on 11 February from New Delhi to coincide with the 81st anniversary of the Corps of Signals.

After drawing rations and making miscellaneous purchases the team concentrated at the roadhead at Mana on 20 May. Recce and ferry to the base camp commenced on 23 May. The base camp was occupied by the team on 30 May.

After the base camp was occupied at Bhagirath Kharak (4570 m) the recce, route opening and ferry to the advance base camp commenced. The route to the advance base camp was hazardous due to heavy snowfall, bad weather and huge rockfalls en route. The advance base camp, with total stocking of food, gear and stores was occupied on 5 June at 5150 m.

Simultaneously recce to and the establishment of C1 (5490 m) commenced by selected members and was finally occupied on 8 June.

In spite of extremely foul weather on 9 June, the members of rope 1 and 2 moved up through ice-walls, crevasses and avalanche-prone areas by fixing climbing ropes for more than 360 m to locate a suitable place for atleast two climbing tents to be pitched. On 10 June, good progress was made to recce and dump the gear and food-stuff, but a suitable site for C2 could not be found, therefore, we had to dump the items in one tent on the approach to C2. Although the slope was exceedingly steep and the loose waist-deep snow made the going very tough, the team members remained undeterred. C2 was finally occupied by the members of rope 1 and 2 on 11 June at 6250 m.

Studying the prevailing weather situation, I decided that the summit should be attempted from 14 June onwards, since 14 to 18 June would provide the advantage of full moon nights.

The first summit party consisting of 3 officers and 1 other rank (Capts Sanjeev Singh, Nadeem Arshad, Vipin Verma and L/Nk Mohammad Ayoub Sofi) left C2 at 0400 hours on 14 June for the summit. As anticipated they had to undertake 7 to 8 hours of steep climbing.

---

1. See H.J. Vol. XXIII, p. 102. The peak has also been subsequently climbed by Indian expeditions — Ed.

Note 9   **42-43.** Kang Guru: Italian route on the peak.

44. Graham Little on the third pinnacle (5500 m) on the
SE ridge of Nilkanth (6596 m).

Note 10

(D. Saddler)

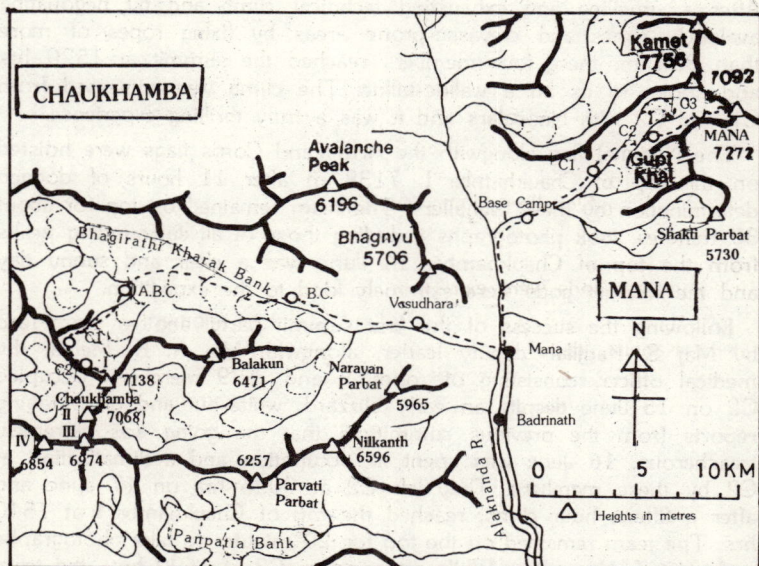

CHAUKHAMBA

Avalanche Peak
6196
Bhagnyu 5706
Bhagirathi Kharak Bank
A.B.C.   B.C.
Vasudhara
Balakun 6471
Narayan Parbat
5965
7138
Chaukhamba
C2
II   7068
III
IV
6854   6974
6257
Nilkanth 6596
Parvati Parbat
Panpatia Bank

Kamet 7756
7092
O3
C2
C1   MANA 7272
Gupt Khal
Base Camp
Shakti Parbat 5730
Mana
MANA
N
Badrinath
Alaknanda R.

0   5   10 KM
△ Heights in metres

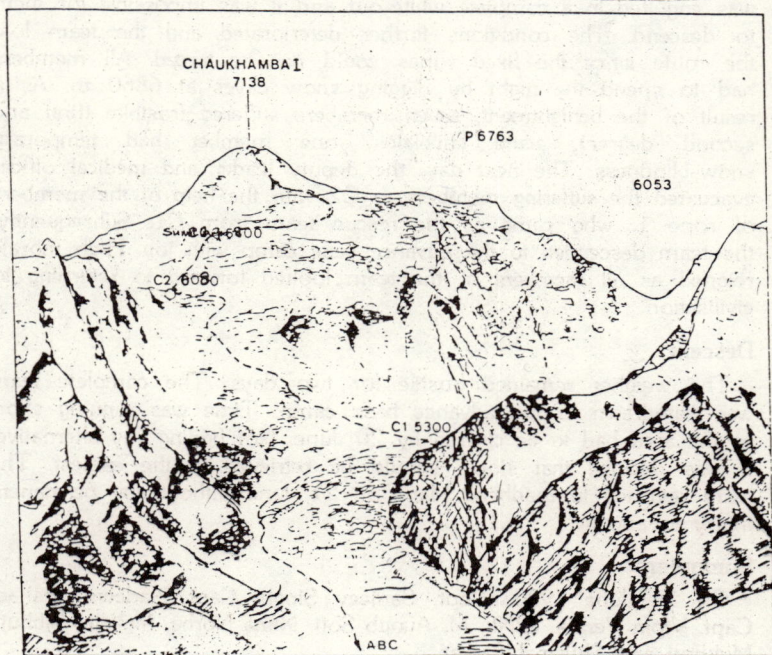

CHAUKHAMBA I
7138
P 6763
6053
Summit 6800
C2 6080
C1 5300
ABC

After a gruelling and exhausting technical climb and by negotiating avalanche-cones and crevasse-prone areas by fixing ropes of more than 300 m, these four members reached the summit at 1520 hrs and spoke to us on a walkie-talkie. The climb was witnessed from C1 and C2 with binoculars and it was a truly thrilling experience.

The National flag alongwith the Army and Corps flags were hoisted on the top of Chaukhamba I, 7138 m after 11 hours of dogged determination by these Signallers. The team remained on top for about 30 minutes, took photographs including those of all surrounding peaks from the top of Chaukhamba. 14 June was a clear and sunny day and the weather gods were extremely kind to the expedition.

Following the success of the first summit party, another team lead by Maj S. Kanjilal, deputy leader, alongwith Maj A. K. Mehta, the medical officer, consisting of ropes 2 and 3 (9 members) occupied C2 on 15 June despite an early blizzard, white-out and discouraging reports from the previous summitters that the going was extremely treacherous. 16 June was spent in occupation and acclimatisation at C2 by these members. They left C2 at 0025 hrs on 17 June and after a fifteen hour climb, reached the top of Chaukhamba I at 1540 hrs. The team remained on the top for 20 minutes to take photographs and started descending. While returning to C2 at 1600 hrs., the team was engulfed in a complete white-out and it was impossible for them to descend. The conditions further deteriorated and the team lost the route since the fixed ropes could not be traced. All members had to spend the night by digging snow caves at 6860 m. As a result of the benightment, seven members suffered frostbite (first and second degree), acute chilblains, one member had temporary snow-blindness. The next day, the deputy leader and medical officer evacuated the suffering members to C2 with the help of the members of rope 1, who came as the rescue team from C1. Subsequently, the team descended to the advance base camp with joy. High morale reigned as all members of the team looked forward to returning to civilisation.

Descent :

The weather remained hostile for two days. The complete team was withdrawn to the advance base camp. Time was running short as the area had to be cleared by 20 June. Not finding any alternative, it was decided that stores should be retrieved at the earliest. The team returned to roadhead Mana on 21 June without any permanent injury to anyone.

Summiters :

On 14 June 1992 : Capt. Sanjeev Singh, Capt. Nadeem Arshad, Capt. Vipin Verma, L/Nk. M. Ayoub Sofi, Nima Norbu, Makalu, Bibhujit Mukhoti and Shyamal Sarkar.

On 17 June 1992: Capt. J. K. Jha, Capt. V. Dogra, Capt. S. P. Sira, Hav. Umed Singh, Hav. R. S. Yadav, L/Hav. Jarnail Singh and Sigmn. C. S. Champawat. Expedition led by Col. Amit C. Roy.

Summary: The ascent of Chaukhamba I (7138 m) by the Indian army Corps of Signals team on 14 and 17 June 1992.

12

MANA PEAK

Capt. S. P. MALIK

MANA IS LOCATED 36 km north of the Badrinath shrine, beyond Joshimath in Garhwal Himalaya which is a serene and impressive mountain range. Mana itself marks the eastern extremity of the Zanskar range and lies between the high Niti and Mana passes, two of the best known, most trodden and traditional land routes between India and Tibet. Rising enticingly into the sky to a height of 7274 m, the mountain stands like an eternal sentinel, ever watchful, on the Indo-Tibet border and is a standing challenge to intrepid explorers and climbers[1].

There are two known approaches to Mana peak; one is the eastern approach through East Kamet glacier and the other is the southern approach through Nagthuni and Banke Kund glacier. The first person to fall under its spell was Frank Smythe in 1937 who was privileged to be the first to stand on the peak of Mana via the southern approach. In 1988 the east face was climbed by the ITBP (Harbhajan Singh) and the south face by a joint Indo-US Army Expedition team (Maj H.S. Chauhan). Again in 1991, an expedition team under Col K Parbhat Singh scaled the peak via the southern approach.

On 15 May 1992, our entire team with complete stores left for roadhead, Mana village, which is 3 km ahead of Badrinath on state highway No 45. The 47 km journey by vehicle took about 3½ hrs through the mountainous terrain. The site was selected near ITBP location and all rations, stores and equipments were neatly stacked to facilitate their onward despatch manually to Musapani east (Intermediate Base Camp). The height of the road head was 3110 m. On 16 May 92, the team had a hot bath in Tapt Kund and paid a visit

---

1. See sketch map in Note 11. — Ed.

to the holy shrine of Badrinath to invoke the blessings of Lord Vishnu and in a brief ceremony prayed for the success of the expedition. Then the team assisted by the porters ferried loads to Intermediate Base Camp (IBC). After establishing IBC and acclimatising properly, the team, moved to occupy IBC on 22 May 92.

Intermediate Base Camp

Intermediate base camp was located at Musapani east and was occupied on 22 May. The camp was located on the eastern bank of the Saraswati river (3780 m). There is a fair weather mule track, during the post monsoon period only when snow melts away, between the roadhead and BC 7.5 km away and it takes 3 hours one way.

The base camp was established at the base of scree of Nagthuni gad. There is a disused track passing over terraced mountainous terrain with big boulders and ice on the way. The total distance is 7 to 8 kms and it takes 4 hours one way. On 28 May a route opening party of three members was sent to open route to a C1 and select campsite.

C1 (5426 m) was occupied on 2 June. This was an icy ledge which formed the base of the three rocky bumps adjoining the large snowfield having innumerable crevasses en route. The route passed over terminal moraine all along Nagthuni gad. The famous Gupt khal (secret pass) was visible from this camp but the pass was hidden till one reached this camp location.

C2 (6035 m) established. It was located on a ledge at the bottom of a rock with steep icefalls on the southern and eastern side. The route passed over a number of open and hidden crevasses. This area is fully glaciated. The team fixed five ropes to negotiate the crevassed patches to reach C2.

C3 (6706 m) was located in the snowfield ahead of a snow clad dome shaped feature which conspicuously stands out in contrast to the razor sharp longitudinal Mana ridge in colour as well as in shape. The route to this camp passed over avalanche-prone, steep, glaciated, slopes which were corniced and crevassed. This involved technical rock climbing in the first phase where six ropes were fixed. The rest of the route is glaciated and covered with 1m of fresh snow passing over a ridge line with cornices. The movements on this ridge were undertaken with extreme care due to the blizzards and dangerous crevasses and cornices. Six more ropes were fixed in this region and going was extremely slow and technically difficult. It took 5½ hrs to reach C3 covering a distance of approximately 6 km. Three tents were pitched on beaten snow which was powdery fresh and approximately 1 m deep. The most conspicuous characteristic of this camp was the strong easterly blizzard which blew unrelentingly throughout the night. Luckily mornings remained encouragingly bright and clear. But it invariably snowed heavily in the afternoons and continued unabated almost throughout the night.

First Attempt on the Peak

The morning of 11 June was bright and clear. Two ropes left at 0500 hrs. It took six hours to fix five ropes in that chilly morning to cross the base of Mana ridge line where the toughest part of the climb had commenced. It involved traversing through soft knee-deep snow which consumed time as well as energy. When the team was climbing the ridge line of Mana from its base it came under an avalanche at 1430 hrs due to movement of snow. NK Balwant Singh and Ex Hav D Lama who were in the lead were swept down by the avalanche and they were fortunately left suspended on the ropes which were removed by the avalanche. They sustained head, leg and rib injuries due to their being hit against boulders and the hard ice. Some other members also sustained minor injuries and bruises. Most of the much-needed equipment was swept away in the avalanche and some of the items were buried under it. NK Balwant Singh and D Lama were rescued.

Both casualties were evacuated to the base camp on 12 June. The entire team was reorganised on new ropes and two ropes were earmarked for another unnamed peak and one rope for Mana as most of the essential equipment had been lost. Hence, it was found possible to send only one rope to Mana.

On 14 June, two ropes left for C1 of Mana. They were occupied on the same day.

Simultaneously, a route opening party was sent to C1 of an unnamed peak under Capt B. P. Singh. Both the groups i.e. of Mana and of the unnamed virgin peak were in communication with each other. Progress was made on both fronts simultaneously. The weather remained inclement beyond.

Both the ropes occupied C2 on 15 June as route had already been opened and ropes fixed. On 16 June weather, became very bad and movement of the team was restricted. On 17 June, these two ropes occupied C3. On 18 June, it snowed throughout the day and the team could not move ahead. The weather cleared up at 2200 hrs on 18 June. Early in the morning on 19 June, both the ropes left at 0430 hrs leaving Govind Singh (HA Porter) and

L/NK D. Limboo behind. The second rope under Capt S.P. Malik, Leader, was positioned ahead of the assault camp near the site of the ice fall where the accident took place on 11 June. It was well prepared and all set to rush for rescue should the occasion arise. The main rope continued to move ahead.

The last 500 m of the climb along the ridge line to the peak was on hard ice which necessitated expert ice-craft on the sharp edge. Though the move on the slippery hard ice was extremely laborious and slow yet the summiters were encouraged by the tell-tale marks of the previous expeditions which served as the route markers. The summiters traversed the last 50 m which happened to be the top of the long razor sharp Mana ridge rising westwards. First summiter Sep NS Rawal reached the lofty peak at 1130 hrs followed by Sep Surbeer Chand, Capt M. C. Jayakrishnan, L/NK S. K. Rao, Rajinder Singh and Kundan Singh. Ultimately on 19 June at 1130 hrs the main rope successfully scaled peak Mana despite the inclement weather. After staying for 25 minutes on peak, at 1155 hrs the summiters commenced their return journey.

The following members on the main rope were the climbers of Mana peak. Capt M. C. Jayakrishnan, (dy leader), L/Nk S. K. Rao, Sep Surbeer Chand, Sep M. S. Rawal, Rajinder Singh, and Kundan Singh.

Assault on 'Shakti Parbat'

As soon as the main rope crossed the site where the accident took place on 11 June, the second rope was withdrawn and moved towards the unnamed virgin peak at 0800 hrs. This auspicious news inspired the other members of the team to forge ahead towards 'Shakti Parbat'. This second rope also scaled the unnamed virgin peak at 1345 hrs and christened it 'Shakti Parbat'. The weather had already packed up with accumulation of dense fog. After staying at 'Shakti Parbat' for 30 minutes the ropes started their return journey to C1. Summitters of both ropes joined at C1 and moved onto the BC. The following members who were divided on two ropes scaled 'Shakti Parbat'.

Capt S. P. Malik, (leader), Capt B. P. Singh, N/Sub S. K. Dogra, Hav ACK Singha, Hav D. Deb, Nk N. S. Tamang, L/Nk D. Limboo, and Sep N. S. Negi.

Summary: The ascent of Mana (7272 m) by the Indian army Ordnance Corps. team on 19 June 1992. An unnamed Peak 5730 m east of their BC was also climbed. They named it 'Shakti Parbat'.

13

YOGESHWAR, 1992

SIMON YEARSLEY

W E CLIMBED IN the Garhwal Himalaya, a four-man British team of Steve Adderley, Malcolm Bass, Julian Clamp and Simon Yearsley.

The latter three made the second ascent of Yogeshwar (6678 m) via a new route on the objectively dangerous south face. The summit was reached on 2 October, 1992. The team thought they were making the first ascent, but were disappointed on their return to the UK where they read that an Indian expedition had made the first ascent via the southeast ridge in the pre-monsoon season of 1991.[1]

Originally planning to approach the mountain via the Shyamvarn glacier, the team's base camp was pitched 2 km short of this because of despondent porters, and they used the Swetvarn glacier as an approach instead. Finding enough good porters in the Gangotri area seems to be becoming more difficult, mainly due to the large number of expeditions operating here.

Base camp was established at 4800 m on 12 September after a three day walk-in from Gangotri.

After acclimatising at BC, loads were carried up the easy but tedious Swetvarn glacier, and advanced base established at 5550 m on 20 September.

Steve Adderley and Julian Clamp made an attempt on the mountain's west ridge on 24 September. They gained this via the north col between Yogeshwar and Chaturbhuj (6655 m), but retreated from between a height of 6200 m in the face of extremely unstable snow on the ridge.

Whilst recovering at base camp, all four members of the team helped in the evacuation of an Indian climber from Chavla Jagiridar's Sri Kailas (6932 m) expedition. The evacuation involved a two day stretcher carry of the climbers suffering from exposure and exhaustion down the difficult Raktavarn glacier.

On 28 September Malcolm Bass, Julian Clamp and Simon Yearsley re-occupied ABC. On the 29th they bivouacked below the horribly

Yogeshwar was named and first attempted by an Indo-French team in 1981 (HJ Vol. 38, p. 91). The first ascent was achieved on 27 June 1991 by an Indian team. See C.H.C. Newsletter 45, p. 16 — Ed.

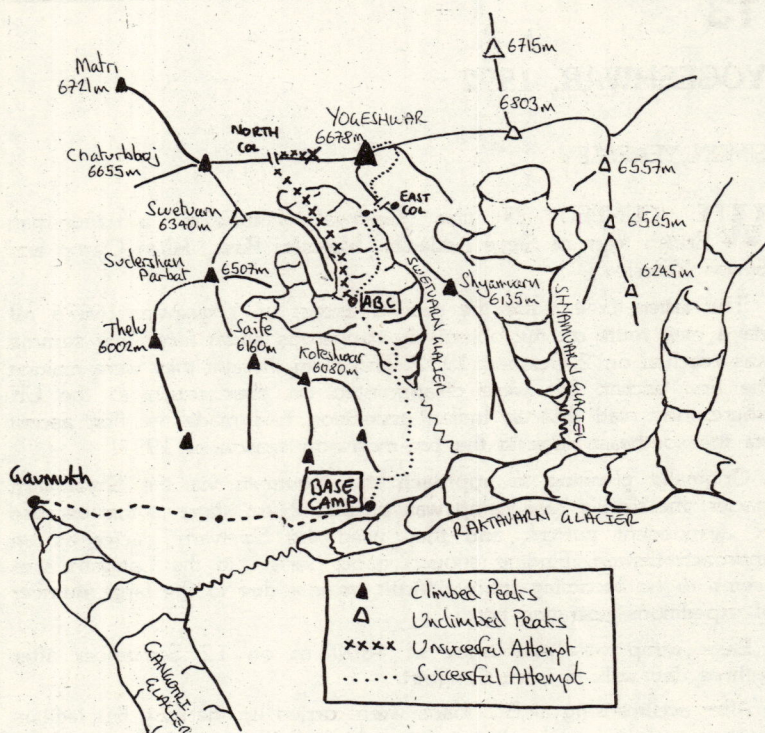

Map labels (as drawn):

Matri 6721m
Chaturbhaj 6655m
Swetvarn 6340m
Sudershan Parbat 6507m
Thelu 6002m
Saife 6160m
NORTH COL
YOGESHWAR 6678m
EAST COL
6715m
6803m
6557m
6565m
6245m
Shyamvarn 6135m
Koteshwar 6080m
ABC
BASE CAMP
Gaumukh
SWETVARN GLACIER
SHYAMVARN GLACIER
RAKTAVARN GLACIER
GANGOTRI GLACIER

Legend:
▲ Climbed Peaks
△ Unclimbed Peaks
xxxx Unsuccessful Attempt
...... Successful Attempt.

loose east col which they had hoped to climb that day, but were unable to because of stonefall.

On the 30th the col was reached, and an extremely comfortable bivi ensued at 5950 m. Whilst having a rest day on 1 October, the team were able to pick out lines on the attractive and unclimbed peaks on the east side of the Shyamuvan glacier. Leaving the bivi at midnight on 2 October, a series of gully lines were followed (Scottish III) from the col onto the south face. The south face was then crossed with straightforward climbing threatened by large serac and avalanche-runnels. The southeast ridge was gained by 7.30 a.m. at approximately 6400 m. Here sacks were left, and the S.E. ridge followed via the east ridge to the summit. This was reached at 11.30 a.m. By 5.30 p.m. the team descended the S.E. ridge, crossed the Shyamvarn glacier and re-ascended to their bivi on the east col. ABC was reached the following morning and cleared of all rubbish, and the team descended to the base camp the same day.

45. South face of Kedarnath (6940 m), from Kedarnath temple.

Note 17

(Harish Kapadia)

46. Rock Tower (6150 m), close up from Kedarnath temple.

Note 17   (Harish Kapadia)

This part of the Garhwal remains relatively unvisited, unlike other areas of the Gangotri glacier. There are still many unclimbed and attractive 6000 m peaks especially around the head of the Shyamvarn glacier.

Summary: The second ascent of Yogeshwar (6678 m) on 2 October 1992 by a British team. The peak stands on the Shyamvarna glacier (Gangotri-Garhwal).

14

MATRI EXPEDITION, 1991

SWAPAN KUMAR GHOSH

THE NINTH EXPEDITION of the Durgapur Mountaineers' Association was to Matri.

We left Uttarkashi on 11 August by bus and reached Gangotri (3140 m). On the following day our trekking started, following the traditional route by the side of the river Bhagirathi and reached the transit camp (3700 m). The camp was 2 km beyond Chirbas and near the Matri nala, by the side of the track towards Gaumukh.

It was decided to establish the base camp on the following morning, 13 August. Thus the team and the laden porters started for the base camp. The boulder-strewn route was through the gorge and towards NE following the right bank of Matri nala. Our movement was slow. At one place we were forced to leave Matri nala and had to climb the left ridge fixing a 40 m rope. Then again we had to get down to the river bed. From there the route seemed to be dangerous. We were to cross the Matri nala, but our attempt to make a bridge by putting boulders on the nala failed. A rope was then fixed across the Matri nala. After crossing the nala we had to climb the ridge on the left of the Matri nala by fixing a 45 m rope. Then, we were to get down from the ridge and reach a flat area near the nala, where we were to establish our base camp at 4300 m.

On the 14th the BC was occupied. The whole BC area was covered with juniper. To the north of our base camp lay the Chaturbhuj and to the south, Manda. After two days' ferry ABC was occupied on 16th and the remaining members occupied BC. Our ABC was at 4740 m on the Matri glacier. On the 19th, a little below the icefall at 5040 m, C1 was occupied. Above this the route was dangerous due to rock-fall, avalanche and crevasses. So the entire route had to be fixed with rope. After six days' hard work of fixing 14 climbing ropes and ferrying the loads, C2 was occupied on 26 August. Our C2 was on the icefield in between two crevasses giving us a place about 7 m broad. It was at 5740 m and below the SW ridge. In between C1 & C2 we made a dumping spot at 5420 m upto which materials were ferried from C1 and then those were carried to C2 by the members of C2.

The SW ridge of Matri in a half circular form connects the peaks Matri, peak 6565 m, Chaturbhuj, Sudarshan Parbat and Thelu. To climb on to the SW ridge was a tough job as we had to fix ropes. After a three day effort we could occupy C3 on 30 August, which was on the ridge and at 6100 m. It was more than a four hour climb from C3.

On the following day, inspite of snowfall with fierce wind the members of C3 could fix seven climbing ropes which ended just below the third hump.

On 1 September Arvind, Subhasish, Sher, Joy and Sangram left C3 at 4.30 a.m. leaving Tarun at the camp. They were on the top of the first hump by 5.15 a.m. Beyond the hump it seemed to be the end of the route beneath a big boulder. The whole route was over the cornice. The second hump was of a gradient above 70^0. After the hump two more tops were climbed and they reached below an ice-wall upto which ropes were fixed on the previous day. They had three more ropes with them excluding those two to which they were roped up. Their climb continued and at 9.30 a.m. they reached the third hump. From here they continued their movement over the cornices and on flat ground. Moving towards the NE and climbing the fourth hump made of rock and ice they appeared before a wall also made of rock and ice. They found no other alternative but to encircle the wall over the dangerous cornice. The route was made safe by fixing a rope and Arvind was saved by this fixed rope as one of his legs got caught in the cornice. They continued their movement towards NE over the cornice and crossed many small humps until they reached a boulder of about 7 m height. One more rope was fixed there and they proceeded further. Then crossing a flat area two big humps were climbed. The route was narrow, about 3 to 4 m broad and in some places it was 2 to 3 m. They moved eastward for some time and again towards NE and at last reached below the summit. There was 15 m more to climb. But a big boulder was obstructing their approach. They first made an attempt from the left by driving a piton on the boulder but failed. Then they started climbing the brittle wall made of rock and ice, on their right and one by one reached the summit of Matri at 2.30 p.m. The national tricolour and the association flag were unfurled. After half an hour they started descending and at 7.30 p.m. they found themselves at C3 leaving behind 3 ropes and the pitons.

Summary: The ascent of Matri (6721 m) by an Indian team in September 1991.

15

ACROSS DHUMDHAR KANDI PASS

SANJIB KUMAR MITRA

DHUMDHAR KANDI PASS, is famous for its tricky location, and unstable weather condition. James Baillie Frazer first came to learn about the existence of the pass in the year 1815. He collected information that since ancient times local villagers and traders and even the invaders used this difficult pass as a short cut to cross over Bhagirathi valley to 'Rawaeen' valley (the upper parts of the Tons valley) and vice-versa. From his account we came to know that the river Sian gad, which flows southeast to meet the Bhagirathi ganga below Jhala village, 'rises in Dhumdhar...... a very lofty and wild range to the north of Bandarpunchh and along which there is a very alarming road leading to the remote parts of Rawaeen'.

A recent attempt to locate the pass was in 1972 by a team from Calcutta under the leadership of Amulya Sen, followed by another group led by Sudhan Bose in 1973. The first attempt was foiled due to inclement weather but the second claimed success though there were doubts in some quarters. In 1984 S. S. Mukherjee and G. Santra also from West Bengal tried to cross the pass from Sian valley. They crossed over the dividing ridge but not exactly through the pass. While the search for exact location of the pass continued, it was revealed subsequently that the pass was marked erroneously in old survey map sheets. The first successful attempt was recorded by a three member team from Calcutta led by Prabhat K. Ganguli in 1987 who could locate and climb the pass correctly.

Our journey to the Tons valley started on 25 August 1990 from Calcutta and we reached Mori on 28 August.

On 30 August morning, we recruited three porters through the Porters' Association and trekked to Taluka (1981 m), 13 km away. We had to cross Tons a number of times after Taluka, as the track was occasionally blocked by tree trunks uprooted during the recent monsoon. So it took us 5¹/₂ hours to reach the Osla forest rest house at Seema (2560 m).

On 1 September, six of us — Rupayan Chatterjee, Tapas Mukherjee and myself along with three porters from Osla — Nikram Singh, Sundar Singh and Surya started from Seema forest bungalow. Rising steeply along with the left bank of Tons, we reached the wide and picturesque meadow of Debsu after two hours. Then we descended to Ruinsara gad. It comes down from the east and joins with Har-Ki-Doon nala, a short distance away. Thereafter it is known as the Tons river.

We crossed the log bridge over Ruinsara at 10 a.m. and trekked along its right bank, and reached Ruinsara lake (3400 m) at 5 p.m. and pitched our tents from the other bank. We left at 9 a.m. on 2 September, negotiated a steep gulley and traversed through the steep slopes of the south face of Swargarohini to Kiyarkoti (3780 m) at 2 p.m. The next day, an overcast sky delayed our start till 10.15 a.m. Continuing steeply over the southern slopes for an hour, we reached a zone of boulders brought down by landslides. We reached Deobasa camping ground at 11.45 a.m. and rested here for half an hour. We could now see almost the entire sweep of the mountain ranges of this region.

Dhumdhar Kandi pass (5608 m) was some where between Barasukha and Yellow Tooth. The Ruinsara gad, the main source of the Tons river originates from Bandarpunch glacier below this range where the horrifying Kalanag icefall joins it at Dharao Udari (4420 m). The Bandarpunch glaicer then flows below the conical snow peak of Ruinsara (5487 m). It continues northwest through a narrow valley separating the two principal ranges of Swargarohini on the north and Bandarpunch on the south.

We resumed our march and passed through a gully on the left. Gaining height steadily along the Bandarpunch glacier over landslide zones and boulders, we reached Dharao Udari (4420 m) at 2.10 p.m. It started raining almost immediately. We quickly erected our tents very close to the wall on the high lateral moraine of the Bandarpuch glacier.

On 7 September, we started at 8.15 a.m. We were going up along our left and we could see the massive icefall of Kalanag with open crevasses, on our right. In 1¹/₂ hours we reached the top of the slope — a vast, open valley. We decided to avoid Arjun Jhari and go up the ridge on our left directly. Negotiating some buttresses and boulder zones we reached an icefield. This was followed by a number of other icefields and a ridge. After crossing a thin stream on our left, the entire Tons-Bhagirathi watershed opened up to view. Kalanag was under the thick monsoon clouds while the Yellow Tooth was peeping through. Dhumdhar Kandi pass was lying hidden between the second rock spire and an umbrella shaped rock to the north of Yellow Tooth. Beyond another icefield, we climbed up the ridge, while snowfall commenced. We went over a slippery zone of loose slates covered by fresh snows.

Now we were on the top of the ridge. We drifted more to our left and climbed over an arc like route. Within a short period we were under the umbrella shaped rock. Between the gate formed by the two rock towers, the concealed Dhumdhar Kandi pass was seen. A long stone pillar marked the spot. We later found out that it is hidden similarly on the other side also. The porters immediately rushed to the pass amidst snowfall though we were moving at our own pace over loose slate stones. After some time we found ourselves atop Dhumdhar Kandi pass. It was then 45 minutes past one.

The concave shaped pass was covered with 6 inches of snow. Snowfall continued and nothing around us was visible. There were few stone pillars planted as cairns. Our porters came here for the first time and we all were very happy to reach our target. We painted 'Rocks & Treks', our club's name, on a small stone and lay it there as evidence.[1] We spent 30 memorable minutes on top before beginning to descend from the other side.

The slope was steep. So we moved to the extreme left of the pass. It was also full of loose slate stones covered by fresh snow. After 45 minutes we were on a small escarpment. There was a massive glacier on our far left. The ridge on the right went down sharply and we continued over the top of the ridge. We descended over the escarpments of several ridges. The valley was closed on all other sides except NNE.

We went over the lateral moraine and crossed a number of dry beds of streams. Since the beginning of our downward trek, it had been raining and when we were fully drenched at 5.30 p.m. we decided to call it a day.

8 September. There was snow everywhere, as far as eyes could see. After drying our tents and clothes and having a heavy breakfast, we resumed our march over the lateral moraine at 9.30 a.m. We moved towards NNE and a number of unknown snow peaks of the

---

1. Surely, a cairn would be more eco-friendly. Such paintings are an eye-sore.
   — Ed.

Lamkhaga range were in front. At 11.30 a.m. we reached an excellent camping ground — a small grassy land surrounded by stones, — it was the Ranla or Rathia camping ground. The valley gradually widened and Sian gad looked like a bright tape in the distance. At 12.15 p.m. we reached an overhang, a cave for six. Further ahead, the Dhumdhar nala turned southeast to join with Sian gad, coming from NNE. We reached the banks of Sian gad at 01.15 p.m. As the river was not fordable at that time, we pitched our 5th camp here, after rearranging the boulders, at a place just above the river bed.

We moved out at 7 a.m. on 9 September and crossed the Sian gad a few yards upstream. Here the river flowed in three streams. We waded through and anchored the rope to ferry the loads. The river flowed southeast and we could see the Sian gorge and the tree line far below. We reached Kiarkoti at 11 a.m. A stream flowed from the right to join with Sian gad on the other bank. Descending through the valley, we pitched our 6th and final camp on uneven grounds, beyond another stream, we later found out that the excellent camping grounds of Tangua were only ten minutes away, on higher ground. Next day, we reached Jhala for a bus to Uttarkashi.

Summary: A crossing of the infrequently visited Dhumdhar Kandi pass from the Tons to the Bhagirathi valley by a team from Rocks and Treks, Calcutta, in September, 1990. The team was led by S.K. Mitra.

16

SAHASTRA TAL

SANDEEP DUTT

Defeat is the touchstone on which the mental make-up of a man is brought out.

Mahabharata

VERY OFTEN DEFEAT is a blessing in disguise, the utility of which is not immediately recognised. It is because of defeat, many people have not ruined themselves. Defeat makes us reflective and self analytical and this is exactly what has happened after our recent attempt to Sahastra tal.

The word 'Sahastra' meaning 'a thousand' in Sanskrit, was given to the area by wandering holy men. It is also the modification of the local Garhwali word 'Sahasyu' which means seven. The topmost and the largest lake on the Bhilangana side is referred to as Darshan tal. The other seven being — Pari tal, Arjuna tal, Bhim tal, Draupadi tal, Gaumukhi tal (or Vishnu tal) and Lam tal, all accommodating the worshippers of Shiva as well as Vishnu. There are of course many other tals like Khukala, Dudhi tal etc. But, perched up at 4752 m Sahastra tal which is also the abode of Vishnu is the holiest.

Our group of thirteen girls, set about to attempt the tal at what was said to be the best time — last week of May/early June; along with a good set of porters, guide and instructors, finally ended up learning more at a lesser height. With a maiden unsuccessful attempt at the stiff uphill to Karki, and great amount of rambling on the meadows, it was felt that we have all come back wiser and better prepared for the hills. It is thus pertinent for me to spell out what we really did in the ten days in which we had meticulously planned to achieve our ambition of reaching the highest tal.

Many of us really do underestimate the hills. With experienced hill walkers, this really is the biggest drawback. Sahastra tal, in fact is more of an expedition and not a simple trek. Surely, technical equipment is not required and the high altitude drawbacks are not there, but the stiff climb over the short distance, makes it far beyond a simple trek/walk.

Having started our ascent from Malla we planned to go up the Pilang gad to Johra and then onto Dharamshala. This is really where we erred first, though being short, the forest cover and steep gradient make this a very unsuitable approach march. Instead, to test the ability of our amateurs and further enable the loads to be brought up, we had to take the longer route via Silla, Chamin Chor, Papar and spend an extra night en route Johra.

On 23 May, we left Malla early and took the 4 km long ascent upto Silla. The uphill path wound across the slope through wheat and poppy fields and we took almost three hours. The climb from Silla to Gheru (chauni or shepherd's lodging) was gradual and through a deciduous forest. The slopes abound with walnut trees, Himalayan oak, rhododendrons 'Kanjal' and 'Kharsei' trees. The dense undergrowth of ferns and the thick carpet of dead leaves along the path, do help relieve the aching feet of the trekkers. There were also the great Himalayan Barbit flying over us. It was around 1 p.m. that we were able to reach our camp at Gheru. In order to improve logistic support for the Sahastra tal attempt, our support staff along with the laden mules marched on to Ghutu.

To encourage the concept of new minimum-impact camping and further instill skills and sensitive strategies for sharing we arranged lectures in geography, weather prediction, first aid, survival skills and other useful information at our camps. The cooking lessons, rope craft and all the sessions of rope knot and rock climbing provided the best back drop for pre-expedition training.

Up the Gawar Dhar towards the meadows of Kush Kalyan, was a beautiful walk through coniferous forests. The elegant and strong 'ringal' or bamboo shoot, the sycamore trees, a variety of lichens on the barks of trees and stones, made the approach to the meadows, very enchanting. The tree line gave way to strawberry blossoms, butter cups, primulas and many other flowers, all covering the entire expanse of the endless meadows. The entire walk now was along ridges and saddles. As the temperature and pressure on our barometer fell and the height increased, it was not only the variety of flowers, but also their colours, as in the case of rhododendrons, changed from pastel shades of purple and pink to faded white and different tints on the sunny slopes across. The ridge walk along the meadows made the valley and ridges stand out sharply and the paths were visible for endless distances.

Along the beautiful paths uphill were rows of beautiful lilies and other deep red flowers. At the higher reaches the flowers and bushes were growing below rock shelters and in clusters under the rock ledges. To further enchant us was the spotting of leopard droppings! The breath-taking walk of 12 km finally ended at Ghutu, a small settling of deserted chappads among the endless meadows. With low night temperatures and absence of the evening sun this place at about 3200 m was our first feel of hostile mountain weather. The cold night and useless sleeping bags of some girls made us think of the hard times ahead after base camp.

Moving along the ridge at 3500 m, our problem was of locating water resources. To establish base camp we set off towards the steep wall of Karki top. At Devta, situated on the saddle was a very small temple of simple rock and one flag. This was in fact a pass which is used by the shepherds in the trans-meadow movement from the Pilang valley to the Dharam ganga valley along the parallel low altitude trek towards the Bhilangana watershed. This is the area being promoted for a ski resort along the Bhagirathi watershed. The bad weather of the afternoon and lack of water now dashed our hopes of crossing on to the Andarban Dhar. The trickle of water, before the base of the black rocky steep above Devta was to be the highest camp for us at about 3800 m.

47. Bharte Khunta (6578 m), SE face from Kedarnath temple.

Note 17   (Harish Kapadia)

48. Kugti pass, right notch, from Alyas camp.

Note 20

49. The last slopes leading to Kugti pass.

On 26 May, a day behind the scheduled attempt for Sahastra tal, a group of four girls with four support staff set off for the ambitious heights of the Andarban Dhar. It was a rocky uphill path and the group walked on at a slow pace, each giving moral support to the other to carry on. Unfortunately the good weather did not keep with us and we were caught in a bad storm. A small rocky outcrop on the steep slope was our saviour from the onslaught of the snow-storm and rain. The white-out and of course the wet, slippery slopes made movement impossible. At this gloomy hour, when we were clinging with all our might to the steep slope up the ridge, our way of retreat was carved. The brisk walk back to base was welcome as we did have better weather now and the joy and jubiliation of meeting the other team members, made us feel as if the Dhar had been attained!

The base camp proved to be a good area for bouldering and rock climbing looking across the Pilang valley was the imposing massif of Bandarpunch and Kalanag. We now decided to climb Kush Kalyan and start going down the valley along the Pilang gad via Mati and Jaura. On the 27 May the high point of Kush Kalyan at 3868 m was the maximum height attained by most of the team members. The usual afternoon storm and rain did drench many of the girls on the way down to Mati, but a fire at Mati camp and the hot meal helped fight fatigue and raise our spirits. When the storm subsided the jungle camp was discovered as the best area for practising monkey crawling, rope traverse and knots. There was enough time to interact with the 'gujars' who needed a lot of medical help too. These nomads were the first of the groups to reach Mati and had come up from Dhaulkhand in the Shivwaliks.

The trail from Mati to Jaura was through dense forest of sycamore and Himalayan oak. There was undergrowth of ferns, bamboo shoots, etc. and as the slopes were wet and devoid of sun it was infested with leeches. On the steep downhill there were the usual slips and sprains and by lunch hour we were all worn out. Hot soup along one mountain stream and applications of ointment provided the necessary relief. Our last camp was pitched just ahead of Jaura on the fields beside Pilang river.

On 29 May we reached Malla and washed away our layers of dirt in the pure water of the Bhagirathi river. There were the usual long hours of packing and sorting out and of course the school at Malla was the camp for night. Badly damaged by the earth quake, with the roof still in place, it provided the peaceful night halt on our return to Dehra Dun on 30 May 1992.

What was so great about this trip?

The honing of the outdoor living skills that keep people safe, comfortable and happy in an environment that is only temporarily their home. We also learnt minimum-impact camping skills that help people leave the outdoors just the way they find it or even better. It was important to get the message across, that outdoor activities mean recreational activities that depend on natural resources (plants, animals, land or water), and outdoor living skills refer to such activities using, understanding and/or appreciating of natural resources.

Summary: A trek in May 1992, to Sahastra tal near Uttarkashi.

17

TEMPTATIONS OF KEDAR

HARISH KAPADIA

'DON'T YOU GET tired of fumes and pilgrims?' my friends always asked me, whenever I planned a trip to the pilgrim centres of Garhwal; namely Badrinath, Gangotri, Jamnotri and Kedarnath. I had been to the former three but the last one had not been visited by me. So there we were, on our way jostling with the pilgrims, along the Mandakini towards Kedarnath.

These pilgrim areas have been visited by the faithful for hundreds of years. Much has been written about them, in vernacular literature also. As a young person every Indian aspires to know about it and is attracted towards it. But as a trekker I was always fascinated by the variety of opportunities these valleys offered. These temples are situated high in the different valleys. Using them as a base, a lot can be done in the surrounding ridges, peaks and valleys.

First the 'fumes', there were none. A comfortable taxi ride of 6 hours dropped us at Gupta Kashi, our first destination. From the lovely bungalow, we saw the gathering clouds and enjoyed the fine temple nearby. We were in the Mandakini valley. A little below us, the Madhyamaheshwar ganga joined the Mandakini and all these waters join the Ganges.

Madhyamaheshwar

Eric Shipton and Bill Tilman will always remain linked with this valley. Though pilgrims visited this temple, NE of Gupta Kashi, it was brought to the notice of the western world by the exploits of these two in 1934.

Starting from the Satopanth glacier near Badrinath, they planned to descend to this valley in 4-5 days, with their Sherpas. After forcing their way through a sheer ice wall they faced some of the thickest forest. As they hacked their way through and crossed and re-crossed many streams, they ran short of food. They struggled to live on bamboo-shoots, but had to compete with bears, for bears also love the shoots. The situation was near hopeless. Finally, one afternoon they climbed up a ridge to have their first glimpse of a village. The Sherpas were joyous. But Tilman greeted the site with a typical dry comment, for which he was well-known: 'We shall be down in time for tea', to which Shipton merely stuttered "Thank heaven for that!"'

In fact, Shipton and Tilman were trying to explore a legend. It was said that, many hundred year ago, the priest at the Badrinath temple crossed over a pass in one day to the Kedarnath temple to perform puja, serving both the temples on the same day. It was believed that there could be a pass joining the temples, known to the priests. Shipton and Tilman decided to investigate this by crossing from the nearest low point with near disastrous results. Their trip exemplifies the difference between knowledge and legends or facts and fiction.[1]

But since reading about the trip, my imagination was always excited about visiting this valley. Two trekkers from Bengal were lost here in 1986 trying to reverse the Shipton-Tilman route and were presumed dead. Hence we did not plan any heroics but wanted to simply to investigate the upper reaches. But we were summarily defeated in the purpose by the untimely rain and fog. Not that one minds that, for the temple and its surroundings are beautiful.

As the legend goes, Shiva was chased by Pandavas of the Mahabharata fame. To run away from them, he assumed the form of a bull. When the Pandavas discovered this, they held the bull-by-the-tail. Shiva buried himself at Kedarnath with only his shoulder visible. This 'shoulder' is worshipped today at Kedarnath temple. Other parts of the bull emerged at four other places, including the centre at Madhya (centre) maheshwar (a name of Shiva). But geographically two rivers flow here. From the north Markand ganga, and from the south Madhyamaheshwar ganga, on the two sides of the hill on which the temple stands. Hence the explanation for the name could simply be; 'Shiva temple on the hill in centre of two rivers'. 'What is the significance of Madhyamaheshwar temple?' my companion Jehangir, a Yoga teacher from Bombay, was inquiring with the only priest at the temple. After narrating two different stories, the priest inquired with Jehangir how

1 See *Nanda Devi* by Eric Shipton, part 4, 'The Second Crossing of the Watershed (Badrinath-Kedarnath).'

to reduce his belly! Each to his own profession. Thinking of the route we had come up, it was a wonder that the priest was fat.

Starting from Gupta Kashi (1480 m), we had descended to Kalimath (6 km). From this ancient temple, dedicated to the goddess Kali, it was up-hill all the way. We trekked on a broad path to Raonalek (8 km), and stopped at Ransi (1980 m — 6 km) for the night. Next day, through some lovely pine forests, the route descended to Gaundar (1400m — 6 km). Here, to the north, was the nala and the valley through which Shipton's party had descended in 1934. Ahead was the steep climb of 1900 m in one continuous slope. In a 10 km climb, we crossed Khandar (2020m 3 km) and Nanu (2330 m — 2 km) to reach Madhyamaheshwar (3290 m — 5 km). All along the route we could get food, and tea shops were aplenty.

We stayed in comfortable quarters near the temple. But as we climbed up to Budha Madhyamaheshwar (3500 m — 2 km) clouds gathered and we were denied the supposedly close and excellent view of the Chaukhamba group. From here a *gaddi* track leads to Kashni tal, a lake at 4730 m. Many other trekking routes are possible from here. A little above the lake some of the various gullies would lead a qualified party across the watershed to the Panpatia Bank and the Badrinath valley. This route was heard of by the locals and, perhaps, Shipton's party was one valley to the north (Satopanth Bank) of a possible crossing.

Towards the east, Maindgalla tal and Pandosera (5120 m) are visited by the shepherds. Crossing a small watershed ridge one can descend to Rudranath which is another temple of Shiva and has an exit to the south.

For two days near the temple we observed the rituals. Two assistants looked after the washings and all the preparations for the simple worship. Our friend the priest then made an appearance for the *aarti* and did the final perambulations, the activity certainly not enough to keep him physically fit! Jehangir showed him some Yoga *asanas*. When we left, we were firmly convinced that the priest may rise spiritually but would not reduce an inch at the belly!

Kedarnath

Back at Gupta Kashi we travelled by taxi to Gauri Kund, the starting point for the Kedarnath temple. Filth, crowds and noise accompanied us for 14 km upto the temple. With so many *dhabas*, pilgrims and sadhus on the way, a trekker can be cheesed off. At every 100 m or so a sadhu sat wishing you *Jai Kedar* (Hail Kedar). But this was the ploy to draw your attention to give alms to him. As the day progressed, the sharpness of tone of the 'Jai Kedar' could clearly tell you how much his earnings had been for the day.

But at Kedarnath (3600 m), if you look away from the temple and the crowds, a majestic range rises within about 4 km, running from east to west. There are great south faces of Bhartekhunta (6578 m), Kedarnath (6940 m), Rock Tower (6150 m), Sumeru Parbat (6350 m), Mandani Parbat (6193 m) ending in the great Chaukhamba massif, (6954 m). These south faces would provide some great climbing to the challengers. The Italians are active here. The only two peaks climbed here are: Kedarnath in 1988 (G. Mandellin, H.J. Vol. 45, p. 45, p. 186) and Rock Tower in 1990 (Stefano Righetti, H.J. Vol. 48, p. 182). Both the climbs were achieved during their second expedition, after their first attempts had failed during the previous years. Within one day of availability of supplies, some serious climbing can be undertaken with Kedarnath temple as a starting point.

On 31 August I climbed up to Vasuki tal (4300 m) on the west. It was a beautiful tarn but its importance to the mountaineers lies in the opportunities it offers nearby. Numerous peaks between 5400 to 6000 m and cross country routes to the Dudhganga and Chorabari glaciers are very tempting. Not much has been done here and, except for army trekking parties, the climbers have not explored it. A lot can be done here in a short time; if you can tolerate the pilgrims, as my learned friend would put it.

Bhilangna valley

About 10 km before Gauri Kund a route bifurcates from Sonprayag to Triyugi Narayan. A beautiful temple nestles here. A well-trodden trekking route adjoining Bhilangna valley joins here.

Almost a decade ago in October 1982, Geeta and myself had landed here. The Bhilangna valley draining the river of the same name, is a beautiful and relatively unspoilt valley between the Gangotri and Kedarnath shrines. The entrance to the valley is from Gamsali and Ghuttu, reached by bus, 194 km from Dehra Dun.

In two stages of 10 km each the track reaches Gangi (via Reeh). This friendly village has a spectacular view. But something is strange about the people here. Due to the close community and inter-marriages, many seemed queer. Ahead, the track proceeds via Kalyani to Bhelbagi and finally to Bhumka, the last camping ground before the Khatling glacier.

One of the early visitors here was Dr. J. B. Auden. During his exploratory visit to the Gangotri area he had finally crossed a pass between Gangotri III (6577 m) and Jogin I (6465 m) peaks from Rudugaira Bamak. He descended to the Bhilangna valley. This col is now called 'Auden's Col' and the route was repeated twice in 1983, from both directions (H.J. Vol. 40, p. 168).

On the NW of the Bhilangna valley lies a group of peaks: Kairi (5435 m), Draupadi-Ka-Danda (5724 m) and even an approach to Jaonli (6632 m) is possible. On the NE, via the Dudhganga Bamak one can join the route at Vasuki tal and descend to Kedarnath.

We retrated to Gangi. The old pilgrim route traversed valleys: from Gangotri to Budha Kedar, descended to Gangi, across Bhilangna valley to climb the eastern ridge, locally called Panwali Kanta. We followed this track. Leaving Gangi early morning, we crossed the river on a *pucca* bridge. A continuous and steep climb saw us on the ridge, at Talli, camping without any water-source. We were on the Panwali Kanta. The route proceeds north on this flattish ridge awarding some of the finest views of peaks: Jaonli, Thalay Sagar and others. After a hard day we reached a small depression called Khimkhola khal and turned east to descend to Mugu Chatti and Triyugi Narayan near the Kedarnath route.

This is just a small selection of the variety of opportunities available for trekkers and climbers in the valleys near Kedarnath. With food and shelter available a trekker can enjoy some fine mountain scenery — if you can tolerate 'fumes and pilgrims'. And if you can say *'Jai Kedar'*.

Summary: Treks and suggestions for the possibilities of climbs in the Mandakini and Bhilangna valleys in Garhwal. Kedarnath and Madhyamaheshwar valleys, visited in August 1992 (Jehangir Palkhivala and the author): Bhilangna valley visited in October 1982 (Geeta Kapadia and the author).

Photos 45-46-47
Panorama E

18

FROM SANGLA TO NETWAR OVER THE RUPIN

WILLIAM McKAY AITKEN

WITH INNER LINE restrictions on tourists being lifted in 1992 for Kinnaur I jumped at the chance to accompany a group from Delhi's St. Stephen's College hiking club led by Romesh Bhattacharjee.

I was puzzled why Bhattoo should be chosen to lead India's future economists when his role in life is to come down with a heavy hand on fiscal inventiveness. 'Don't be late' he told me and I leapt out of a taxi at 5 in the morning of 4 October 1992 to pick up Bhattoo and Chetan, father and son. They were both tucking into a breakfast of fried eggs which seemed a bad omen to one who always finishes his trek with ovarious fare. I should have remembered that the lean and hungry look on Bhattoo's face denoted the agony of the only man in the entire length of the Himalaya who does not eat dal-bhat, our staple for the next ten days.

The Himalayan Queen whisked us to Kalka where, on finding the narrow-gauge link train bulging with Dushera passengers, we had to take the bus to Shimla. Our party of a dozen yielded a rare mix of types and regions and some were on their first Himalayan outing. Norden was the strong-man of the group and our public relations spokesman in view of his father's seniority in Shimla's charmed circle of bureaucrats. Shah was equally muscular and stoutly maintained the expedition accounts against daily anarchic suggestions. Next morning there was no bus to Sangla and we had to debate financing a taxi to assure our waiting porters that we were on our way. As the taxi drove up it got a flat. Commending its chagrined driver to St Michelin (the patron saint of the deflated) we unscrupulously piled on to a bus going to Tapri within striking distance of Sangla. Our bad karma caught up with us at Rampur Bushair as the bus swerved wildly on beholding the Satluj. Not one but two punctures stalled our plans and worse was to follow on the third morning out of Delhi when we eventually made it to Sangla but with our porters nowhere to be seen.

. We put up in the forest bungalow which overlooked the river and faced the splendid march of cedar-timbered houses that gave Sangla so much character. Behind, the grey polished pinnacles of the Kinner Kailash clamoured for attention though I noted the younger male trekkers in the group - Mylin, Gaurav and Vivek — preferred the equally daunting challenge of overcoming the indifference of the three ladies in the party Ruchika, Delicia and Diane. We managed, after a lot of haggling (caused by the apple season) to hire two Nepali porters but they were not properly equipped for the Rupin. The temples at Sangla were ablaze with colour at the big annual *phuletch* fair and architecturally the village was a great joy.

Owing to a late start we moved up to spend the night at Kanda Dogri where the villagers tend seasonal plots. The views of the Kinnaur pinnacles grew more spectacular but shepherds we spoke to urged us to get over the Rupin before the present dusting of snow turned to winter's snuffing out of the route. Progress to the crest of the range that in theory divides Himachal from Uttar Pradesh — in practice the border lies a long way down the Rupin valley and must reflect the boundary of an earlier hill fiefdom — was slow owing to the newcomers finding their hill legs and the *ustads* (Ranu and Bill) running everyone else off theirs in false trails. When a porter decided he could go no further, we all said Amen and found a camp site well under the lee of the pass but near enough to hope for a group photograph on top at lunch next day, 9 October.

The camping arrangements among such a mixed group, confounded by the absence of a tried cook, could have led to a lot of friction but not once did anyone blame or blow his top.

Possibly Bhattoo's bold hairstyle had foreclosed that option. Remarkably, in view of the setbacks, slow progress and doomsday predictions about the inadvisability of bringing freshers on demanding trails, the group gelled magnificently. Bhattoo forever brought up the rear and magnanimously shepherded the struggling girls over the pass exactly as scheduled. Ranu had to get back to Chandigarh in two days for an exam and I also planned a brisk return to Mussoorie. The easy sweeping approach to the head of the Rukti gad which we had followed all the way from Sangla steepened for the final pull. The climax yielded a steep drop southwards where the Rupin rose in a dried up lake surrounded by a saucer of tortuous terrain, unappetisingly rugged and snowswept. Eastwards from the cairns on the pass the ridge angled up steeply and settled any doubts that the Nalgan ghati a neighbouring pass lay close at hand. Westwards the ridge did not run so high but seemed just as loathe to allow easy passages. The shepherds warned against straying towards the Buran pass leading to the Pabbar valley since in the tangle of options it was easy to end up back in Sangla.

Nobody seems to agree on the position or height of the Rupin and while our objective bore all the right credentials its height couldn't be much above 4300 m, if that. Confirmation that it probably was the real Rupin pass came from W.E. Buchanan's account in the second issue of the *Himalayan Journal*,[1] vouched for by H. M. Grover a senior forest officer familiar with the area. Buchanan chose the harder part and crossed from the south in mid-September. It was from the miseries of his party's steep ascent where the porters had to let their hair fall over their eyes to prevent snow-blindness that convinced Ranu and I of the sameness of our route. We left the main party

1. H.J., Vol. II, P. 74.

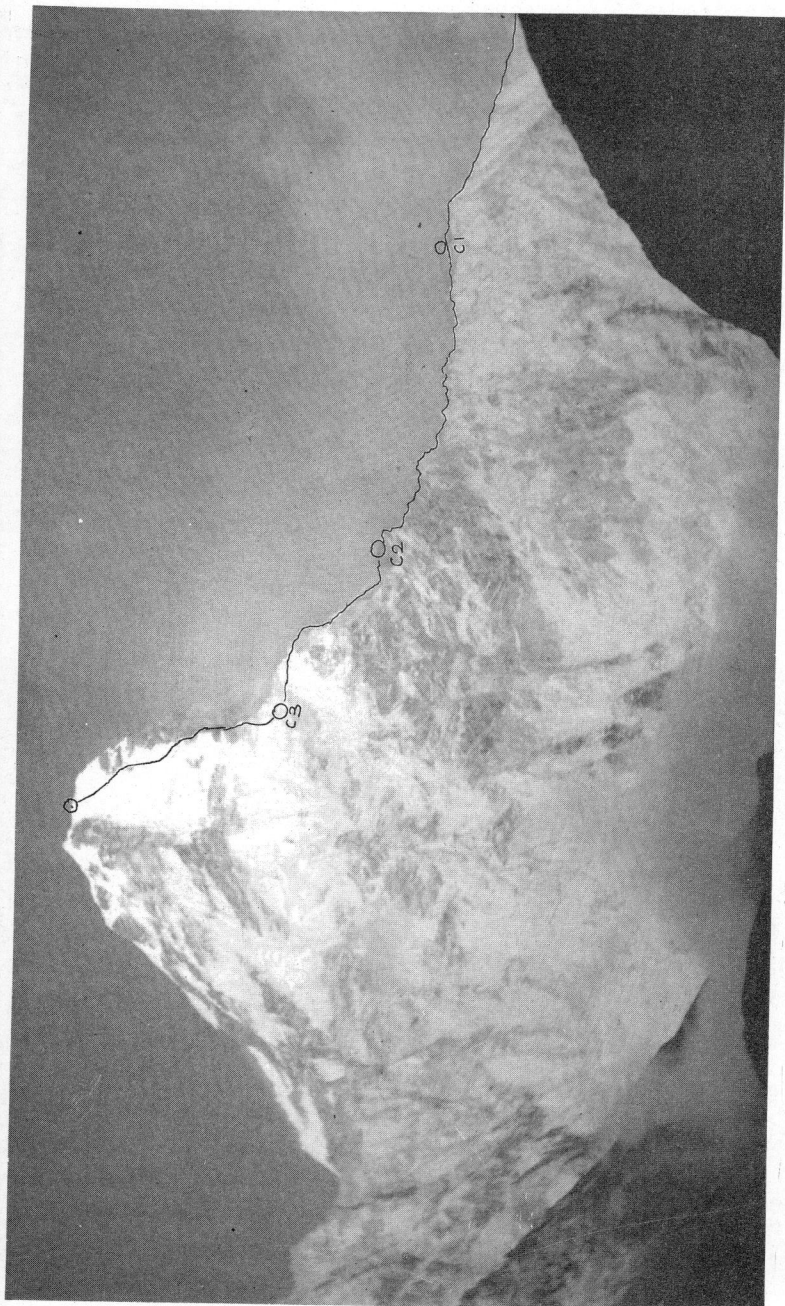

Illustrated Note I

Ama Dablam (6812 m)

Many expeditions climb this peak every year. There are various routes, the southwest ridge being the most popular. Here it is the route of the Spanish expedition of Carlos Goni Mendibill in 1991.

Illustrated Note 2
Numbur (6957 m)
Two member German team of Helmut Muller and Mathias Rau climbed the peak via th
southwest ridge on 7 November 1991.

Illustrated Note 3
Annapurna I (8091 m)
Unsuccessful attempt on the Dutch route on the north face by the Austrian team led
Arthur Haid in April 1991.

on the pass and it was a truly testing descent with no question of our hair being in any state to fall over our eyes. Most of the time it was standing on end! From the cairn a sheer chute of splintered rock had to be negotiated that led to the flats where the river Rupin took birth, Ranu and I fairly flogged our way down steep narrow passages bypassing some of the most gorgeous fanned-out waterfalls it has been our privilege to see. Snow-bridges of surprising girth considering the lateness of the season stalled our impatient progress. Neither of us was shod very sensibly for the occasion, having totally underestimated the seriousness of the trek.

We puzzled over how the hell Lady Canning, the vicereine had managed to glissade down these slopes to the astonishment of Queen Victoria who kept her letters — now in Harewood House. Charles Allen's book about Lady Canning's tours fails to convey that she was in fact rather vague about her route. The ladies of our party were convinced she had crossed by an easier pass and they should know because behind us, the main party was forced to camp around the incipient lake, a howlingly bleak choice brought on by nightfall and made more miserable when neither of the expedition stoves worked. Meanwhile down in the spectacular valley which swung drunkenly from the perpendicular to a long run of meadow before plunging us into a tangle of autumnal forest, Ranu and I were still legging it like mad into the gloaming. To avoid further embarrassment on the snow-bridges we skirted them by soul-numbing river crossings, a horrible way to prepare for bed.

Darkness, a disintegrating path and a close pounding river forced us to take one risk too many and quaking with fear at the close shave we bivouacked, optimistically draped around a willowy shrub to prevent us rolling down the sheer conifer hillside. We even managed to sleep though we took turns to wake up to let out maniacal groans at our immaculate absurdity in lacking a box of matches between us. According to Ranu this therapy would deter bears — as if any wild animal would be so rash as to set foot on our impressive angle of incline.

Next morning we zapped down the dessicated river bank to arrive in the first village of Jhaku by 10. Marvellously sited deodar village houses overlooked riotously red hanging valleys of Ramdhana, the ripening cereal crop of these inaccessible villages. Below, the Rupin a peerless jade, purled with enough benevolence to make us overlook our devastated knees and purple toe-nails. Down and down we jerked until we came to a startlingly expensive temple of opulent cedar logs at the first village in Uttar Pradesh — Seva Dogri. Civilisation announced itself when we turned a corner and saw the feudal equation updated. The local bigwig was flaying the bowling of half a dozen tiny-tot minions who were queueing up to send down full tosses so he could score a century in three overs.

Astoundingly we learned at the teashop that the sale of illicit opium had paid for the cost of the temple — and the cricket bat. Amusingly, Bhattoo who is supposed to prevent such things walked through the village two days later (after roping up the party to get them off the dicey passages), unaware the dope scene was so rampant. Ranu was given a few complimentary shavings of raw poppy gum as a conversational gambit for Delhi drawing rooms. Also best-quality *charas* could be had for a song. The flip side to these junkie encounters was to arrive at the teashop at Peesa for the night and roam around for half an hour (again getting our feet wet) bawling for help. The owner sat watching us from 50 yards away thinking we were a narcotics raiding party.

The final day along this sumptuously endowed river with its appallingly vertical trail was aided by some mules. From Netwar which we hit by midday we caught a bus to Naugaon in the Yamuna valley. The gods smiled and an empty taxi returning to Mussoorie whisked me home by 7 p.m. This enabled Ranu to meet his deadline. The rest of the group also managed to report back at St. Stephens by the due date, with a delightful quotation attributed to Delicia, the most petite of the party. She had shied away at the sight of some white pack horses and Bhattoo had queried her violent reaction. Did she associate them with the classic climbing archetype 'Dream of white horses?' Disconcertingly her reply referred to a different ball-game. She said they reminded her of Boris Becker!

Summary: A trek across the Rupin ghati pass, in October 1992.

19

RUBAL KANG EXPEDITION, 1991

APURBA CHAKRABARTI

RUBAL KANG IS SITUATED north of Parbati valley in the Kullu Himalaya. It stands southwest of Kulu-Makalu, on the divide of Kullu and Spiti valleys. Practically Dibibokri west glacier starts from the foot of these two peaks.

We started along the traditional trail on the right bank of the Parbati river. We reached Raskat within an hour. We passed Ghatighat and Tauk, and reached village Barsheni (2100 m) at 3 p.m. The environment of the village looked unhygienic. Our only shelter was the school building. The view of village Pulgaon on the opposite bank of Parbati was very nice.

On 1 September, we proceeded east along the trail, gradually downward upto the confluence of Tos nala and the Parbati river. Crossing the nala, the trail goes up through the terraced fields. We reached Rudranag at 11 a.m. and had lunch from the *langar* of the temple of lord Shiva. The view of the roaring Parbati passing through the gorge was enchanting. Crossing the river we faced a steep climb through a forest of typical Himalayan trees, till we reached the grassy fields of Khirganga (2950 m). From here, there are two trails towards Tundabhuj. The lower one is generally used by the cattle owners. The upper one, which we chose, passed over a rock slope to traverse diagonally. We crossed Tundabhuj nala and established our transit camp (3300 m) beside the boulders at west of the grassy field. On 3 September, we started for Thakur Kua. At about 1 p.m. we reached the rope bridge to across Parbati river. The trail towards Mantali and Pin Parbati pass goes along the left bank of Parbati river. We crossed Parbati along the single steel rope bridge with a basket hanging from a rusted pulley and set up a camp on the right bank of Parbati. The confluence of Parbati river and Dibibokri nala was at a distance of about 200 m from our camp. On 4 September, we packed up and started, initially on the trail towards northeast, steep up along the grassy slope and loose boulders. We passed through gradual grassy slope along the right of Dibibokri nala. At about 2 p.m. we all reached the base camp (4060 m) area just before the confluence of Ratiruni nala and Dibibokri nala.

The trail towards C1 was along the boulders up to the confluence of Dibibokri and Ratiruni nalas. Then it turned a little to the left towards the north and over huge boulders. At 4500 m, we found the camping spot and dumped all the loads in a tent.

On 7 September, 5 members and 3 HAPs who had stayed at C1, moved north along the stream upto the high point of loose rock barrier, on the other side of which the stream, wide enough, from the snout of west glacier, looked like a glacial lake. Little before the west glacier, they crossed another stream coming from the first tributary glacier from peak 'West Horns'. Then they moved over the right lateral moraine of west glacier. Site of C2 (5060 m) was chosen at the foot of third tributary glacier on the right of West glacier. C2 was established on right lateral moraine on West glacier bed.

Chaman Singh identified the rock peak to NNE as Rubal Kang. And this peak is being climbed since 1986, Chaman added. Kulu Makalu was out of sight as it was obstructed by the west ridge of the peak. We studied our sketch map carefully and felt doubtful about identification of the peak 'Rubal Kang'. On 9 September, initially we proceeded along the right lateral moraine and then crossed the West glacier diagonally. After one and half hours of trekking, we saw Kulu Makalu, the chief peak of the basin, as if it dominates the entire area of West glacier. On its SW was a snow peak with a rocky top. The west ridge of the peak ends at a col and again continues to SW, upto the rocky peak. We again discussed the identification but Chaman Singh declared the rocky peak as 'Rubal Kang'.

We proceeded towards the rocky peak. At 2 p.m. we reached C3 (5240 m) at the foot of this rocky peak. After sun-set, monsoon clouds appeared in the gap between Kulu Makalu and its subsidiary peak. We came to a conclusion that this subsidiary peak is the real Rubal Kang (6115 m).[1]

But Chaman kept firm in his opinion. He is a famous guide of this region. We wanted to attempt the real Rubal Kang. But Chaman did not agree to accompany us for want of climbing shoes.

On 10 September, we decided to climb the 'false' Rubal Kang. First five members namely Gautam Baxi, Amitav Ghosh, Pulin Dey, Prasun Pan and Krishnamoy Nayak along with Chaman Singh and three HAPs left C3 at 6.30 a.m. They covered the slope full of boulders. After two hours of climbing they reached the middle of the V-shaped top of the peak. Traversing left they reached the highest point on the rocky top (5700 m). Photographs of the surroundings were taken. The West glacier and Tichu glacier in the west looked beautiful. Photographs of Kulu Makalu and the real Rubal Kang were taken to establish the correct position of the peak 'Rubal Kang', which was visible clearly from here.

In the meantime, on the same day Samar Barua, Gautam Banik and myself packed up and left C3 at 8.30 a.m., and marched towards the real Rubal Kang. We planned to establish a summit camp on the fourth hump of the ice-plateau below the centre of the west ridge of Rubal Kang. We turned right towards the east, passed over the first two humps. A large number of crevasses were faced beyond the second slope. The only possible route to be followed was to our left, below the hanging ice-wall on the rock band. We had alreadyobserved 4-5 avalanches on this within an hour. We proceeded further upto the end of the rock-wall below the ice-mass. But we

1. See the article 'A Dawdle in the Dibi' by Aloke Surin in the present issue also. — Ed.

could not find any possible way to proceed further. At about 2 p.m., as we decided to give up our attempt at 5660 m the weather deteriorated rapidly. We returned to C3 at 5.30 p.m.

On 11 September, we three attempted the rocky peak (false 'Rubal Kang') that our members had already climbed. We succeeded and returned on to C3 at 10.30 a.m. On 12 September we all gathered at base camp.

The position of the real Rubal Kang is very close to Kulu Makalu in SW. But at first sight, Kulu Makalu and Rubal Kang seemed to be the same peak. For this reason the rocky peak with twin tops (5700 m) is being climbed as 'Rubal Kang'. Chaman Singh knows this fact, and he has been misguiding teams about Rubal Kang. We tried out best to attempt the real peak (6115 m) but failed.

Summary: A climb of a rocky peak 5700 m and an attempt on Rubal Kang (6115 m) in Kullu area in September 1991 by an Indian team from West Bengal.

20

KUGTI PASS

PRASHANT M. TALE

PIR PANJAL RANGE runs on the borders of Kashmir and Himachal Pradesh. The average height of the range is about 5500 m. We crossed over from Chamba valley to Lahul valley, from basin of Ravi river to Chenab river, via Kugti pass (5120 m).

We followed the following route: Chamba-Bharmaur: (1) Hadsar 2740 m, (2) Kugti 3050 m, (3) Duggi (Rudi) 3660 m, (4) Glacier Camp 4270 m, (5) Kugti Pass 5120 m, (6) Marika Got 3966 m, (7) Rape 3350 m, (8) Keylong Manhhi.

It is also famous for its many ancient temples. These were built in 7th century. We visited the temples of Chamunda, Laxminarayan and Shiva and offered our pooja.

18-19 September 1992

We reached Chamba by bus from Pathankot. We boarded the Chamba-Bharmaur bus. The route was through narrow valley and on the banks of Ravi. We left Ravi at Khadamukh and entered the Budhil nala valley.

Bharmaur is very beautiful village in background of snow-capped peaks. There are a few famous ancient temples. We were happy to know that a jeepable road now links Bharmaur to Hadsar. We kept out luggage at Hadsar and started on the famous trek to Mani Mahesh lake (4420 m). The route was very steep, but safe. We reached Dhanchoo camping ground, which is 8 kms. from Hadsar and stayed for the night.

20 September

We left Dhanchoo early for the onward trek. It was cold and windy. The trail was steep and without any trees. We reached Gauri Kund at 10 a.m. and Mani Mahesh lake at 10.30 a.m. A beautiful lake and magnificient view of Kailash peak (5656 m) was breathtaking. We reached Dhanchoo at 1.30 p.m. and Hadsar at 4.00 p.m.

21 September

Today our real trek to Kugti Pass started. We hired 3 porters. We left Mani Mahesh nala and reached very close to Budhil nala. Then we climbed a very steep route. The towering mountain walls and water falls were a frightening sight. We reached Dharol, about half the distance and had our lunch. Then the strenuous climb continued for next 3 hours. We got a view of gigantic snow covered Pir Panjal range. A view of Bhujala nadi was fascinating, from here one route also goes to Mani Mahesh lake from east of Kailash peak. We stayed at the forest rest house.

22-23 September

Our next camp was at Duggi (3660 m). The route was steep but well marked as many of the villagers trek via this route to Kartikeya temple. This beautiful wooden temple is worshipped by many in this and nearby valleys. A rear view of Mani Mahesh Kailash peak was great. Similarly a grand view of Duggi pass and the snow peaks were visible from the temple. We halted at a natural cave (3660 m).

Next day we reached Duggi Ralling and a grand panorama opened in front of us. A grand view of snow peaks on Pir Panjal range and Kugti pass was visible. Porters were complaining about weight (about 15 kg). We tried to convince them but they started blackmailing us and asked for more money. This was the first experience of this kind for us in the last 10 years. After discussion between ourselves, we decided to dismiss them.

Now it was tough trek to carry about 35 kg extra load in addition to the personal one. We decided to make load ferrys. A camp was established at 6 p.m. on the moraine of Kugti pass glacier.

24 September

We reached the base of the glacier at 8.30 a.m. As usual we found that unlike the distant view the actual glacier is quiet, large and steep. It had taken us 5 hours to climb that steep icefall before the vertical gully. We reached the top of the icefall at noon.

The last portion of the climb was through a wide gully. We were making very slow progress, and were struggling to trace the route. It was miserably cold when reached the pass at 4 p.m. As we were standing in the pass a thundering wind was blowing from Lahul valley to Chamba valley. We pitched our tent at the pass itself. The barren Lahul valley was clear. We could see famous peaks such as Gangstang, Phabrang and peaks near Menthosa.

25-26 September

We woke up at 7 a.m. The weather was very clear and we felt as if we were on the top of the world. We were stunned to see the steepness and the glaciers on both the sides.

We descended towards Lahul by traversing the glacier on rocks and icy slopes. It took us 3 hours to traverse, then we reached the icefield. We were very cautious and used snow-bridges to cross 3 main crevasses. We reached the base of the glacier at 2.00 p.m. and walked on a giant moraine field. It took us 3 hours to cover that moraine and we reached Mrika Got at 5.00 p.m.

The 26th was the last day of the trek. After 3 hours of descent we could see an unmetalled motorable road on the other bank of the Chenab river. After another two hours we reached village Rape. We crossed the Chenab on a suspension bridge and reached the motorable road at 2.30 p.m. We went to Keylong by bus for our onward journey to Manali.

Members: Prashant Tale (leader), Shashikant Aminbhavi, Sanjeev Shukla and Pravin Tale.

Summary: A trek to Mani Mahesh lake and across Kugti pass (5120 m) in Himachal Pradesh in September 1992.

Photos 48-49

21

KARCHA PARBAT EXPEDITION, 1991

SATYAJIT KAR

THIS YEAR WE decided to make an attempt to climb Karcha Parbat (6270 m) in Lahul Himalaya. This peak was first scaled by an expedition team from Ireland[1] and Diganta, Calcutta[2] was the first Indian team to climb the peak in the year 1986.

Four members of our club, the Calcutta Trekkers Youth, West Bengal, left for Manali as advance party on 21 August. The remaining members of our team left Calcutta on 23 August, and met the advance party at Batal on 27 August. In the meantime, the advance party ferried their loads upto Grelu Thaj (4270 m) which was made a transit camp for the expedition team on 28 August. Grelu Thaj is on the left bank of Karcha nala. First we came to the confluence of Karcha nala and Chandra river after 20 minutes walk from Batal. Then we continued for 3 hours and came down to the riverbed to cross an ice-bridge. The path was steep and on a scree slope on the right bank of the nala. After crossing the ice-bridge we went towards the northeast along the left bank of Karcha nala. After a 2 hour walk we reached Grelu Thaj.

On 30 August, we started for the base camp, early in the morning. Just after an hour's walk from transit camp, crossing a ice-bridge, we came to the right bank of Karcha nala. After another 45 minutes through heaps of moraine and loose boulders, we reached a piece of flat land and established our base camp (4450 m).

We established ABC (4900 m) and C1 (5330 m) by 1 September. On 2 September, we took the route through the southwest ridge of Karcha Parbat. Through boulders we went on. After about 5 hours we found a shelf beside a big rock and established C2 (5730 m). We did not want to waste any time as the weather was favourable and decided to attempt the summit very next day. So we began to prepare ourselves from 2.45 a.m. on 3 September for the journey to the summit. At 4.15 a.m. Ashim, Gopal, Sabbya and Monika alongwith the 3 HAPs left C2 and started for the summit. First they traversed

1. See H.J. Vol. XXI, p. 97, Vol. XXXV, p. 298.
2. See H.J. Vol. 44, p. 102. — Ed.

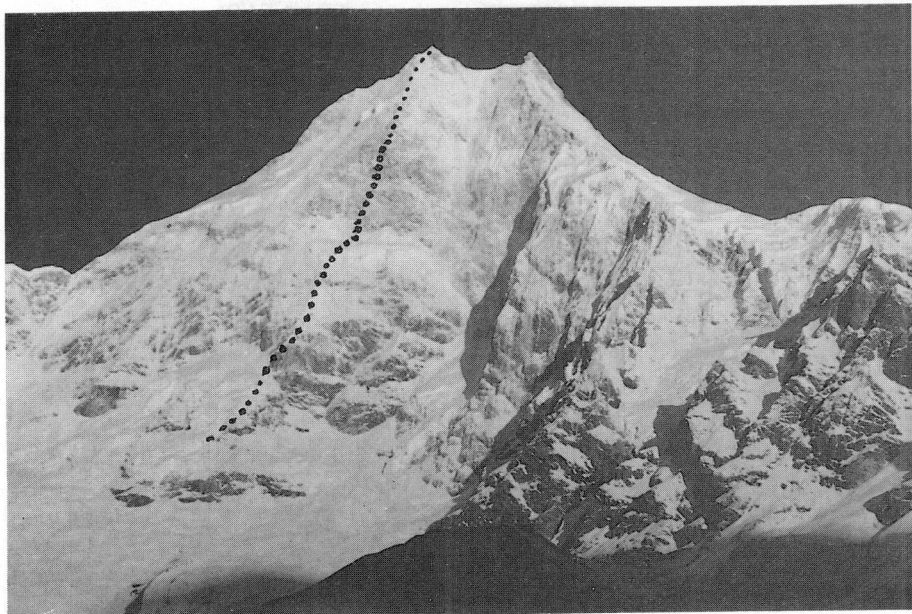

Illustrated Note 4
Manaslu (8163 m)
The first Ukranian Himalayan expedition was led by Prof Vladimir Shumichin. They tried a new route, on east face. After three tries they changed to the southern ridge and descended the normal north route. Three climbers reached the summit on 6 May 1991.

Illustrated Note 5
Himlung Himal (7126 m)
Peak climbed by Japanese expedition led by Yukio Niwa. They followed the northwest ridge. Two parties reached the summit on 3 and 6 October 1992.

Illustrated Note 6

Cheo Himal (6820 m)

First ascent by a Nepal-Japan team led by Masanobu Okazaki and Gupta Bahadur Rana. Four climbers reached the summit on 13 October 1991. The peak lies to the east of Himlung Himal.

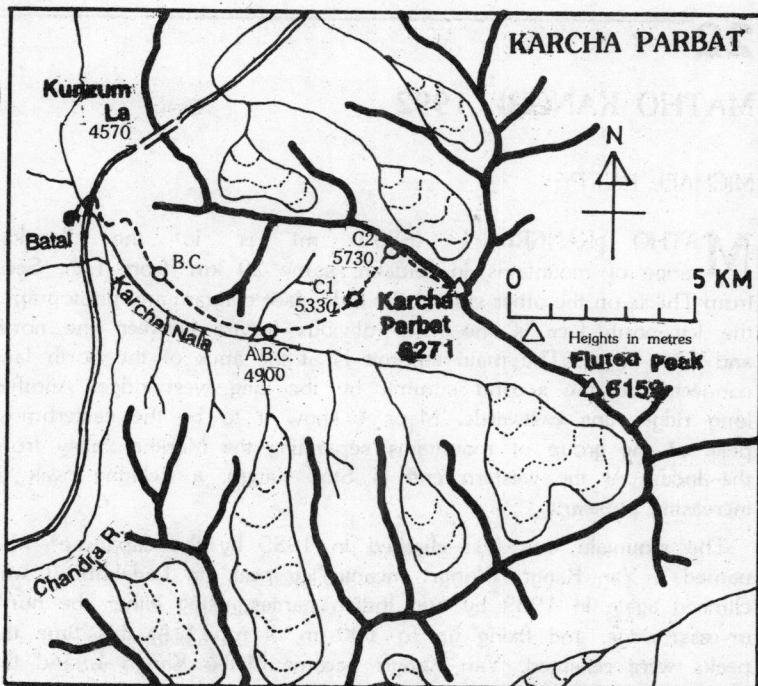

KARCHA PARBAT

Kunzum La 4570

Batal

B.C.

Karcha Nala

A\B.C. 4900

C2 5730

C1 5330

Karcha Parbat 6271

N

0   5 KM

Heights in metres

Fluted Peak 6159

Chandra R.

some rock, and made their way through loose boulders. After overcoming a big rock they came on the top of the main ridge. Later they arrived at two snow-patches and crossed cautiously. Though the route was through loose rocks, the gradient was moderate, which helped them progress without any disturbance, Crossing the last snow patch they reached a big boulder. This was also negotiated and from there the peak was about 50 m away. They took some rest and reached the top at 7.20 a.m. The summit was about 3 m long and 1 m wide. They stayed on the summit for 70 minutes, then they came down to C2 and after lunch came to ABC.

On 4 September all of us met at camp and on 6 September we returned safely to Manali.

Members: Satyajit Kar (Leader), Manjul K De Sarkar, Gopal Roy, Ashim K Ghosh Chowdhury, Pradip K Dey, Ajoy Kumar Singh, Sabya Sachi Bose, Moloy K Ghosal, Bhaskar Das, Ms Monika Kar and Dr Dipankar Majhi.

Summary: The ascent of Karcha Parbat (6270 m) by an Indian team in August-September 1991.

22

MATHO KANGRI, 1992

MICHAEL RATTY

MATHO KANGRI I (6230 m) is in the Zanskar range of mountains in Ladakh, some 20 km. from Leh. Seen from Thikse on the other side of the Indus (see diagram and photograph) the icy north face is the most obvious feature between the north and west ridges. The main summit is at the apex of the north face connected to the second summit by the long west ridge. Another long ridge runs eastwards. Maps[1-2] show it to be the easternmost peak of the group of mountains separating the Markha valley from the Indus. At the western end is Stok Kangri, a trekking peak of increasing popularity.

The mountain was first climbed in 1985 by the Japanese[3] who named it Yan Kangri (Kangri means 'icy peak' in Ladakhi). It was climbed again in 1989 by two Indian parties, using either the north or east ridge, and fixing up to 100 m of rope.[4] At this time the peaks were renamed. Yan Kangri became Matho Kangri I, and the pair of summits on the west ridge, Matho Kangri II. The account also mentions Matho Kangri III and IV, but we were unable to identify these, either on maps or from the summit.

Our expedition had the simple objective of making the first British ascent of the mountain. The team consisted of four British members. M. Ratty (leader), T. Willis, J. Shelley, and A. Rowland. Our other member was Deepak Jhalani, the liaison officer. Although the team was experienced in Alpine climbing, only Michael Ratty and Deepak Jhalani had Himalayan experience. Local knowledge and experience was provided by Phunchok Tangias, a local guide and climber.

The mountain is close to the road, so for acclimatisation we undertook a ten day trek, which effectively circumnavigated the range of mountains of which Matho Kangri is a part. It followed the well trodden route over the Ganda la to Skiu in the Markha valley, and along the valley to Hankar. We climbed to the Nimaling plain, and returned to the Indus valley over the Kongmaru la. Apart from getting everyone used to the altitude, it also provided an opportunity to study the geography of the mountains. For some of the team it was an introduction to a remote and beautiful part of India.

Base camp was established in the Mirutse valley, at 4100 m on 13 August. It is a few hours' easy walk from the roadhead at Matho village, altogether just one day away from the comforts of Leh. The valley has several houses in it, and is used for grazing sheep and goats. The following day, we climbed to a flat area below the north face, and set up advanced base camp (4700 m).

We intended first to climb the mountain via the west ridge, which appeared straightforward, and to follow this with further ascents via the north face or the gullies to either side. That same day, Trevor Willis and Deepak Jhalani continued to the col on the west ridge, where they set up a tent at 5300 m. C1 was intended to provide rest during future descents, and useful acclimatisation. The route to the col follows a gully descending from the lowest point on the ridge. It was icy in parts, but presented no problems.

On 15 August the remaining three members accompanied by Phunchok Tangias, joined the other two on the west ridge, and all continued to the summit. There was little or no snow on the ridge, and the remainder of the ascent was on scree and loose rock. The summit itself was gained by a short scramble up a rock rib. Having decorated the summit cairn with Indian and Union flags we descended without incident.

During the ascent and descent we reconnoitred possible technical routes. The north face is icy, but not excessively steep, and we saw

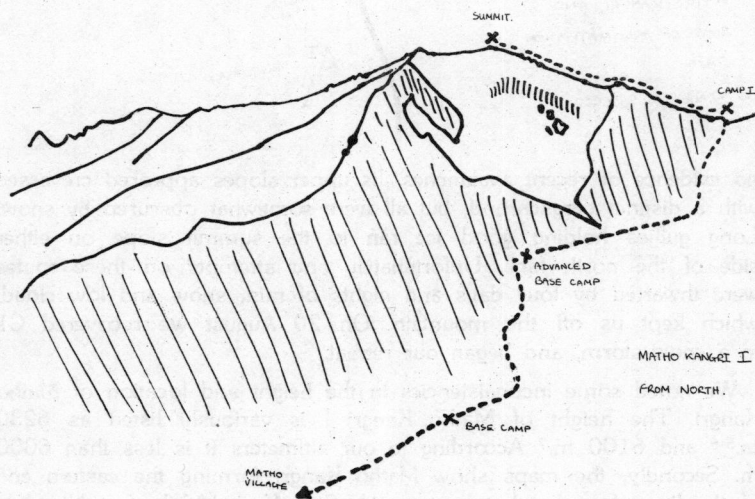

MATHO KANGRI I
FROM NORTH.

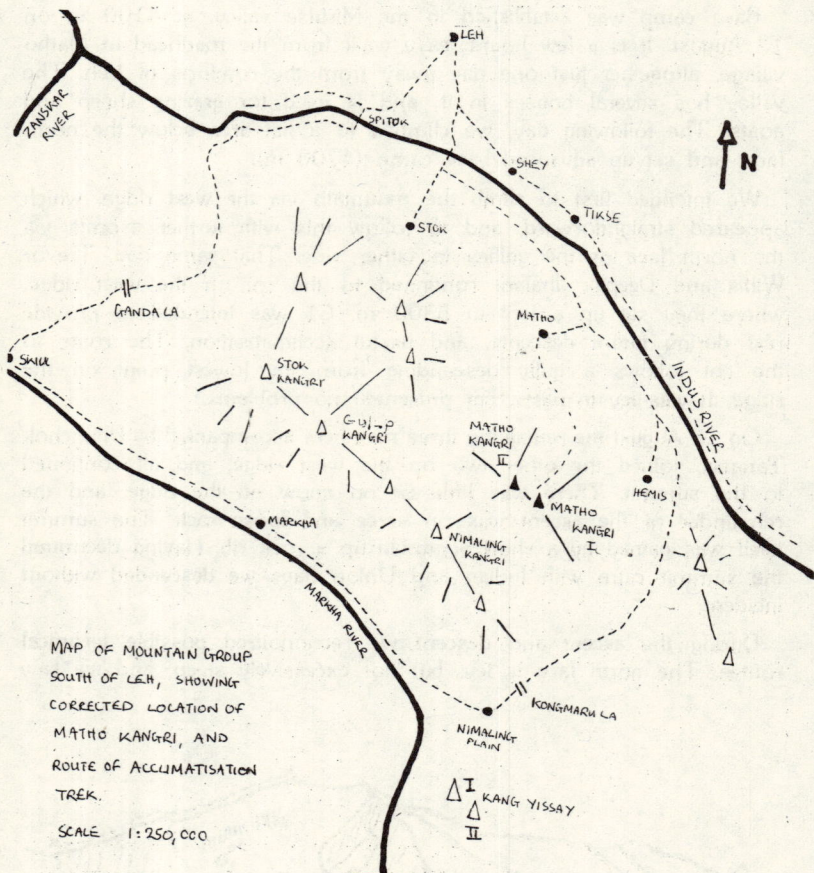

MAP OF MOUNTAIN GROUP
SOUTH OF LEH, SHOWING
CORRECTED LOCATION OF
MATHO KANGRI, AND
ROUTE OF ACCLIMATISATION
TREK.

SCALE 1:250,000

no evidence of recent avalanches. Its upper slopes appeared crevassed with a distinct bergschrund, but all were somewhat obscured by snow. Long gullies holding good ice ran to the summit slope on either side of the north face. Unfortunately any attempts on these routes were thwarted by four days and nights of rain, snow and low cloud, which kept us off the mountain. On 20 August we recovered C1 in a snow-storm, and began our retreat.

We noted some inconsistencies in the height and location of Matho Kangri. The height of Matho Kangri I is variously listed as 6230 m.[5-6] and 6100 m.[7] According to our altimeters it is less than 6000 m. Secondly, the maps show Matho Kangri forming the eastern end of the line of peaks that begins with Stok Kangri.[8,9] In fact Nimaling

(Kangri?), not named on the maps, is the end-most peak, and Matho Kangri I and II are northern outliers, separate from the rest.

Reference:

1-8   U.S. Army Map Service, (1962), series U502, sheet NI43-12.
2-9   Chabloz. P., (1989), Carte Artou *Ladakh Zanskar* Editions Olizane.
3-4-5   Bawa; Major H. S., Singh, B. P., 'Matho Kangri Expeditions 1989', (1989), *Himalayan Journal*, 1988/89, pp. 192-4.
6   Alpine Club (G.B.) Himalayan Index.
7   Genoud, C., (Ed.) (1984), Ladakh Zanskar, Editions Olizaine, p. 208.

Summary: The ascent of Matho Kangri I (6230 m) by a British team on 15 August 1992.

23

SANI PAKUSH

HUBERT BLEICHER

ON 13 JULY WE REACHED BAR, at the end of the dusty road from Chalt in the Hunza valley. Following the course of the Kukuar glacier we walked for 5 days to the base camp at 4200 m (with 27 porters). We found lots of old snow. We intended to make an attempt on the summit, following the route a Japanese expedition had explored in 1988.[1] After advancing through the first two ice walls and after spending one night at 5000 m we decided to make an attempt in alpine style.

We left base camp on 25 July in rather poor conditions and in snowfall. Hans Jud could not come with us since he was suffering from diarrhoea. On the second day we set up our second camp just above the ice wall (at about 5700 m). On the third day Braun and Bleicher climbed the 400 m ice-face (up to 65°) above C2 in very poor conditions (powdery snow). Since we had only light equipment with us we couldn't fix ropes on the ice-face. Therefore, we installed another route across the steep rocks to the left of the ice-face, returning to C2. That day Ketterer and Klimmer went down to get more equipment (ice-screws and ropes) from C1. In the evening we had a cloudless sky and it looked as if we could expect a spell of excellent weather for some days to come.

On the fourth day, four of us climbed the ice-face and we also managed to fix about 200 m above the very steep ridge which is

1. See H.J. Vol. 40, p. 204.

formed by the western face and the north face (upto 65°). At 6300 m we managed to find some room for both our tents at the edge of a crevasse. We had expected to reach the summit on the fifth day, but the last day had been rather hard and since there was no sign of weather conditions worsening we decided to take a rest in C3. The sixth day was a beauty and we had no difficulty reaching the summit within 5 hours inspite of the deep powdery snow on the steep north face. It was not possible, though, to actually get on top of the highest point due to its steepness and since a huge snow-cornice towered above it. So we had to stay roughly 5 m beneath the actual summit.[2] We were able to enjoy the spectacular view in absolutely calm weather for a considerable time before we finally returned to C3. On the seventh day (30 July) we succeeded in reaching base camp in 9 hours in steadily worsening weather conditions. Unfortunately we were forced to leave behind 200 m of ropes including abseil-loops. Jud and myself were still badly suffering from diarrhoea (since reaching C3) and therefore we had to return as fast as possible for medical treatment to Gilgit.

Members: Arnfried Braun, Hans Jud, Daniel Ketterer, Leo Klimmer and Hubert Bleicher (leader).

Summary: An ascent of Sani Pakush (6885 m) by a German team on 29 July 1990.

---

2. See correspondence on a similar situation on Swargarohini peak and the opinion by U.I.A.A., H.J. Vol. 48, p. 241. — Ed.

24

SHIMSHAL-MALANGUTTI GLACIER EXPEDITION, 1991

PAUL HUDSON

THE YORKSHIRE SHIMSHAL Malangutti Glacier Expedition set out to provide high-mountain experience for its members and hoped to reach and climb Pyramid peak which lies at the top of the glacier under Disteghil Sar. There were seven members who spent about 6 weeks in Pakistan. (23 July to 31 August 1991.)

The Shimshal valley lies north of Gilgit just above and to the east of Pasu. The Karakoram Highway. provides reasonable access to this area. Local buses and minibuses for private hire are available from Gilgit. The Shimshal gorge through which all visitors travel has steep sides with the path being built out from the rock face in certain places; it is generally dusty and has the effect of channelling the winds. Its bridges, which vary in construction are all interesting. We were told that the present inhabitants came to the valley around 400 years ago finding that it had previously been inhabited, then deserted. Trekking groups are now beginning to use this valley on a regular basis but many glaciers and side valleys remain unexplored. Shimshalis are subsistence farmers who grow crops in the summer months by irrigating their fields every two days or so via a series of diverted streams. The crops we saw included peas, potatoes, wheat, barley and apricots. In the winter when the work in the fields is at a minimum the men weave yak hair rugs and the women knit. We employed a young Shimshali teaching student from Gilgit, Quadrat Ali, as cook/guide.

We chose this area because of its peak possibilites and because it is rarely affected by the annual monsoon, an important factor as some members were available only in August.

As no-one had been on an expedition prior to this one, we all had a lot to learn, and learn we did. Some members are already planning to use this new knowledge in new ventures.

Research had identified a peak lying at the head of the Malangutti glacier, under Disteghil Sar the 7884 m peak which dominates this area. Pyramid peak had not, as far as we knew, been reached let alone climbed and at 5500 m provided us with a realistic aim. As well as this primary aim it was evident that a number of other options would be available and both virgin and previously climbed peaks were noted.

The team visited Shimshal village at the start of the expedition as guests of Quadrat Ali and then concentrated on the mountain area itself. Some time was wasted by looking for a non-existent path on the west side of the glacier before using the central moraine as a way of getting to Madhil Sar. From a camp at glacier level (ABC) below Madhil Sar we moved up to a high meadow at the bottom of the Adver Sar circ.

This was C1 and provided us with some acclimatisation peaks. Everyone climbed a 5200 m peak above a valley looking down onto Shimshal village. Three members also examined the lower slopes of Madhil Sar and Shiffkitten Sar but did not make attempts on these peaks. Two members climbed a second rock peak from C1 on loose and overhanging rock.

In preparation for Pyramid peak the glacier was explored a second time and thought to be difficult above the highest point reached. On the day of the attempt to force a way through the icefall to Pyramid peak the team reached an ice meadow and sent two people off to find a route. This proved impossible and after taking two hours to gain around 500 m they returned to the main party.

A route to the west edge of the glacier was then found and the party established C2 on a flowery meadow, below a good looking peak of snow and rock. The following day a bivi was reached on a stone covered glacier. At 3 a.m. on 20 August the whole group set off for the last peak believed to be 5800 m and unclimbed. Three turned back at a col but three others continued up a steepening snow slope and reached the top. Clouds stole the hoped for views. If unclimbed the peak has been named 'Straker Sar'. The altimeter reading at this peak was 5500 m.

Two members also put up a rock route 120 m above C2, they graded it III and named it 'Special K'. The buttress was named '3K Buttress.'

The weather experienced should encourage others, as we had 18 fine days out of the 23 spent in the mountains.

The area still abounds in interesting challenges at below 6000 m height and a number of smaller unexplored valleys could provide interesting diversions. If our altimeter reading is correct then some peaks in the area could well fall to a sub-6000 m height and be accessible on a trekking permit.

Summary: Climbs on the Malangutti glacier by a British team in July-August 1991.

BOOK REVIEWS

HIMALAYAN CLIMBER, By Doug Scott. Pp. 192, many colour illustrations, 1992. (Diadem Books, London, £20).

This is a beautiful and profusely illustrated story of the climbing career of Doug Scott. It depicts Doug's early adventures on rock and ice in Britain, through to alpine walls in winter and summer and follows his progress into the greater ranges. Starting in North Africa and Turkey on the steep faces of the Tebeati and Cilo Dag, we climb with Doug and his friends in the Afghan Hindu Kush — then onto Everest. The story side-tracks via big walls in Yosemite, Norway and the British Hebrides to Arctic Baffin Island, British Columbia and Alaska. On to the Karakoram, via East Africa — and so expedition follows expedition in this breathtaking book.

Twenty-seven major expeditions are described and illustrated - twenty of these in the Himalaya and many are multiple objective trips. Most climbers would think that this was enough but in between trips, Doug describes climbing and travelling forays all over the world. Mountains in Australia, ice in Scotland, unclimbed rock in India and bush-whacking through the rain forests of Canada.

The pictures are superlative. I wonder if Doug appreciates what a talented photographer he is — with these marvellous pictures he shares his memories of the harsh, hostile and sometimes quirky world he has chosen to inhabit.

The format is complex, ther is page after page of story telling photographs, many of them unfamiliar insights of little-known mountains. There are action packed photos of legendary climbs. You can almost feel the rope and the cold. There are familiar mountains and countries of the Himalaya captured by Doug's lens in a new and refreshing way. The mountain pictures are puctuated by a wealth of laughing, graphic titbits — children, tribesmen, sacred cows, holy places, friends in groups, friends relaxed, friends in extremis. The images of local people jump out of the page with the same vibrancy of the climbing shots.

The great pictures capture the sheer exhilaration of hard climbing in lonely places whether on arctic rock or Himalayan giants. Most pictures are glamorous but some depict the gripping struggle to survive in these eternal snows. Chris Bonington and Doug on the Ogre retreat, Nick Kekus attempting to find a snow-hole in an Everest blizzard, fighting a retreat from Makalu's eastern cwm and desperately searching for the body of Doug's friend, Ang Nima.

The captions are all good — usually understated and sometimes humorous. The book mirrors Doug in many ways — the sheer immensity of his achievements and travels are confusing to keep pace with. Sometimes the climbs are grouped chronologically, sometimes ethnically and sometimes geographically — which leads you to jump backwards and forwards in time throughout the book. The effect is that of a captional kaleidoscope of mountaineering. The texts that preview each chapter almost merit a book on their own. Consequently they are a brief pastiche of fact, personal observation and spiritual insight. We catch glimpses of some one who can achieve peace and insight walking the razor's edge between life and death on the high windswept summits of the world. This same man, through his very powers of survival, returns again and again to the confusing world below.

Part of that confusing world seems to be Doug's analysis of high mountain ethics. He states clearly his views against the use of fixed ropes and large expeditions and yet, and yet — fixed ropes and big teams abound here. We even find Doug's ascent of Lobsang Spire drilling holes up the summit block. If alpine style is a team of two with no fixed rope and no base camp support, there are murky ethical waters here, I fear. However, ethics are for tired sports and climbing is not yet tired. In terms of aesthetics Doug's style is to be admired. Great Britain may not be the greatest mountaineering nation in the world but there is a long tradition of innovative, adventurous and sometimes eccentric mountaineering. This is the illustrated handbook of that tradition.

The huge content of the book and the wealth of thoughts and stories that must lie under this iceberg's tip leave the reader anxiously waiting for the full autobiography promised in the foreword. This is a marvellous film and I for one would like to read the book.

The postscript catches some of Doug's complexity and his attempt to make sense of his climbing life. He quotes Tao Tsu in defence of climbing being unexplainable but truly the pictures capture what words will always fail to tell. I quote from the same Chinese sage;

The very highest is barely known by men

When actions are performed without unnecessary speech

People say 'We did it'.

JIM FOTHERINGHAM

MY VERTICAL WORLD. By Jerzy Kukuczka. Pp. 189, 19 colour
illustrations, 3 maps and 19 sketches, English edition 1992.
(Hodder and Stoughton, London. £16.99).

When, in the early '60s, Walter Bonatti wrote his first autobiography
On the Heights, he produced a classic account of great daring and
total commitment at what was then the cutting edge of alpinism.
Chapter after chapter sent shivers down the spine, because, above
all, this was a book stacked with legendary epics. *My Vertical World*
is the '90s equivalent. That same cutting edge has moved 4000
m higher and margin for error has narrowed considerably. Bonatti
survived due to his extraordinary ability, resilience and a large dollop
of luck. Although always a complex character, he was able to come
to terms with this, finally bowing out while the going was good.
Kukuczka, who had a more simplistic approach to life, unfortunately
did not.

Before he died on the south face of Lhotse in 1989, Kukuczka
had climbed all fourteen of the eight-thousand metre peaks and his
book describes those successes. It could hardly be classed as great
literature; a straight translation does nothing to improve the sometimes
clumsy sentences, and the final text could have been better proofed.
But it is an incredible story, told simply and with great honesty.
There is no attempt to conceal the race to be first, yet while Reinhold
Messner continued to pick off the normal routes, Kukuczka would
allow himself no compromise in standards: each summit must be
achieved by either a first winter ascent or a new route (remember
also that Polish winter ascents take place in the 'deep' winter of
January/February, and not in the relatively hospitable weeks of early
December, as is normal with virtually all other foreign expeditions
to Nepal). It was only his first eight-thousander, Lhotse, that failed
to meet this criterion, and it was to rankle Kukuczka throughout his
career.

This is a book that gives some insight into the difficulties in organizing
major expeditions from Poland; the 'under the counter' tactics to gain
funds, provisions and even, on occasions, summits. It is illustrated
by fourteen excellent and informative mountain sketches (by Alex Spark)
which contrast strongly with a disappointing collection of colour prints.
Now and again there are some revealing statements about his attitude
to both climbing and other climbers, though some of these fill one
with incredulity. For instance, he refers to the ever reliable Zyga Heinrich
as one of the leading figures of Polish, Himalayan and Alpine climbing,
but someone with little push who had rarely set foot on a summit;
this about a man who was reputed to have climbed more than 25
peaks of over seven-thousand metres, including new routes on Kungyang
Khish and Cho Oyu.

However, the overriding impression of Kukuczka is that of a talented
mountaineer with superhuman strength and an almost fanatical drive.
This is perhaps most apparent during the winter of 1984-85. Kukuczka
arrives in Kathmandu some weeks after the expedition has departed
for Dhaulagiri. By taking a short cut and ploughing through deep
snow on two high passes, he joins the team in late December, goes
straight onto the mountain and climbs it in appalling weather. Descending
from the summit he is forced to spend two nights out in the open,
with temperatures below 40°C and without food, drink and equipment,
before struggling down to base camp with frostbitten feet. Even Mr
Messner would, I am sure, have been perfectly happy to retreat to
the armchair in his alpine castle for a few months; but not Kukuczka.
The next day he is off on his own, racing back along the short
cut; racing to Kathmandu; racing to Cho Oyu where another Polish
expedition has nearly completed a new route up the south face. He
reaches the summit on the last day of winter, spending more unplanned
nights in the open and having more near misses. He returns home
for treatment of his badly frostbitten feet, yet two months later we
find him en route to Nanga Parbat and perhaps the most dangerous
ascent of his career. And so it goes on: a single-minded approach
to the mountain, an immense drive that is hardly dented by the
various deaths to fellow team members, a drive that often takes him
upwards into truly dangerous terrain when other powerful and experienced
colleagues are sounding the retreat with words such as 'unjustifiable'.
However, don't attempt to look for any underlying philosophy in the
text. Kukuczka's ideals were simple. I leave you with his own words.
'There is no answer in this book to the endless question about the
point of expeditions to the Himalayan giants. I never found a need
to explain this. I went to the mountains and climbed them. That
is all.'

LINDSAY GRIFFIN

THE CLIMBERS. A History of Mountaineering. By Chris Bonington.
    Pp. 288, 40 colour and 82 b/w illustrations, 6 maps, 1992.
    (BBC Books and Hodder & Stoughton, London, £16.95).

SEA, ICE — and — ROCK. Sailing and Climbing above The Arctic
    Circle. By Chris Bonington and Robin Knox-Johnston. Pp. 143,
    41 colour and 15 b/w illustrations, 3 maps, 1992. (Hodder
    & Stoughton, London, £15.99).

When Bonington visited Bombay in May 1992 he carried a copy
of The Climbers, his 12th book. When he returned in September
1992, he brought his 13th book: Sea, Ice-and-Rock. Not many writers,
especially mountaineers can boast of such prolific writing achievements.

The second book is about about a sailing-cum-climbing expedition above the arctic circle. A small group sailed and climbed in Greenland. The sailing skills of the master mariner, Robin Knox-Johnson and mountaineering skills of Chris Bonington combine. Robin Knox-Johnson with 9 previous books to his credit, matches Bonington's writing skills too. The result, an interesting book. But it is the former book, *The Climbers* that would interest the readers of the *Himalayan Journal* more.

The Climbers deals with 'A History of Mountaineering'. There have been few books in this genre, starting with the most celebrated of them all, Kenneth Mason's *Abode of Snow*. Mason's book covered the period from the earliest time till the first ascent of Everest in 1953. He covered only the Himalayan and transhimalayan ranges. Chris has a different line up. He covers both the Alps and the Himalaya starting from 1881 to 1990. The bulk of the book, 200 pages, covers the adventures till 1953. The prolific period of climbing for the last 37 years is covered in 68 pages. 'A brief History of Mountaineering', compiled by Audrey Salkeld towards the end, ensures a complete record of adventure.

If Mason's book is a thorough experience, like a symphony playing, with all the pieces, Bonington's book is to be read on an arm-chair with a cup of tea and a violin concerto playing lively tunes. The difference is obvious, but what is lost by way of complete coverage, Bonington makes up by way of extremely good reading and fun. Here is a part of the history. Bonington, narrating the history, and he knows it:

It is difficult for me to be completely objective since I have been closely and directly involved with the development of climbing in the last forty years. It has filled my life, given me that combination of joy, excitement, wonder and inevitable sorrow at the loss of all too many friends, but I hope that has enabled me to empathize all the better with those early climbers who first explored the mysteries of the Alps and traced the course of this serpentine river of ours.

So, turning familiarity to an advantage, Bonington writes about the climbers (not explorers). For the younger generation, particularly, the first 200 pages tell all the well-known stories and weave different patterns. This is enjoyable and exciting with the right mix of events and stories.

The latter pages consider the last 37 years, a long period. The chapters present three main issues as such, leaving behind the attempts to be exhaustive. The major climbs and development of climbing the mountains the 'hard way up' are considered. In the next chapter 'The Art of Suffering' extreme climbing is taken up. Exploits of Messner, Kurtyka and Kukuczka and the death of Boardman, Tasker and MacIntyre are covered in detail. But the last chapter is a stealer: 'Always a Little Further'. Here Bonington considers the major developments, which may affect the future attitudes. Sponsorship, commercial climbs, sport climbing and various developments in rock climbing advancements are touched upon. We are left with a vision of the future.

In his opening sentence itself, Bonington declares the scope of the book: 'In writing a one volume history of mountaineering I have had no choice but to be selective'. It is here that some can have a grouse against this book. To a lay reader it may appear that mountaineering is still a British preserve, or that only Americans and Europeans indulge in the sport. Not enough mention is made about the Japanese climbers or of climbers from many other countries such as South Korea, India and others. This has led to certain specific achievements of these nationalities being ignored. For example the traverse of the Nanda Devi peaks by the Indo-Japanese team, climbs of many high peaks in the East Karakoram by the Japanese in the 1970s are not mentioned. They marched for weeks to reach the base camps over high passes and climbed giants like Singhi Kangri, Teram Kangri and others. One may not like the fixed-ropes but they are there, even as a style.

The personal selection necessarily misses out on some areas. The entire Himalayan range from Nepal to Karakoram is covered by one sketch-map of Changabang, the peak climbed by the author. Thus Paul Bauer's attempts on Kangchenjunga from Sikkim by the northeast spur is taken up, but not the completion of the route in 1977 by the Indians. The 1979 British route by the north face gets a mention.

Considering the style and, as a major event for the development of attitudes, small teams and smaller, independent climbs, deserved a passing mention at least. The achievements of Shipton and Tilman still attract many. Stephen Venables' climb of Kishtwar-Shivling with Dick Renshaw and even Bonington's own ascent of Shivling West with Jim Fotheringham, were trend-setters, and this brand of climbing should be emphasised. That would be really looking into the future.

But then these are only small personal observations and do not detract from the merit and enjoyment of the book. To write 'the' history of mountaineering some one would have to fill half a dozen volumes and the author would still not be able to include everything.

The history of climbing is wonderfully rich — it is not
  so much a matter of hanging on to the tradition and

distrusting new developments, for these must occur as they
do in all forms of human development.

Bonington, even at his age and with his experience, refuses to
be 'pickled' and looks forward to the future with an open mind and
welcomes change. I am sure readers will look forward to many more
books from Bonington in future.

HARISH KAPADIA

K2 THE 1939 TRAGEDY. By Andrew J. Kauffman & William L.
   Putnam. Pp. 224, 36 b/w illustrations, 2 sketches, 3 maps,
   1992. (The Mountaineers, Seattle and Diadem Books, London,
   £14.99).

Most British climbers know far less about the history of attempts
on K2 than they do about equivalent attempts on Everest, mainly
because the latter were predominantly British, so a potted history
of K2 may be relevant. K2, only a few hundred feet lower than
Everest, is considerably steeper and more difficult, and a much greater
challenge to serious mountaineers. It has quite an early history.

The first attempt to climb it was ahead of its time, an expedition
in 1902 led by the controversial Englishman, Alastair Crowley. They
did some reconnaissance and climbed the lower part of the N.E.
ridge. Next was a big Italian expedition in 1909, led by the Duke
of Abruzzi. They did a little better, getting to 21,870 ft (6666 m)
on the Savioa Saddle at the start of the N.W. ridge, and to 20,300
ft (6200 m) on the S.E. (Abruzzi) ridge.

Then a gap followed until Charles Houston's excellent expedition
in 1938. His party was first to get high on the mountain. They
climbed the most difficult part of the Abruzzi ridge, and reached a
high point at about 26,000 ft (7920 m), only some 2,000 ft (600
m) from the top. The 1939 expedition was a follow-up of the previous
trip, but with a weaker party which nevertheless got to about 27,000
ft (8230 m).

Another American attempt was made in 1953, also by Houston,
and the mountain was finally climbed by a big Italian expedition in
1954 via the Abruzzi ridge. Over subsequent years, most of the other
ridges, and a few faces have been climbed, with a rush of activity
in 1986, when there were more ascents of, and more deaths on
the mountain than in all of its previous history.

The topic of the book under review is the 1939 attempt, noted
for its controversial disaster involving the deaths high up of Dudley
Wolfe, a rich but incompetent American climber, and three Sherpas.

I was myself on K2 in 1986. After my brush with the mountain, less conclusive either way than many others that year, I do have an active interest in most K2-related writings. But I did not find this book to be compulsive reading. I think the authors intended their book to be a historical work, putting the record straight, rather than a gripping yarn. The style of writing certainly indicates this, with painstaking attention to detail, rather than an easy-flowing narrative.

They wished to throw light on the complex circumstances leading up to the disaster, an objective they pursued with meticulous care, but only limited success due to incomplete factual information. They did make good use of a number of fresh sources of original information, notably the expedition diary of Jack Durrance, one of the expedition members. The diary was previously unpublished due to Jack's reluctance to become caught in the web of post-expedition recriminations which had ensnared others. Although the diary cannot be regarded as completely impartial, it does seem to absolve Jack from much of the blame for the tragedy, that had previously and unfairly been laid on him. On the other hand, expedition leader Fritz Wiessner was, it seems, only human after all, and must shoulder his share of the blame. Much remains unanswered.

Personally, I was interested less in such detailed fault-finding, and more in general long-term matters which the authors touched on, but did not emphasise. The main blame for the tragedy was in the weakness of the team. Fritz was the only one who was really qualified for such an ambitious objective. A naturalised American of German origin, he had much experience in the Alps and Rockies, and in 1932 he had been to 23,000 ft. (7000 m.) on Nanga Parbat with Willi Merkl. The other five members of the team were much weaker, none had previous Himalayan experience (but who had in those days?), most had climbed in the Alps or Rockies, but unexceptionally, and some only in the company of guides. The 1938 expedition members, mostly with stronger credentials, were unable to get away again so soon. No doubt Fritz realised the limitations of his colleagues, but his optimism, ambition and Teutonic stubbornness prevented him from cancelling the expedition, or withdrawing the party from the mountain when things were going wrong, but disaster might still have been averted.

The American Alpine Club, officially organised this expedition and the previous one, should also take some of the blame, for sending so inexperienced a team on so major an undertaking. They should surely have been more objective in their appraisal of the party's chances than the ambitious and headstrong Wiessner. But the authors, both experienced mountaineers, fail to give this point due stress. They were

both former dignitaries (one a president, the other a vice-president)
of the A.A.C., and failed to bite the bullet of blaming their own
organisation.

An extenuating factor was the late withdrawal from the expedition
of three of its strongest potential members. But they were not very
much stronger than those who did go, so I feel the authors overstress
this point. The A.A.C. should have made the hard decision to cancell
the trip, or divert it to a more appropriate and lesser objective.

The book would best be read not for its weak narrative worth,
nor for its strong attention to historical detail, but rather as an insight
into what can go wrong on a big mountain with a party most of
who have the wrong sort of experience. You wouldn't fill an Olympic
marathon team with 100 metres runners.

DAVE WILKINSON

LADAKH THROUGH THE AGES. By Shridhar Kaul and H. N. Kaul.
    (Pp. 368, 38 b/w illustrations, 1992. (Indus Publishing Co.,
    New Delhi, Rs. 450).

Begun by Shridhar Kaul, this book was completed by his son
H. N. Kaul and represents a labour of love for both. In trying to
squeeze between its covers the full sweep of Ladakh's history, geography,
heritage, political and administrative neglect, the book aims to present
and impassioned plea to grant the Ladakhis power to steer their
own destiny.

The first half of the book serves only as a backgrounder: the
centuries of Ladakhi kings, the rule of the Dogras after the exploits
of Zorawar Singh; the complex social organization of the Buddhist
community and the rise of a few modern leaders like Kushok Bakula:
all these are covered rapidly, with a pedantic, linear approach. The
material is sourced from the Ladakhi chronicles, early British commentators
like Cunningham, Drew and Moorcroft, the Tarikhi Rashidi and, except
for the last named, does not offer any new insights.

The real significance of the book lies in the chapters covering the
pre and post-Indian Partition events in Ladakh, events in which Shridhar
Kaul participated personally: thus we get a ringside view of the historic
upheavals from a civilian point of view as opposed to the plethora
of memoirs by the army brass who over the years have told their
'untold stories' to the nation.

As the second half of the book, penned by H. N. Kaul, takes
over, political events gather momentum and here the author has been
quite successful in detailing the sins of omission and commission

of the successive state Chief Ministers — beginning with the 'Lion of Kashmir' Sheikh Mohamed Abdullah right through to the mid-eighties when his son Farookh Abdullah held the reins of the state government — and their betrayal of the faith of the Ladakhi people. Thus we have the glaring contradiction that even 45 years after the Indian Independence, a Buddhist Ladakhi child is taught in Urdu in the few state schools when Bodhi, his mother tongue, has a perfectly sound script and literature; whereas in the Kashmir valley, a Kashmiri script was evolved and used to replace Urdu as a medium of instruction. This section of the book is a disturbing litany of neglect, discrimination and corruption; brought up to date and including the disturbances that rocked Leh and shocked the rest of India in 1989.

Underlying the apparently partisan accounts, biased in favour of the Buddhist majority of the Leh district, it is the author's firm belief that they are the wronged people: and he argues logically and also substantiates his claims. What ultimately emerges from all this is that unless the Ladakhis run their own affairs, instead of being victims of a state power which is far removed from them, in distance sympathy and understanding, there is little hope that the poverty, backwardness and extremely hard life of its simple, cheerful and hardy people will improve. In the world's largest democracy, it is the least that the nation can do for them. Except for a total lack of maps and rather slipshod proofreading, the message the book aims to deliver, hits the target.

ALOKE SURIN

ISLAND AT THE EDGE OF THE WORLD. By Stephen Venables, Pp. 177, 32 colour illustration, 3 maps, 1991. (Hodder & Stoughton, London, £ 16.99).

Island at the edge of the world is not only a narrative of a five man expedition to South Georgia. It also provides a perceptive insight into the history of the island and a description of the abundant and varied species of wildlife found in the Antarctica, which are quite unfamiliar to most of us. It is a multifaceted book — a work which reflects the sensitive and perceptive nature of the author.

It was around the time that Stephen got back from his ascent of Everest and visited his friend Julian Freeman Attwood towards the end of 1989 that they discussed the possibility of an expedition to South Georgia. Ever since 1775, when Captain James Cook had landed in Possession Bay and taken possession of the country in his Majesty's name (George III), South Georgia has belonged to the U.K. Over the years Argentina made several claims to the island.

Since 1968, MMS Endurance, an ice patrol vessel, had symbolised Britain's presence in the Antarctic. Every year on its southern journey via the South American ports, it had been traditional for it to take some civilian passengers along. Julian and Stephen decided to persuade the Navy to take them along.

When it was clear that the expedition was definite, Julian and Stephen got down to choosing the team. They had been set a maximum of 5 members by the Captain of the Endurance. They decided on Lindsay Griffin and Brian Davison, both experienced climbers who had climbed in Tibet with them and Keest Hooft, a Dutch film maker to get video footage for the expedition. 'Hooft's sensitivity as an observer would probably be more valuable than the technical skills of a seasoned cameraman'.

When the team was finalised, they decided to find out more about the mountains in South Georgia. Who could be better informed than Duncan Carse — after whom Mt. Carse, the highest peak in South Georgia was named. Duncan Carse had gone to live alone in South Georgia for 18 months. One night, Carse's hut was completely destroyed by a freak wave and this left him in a tent, surviving 116 winter days before a passing sailing vessel rescued him. Carse gave them valuable information on the island.

On Sunday, 3 December, 1989, the 5 man team left Britain for South Georgia. They first flew to the Falklands, stopping at Ascension Island to refuel and then joined the Endurance to sail 850 miles to South Georgia.

South Georgia's main mountain range is at right angles to the wind. However, there is a mile-wide break between the ranges, the Ross pass, which was the expedition's proposed base from where they would attempt the unclimbed peaks. Ross pass was also a wind funnel directing all the force of the notorious westerlies down Ross glacier and into the Royal Bay. It was at Royal Bay that they learnt about the wind. 'It was a new malevolent force, battering mercilessly at our tents, flinging storage barrels across the valley, whipping sand and snow in our faces, and when it got the chance throwing us bodily to the ground.'

They started ferrying supplies to Ross pass and also built a snow cave to move into (because a tent had already been wrecked at Royal Bay). However, an unusually warm wind melted the ice and the cave got submerged in the lake that formed, forcing them back to Royal Bay. The weather was bad for the next few days, but it got better on Dec. 30th Brian and Stephen set out for Ross pass, to build an 'Ice Palace' while the other three followed later. By the next day

---

the 'Ice Palace' was completed and was to be their home for the next twenty one days.

The first peak they attempted was Vogel. However by following the prospective route, they realised that a deep trough separated them from Vogel. It was Friday morning, 4 a.m., Brian woke the rest as the weather was clear and there was time to climb a virgin peak they had been eyeing. Their first summit was called 'the Thing' or the 'Blob' and this success was followed by another one — Vogel peak, approached this time round the southwest flank. By the time they had climbed Vogel, they had spent 16 days in the 'Ice Palace' and had only a week's supply of food left. Brian and Stephen were the optimistic ones, aiming for Mt. Carse, while Julian had his eyes on Mt. Kuing — a closer, unclimbed peak. But the weather was not on their side. Three days of relentless rain, and the snow cave dripped incessantly. A slight clearing allowed them to conquer point 2422 and then the wind changed direction, the barometer showed some encouraging signs — would there be time for Mt. Carse? Brian and Stephen were up at 4 the next morning. None of the others were anxious to go. They left by 7 and made their way up Spendley glacier. By one, they reached the final pass and studied the mountain — and decided on the northwest ridge. They decided to press on while the weather was good, and 'take the mountain by storm before it knew what happened.'

Island at the Edge of the World is about a dream. A dream which unlike many others, was fulfilled. Stephen Venables writes with easy informality, vivid expression, humour and a human touch. This is not a mere technical account of an expedition. It is also an account of the history (could he have been more brief?) of South Georgia, its unique wildlife and its landscape. The photographs were a pleasure, some breathtaking. The one of lenticular clouds in East Cumberland Bay stays in one's memory like a beautiful painting.

RAMANA NANDA

THE CALL OF EVEREST. First ascent by an Indian woman. By Brig. D. K. Khular, Pp. 200, 8 b/w and 6 colour illustrations, 2 maps, 1992. (Vision Books, New Delhi, Rs. 190).

Here is a small sized book without any pretence to aesthetic excellence or quality of pictures, purporting to be an account of the officially sponsored Indian men-women expedition to Everest in 1984. However, it deserves special attention since the style and contents of this book lay bare the unsavoury story of a major Indian expedition, which is generally not found in print, being preferred to be pushed under the carpet.

Mountaineering activity in India whether official or otherwise is undertaken with an overdose of glorification and national pride. More so on Everest, which promises a passport to places and privileges to a summiter. In narrating this race the author has gone counter to the element of glorification. He admits alarmingly to serious short-comings in administration, organisation, material and financial resources, the process of selection of the leader and members, the Sherpa teams, and above all the clashes of ambitions of the personalities that were pitted on the highest mountain in the world. As Brig. Gyan Singh states in his opening remarks, 'Competition, jealousies, vaulting ambitions seem to have replaced camaraderie and team spirit in many cases, particularly in prestigious ventrues.' It is significant that the book was published seven years after the event.

The author was the Principal of the Himalayan Mountaineering Institute at Darjeeling from 1981 and commences his story with the goings-on there and the process of selection of the leader and members of the team. There is the strain of bureaucratic reporting in the prose, interspersed with titbits of gossip on the frailties of men and women. The reader becomes restless with such pages filled with innuendoes fit in a memoir but not germane to the main story. Expedition writers in India seem to be bogged down too much with the irrelevant bureaucratic process which may be dispensed with in a few lines in the preface. True mountain literature would emerge if only the writers describe the action of men and mountains as their principal theme and not how they were assembled and announced simultaneously from Delhi and Kathmandu, where then the I.M.F. President, H. C. Sarin, was on a posting as an Ambassador. The author describes at length the goings-on at Delhi for fund raising, purchases and packing.

It ws a tragic expedition. A strong team of climbers were selected. An advance party had negotiated the icefall in five days with deputy leader Prem Chand. The author disarmingly narrates the loss of personal understanding between himself and his prospective summit climber Dorjee Lhatoo, who was also his subordinate at the mountaineering Institute. There are numerous anecdotes which caused friction between them before the expedition left Delhi, largely due to certain behaviour that infuriated the leader which nearly ended in Lhatoo threatening to leave the expedition a few hours before the departure. Eventually this did not take palce. Writing with hindsight, the leader felt that this was a precursor of the rift that was caused with the deputy leader, upon instigation by this member.

The expedition's advance party was dogged by lack of proper provisions, administrative and financial support that caused a near rebellion by one of the Sherpa teams. As the leader's party was on the march

to the base camp, news came of an avalanche tragedy causing the
death of a Sherpa and injuring five others. On top of that, the cook
was found dead near Lobuje. The lack of funds compelled the leader
to send his lead climber with an S.O.S. to Kathmandu to meet I.M.F.
President/Ambassador. Upon arrival at the base camp the leader received
a long note from the deputy leader, from a lower resting place,
pouring out his mind at the chaotic nature of the expedition.

Eventually the expedition got going and quickly set up a series
of camps up the Western Cwm and even reached the Sourth Col
as early as 29 April. It was still beset with Sherpa porter shortage
to carry loads as different teams of them apparently did not pull
together. To top it all, the oxygen equipment which reached the expedition
was deficient, forcing the leader to trade-off a sporting offer from
a Bulgarian team climbing the West Ridge and desiring support for
a traverse by the Indian route, in exchange for lighter and more
efficient Russian oxygen equipment, so vitally needed for the Indian
push. When the leader and the deputy leader announced the first
summit teams there was discord from those who were not included
in the first push, to the extent of a lady declaring her desire to
quit!

The summit party was all set on 9 May. By a strange turn of
events the two Bulgarians on their way down from the summit traverse
found themselves benighted on the SE ridge. The leader of the Indian
expedition had to respond to a call for emergency help from the
second summit team of Indian climbers at the South Col who were
in position. The second summit party of Bulgarians met lone Indian
climber Phu Dorji below the summit. Two others from the Indian
team had earlier retreated. After reaching the summit without oxygen
an the last sections, Phu Dorji descended to the South Col, meeting
Bulgarians on the way. The two Bulgarians escorted a benighted member
of their first traverse party to the South Col.

The Indian leader called-off the second summit party poised for
the attempt and diverted the manpower and resources for the rescue
operation for the two Bulgarians who were left in their hands at
the South Col, the second Bulgarian party having left for the base.
This dramatic turn of events fatally affected the destiny of the Indian
expedition. The Bulgarians had co-operated considerably with the Indians,
giving them oxygen equipment and walkie-talkie sets. It was the Indians'
turn to express gratitude and sacrifice.

It should be mentioned here that one of the principal assignments
of the Indian Everest expedition 1984 was to place a minimum of
two Indian girls on the summit. This was drummed into each member
of the team. However the leader notes with regret that when Phu

Dorji in the lead found Rita and Ang Dorji trailing behind (all unroped), he did not bother to communicate with them and instead dashed alone for the summit, ditching the principal objective of taking the girl along. Ang Dorji had to turn back as his feet got cold. Rita had no other alternative but to give up.

On the part of the ladies there was keen contest to be on the summit team. On a trial run two ladies claimed to have reached C3 when they had turned back for short of it, as seen by the leader from the advance camp. 'A small lie is not much of a price, if it secures a summit birth'.

After regrouping, two summit teams were put to action only to be foiled by a severe avalanche which hit C3. It was occupied by one summit team. Members and Sherpas were badly injured. The Indian penchant for records is evident in a short quote attributed to Sanjeev Saith. While waiting for the injured being attended and with the avalanche debris strewn all around, he had something else to do.

> Pretending not to be breathless, I pulled out my flute and proceeded to play a Bhairavi for the sherpas, thereby establishing a high-altitude record for an Indian classical flute recital. I had to. I wouldn't have been invited to the IMF parties in Delhi without some sort of record to my credit.

Shades of Nero playing the fiddle while Rome was burning?

The rescue effort was heroic but this made the team's objective almost unattainable now. The earlier team at the South Col retreated in bad weather. Morale was low. Fear had gripped the party. However, the objective to put a girl on the summit looked attainable with the enthusiasm showed by Bachendri Pal who, although involved in the avalanche at C3, was undaunted in spirit. It was decided that she would participated in the final push with two men and with two more in support. A follow up summit party of Lhatoo and Paljor was also planned a day after. However what followed was bizzare. The second party using oxygen in full throttle, instead of halting at C3 as ordered, overtook the first party to occupy the South Col along with the latter. Next day there was a shameless show down with the second party not giving up their scarce oxygen cylinders for the first party — six left-over cylinders were found to have mysteriously leaked! The leader suspected foul play by the second summit party, having sabotaged the leak earlier, but he is not definite. He writes a special Appendix 4, titled 'Leaked Cylinders'. There was one girl

in the crowd at the South Col and the second party was fitter than
the others. The leader's order on walkie-talkie to Paljor to hand
over oxygen cylinders to Magan Bissa was disobeyed. Paljor walked
away to the summit. The leader instructs Kiran Kumar, the member
of the first team to hand over the remaining Bulgarian oxygen cylinders
to Lhatoo, who by now had attained the position of strength. The
leader remarks:

> There was a basic dichotomy in our team, which surfaced
> quite unmistakenly now. There were the professionals who
> had clean and simple single-minded motives, get-to-the-top-
> and-back-safely-looking-after-myself-first-and-then-after-others,
> and then there were the amateurs, who had mixed-up notions
> about friendship and decency and chivalry and sportsmanship
> and sacrifice and fair play.

The race that commenced on the 22nd ended on 23 May when
on a magnificent day the first Indian girls set foot on the summit
of Everest at 1.07 p.m. along with two men and one more to follow
after some time — Lhatoo, Ang Dorji and Paljor. (Ang Dorji was
rewarded Rs. 15,000 for roping up the girl to the summit).

There was rejoicing all around in I.M.F. quarters at Kathmandu
and Delhi. The I.M.F. President exhorting the leader to put one more
girl to the top to make the lady 'P.M. and I.M.F. happy' and that
will win 'the leader, deputy leader, the team a welcome given only
to big heroes'. But the depleted team was in shambles, physically
and psychologically. The leader called off the expedition. It is indeed
comical to find attempted backseat driving from Delhi and Kathmandu,
as if the leader was a babe in the woods. Even answering the press
conference at Kathmandu on leader's return was taken over by the
I.M.F. President.

The expedition ended in disenchantment all round. The leader published
his story after a seven year digestive process. There could be many
facets of this sad story. The author has revealed his inner thoughts
and frustrations. He even admits his own misjudgements and errors.
He had not hesitated to comment on the frailties of his team members.
Although the book cannot be included in memorable mountain literature,
it has the unique distinction of laying the affairs of the expedition
bare. The leader has listed the lessons of this expedition and some
of self-critical comments by members. He also gives a verdict as
seen through the comments by members, 'Avoid mixed expeditions.
It turns out to be a honeymoon'. A sad commentary on Indian morality,
in the second last decade of the 20th Century. The book has a
lot to ponder over.

JAGDISH C. NANAVATI

Note: Please also refer to the letter on the same expedition by Dorjee Lhatoo
in the 'Correspondence' section in the present volume. — Ed.

GANGA DESCENDS. By Ruskin Bond. Pp. 95, 12 sketches, 1992.
(The English Book Depot, Dehra Dun, Rs. 50).
SEVEN SACRED RIVERS. By Bill Aitken. Pp. 196, 16 b/w illustrations,
1 map, 1992, (Penguin Books, New Delhi, Rs. 75).

Ruskin Bond has done more to introduce Nature to Indian children
than any government department or enthusiastic environmentalist. Trees,
animals and birds play an important role in his stories. His forte
is simple language and short, easy descriptions. Bond lives in Mussourie
and it is the vicinity of his home that he describes in *Ganga Descends*,
a book comprising a collection of essays about folk-lore, lives of
villagers, birds, rivers and his own personal experiences in the Himalaya.
As the start and end of the book, he has included chapters about
himself as a writer and mountain-dweller, and his lifestyle. In two
chapters, he has written about the history of Dehradun and Mussourie.
By telling the reader about a young lad waiting for a letter, about
an old man selling peanuts in a bazar, about the pilgrims that struggle
to Badrinath, with only their faith to keep them going, Bond had
brought out the difficulties of living at such great heights. Unkind
weather and little food, bad transport and loneliness are overcome
by a certain ability to endure.

Besides spurts of descriptions, always crisp and short, he frequently
includes mentions of Englishmen who visited the areas he has been
to, as well as the towns along the way. The book is good to take
a peek at the living conditions in Garhwal Himalaya. The view offered
is of a lay-person, part-naturalist, part-trekker, part-writer. The book
is easy to read, easy to finish.

Bill Aitken's name is a familiar one amongst readers of national
dailies and magazines in India, published in English. His theme is
travel, his talent, humour. Though Scot, he has made India his home
for over three decades, we has imbibed the traits and attitudes of
his adopted countrymen. The mixture has resulted in a refreshing
approach towards people, experiences, cultures, problems, and Aitken
pens them lucidly in his essays.

In *Seven Sacred Rivers*, Aitken has described his journeys up and
along the Ganga, the Brahmaputra, the Mahanadi, the Narmada, the
Godavari, the Kaveri and the Indus. He has traced the rivers upto
their source, be it in the lofty, inaccessible heights of the Himalaya
or the primitive wilds of Madhya Pradesh. He has 'travelled along
India's rivers by foot, motor-bike, bus and train for the sheer pleasure
of proximity'. In the process, he has faced hardships and seen Indian
life at grass-root level, and most of the time with little money to
spare. The book reveals more than just the flow of the rivers; it

is a fine comment on the social fabric of Indians from Assam to
Rajasthan to Tamil Nadu. Whilst glorifying the abundance and variety
of Nature's bounty along the banks of the rivers, the author' has
brought out the extent of environmental damage wherever he has
witnessed it.

Philosophical paragraphs are interspersed with autobiographical ones.
He has met and expressed his opinions (often unflattiering) on various
important personalities, both political and social. The geography and
history of the places he has journeyed through have been well-researched
and briefly given — enough to acquaint the reader, not bore him.

What makes the book different is the way Aitken has treated his
theme. He has compared each river to a human female form. Thus
he 'fell in love with the Narmada the moment (he) saw her. She
was incontrovertibly feminine, more so than any other river I have
seen..... The blueness of the Godavari was a lighter, more spiritual
shade while the dark blaze of the Krishna was openly erotic. Only
the Narmada seemed to offer a lasting relationship based on warmth
and affection. Who was she?'

Aitken's journeys on motor-bike, alone, and with little money to
spare have enriched his experiences (and the book) and he has injected
his work with plenty of anecdotes, too. Aitken's other writings have
ranged from complaints about and against the Indian tourism industry,
to descriptions of the 'toy' trains that carry vacationers to hill-stations,
to life in the Capital, to.... Seven Sacred Rivers, indeed a worthwhile
addition to any library.

The selection of the seven rivers narrated here itself shows a deep
understanding of the Hindu psyche by the author. It is the blessings
by these rivers that a traditional Hindu marriage is solemanised and
the ancient texts give mantras which state these. The author makes
the readers understand why these rivers were selected by the sages.
This is a commendable job for a Scotsman turned Indian. Both the
authors, Bond and Aitken, live near each other at Mussourie and
between them understand Indian culture and write about it more than
anyone else.

                                                SHEELA JAYWANT

100 HIMALAYAN FLOWERS. By Ashwin Mehta. Text by Prof. P.
    V. Bole. Pp. 144, 100 colour illustrations, 1991. (Mapin Publishing
    pvt. ltd., Ahemdabad, nps).

Last summer I had the good fortune to visit the Kumaon Himalaya
for the first time. That expedition to Panch Chuli is extensively documented
in this journal, but the articles are reports mainly on the climbing

that took place. The mountains were indeed very fine and the glaciers impressive, but for me the real treat was to travel through primal virgin forest and up onto alpine meadows that were probably identical to Smythe's famous 'Valley of Flowers'.

The flora of Kumaon is the perfect Everyman's compromise, encompassing most of the Western Himalaya species and a good smattering of flowers associated with Nepal and the far eastern Himalayan. Ashvin Mehta's beautiful new book is drawn from this wealth of variety, presenting a personal selection of 100 better known species. Most readers will be familiar with Mehta's earlier photographic study, *Himalaya: Encounters with Eternity.* His new book focusses down from the grand view to the intimate, but is printed to the same high quality.

The book is not a botanical reference work. For plant identification, one turns to the standard work by Polunin and Stainforth. Mehta's photos are deliberately subjective, artistic rather than botanical, frequently isolating flowers without accompanying foliage. Although each photograph is backed up with a precise botanical description, the book is essentially an aesthetic celebration of the glories of the Himalayan flora, to titillate the beginner.

I was thrilled to see his massed pink polygonums, reminding me of the high meadows of Kishtwar, his close-up study of a blood red potentialla and his tight cluster of Iris Kumaonensis, bringing back a flood of memories from the Panch Chuli expedition. By contrast, I was disappointed by his Primula macrophylla, which did not seem to extract the deep, vibrant purple I recall. However, one has to remember that there are numerous variables, not only in the flowers themselves and the particular light in which they are photographed, but also in the colour film and the many processes that lead to the final printed page. By and large the colours seem vibrantly accurate: to give one specific example, the unique, exquisite, electric blue of Corydalis kashmeriana is captured perfectly.

If I have one criticism, it is that sometimes the depth of field is so restricted as to leave nine tenths of the picture blurred. However, these photographs are not studio portraits — they were all taken in the field, making do with available light and the blurring tendencies of wind. In any case, the book is not intended as a scientific study. The introduction and notes at the end are directed at the amateur like me, who can be driven to ecstatic rapture by the Himalayan flora, without necessarily knowing a great deal about it. Mehta's beautiful book certainly tempts me to return and has made me desperate to find the wonderful crimson spotted Lilium polyphyllum.

STEPHEN VENABLES

THE HANDBOOK OF CLIMBING. By Allen Fyffe and Iain Peter,
    Pp. 373, many b/w and colour illustrations, sketches, 1990.
    (Pelham Books, London, £20).

A handbook which has been endorsed by the British Mountaineering
Council. It is useful for those who want to learn to climb and for
those who wish to improve their skills and technical knowledge of
climbing.

Many books on the climbing, techniques have been available for
many years. Some cover specific areas like ice-climbing and related
techniques. Many cover specific aspects like leadership for children
or organising small expeditions. Few are exhaustive, hoping to cover
almost all a climber should know. One such well known book over
the years is *Mountaineering* by Alan Blackshaw. But techniques change,
attitudes change and equipment is upgraded. Thus it is always welcome
when someone who is in forefront of climbing writes about it from
experience. Here we have two of them.

Both authors are fully qualified to undertake such an exhaustive
work. Allen Fyffe is a full time climbing instructor at Glenmore Lodge,
Scotland. He has made a number of ascents in the higher ranges
also. Iain Peter is, at present, training administrator of the British
Mountaineering Council's Mountain Walking Leader Training Board. He
also has pursued a full-time career in instructing and guiding all over
the world. Thus what they write here is backed up by experience
and authority.

The book has been divided into three major sections and appendices.
Section one is on 'Rock Climbing' and section two is on 'Snow,
Ice and Winter Climbing.' Both these sections cover major aspects
like equipment, technique, protections and belay. The section on rock
climbing also covers Emergency Procedures and Pegs and Artificial
Climbing. Section three is on 'Alpine Climbing' divided into chapters
on The Alpine Experience, Glacier Travel; Alpine Rock, Ice and Mixed
Climbing; and Mountain Huts and Bivouaking. The appendices cover
chapters on Guides, Grades and Games, Sea Cliff Climbing, Navigation,
Snow & Avalanches, Snow Shelters, Training, Psychological Skills in
Climbing and First Aid.

All sections are written in a simple clear and logical manner and
are supported with illustrations and photographs. The sections on
equipment, technique, protections and belay are exhaustive and cover
the latest developments. 'Emergency procedures'. The chapter on first
aid could be well complemented with a section on search and rescue.

In the chapter on 'The Alpine Experience' the authors have described only the alpine style of climbing. The book could have also covered the traditional style of climbing mentioning the trend towards alpinism. In reality, many of the climbs to the high mountains end up as a mix of different styles of climbing. This chapter would be useful to those who are starting out on their alpine experience, for those who wish to extend this alpine experience to the high mountains, the authors could have also described the procedure of organising an expedition to the high mountains with its related problems of travel, equipment, medical background and logistics. From its title one would look forward to an insight into all aspects of climbing, including that of the high mountains of the Himalaya, Karakoram etc. but is restricted to purely alpine climbing.

The Appendices are informative and cover various related topics. A chapter on weather patterns and forecasting would have been useful. Much credit needs to be given to the authors for including the chapter on Psychological Skills, since this subject has been neglected in the past. The chapter on First Aid touches only a few areas. One must go through a good book on first-aid for mountaineers in addition.

Hamish Macinnes aptly writes in the Foreword to the book, 'But it is not just a book for the beginner, even the experienced mountainer will find gems of information and the excellent Glossary and Index make it also a comprehensive reference work.'

Finally as the authors say in introduction, 'The best aspects of climbing are your personal experiences. No attempt has been made in this book to describe what climbing can give its participants: that is for you to discover, and it has been very well described by others.' This book will certainly make attaining that experience safe and possible.

DIVYESH MUNI

AS I SAW IT FROM SHANTI NIVAS By Jack Gibson, Pp. 191, 6 colour illustrations 1992, (Published by the author, Ajmer, Rs. 200).

The author came to India in 1937 to join the teaching staff of the newly opened Doon School in Dehra Dun. Till he retired in 1969 from Mayo College as its Principal he worked with educational and military institutions from time to time. He had keen interest in out-door life and introduced his pupils to skiing and mountaineering. He was the President of the Himayan Club from 1970 to 1973. This period of his time in India is covered in his early book *As I Saw It* published in 1976.[1]

1. See H.J. Vol. XXXIV, p. 203, for the review. — Ed.

The author decided to retire and settle in India. For most of the period till today he has resided at Ajmer in Rajasthan. This new book *As I Saw It From Shanti Nivas* records his experiences mainly in India from 1969 to 1984.

The book offers a bird's eye view of a British educationalist, of what it has been like to stay on, after 32 years of work in India, both during the time of British Raj and after the Indian Independence. His views are freely expressed on political, judicial and social systems, educational and moral standards. These are of great value but to those who are interested in genuine introspection. His love for his kitchen gardern his struggle to adjust with the deteriorating values, not only in the India but the world over, his deep concern for the protection of environment and well-being of India come out very strongly.

The author has preferred to tell his story in the form of letters in chronological order. Though the continuity is lost in this format he believes that a better picture is painted in this way.

His views are not pessimistic but one definitely comes across a feeling of hurt and sadness in his writings as people around him and the turn of events keep failing to stand up to his high expecttations. Just to quote an example he handed over hundreds of meticulously prepared, valuable exercises he had set in Geography and English to masters at Mayo College in 1984, a part of his heart hoping that they could be put to good use. At the same time, however, the other part of his heart very well knew that the papers would be probably chucked into a waste paper basket. And he felt perhaps that was what he should have done in the first place. But everything is not lost. Gibson has created awareness and passed on his values to many in the next generation.

ARUN SAMANT

THE MERRY-GO-ROUND OF MY LIFE, Pp. 219, b/w illustrations 1991, (Vantage Press, New York, £13.95).

The book is an account of Richard Hachtel's various climbs, expeditions and excursions in various parts of the world over a few generations. The author Richard Hachtel was born in 1913 at the small town of Schwabach, near Nuernberg in what today is the Federal Republic of Germany. He belongs to the revolutionary era of World War II when concepts of sports and life in general were constantly changing. Mountaineering as a sport was not very well recognised and there was no special clothing or climbing equipment available to climbers unlike today. He has well brought out these changing concepts in attitudes and equipment over the last few decades.

He used to ride a bicycle upto whatever distance possible to reach the base of the mountains on dirt tracks because in those days there was no means of easy transport to the base of some of the climbers in the Alps. From his narrations of adventure the reader shares his feelings of fulfilling the spirit of adventure and the satisfaction of enduring physical hardships. In addition to all the drawbacks of that time the author is consciously aware of his clumsy physical appearance. Through his determination and strong will power these never came in the way of his mountaineering.

He climbed in different parts of the world. Though the climbers are distinct, his narration is plain and sometimes it is tiring to read details of excursions. He rarely expresses his feelings while on the mountain thus not allowing the reader to be an active participant of his adventure. However, his stories bridge the generation gap between climbers of past and present as he is well aware of techniques, grading systems for rock climbing, and clothing of modern mountaineering which may be attributed to the fact that he has climbed with different generations of climbers with ease.

His major expeditioning period was between 1961 to 1978. He turned seventy in 1983. Reading his adventures from 1983 till the publication of this book in 1991 one admires his perseverance.

In the last outing mentioned in the book, he only says 'You cannot win them all' but is contented with his life. He has aptly called the book an adventurer's diary and not an autobiography to suggest that the spirit of adventure is immortal.

VINEETA MUNI

BUDDHIST MONASTERIES IN HIMACHAL PRADESH. By O. C. Handa, Pp. 216, 37 plates, 54 sketches, 1987. (Indus Publishing Co., New Delhi, Rs. 150).

This book is a detailed study of the Buddhist monastries in Himachal Pradesh, a historical record from ancient India to medieval Renaissance, and to modern transformation.

The author has divided the romantic centres of Himachal Pradesh into four valleys.

The author starts from Lahul Valley where Buddhism must have entered around the 2nd century A.D. The Vajravarahi temple, Trilokinath temple, Guru Ghantal monastery have all the common link of carvings of the same era. The present structure is a fascinating monument of Hinduism and Buddhism through the ages.

Lahul monasteries adopt the Tibetan construction technique marked by flat roofs and sun dried brick walls. But in the layout they follow the ancient Indian scheme as a matter of tradition.

Spiti valley has seven monastries which profess the unreformed form of Lamaism, the Nyingmapa order. There are 21 monastries belonging to the Ge-Lug-Pa order. The author studies each in great depth, about the structure layout, comparison with Tibetan and Indian temples. Well drawn sketches accompany each section.

Satluj valley: This is the Kinnaur region, narrated in the Indian epics and *Puranas*. Here the Buddhist influence can be seen on the demoanical Kinnaur dieties.

In Kinnaur, the primitive deities are propitiated and the Mahanayanist pantheon worshipped by all. This region is a socio-economic divide between the Buddhist Tibet and the Brahmanic India.

Beas valley: It was till the 9th century that Buddhism thrived here, then the Brahamanism held sway again in the 14th century Lamaism found its way, and the most prominent example is of Rawalsar.

The explanation of a minor structure like chorten, its significance, are in details with diagrams. Further chapters explain the educational, social economical and political aspects of this region. The architectural development with local construction technique is studied in detail.

The monastic art makes interesting and knowledgeable reading about the paintings in thanks, the motifs, and the different types of casting and carving of statues.

This history of this the Western Himalayan region is well preserved in minute details by O.C. Handa in this book.

GEETA KAPADIA

LAHAUL-SPITI. A Forbidden Land in the Himalayas. By S.C. Bajpai. Pp. 164, 10 b/w illustrations, 1 map, 1992. (Indus Publishing Co., New Delhi, Rs. 200).

KINNAUR. A Restricted Land in the Himalaya. By S.C. Bajpai. Pp. 240, 13 b/w illustrations, 1 map, 1991. (Indus Publishing Co., New Delhi, Rs. 250.)

A HANDBOOK OF THE HIMALAYA. By Dr. S. S. Negi, Pp. 350, 34 b/w illustrations, 18 maps and sketches, 1990. (Indus Publishing Co., New Delhi, Rs. 400).

HIMALAYAN RIVERS, LAKES AND GLACIERS. By S. S. Negi, Pp.
182, 8 sketches, 1991. (Indus Publishing Co., New Delhi, Rs.
200).

The Britishers, during their rule in India, compiled information about
each district. These were published in the District Gazeteers and covered
each area in great details. The details generally covered location, geography,
social attitudes and political events, economy and revenue matters.
These gazeteers were an invaluable reference to the areas, its history
and administration. They were periodically updated. In recent decades
these gazeteers are not published regularly.

The above books, particularly the first two, cover their respective
areas in similar details. They cover most of the items of the early
gazeteers and update it till the present day. These books will be
a good source of reference about these areas. The title 'Lahaul' is
not in conformity of the accepted spelling 'Lahul' on the maps. And
it must be the 'Himalaya' (not s), particularly for an Indian author.

The last two books covers the entire Himalayan range systematically
regionwise at first. Then all the subjects like forests, geology, wild-life,
environmental problems, etc., are covered. Rivers of India, Bhutan and
Nepal with some of the lakes and glaciers are covered in the last
book. The style of all these books are more suited for reference.

These books also represent a sample of mountain-related literature
now being published in India by Indian authors and Indian publishers.
The photographs are of rather poor quality, but the information makes
up for it. For those interested in these areas and the range of the
Himalaya, more than just climbing mountains, the titles will prove
useful.

HARISH KAPADIA

THE STATE OF THE WORLD'S MOUNTAINS: A Global Report.
Ed. by Peter B. Stone on behalf of Mountain Agenda. Pp. 391,
i-xx, 1992. (Zed Books Ltd., London and New Jersey, SFR.
25).

This complete, well-illustrated report was prepared by a group of
people, collectively known as Mountain Agenda, as a 'back up' to
a shorter document submitted to the Rio Summit Conference on
Environment and Development. It is a detailed analysis of the impact
of human activity on mountain regions, describing what is going wrong,
why, and what can be done.

The report covers all the mountain regions of the world: the Alps, the Himalaya, and the Andes, of course, but also the mountains of Iceland, of Papua New Guinea, of Hawaii, the Appalachians, the Scottish Highlands and others. It deals with maximum global diversity, from sea level to almost 900 m, from the tropical rainforest to extreme highaltitude deserts.

The report sets out to answer three key questions:

1. What is the role of mountains in the global environment and in development?

2. What are the present threats to the highlands of the world?

3. What needs to be done for the world's mountains and their inhabitants?

The section on the Himalaya was prepared by J. Bandyopadhyay of the International Centre for Integrated Mountain Development (ICIMOD) in Kathmandu with the help of his colleagues. It deals with the 'Himalayan Dilemma'; the need for accelerated use of natural resources to deal with poverty on the one hand, and the need to protect the ecological fragility of the region, on the other.

His description of what is happening is familiar: increased accessibility leading to 'fast-changing patterns of socio-economic development and exploitation of natural resources'; felling of forests; increased exports of medicinal plants; the construction of water resource works; mining of minerals; tourism; commercial farming; urban industrial growth in the foothills. He complains that the forms of development were decreed by people from the plains, not those who live in the mountains.

The forests are a most important repository of one of the world's richest stocks of bio-diversity and have been used for thousands of years as sources of food, fodder, fuel and other biomass by the Himalayan people. Extensive commercial felling is destroying this valuable resource.

He lists the environmental constraints on the use of resources: seismicity; mass wasting (large masses of earth material moving downhill); glacial lake outburst floods; climatic extremes; erosion and sedimentation; and floods. He is cautious about the common belief that deforestation of the Himalayas is responsible for the floods downstream, as in Bangladesh.

The multiplicity of ethnic and linguistic groups in the Himalayan region adds another dimension to the problems of sustainability. 'The very diversity which, under conditions of peace, may be a positive resource for sustainable development can, under certain conditions, be the cause of widespread socio-economic instabilities which encourage hostility between the various mountain communities.' What is happening, alas, in Bhutan is an example. 'Once ethnic conflicts emerge as a dominant social process, concern for sustainable development becomes the first and easiest victim.'

In suggesting an approach to sustainable development, he suggests that the Himalayan region is not in a hopeless condition in spite of population pressures, but it does need the concerted efforts at all levels, micro and macro, to 'face the dual challenge of acute poverty and the need for ecological rehabilitation.'

The agenda for the region can be divided in three levels: macro, meso and micro. The natural resource dimension of the Himalaya, 'the water tower of Asia', extends beyond the eight countries of the region, and needs a collaborative approach. National efforts must evolve towards enhancement of specific ecological research, particularly the conservation of biodiversity. At the micro level, the marginalisation of people from the decision-making processes for development must be countered. 'Any attempt to replace the micro-level actors by the macro-level ones will be a sure prescription for unsustainability, a luxury the Himalayan region cannot afford any more.'

The book attempts to indicate what needs to be done to protect the mountains of the world. It must be hoped that the Commission for Sustainable Development, resulting from the Rio Summit, will pursue this vigorously. Ultimately, however, it is the peoples and governments of the countries themselves that must bear the major responsibility.

AAMIR ALI

ANTARCTICA — BOTH HEAVEN AND HELL: By Reinhold Messner. Translated by Jill Neate. Pp. 381, 129 b/w, 75 Colour Illustrations, 1 map, 1991. (The Mountaineers, Seattle, $ 35).

Reinhold Messner first made it to the Antarctica in December 1986 — after three earlier attempts since 1983. With two friends, he climbed Mount Vinson (5000 m), the highest mountain in the Antarctic. This was a climb in the game of making it to the top of the highest mountain in each continent. After this climb, Reinhold began to think about a traverse of the Antarctic continent. This would mean a walk of 3000 km in a maximum of 120 days (the short Antarctic summer). From the first beginnings of the expedition as an idea to its taking shape, took almost three years. In November 1989, the traverse had begun.

Following the climb of Mount Vinson, while Reinhold went into the history of the attempts to explore the Antarctica, it was the early adventurers Amundsen, Shackleton and Scott who fired his imagination. In particular, Scott's brave journey, the team pulling sledges rather than using motorised transport or dog traction, was the model for Reinhold. Scott and four others reached the South Pole on 17th January 1912. Amundsen and his team had beaten them to the Pole and Scott found the Norwegian flag there before he could plant the Union Jack. The return march of Scott's demoralised team was a catastrophe. Two members of the team died early on, during the return. The three others including Scott, weakened and unable to make progress because of the snow storms froze to death thirteen kilometers from One-Ton-Depot. Their corpses were found eight months later. Also found, was Scott's diary, which was to immortalize him as a tragic hero.

The expedition's original plan to start from the edge of the RonneShelf Ice had to be modified because their departure for the Antarctic had to be put off repeatedly on account of bad weather. Already two weeks late, they landed at 'Patriot Hills', a camp run by a private organisation, Adventure Network. They set out for the South Pole on 13 November 1989. Their first supply point was planned in the Thiel Mountains and the second at the South Pole. From the South Pole onwards, they had planned the expedition without a supply point as they felt that the prevailing winds would help them carry a heavier load with the help of a specially designed sail to speed them along on their skis.

Reinhold and Arved were lucky to find the first supply dump at the appointed place in the Thiel Mountains. After days of poor weather, the plane had just been able to make it and was still there when they arrived after endless running through fields of Sastrugi — snow waves. They were behind their schedule and not progressing fast enough to make up on lost time. Arved Fuchs with his bruised feet was considering the South Pole as a destination rather than the traverse to McMurdo. The narrow summer window did not help to make a decision any easier. For Reinhold, however, with his indomitable spirit there was never any doubt about the destination.

The two man expedition made it to the South Pole, on 30 December. Excitement, relief, the pleasure of meeting other people and comfort of the permanent Summer Camp at the Pole, all came in a rush. 'One experience richer, I stood at the geographical South Pole. Arved and I hugged each other. I liked this man. He had given me much. He was, despite everything, the ideal partner. We would also make the second half.'

Reinhold and Arved set off on the last and longest leg of their journey on 3 January 1990. They planned to reach McMurdo not later than 15 February. 'We ran towards the South. There were no farewells. As we had arrived, so we disappeared again.' This was the leg on which the two had planned an extensive use of their sails. 'We had developed three types of locomotion, as I noted in the margin of my diary.

1. Donkey, i.e. pulling the sledge in the conventional way (speed 2 mph max).

2. Swallow, i.e. sailing, standing on out skis and being pulled along by the sail/wind together with the sledges (speed 5-8 mph).

3. Penguin, i.e. skiing with outstretched sail, as if we were trying to sail (fly) but couldn't (speed 3-4 mph).

The wind helped on occasion, assisting them to cover 100 km on one day and yet on many other days it wasn't there and their progress was worryingly slow. They had to ration food and march upto 30 km per day. The images from Scott's diary of the return from the South Pole were with them. On 12 February, they had made it to McMurdo.

As with many other expeditions, Reinhold and his partner were involved in controversy following its end. Reinhold has mentioned it only briefly and there is no need to go into it here. The traverse of the Artarctica — 2800 km in ninety two days was a tremendous triumph of their spirit of adventure and will to succeed.

Antarctica — Both Heaven and Hell is a record of a long, lonely and successful struggle by two men to traverse the Seventh Continent. It is an inspiring book as one of such human achievement should be. The excessive use of quotations from the diaries of previous expeditions and the repetition in dealing with the history of exploration in the Antarctica do detract from its readability. However, the story itself, the historical summary of Antarctic exploration and the details on the Treaty make it both a record of a great expedition and an exhaustive store of information on the continent — a good addition to the library.

NAREN NANDA

ZEN IN THE ART OF CLIMBING MOUNTAINS. By Neville Shulman. Pp. 117, 17 b/w illustrations, 1992, Paperback. (Element, Shaftesbury, Dorset, £ 6.99).

With no prior climbing experience Shulman, a director of the British International Theatre Institute and dedicated Zen follower, perceives a certain affinity between mountaineering and the Way of Zen. He feels an irrational compulsion to join a commercially guided party attempting Mont Blanc. He is, by his own admission, a poor natural climber and in the ensuing struggle is only carried upwards, both spiritually and physically, by the strength of his *Shin* — the driving force within.

I read this book first as a mountaineer and guessed that most alpinists would cringe: I tried to read it again as someone who had never seen a snowy peak nor mixed with Oriental culture. The drama of mountaineering was there allright — if somewhat over the top, the introspection, the frustration, the struggle for apparent survival .... and I was 'enlightened' on the fundamental teachings of Zen. In fact, this is a surprisingly uncomplicated book. Unlike Robert Pirsig's cult bestseller of the mid-seventies (pre-dated by the model *Zen in the Art of Archery*), there is no profound or complex philosophy, nor indeed is there any need for an in-depth knowledge of Homer (or even motorbikes!). This is a book of the Self. Other characters are totally anonymous, at times almost superfluous. Never once is a personality touched upon. 'My relationship cannot be with any of the other climbers; I can only climb alone, my relationship is solely with the mountain'. We are told throughout the book that this ascent is a one-off; the pain, the misery, the fear — all part of the Way that must be experienced. Yet suddenly on the penultimate page he is talking of a return match — a desire to be tested once more by the mountain. Could this be metaphorical? No, for we see in the short biography of the author that he has gone on to climb Mounts Kenya and Kilimanjaro. The seed has been sown. 'The mountain could explain all the tenets of Zen to those who wished to listen': Yes, I could relate to that!

LINDSAY GRIFFIN

SHERPAS: The Brave Mountaineers. Compiled by Padma Sastry. Pp. 76, 13 b/w illustrations, 1991. (Himalayan Mountaineering Institute Publication, Darjeeling, nps).

The book pays tribute to the Sherpas, (Shar-pa) which means easterner, the original settlers of eastern Tibet. The book describes the lives of twelve Sherpas (Tenzing Norgay, Nawang-Gombu, Ang Tshering, Ang Temba, Nawang Topgay, Dorjee Lhatoo, N. D. Sherpa and others) and enlightens us on their upbringing, the hardships encountered by them and the strength, courage and devotion displayed by these 'brave mountaineers'. It traces their lives from their humble homes to the summits of the mighty Himalaya.

Sherpas is a biography of twelve men and a race of people whose actions speak for themselves. The compiler Padma Sastry has done a commendable job in honouring these twelve men and enlightening us on their lives.

KAIVAN MISTRY

JOHN MUIR: THE EIGHT WILDERNESS DISCOVERY BOOKS. Pp. 1030, 15 b/w illustration, 1992. (Diadem Books, London and The Mountaineers, Seattle, £ 16.99).

This book is about discovering the wilderness, not in the Himalaya but in the U.S.A. John Muir (1838-1914) is a legend in America. A name that has become synonymous with the preservation and protection of wildlands in the U.S.A. and Britain. Muir was a philosopher, naturalist and a man of great vision. He realised in the late 1800s that: 'Thousands of tired, nerve-shaken, over-civilized people are beginning to find out that going to the mountains is like going home. Wilderness is a necessity and the national parks and reservations are useful not only as fountains of timber and irrigating rivers but as fountains of life.' Muir was a prolific writer with a passion for detail that leaves the readers with vivid excitement. The writing is also full of humanity in its warm character-sketches and anecdotes. No wonder that generations of Americans have been influenced by him. Muir talks about his excursions right from his childhood in Dunbar, to his later ramblings in Alaska. Many of these stories are based on and devoted to Sierra Nevada and Yosemite, his favourite areas. Even though many decades have passed since his writing, his work is remarkably relevant even today. 'Few in these hot dim times are quite sane or free' he writes. 'Choked with care like clocks full of dust, laboriously doing so much good, making so much money — or so little, that they are no longer good for themselves.' John Muir was the founder of the Sierra Club which today is popular as an organisation devoted to protecting America's wildlands. The publishers have done a remarkable job of compiling these eight books into one volume. Definitely worth reading if one is interested in America's wilderness areas.

KRISHNAN KUTTY

IN MEMORIAM

THE HIMALAYAN CLUB OBITUARY

D. F. O. Dangar	(H. 1964)
Chris B. Briggs, B.E.M., D.L.	(L. 1970)
Gordon Whittle, M.Sc., F.R.G.S.	(L. 1944)
Robin Drake	(O. 1973)
Katsumasa Itakura	(O. 1966)
Mahinder Lall	(O. 1951)
Surinder Lall	(O. 1949)

(H.: Honorary, L: Life, O: Ordinary)

D. F. O. DANGAR
(1902-1992)

FRED DANGAR was born in 1902 and died shortly before his ninetieth birthday. His climbing career started with his first visit to the Alps in 1922. To use his own words he climbed in the old fashioned way with a guide. He had 26 seasons in the Swiss Alps in the course of which he climbed most of the major peaks as well as a host of others. He also climbed in the Austrian and French Alps. He always regretted that he never had the opportunity of visiting the Himalaya.

Fred was elected to the Alpine Club in 1931 and became an honorary member in 1969. He was also a member of the Swiss Alpine Club and the Osterreichischer Alpenklub. He was Assistant Editor of the *Alpine Journal* for 21 years, during which time he produced two consolidated indexes and many volume indexes.

It was in the late fifties that he came into contact with the Himalayan Club. The earlier volumes of the *Himalayan Journal* had not been indexed and it was agreed during discussions in London that the Club should endeavour to find someone with the necessary knowledge and experience who would be willing to undertake the job. Trevor Braham approached Fred Dangar who willingly agreed to take it on.

Photo

Illustrated Note 7

'Saraswati' (6940 m)
Indo-Japanese ladies expedition 1992 was led by Ms Reiko Teraswa and Inspector (Ms) Santosh Yadav. This unnamed peak in the Saraswati valley, on the Tibetan border, was climbed by the south ridge from the Balbala glacier — a first ascent.

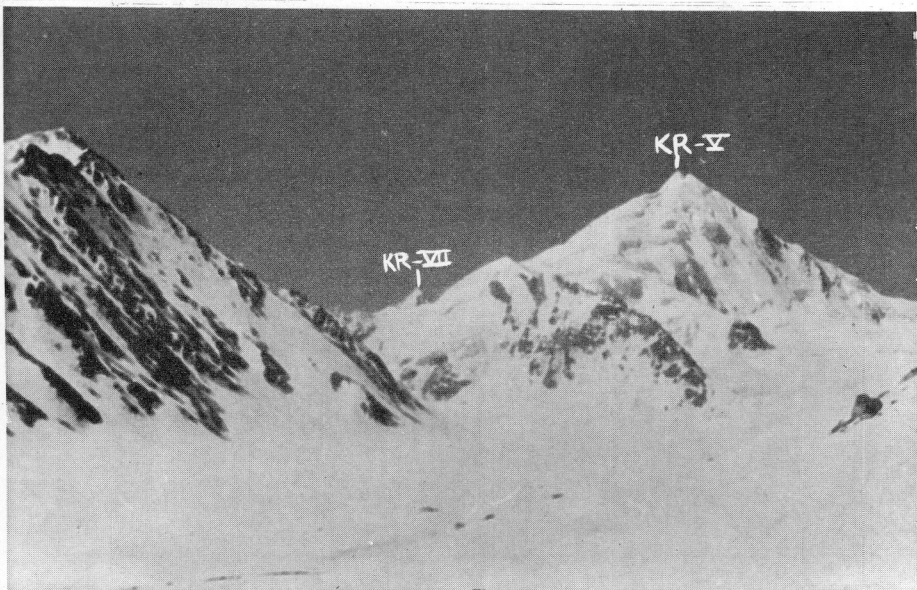

Illustrated Note 8

K.R. V (6258 m)
Indian ladies team from Calcutta was led by Ms Purnima Dutta. They climbed the peak on 2 July 1991 in the Koa Rong nala, Lahul.

D.F.O. Dangar

His first task was to produce a consolidated index covering Vols I to XXI. Individual volume indexes followed for subsequent volumes and he also brought out a further consolidated index covering Vols XXII to XXXII. After Vol. 39 in 1982, Fred understandably felt that it was time for someone else to take over.

Fred Dangar brought tremendous enthusiasm and devotion to the task and I look back with a great deal of pleasure upon the many discussions we had in the early days. His meticulous attention to detail and accuracy set a high standard for his successors to follow. The Club was indeed fortunate in having his services so generously given for more than twenty years. He was elected an honorary member of the Himalayan Club in 1964.

Our deepest sympathy goes to his wife and family.

V.S. RISOE

SIR GEOFFREY CHARLES FRESCHVILLE RAMSDEN[1]
(1893-1991)

GEOFFREY RAMSDEN became a member of the Himalayan Club very soon after it was formed in 1928.

After leaving Cambridge he served in the Army throughout the First World War. He held the rank of Captain in the 1st Batallion of the Royal Sussex Regiment in the N.W. Frontier of India from 1915 to 1919. After the War in 1920 he joined the Indian Civil Service in which he had a distinguished career. He was Secretary of the Indian Tariff Board from 1923 to 1925, after which he held various senior posts until his retirement in 1948 when he was Financial Commissioner in the Central Provinces and Bihar.

During his years in India Sir Geoffrey paid many visits to the Himalaya and took a particular interest in the flora of the region. His beautiful garden in Hindhead contained many flowers from the Himalaya. He was a keen photographer and took some striking photographs of the Himalayan peaks.

He continued to take an interest in the Club after his retirement, and he and his wife, Margaret, came regularly to the Annual Reunion Dinner in London during the sixties and early seventies. His wife died in 1976.

V. S. RISOE

---

1. Hon. Member of the Himalayan Club.

JILL HENDERSON

FOR ALMOST six years, from 1951 to 1956, Jill Henderson acting as the Club's Honorary Local Secretary in Darjeeling fulfilled a central role assisting organisers of expeditions large and small, and establishing a unique relationship with the Sherpa community whose trekking and mountaineering activities at the time emanated almost exclusively from Darjeeling. She encouraged the best of them to develop the status of guides and leaders and to acquire the independent skills which made them the forerunners of the agencies that proliferate around Kathmandu today. Her consideration and generosity to the younger and less gifted amongst them earned her a sort of head-of-family status within the Sherpa community. Her kindness, understanding and care for their problems touched equally the smallest and the greatest of them. In those days most Sherpa families possessed little or no means of livelihood during the long winter months. I can recall Angtharkay's moving references to her when I travelled through Sikkim with him in 1952. I am certain that without Jill Henderson's gentle but wise persuasion Tenzing would not have agreed to join the 1953 Everest expedition, finding himself utterly spent both physically and in spirit after two determined attempts to climb Everest with the Swiss in 1952. I, personally, like other members of the 1954 Kangchenjunga Reconnaissance team, was most grateful to Jill Henderson for placing at our disposal her large bungalow at Rungeet Tea Estate as a starting point for our expedition, although she and her husband were away at the time. She extended the same hospitality to Charles Evans and his expedition in 1955. By a happy co-incidence in Janaury 1954 Jill Henderson co-hosted, with the Club's President Charles Crawford, a tea party in Darjeeling for Sherpas with their wives and families. The occasion, believed to be only the second of its kind (General Bruce hosted the first on 1924) and almost certainly the last, marked the presentation of Coronation Medals awarded by H.M. The Queen to 22 Sherpas for their valuable contribution to the 1953 Everest expedition. In addition 8 Sherpas were awarded the coveted H.C. 'Tiger' badge for outstanding services.

Jill Henderson left India in 1958 upon her husband's retirement. After a short spell in East Africa she and her husband returned to England. During the last few years of her life Jill Henderson lived in America, where she died in 1991.

TREVOR BRAHAM

CHRIS BRIGGS

A LL THOSE who knew Chris Briggs will be very sorry to know that he died in October 1992. He was a Life Member of the Himalayan Club and of the Mountain Rescue & Climbing Clubs of Snowdon and he and his wife ran the Penny Guryd Hotel in North Wales and were well known. And there was, among other things, the Annual Reunion of the Everest 1953 party, with Sir John Hunt and Sir Edmund Hillary taking a large part in the proceedings. Chris did a lot of work among climbers in the Himalaya and in Snowdon, where he was awarded the BEM and was High Sheriff of Cumberland. He and his wife ran a hotel which was very popular among climbers and others. Once when the Earl of Snowdon brought the Prince of Wales in unexpectedly, the latter asked if 'shepherd's pie' which was on the menu was a good dish; and Chris replied that Welsh shepherds were usually very tender.

R. E. Hotz

KATSUMASA ITAKURA
(1915 — 1992)

K ATSUMASA ITAKURA was a distinguished scholar and moutaineer. He was born in Tokyo as member of distinguished Samurai family which served Tokugawa Shogunate (1615-1868). He graduated from the Tokyo Imperial University (Faculty of the Western History) in 1937. He worked as a professor of the Ancient Oriental History in Hokkaido University and Chuoh University in Tokyo. He co-founded with Prince Mikasa 'Japan Oriental Study Association'. He led a successful Hindukush mountaineering expedition 1967 to Koh-i-Bandakor, organised by Chuoh University Alpine Club. He was a distinguished member of the Japanese Alpine Club, and was its Hon. Secretary in 1974-1975.

He published many scholarly books on ancient Middle-eastern history including the translation of 'They Wrote on Clay' written by Edward Chiera, 'The Genesis Mystery' written by Jeffrey Goodman which are still good sellers.

JIRO TAGUCHI

CORRESPONDENCE

Himalayan Mountaineering Institute,
Darjeeling-734 101

17th March, 93.

The Editor
The Himalayan Journal
P.O. BOX 1905
Bombay 400 001 (INDIA)
Dear Sir,

With Brigadier D.K. Khullar's book the call of Everest, on the Indian man and women's Indian Everest expedition, 1984, doing its rounds of the world's mountaineering circles, I find myself unable to remain silent any longer. Besides being an exercise in slander the book is full of contradictions. His story, which has taken him eight years write is quite sickening in its dishonesty. I feel compelled to write my side of the story, set the record straight.

On the one hand Khullar profusely flatters the pundits and personalities of Indian mountaineering, all those who are in a position to enhance his career once he is off the mountain. On the other, he chooses a set of people and an individual, namely the Sherpas and me, to constantly ridicule, depreciate and malign. I am an object of controversy from the first to the very last page of his book. Indeed, with his liberal use of borrowed rhetoric, coarse humour and unhealthy interest in the personal lives of expedition members, Khullar's book reads more like one of Jackie Collins less inspired pulp novels than a truthful account of a mountaineering expedition.

The expedition was supplied entirely with the latest American and European climbing equipment and clothing. Food above the base camp was imported. Fifty-two selected professional high altitude porters were employed, an uncommonly large number. The team of men and women, prepared after a painful six year's process of training and observation by Col B S Sandhu, was arguably the best the country has ever seen. With such resources at his disposal, there was nothing to stop the expedition from becoming a tremendous success. The tragedy of this expedition, however, was the weakness of the head attached to such a strong body.

---

1. Refer to the review of this book in the present Journal (vol. 49), 'Book Review' section. — Ed.

272

Khullar's conjecture regarding the leaking of oxygen cylinders at the South Col (he has even had the temerity to publish an annexure on the issue) is totally false, with the singular intent of maligning Paljor and besides being a shabby attempt to divert attention from his failure.

On the 8, 9 and 10 whilist the Indian summit teams were positioned on the South Col after Rita and Ang Dorji's unsuccessful attempt on the summit (and Phu Dorji's return) the Indian camp, including the summit camp and the south Col camp, were in a bit of a mess, to say the least. The Bulgarian climbers, having descended along the Indian route after their West Ridge climb, found the Indian camps well stocked with food, fuel and oxygen. Indeed, some of these fatigued climbers were still in these camps after the retreat of the Indian summit parties, enjoying high altitude Indian food and hospitality. It is all very well for Khullar to rhapsodise over these times in terms of true mountaineering spirit, fellow feeling, Indo-Bulgarian friendship, etc, but he fails to acknowledge the crucial problems here; namely the confusion that arose as a result of this activity. There was no account of how many full, half or empty oxygen cylinders were lying available at the South Col. Six male members, three female members, eight Sherpas and four Bulgarians passed by the South Col. Lying in his tent at the base camp, Khullar was surely the last person one would expect to be in a position to correctly specify who was using what miles above him at the South Col.

On 15, May when Rattan, Paljor, Rekha and I went to the South Col supported by just two Sherpas, the area was a scene of chaos, with oxygen cylinders lying scattered around the camp (as seen in our south col photographs). The tents were a confusion of oxygen masks, life support bottles, half eaten food, Salewa noodles, pee-bottles of frozen urine and every sort of high altitude junk one could think of. Fatigued as we were, we did little to clear up the mess — which is the normal reaction expected of any climber at such an altitude.

Now, in retrospect, I must mention that I regret obeying Khullar's orders that day. Had I followed my own judgement as a professional climber and acted at my own discretion (as I was to do later on 23, May), all four of us would have reached the summit on 16, May. When we left the South Col on the 16th in the morning, Rattan, Rekha and myself and Paljor, in the same order, we were in line, each almost within touching distance not in the manner Khullar assumes from his catbird seat at the base camp.

The Sherpas, for whom he expresses such contempt in his book, paid no heed to his authority because they considered him undeserving of their respect. He never carried his rucksack beyond the Base Camp, and even had his gaiters and crampons fitted onto him by three personal Sherpas. He made it a habit of paying for every little favour done to him with money, apparently to earn the Sherpas' respect and win them over to his side. The result, unfortunately, was quite the opposite.

After 30 years of professional dedication and proficiency in my work, I see Khular's attitude towards me as nothing short of a scathing attack, Providing, perhaps some sort of outlet for his personal frustrations.

As a member of the Himalayan Club, and it's Hon. Local Secretary, a member of the IMF and a life member and a senior staff member of the HMI, I hereby request that this letter, alongwith the true account of the incidents of 1984 herewith attached, may please be published in your esteemed Journal.[2] It is my firm belief that truth shall prevail and I have full faith in the mountaineering fraternity's ability to judge for themselves. The facts have only to be laid before them.

Yours faithfully,

Dorjee Lhatoo
Deputy Director, Field Training
Himalayan Mountaineering
Institute, Darjeeling
West Bengal (India)

'Parikrama', Talla Danda,
Nainital — 263002.

Dear Harish Kapadia,

I enjoyed HJ 48 and would like to correct a few factual mistakes in the articles written by William Mckay Aitken and Sandeep Dutt. (p.58 and p. 196)

1. Gandhiji came to the different parts of Kumaon in June-July 1929 for the collection for the Harijan fund. The crusade against forced labour was already completed in January 1921, at a time when Gandhiji had abandoned the non-cooperation movement and the Khilafat initiative too had proved to be unsuccessful. The 'Begar (forced and unpaid labour) Abolition Movement' was unmatched for its strength and participation, leadership and organisation. It started as a local / regional movement and finally became the part of Indian struggle for freedom. Gandhiji called this movement the 'bloodless revolution' in 1929.

---

2. The account of the incidents is available with the club in the library — Ed.

The commentary Gandhiji wrote on 'Geeta' at Kausani on 24th June 1929 is known as 'Anashakti Yoga' and the house where he stayed is now known as 'Anashakti Ashram' The tributary of Ramganga, which orginates from Bhutkot range is Gagas and it does not flow through Dwarahat town. The seasonal lake en route from Dunagiri to Ganai Chaukhutia is Taragtal.

2. Lord Curzon trekked from Almora to Kuari or Ramni (though the road was constructed up to Dhak Tapovan via kuari pass and bugyal) via Kausani, Garur, Gwaldam, Deval, Kanaul in 1903, not in 1905. (See Correspondence of Curzon, 1903, Reel 4, Micro Film, National Archives of India, New Delhi.)

With regards and best wishes to you and the HJ family from my point in the Himalaya.

Shekhar Pathak
Editor PAHAR

Indian Mountaineering Foundation
Benito Juarez Road, Anand Niketan,
New Delhi - 110021

No. 39(FE) — IMF/92 Pt. I   20 October 1992

Dear Shri Kapadia,

Kindly refer to your letter dated 29th September 1992, and previous correspondence, regarding wrong claims of ascents of Panch Chuli III, IV and V by the 1964 Indian expedition, led by late Capt. A.K. Choudhury.

This Foundation has gone into the details of the 1964 Panch Chuli expedition and also of the 1972 ITBP expedition which succeeded in climbing Panch Chuli I, and has arrived at the conclusion that it would not be possible to approach peaks Panch Chuli IV and V from the junction point of Uttari and Dakhini Balati glacier where the camp was established by the 1964 Panch Chuli expedition and even Peak III is extremely difficult to be climbed from the said route.

The IMF 1964 expedition led by the late Gp. Capt. A.K. Chowdhury, seems to have been mistaken in identifying the Panch Chuli III, IV and V, perhaps due to poor visibility and inadequacy of maps. This has now been proved by the joint Indo-British expedition in 1992 jointly led by Harish Kapadia and the world famous British climber

Chris Bonington. Therefore, the claim of the 1964 expedition having scaled Panch Chuli Peaks III, IV and V from the said route within the reported time, is untenable and IMF nullifies their claim and treats Panch Chuli III, IV and V as unclimbed peaks.

   With regards,

                                                    Hukum Singh
                                                    Hony. Secretary, IMF

                                                    25 October 1992.

Dear Shri Hukum Singh

   Thank you for your letter of 20, October, 1992 No. 39 (EF)—IMF/ 92 -Pt. I.

   It is noted that the I.M.F. agrees with the view that the peaks Panch Chuli III, IV and V were *not climbed* by the 1964 Indian expedition led by late Group Captain A.K. Chowdhury and sponsored by the Indian Mountaineering Foundation. We are happy to note that the IMF has taken this objective view to correct the records of their own sponsored expedition.

   It may be noted that the first ascent of the Panch Chuli V was made by the Indian-British Panch Chuli expedition this year (1992). Peaks III and IV remain unattempted.

   One of the so-called summiteers Sheo Raj Singh in his letters to J.C. Nanavati, Hon. Secretary, ·The Himalayan Club and Harish Kapadia, Hon. Editor, The *Himalayan Journal,* wrote that 'they (Nanavati and Kapadia) are not competent to seek clarifications from him or doubt the climb of Panch Chuli III, IV and V.' In his view 'the I.M.F. is the only competent authority' to decide the matter'.

   With the result of our studies now corroborated by the IMF the matter is now concluded. It is evident that it was Sheo Raj Singh and his 1964 team members who were not competent — for 28 years.

                                                    Harish Kapadia
                                                    Hon. Editor
                                                    The Himalayan Journal

CLUB PROCEEDINGS, 1992

THE HIMALAYAN CLUB COMMITTEE, 1992
(Founded on 17th February, 1928)

Officers

President	K.N. Naoroji
Vice President	K.K. Guha
	S.P. Mahadevia
	G. Ramchandani
Honorary Secretary	J.C. Nanavati
Honorary Treasurer	Arun P. Samant

Members of Committee

M.H. Contractor	A.D. Moddie
Harish Kapadia	S.R. Shah
Sharavati Prabhu	M.S. Soin
Joydeep Sircar	Naren Nanda
Sudhir Sahi	Dr Rodhan Shroff

Honorary Local Secretaries

India

Almora	N.B. Parekh
Bombay	Dhiren M. Pania
Calcutta	Prabhat Ganguli
Darjeeling	Dorjee Lhatoo
Delhi	Sudhir Sahi
Jammu	Sat Paul Sahni
Manali	John Banon
Shimla	Col B.S. Sandhu
Nepal	Elizabeth Hawley
Pakistan	Nazir Sabir
Australia & New Zealand	W.M. Deacock
Czechoslovakia	V. Smida
France	Bonneau Yves
Great Britain	R.G. Pettigrew

Japan	H. Ohtsuka
Italy	Prof Ardito Desio
South Africa	Dr. S.A. Craven
South Korea	Sae Bae
Spain	Jose Paytubi
Switzerland	Eric Bernhardt
U.S.A. West	Nicholas Clinch
East	H. Adams Carter

Honorary Editor	Harish Kapadia
Honorary Assistant Editor	M.H. Contractor
Honorary Librarian	W.M. Aitken
Hon. Asstt Librarian	
Bombay	Suhas Kharde
Calcutta	A. Guha Thakurta
Hon. Equipment Officer	Arun P. Samant
Hon. Asst Equipment Officers	
Bombay	Ashok Shenvi
Calcutta	Prabhat Ganguli
Delhi	Sandeep Kapur

CLUB NEWS

An active year for the Himalayan Club, as usual, with many sectional meetings at Bombay (4), Calcutta(2), and Delhi. *The Himalayan Journal* Vol. 48 was published in April while *The Himalayan Club Newsletter 46 was published on 17 February.*

The Grindlays Bank Mountain Scholarships were awarded to various trainees. Many new books and items of mountaineering equipment were added to the store.

The Club membership continues to grow beyond 900 members' spread over various parts of the world and consisting of many leading mountaineers. The membership is open to all who are interested in various aspects of the Himalaya and are qualified to be members. Full details and forms are available from Hon. Secretary. The Himalayan Club. Post Box. no. 1905, Bombay 400001, India. (Full details of the club activities, 1992 are available in the *Himalayan Club Newsletter 46)*

THE HIMALAYAN JOURNAL

Volume 49
(1991-92)

Honorary Editor
HARISH KAPADIA

Honorary Assistant Editor
M.H. CONTRACTOR

Assistance

S.P. Mahadevia (Buisness)   Naren Nanda (Proofs)
Arun Samant (Sketch-maps)   Kaivan Mistry (Proofs and Index)
Dhiren Pania (Despatches)   Kekoo Colah (Proof and Index)
                               Rashmi Palkhivala (Editing)

Trade inquiries with Oxford University Press, Post Box No 31 Oxford
House, Apollo Bunder, Colaba, Bombay 400001, India.

Stop! Your search for a perfect typewriter ends here!

PRIMA from *Godrej*

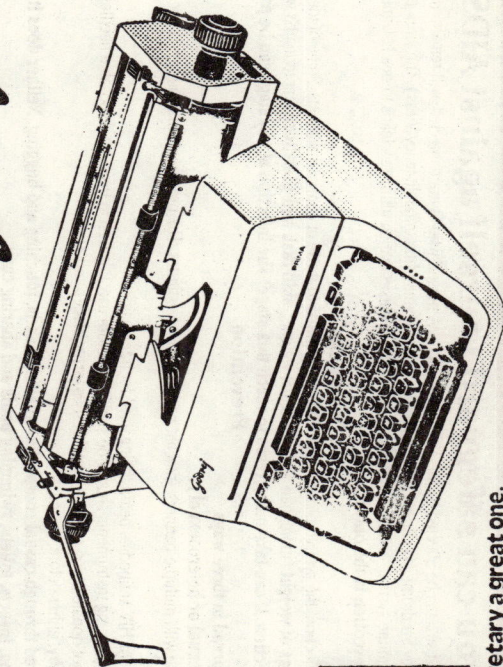

Godrej
PRIMA

Makes a good secretary a great one.

ULKA · GB · PR · 9 · 83

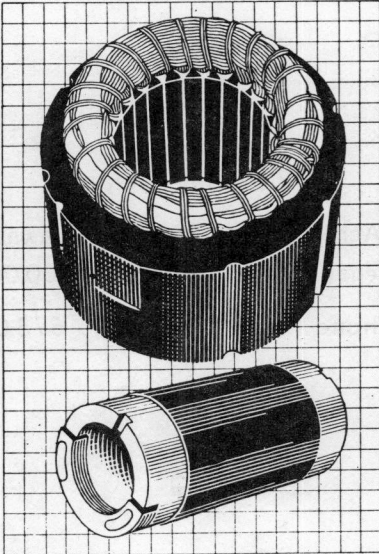